Charlotte Brontë's Life Through Clothes

PRAISE FOR *CHARLOTTE BRONTË'S LIFE THROUGH CLOTHES*

"As expertly constructed as a Chanel suit. The clever ploy of exploring Charlotte's life through the unique prism of her clothes uncovers a whole new landscape beyond the standard biography. I thought I knew Charlotte, but now I feel I understand her better."

TRACY CHEVALIER, bestselling author of
Girl with the Pearl Earring and *The Glassmaker*

"In this revelatory biography, Eleanor Houghton recreates the life of Charlotte Brontë less through the words that she wrote, but instead the clothes that she wore [...] Houghton's exquisite drawings of surviving garments truly set this biography apart, and make it such a pleasure to savour."

SUSAN HOLLOWAY SCOTT, bestselling author of
I, Eliza Hamilton and *The Secret Wife of Aaron Burr*

"No longer must we picture her slogging through life in dull tones of sepia. In Houghton's enlightening and compassionate analysis, even Brontë's dark 'Quakerish' governess dress emerges as an emblem of deliberate self-expression rather than repression."

CHRISTINE NELSON, curator of *Charlotte Brontë: An Independent Will*, Morgan Library & Museum, US, and author of *The Brontës: A Family Writes*

"Houghton's writing is personable and vivid, and her intricate illustrations imbue this book with an artful kind of magic. A true delight."

RUBY GRANGER,
Educational YouTuber and Content Creator, UK

"This beautifully written, brilliantly argued study unlocks the secrets of Charlotte Brontë's wardrobe – a collection of signifiers as compelling, Houghton reveals, as her novels. An indispensable book for lovers of fiction and fashion alike."

CAROLINE WEBER, Barnard College, Columbia University, US and author of *Queen of Fashion: What Marie Antoinette Wore to the Revolution*

"Beautifully illustrated and fluently written, Eleanor Houghton reveals just how central Charlotte Brontë's relationship with clothing was to both her self-image and the ways in which she shaped her most famous characters. This book offers a distinctive and original contribution to Brontë scholarship."

MARIA HAYWARD, Professor of Early Modern History, University of Southampton, UK

"Not simply the definitive reading of the contents of this archive, but a fascinating model for integrating fashion and literary history."

MICHAEL MEEUWIS, Assistant Professor of English, University of Warwick, UK

"Houghton's meticulous analyses and illustrations of an extensive, widely overlooked body of evidence reveal the local and global underpinnings of the Victorian authors prints and patterns, fabrics and furbelows, and the manifold complexities of Brontë's public and private self-fashioning."

CORNELIA PEARSALL, Professor of English Language and Literature, Smith College, US

"Eleanor Houghton's genius for evoking other worlds is revealed through her prose and the affecting delicacy of her illustrations, which capture the unfolding of both the Regency and Victorian eras, and Charlotte's life. This is an unforgettable portrait of a woman whose intelligence and unyieldingly romantic idealism would culminate in a masterpiece of English literature."

ANTONELLA GAMBOTTO-BURKE, journalist and author of *Apple: Sex, Drugs, Motherhood and the Recovery of the Feminine*

Charlotte Brontë's Life Through Clothes

Written and Illustrated by
Eleanor Houghton

BLOOMSBURY VISUAL ARTS
LONDON · NEW YORK · OXFORD · NEW DELHI · SYDNEY

BLOOMSBURY VISUAL ARTS
Bloomsbury Publishing Plc, 50 Bedford Square, London, WC1B 3DP, UK
Bloomsbury Publishing Inc, 1359 Broadway, New York, NY 10018, USA
Bloomsbury Publishing Ireland, 29 Earlsfort Terrace, Dublin 2, D02 AY28, Ireland

BLOOMSBURY, BLOOMSBURY VISUAL ARTS and the Diana logo are trademarks of Bloomsbury Publishing Plc

First published in Great Britain 2026

Copyright © Eleanor Houghton, 2026

Eleanor Houghton has asserted her right under the Copyright, Designs and Patents Act, 1988, to be identified as author and illustrator of this work.

For legal purposes the Acknowledgements on p. xiii–xiv constitute an extension of this copyright page.

Cover design: Holly Capper
Cover illustration: Charlotte goes to London © Eleanor Houghton, 2026
Figure 0.1 (opposite): Knitted purse with brass closure thought to have been made by Charlotte Brontë for Ellen Nussey, D191

All rights reserved. No part of this publication may be: i) reproduced or transmitted in any form, electronic or mechanical, including photocopying, recording or by means of any information storage or retrieval system without prior permission in writing from the publishers; or ii) used or reproduced in any way for the training, development or operation of artificial intelligence (AI) technologies, including generative AI technologies. The rights holders expressly reserve this publication from the text and data mining exception as per Article 4(3) of the Digital Single Market Directive (EU) 2019/790.

Bloomsbury Publishing Plc does not have any control over, or responsibility for, any third-party websites referred to or in this book. All internet addresses given in this book were correct at the time of going to press. The author and publisher regret any inconvenience caused if addresses have changed or sites have ceased to exist, but can accept no responsibility for any such changes.

A catalogue record for this book is available from the British Library.

A catalog record for this book is available from the Library of Congress.

ISBN:	HB:	978-1-3505-1408-9
	ePDF:	978-1-3505-1407-2
	eBook:	978-1-3505-1409-6

Typeset by Integra Software Services Pvt. Ltd.
Printed and bound in India

For product safety related questions contact productsafety@bloomsbury.com.

To find out more about our authors and books visit www.bloomsbury.com and sign up for our newsletters.

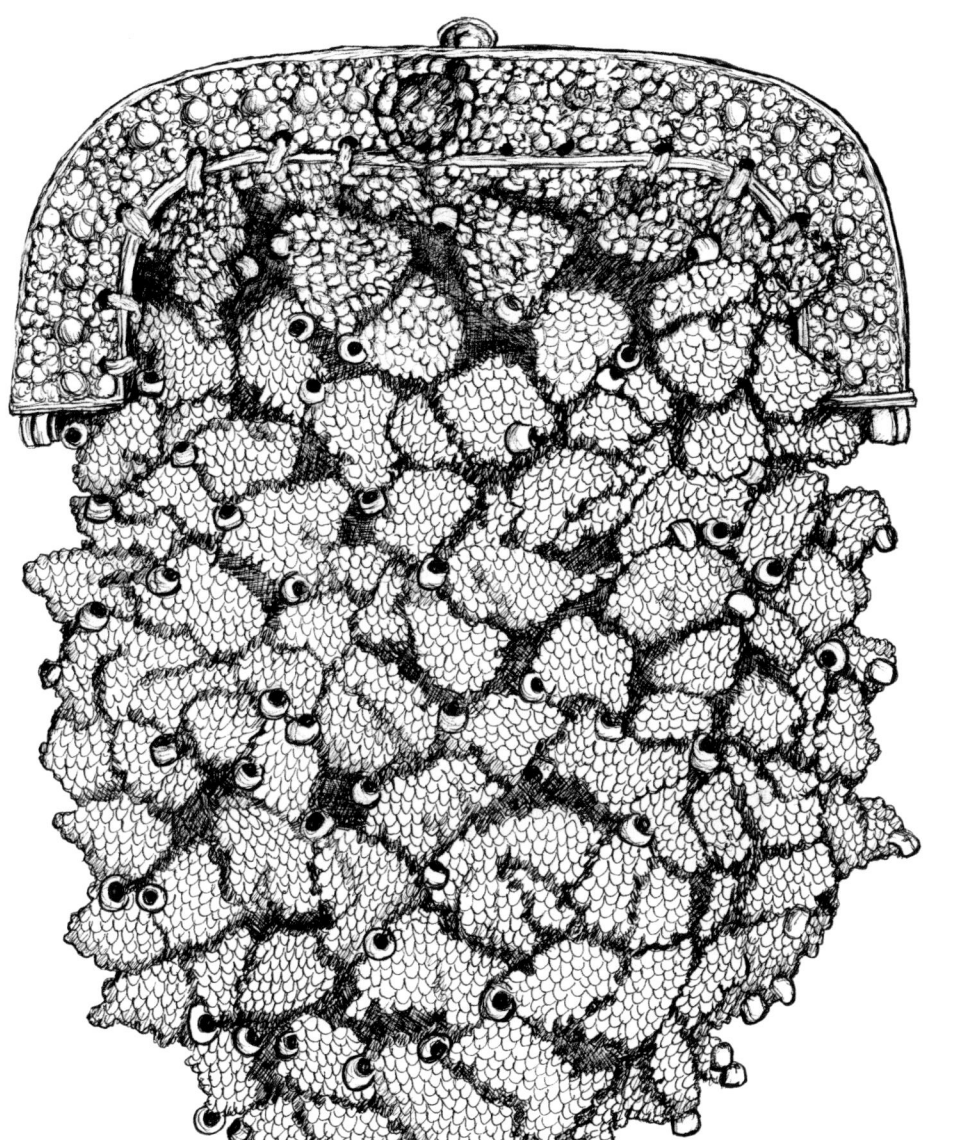

Contents

List of Figures x
List of Tables xiii
Abbreviations xiii
Acknowledgements xiv

1 Recalled to Life 1

2 The Receiver 5

3 Romance and Reality 27

4 The 'Governess Dress' 53

5 The Corset 73

6 In Print 101

7 Mourning 131

8 Fame 157

9 The Wedding Dress 187

10 The 'Going Away Dress' 211

11 Afterlives 239

Glossary of Terms 248
Tables 253
Notes 259
Select Bibliography 322
Index 346

Figures

Unless otherwise stated, all illustrations, including endpaper and cover images, are by Eleanor Houghton. © Eleanor Houghton, 2026.

0.1 Knitted purse with brass closure thought to have been made by Charlotte Brontë for Ellen Nussey, D191 v
0.2 Charlotte Brontë's pale pink satin, drawn bonnet, D141 xiii
1.1 Charlotte Brontë's 'Paisley Dress', D8 xiv
2.1 Charlotte Brontë's christening bonnet, 1816 7
2.2 Clothing of a young girl c. 1820 10
2.3 Child's leather mules, c. 1820s, 2004.33.1 12
2.4 Haworth Parsonage 14
2.5 Charlotte Brontë's sampler, July 1822, S15 18
2.6 Girl wearing winter uniform of the Clergy Daughters' School, Cowan Bridge 21
3.1 Sand, orange, red and green wool shawl, D64 37
3.2 Charlotte Brontë's hand-sewn needle case, D154 41
3.3 Patrick Branwell Brontë, *The Brontë Sisters*, c. 1834. Oil on canvas, 35½ × 29⅜ inches. Located in the National Portrait Gallery, London, England, UK. Recently restored. (Photo by VCG Wilson/Corbis via Getty Images) 42
3.4 Regency man's shirt 49
4.1 Charlotte Brontë's 'Governess Dress', back view, D11 52
4.2 Charlotte Brontë's 'Governess Dress', front view, D11 59
4.3 Inside of Charlotte Brontë's 'Governess Dress', D11 61
4.4 Embroidered pockets, early nineteenth century 65

Figures

5.1 Charlotte Brontë's corset, *c.* 1842, D116 72
5.2 Inside view of Charlotte Brontë's corset showing bust enhancers and metal eyelets 80
5.3 Impenetrable busk of Charlotte Brontë's corset 85
5.4 Charlotte Brontë, Self portrait contained within 'Letter to Ellen Nussey, 6 March 1843', © Brontë Society 90
5.5 J.C. Russell, *Russell's General Atlas of Modern Geography*, unnumbered page, sketch of an unnamed girl. The Morgan Library & Museum. PML 129886. Bequest of Helen Safford Bonnell, 1969 96
6.1 Front view of feasible design of Charlotte Brontë's 'Muslin print dress' 100
6.2 Charlotte Brontë's Berlin wool work bag, D31 108
6.3 Front view of Charlotte Brontë's 'Paisley Dress', D8 110
6.4 Fragment of floral muslin worn by Charlotte Brontë, D148 112
6.5 Heavy woollen cloaks belonging to the Brontë sisters, D16, D17 114
6.6 Front view of D102 116
6.7 Inside view of D102 showing pieced sleeves 118
6.8 Charlotte Brontë's paisley parasol, D133 127
6.9 Charlotte Brontë's black-and-white silk parasol, D106 128
7.1 Charlotte Brontë's hair and brass bracelet made from Emily Brontë's hair, J13 136
7.2 Charlotte Brontë's blue silk ugly bonnet, D21 141
7.3 Charlotte Brontë's Iroquois moccasins, D124 144
7.4 Charlotte Brontë's black lace veil, D169 149
7.5 Charlotte Brontë's whitework blouse with black trim, D171 152
7.6 Charlotte Brontë's printed wool shawl, D12 154
7.7 Charlotte Brontë's tortoiseshell comb, J73 155
8.1 Charlotte Brontë's 'Thackeray Dress', D129 159

Figures

8.2 Front view of Charlotte Brontë's 'Thackeray Dress' 161
8.3 Microscope images of D129 taken using Nikon Eclipse LV100ND microscope, x2 objective. University of Southampton 163
8.4 Charlotte Brontë's blue-and-cream striped silk gown, early 1850s, D10 174
8.5 Ribbon and faux flower detail on lower bodice of D10 176
8.6 Jacquard ribbon tie, D184 180
8.7 Charlotte Brontë's pink-lined leghorn straw bonnet, D140 184
9.1 Annotated drawing of Charlotte Brontë's reconstructed wedding dress, 2003/17 195
9.2 Charlotte Brontë's wedding bonnet, D2 202
9.3 Charlotte Brontë's wedding bonnet veil, D97 205
10.1 Charlotte Brontë's 'Going Away Dress', D74 210
10.2 Microscope images of D74 silk taken using Nikon Eclipse LV100ND microscope, x2 objective. University of Southampton. Images taken by Danai Panagoulia, Alex Keeler and Eleanor Houghton, University of Southampton 213
10.3 'Fringed Silk Day Dress', 1854/6, York Castle Museum, York 218
10.4 Charlotte Brontë's pink cotton wrapping gown or 'wrapper', D51 222
10.5 Surviving sleeve of Charlotte Brontë's green spot barège gown, D119.2 224
10.6 Front view of feasible reconstruction of Charlotte Brontë's 1850 barège spot dress 226
10.7 Knitted baby socks sent by Elizabeth Smith for Charlotte Brontë's unborn baby, SG35/6B 235
11.1 Charlotte Brontë's spotted canvas and leather boots, D96 238
11.2 Feasible reconstruction of 'Muslin Dress' 244

Tables

1 Clothing requirements in accordance with events detailed in Charlotte Brontë's extant letters 255
2 References to the making, receiving and buying of Charlotte Brontë's clothing in her surviving letters 258

Abbreviations

BPM – Brontë Parsonage Museum
V&A – Victoria and Albert Museum

Acknowledgements

This book stands on the shoulders of countless giants. Five deserve special mention. Juliet Barker is a doyenne. Not only is her work invaluable, but she has also proved herself a kind and generous mentor. The late Margaret Smith's *Letters*, compiled and edited over decades, have made new revelations possible, as has the meticulous research of Christine Alexander and Jane Sellars.

A huge debt of thanks is also owed to the Brontë Society and to staff at The Brontë Parsonage Museum, most notably to Ann Dinsdale, Sarah Laycock, Linda Pierson and Amy Rowbottom. Despite my repeated upending of the library, they have remained unstinting in their sharing of expertise, tea and friendship.

I will remain ever grateful to the Wolfson Foundation for financially supporting my doctoral studies and thus a significant proportion of this research. Thanks must also be extended to Leen Van de Wiele for braving the Lokeren archives on my behalf and also to weaving and textile expert Jim Laycock who helped me unlock the secrets of Charlotte's corset.

I wish to express my sincere appreciation of my agent, Juliet Mushens, and also Liza DeBlock, Kiya Evans and Emma Dawson for their perpetual help and guidance. I am also grateful to Georgia Kennedy for answering a thousand questions without complaint and to Maria Hayward, Mary Hammond and Andrea Russell for their scholarly contributions.

To Alastair and Rachel Anderson, Sheila and Geoffrey Ractliffe, Val Osmond, Polly Read, Anne Sophie Darlington, Kit Byford, Alexis Wolf and Anna Hewitt – you have been steadfast, loving and supportive friends, and for that I will always be grateful.

To Mum, no words are enough. Thanks also to the rest of the Houghton clan, but specifically to Wills for his persistent encouragement, graphic wizardry and inappropriate memes; to George for rescuing me from the ravages of Microsoft Word and to Grace for minding enough to ask if I'm nearly finished every day for nine years.

Finally, to my dogs past and present, though your squeaky toys and postman patrols have, without doubt, slowed proceedings, thank you for reminding me what really matters.

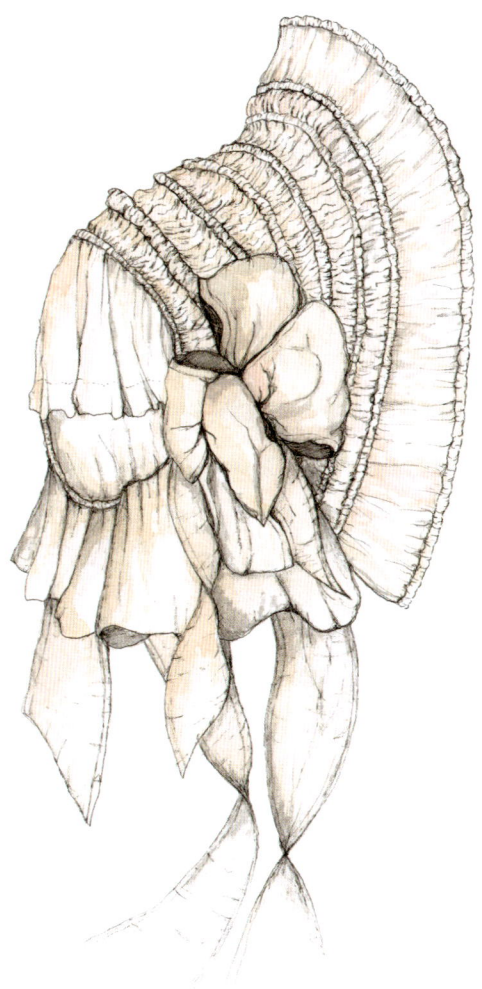

0.2 *Charlotte Brontë's pale pink satin drawn bonnet, D141*

1.1 *Charlotte Brontë's 'Paisley Dress', D8*

1

Recalled to Life

Nearly 170 years have passed since the nineteenth-century novelist, Charlotte Brontë, took her last breath, but, astonishingly, witnesses to her life still survive. These were present as she penned the first lines of *Jane Eyre*, as she walked the cobbled streets of Haworth with her sisters, as she railed at fellow author William Makepeace Thackeray or as she joined fiancé Arthur Bell Nicholls at the altar in the summer of 1854. Yet, revealing and powerful as their stories are, until this book was written, their testimonies had remained unheard.

Few would argue that Charlotte Brontë's novels constitute some of the most forceful and vivid literature of the nineteenth century. When her most famous book, *Jane Eyre*, was published in 1847, it 'set all the literary world of that day vibrating'.[1] For the dark, rags-to-riches tale had an extraordinary heroine at its heart – a plain, poor, rebellious governess who flew in the face of convention to speak out her passion, her anger, her pain and her frustration. Quickly deemed a 'naughty book', it was an instant bestseller, but sensation only mounted when it was revealed that the creator of this audacious heroine was, in fact, a woman. What is more, she was a diminutive, socially anxious, evangelical clergyman's daughter from the West Riding of Yorkshire.

Brontë would go on to write two more successful novels, *Shirley* in 1849 and *Villette* in 1853, before her premature death on 31 March 1855 at the age of just thirty-eight. Two years later, novelist Elizabeth Gaskell (*Cranford* and *North & South*), keen to capitalize on Brontë's fame and tragic life story and to liberate her friend from accusations of coarseness, released a biography of Charlotte's life that was every bit as engrossing as *Jane Eyre* itself. But, for all that this biography revealed, quite as much was obscured. Gaskell's Charlotte emerges as a long-suffering, fragile, sexless, saint-like being, forever enshrined in an isolated parsonage perched high on the wild Yorkshire moors. Silenced and sanitized, *this* Charlotte was far removed from the complex, passionate, radical who had dared to pen *Jane Eyre* or to hanker after her married, Belgian professor, Constantin Heger. Yet, in spite of the reality, it was *Gaskell's* Charlotte that would become firmly cemented in the minds of the majority for generations to come.

In more recent years, numerous biographers have been preoccupied with the slow exhumation of the real Charlotte Brontë from beneath the layers of myth, under which she has, for so long, been buried. This biography continues in their wake and, like those that have gone before, draws heavily upon the huge wealth of sources that relate to the lives and works of Charlotte and her family. There remain hundreds of letters, childhood writings, novels, poems, self-portraits, portraits, the reminiscences of their contemporaries, artworks, catalogues, logbooks, account books, memoirs, journals, diary entries, newspaper articles and, of course, even the house in which the Brontës lived for much of their lives. But in a new departure, this highly innovative study also draws upon an enormous and previously unresearched body of first-hand evidence that offers an entirely new perspective on the fascinating, paradoxical, complex life of the novelist Charlotte Brontë. This evidence takes surprising form, but after nine long years of meticulous study, the bonnets, cloaks, gowns, shoes, boots, corset, corset covers, shawls, stockings, and other garments, jewellery, fragments, and accessories that make up Charlotte's surviving wardrobe have proved themselves astoundingly communicative witnesses. So too has the body of clothing that no longer exists in physical form but rises up from the past to testify from the pages of her novels, from her letters, from within a school prospectus or on the surface of a canvas. Though these once real garments now exist only in shadowy form, they play a vital part in joining the dots of Charlotte's history.

One might be led to wonder how the things a person wore so long ago could possibly reveal anything meaningful – after all, clothing is surely just a mass of fabric and buttons and seams and thread. But, to reduce it to this is to miss its power. Clothes are, and always have been, a vital part of our daily lives. Few things walk with us so closely. The garments that we wear literally mould themselves to our bodies, even becoming imbued with our DNA. Part of us and yet not part of us, they form inexorable links between the material and the immaterial.[2] They are an extension of who we are, and yet can be changed to suit our own needs or the expectations of those around us. Though we are often unconscious of it, they are able to communicate a huge amount of personal information about our status, our financial circumstances, how and where we live, our values and religious beliefs, our sensibilities, and our tastes. They can convey how we feel about our bodies, our appearance and even reveal some of our most private, innermost conflicts. They can disclose intimate details about our physical size and shape – the length of our legs or the width of our feet. And, in more generic terms, our clothes can also expose much about the society that made them, about the culture that demanded them and the political, technological, environmental, or geographical factors that helped shape them, or the many individuals or businesses involved in their production.

The items that make up Charlotte Brontë's wardrobe have, then, borne witness to, and indeed been active participants in, a remarkable life – one that was at once both ordinary and extraordinary, public and private, obscure and famous. Secrets have been found within their very fibres. Charlotte's iron busked corset tells the story of corporate espionage and forbidden love, whilst her highly embellished, striped, silk dress showed how she coped with the new-found pressures of fame as a shy, plain woman. When exposed to twenty-first-century technology, a tiny sample of fabric from her blue-and-white 'Thackeray Dress' reveals important innovations of the Industrial Revolution going on around her, and a black lace veil, worn after the deaths of her siblings, tangibly conveys how she dealt with repeated familial loss.

The sheer size and scope of Charlotte's surviving wardrobe is nothing short of remarkable. The vast majority of these garments, fragments and accessories, amounting to more than 150 items, are housed at the Brontë Parsonage Museum in Haworth.[3] To find such a large and varied collection of nineteenth-century, middle-class clothing, particularly one that can be attributed to an individual, is exceptionally rare. Most clothing of this kind was not kept. Rather, it is often only solitary, treasured garments, such as wedding dresses, that stand the test of time. These are not, of course, without merit. Much can be gleaned from the study of a lone garment, but the benefits to having such an enormous and diverse 'cloud of witnesses' to a single existence are many. If only Charlotte's drab, brown bonnet had survived, a familiar, sartorial stereotype would have been confirmed. Brontë would have fully morphed into her protagonist, Jane Eyre. But, in reality, her surviving wardrobe defies all expectations. Yes, there are the anticipated neat, dark gowns, but there are many other pieces too. Some startle with their pattern, texture and exoticism. Some are Pepto-Bismol pink, some cerulean blue. There are bold, sarape-inspired cloaks and heavily beaded, Mohawk moccasins. There are garments that mark the first months of life and garments that mark the last. There are clothes for work and there are clothes for fame; some worn in celebration and some in times of grieving. Closely studied, both as individual items and en masse, patterns emerge, tastes are perceived, a life is chronicled and a personality revealed.

Now, at long last, the clothes that covered Charlotte's body, some of which still bear the imprint of her foot or the sweat from her pores, have been summoned to the witness box to give their testimonies. There, myths are shattered, long-held preconceptions challenged, and a breathing, thinking, feeling, three-dimensional woman is recalled to life.

2

The Receiver

The weather was unseasonably cold in April 1816 when Charlotte Brontë made her way into the world. Winter had not yet loosened its fierce fingered grip on the West Riding of Yorkshire. Snow and ice had travelled south as far as London and had hampered the growing of crops up and down the land.[1] But, despite the unceasing cold and gloom, the twenty-first of the month, the day of Charlotte's birth, also saw hope brought in quite another form, for it was the day the swallows returned, to fill the skies with their euphonious song.[2]

The baby, a third child and daughter for the Reverend Patrick and Maria Brontë, was born at home in the small town of Thornton – a place the indomitable Mrs Gaskell would later describe as 'desolate and wild', perched high on the hillside overlooking the mills and mines of Bradford.[3] Clothing would, as it does for us all, play a significant role in the young Charlotte Brontë's life from the outset. For almost as soon the cord was cut and the new-born girl was separated from her mother, Charlotte was clothed in her first ever garment – a new, soft, flannel cloth, sometimes lined with linen, known down the centuries as a 'receiver'.[4] No biography through dress would be complete without mention of it, for there are few items of clothing more important than that in which we are swathed as we emerge, blue and breathless, from the darkness and the quietude of the womb. Rarely do we keep this square of cloth for, covered in blood, it is not a thing of beauty. But, enveloped in this raiment we are marked out as human – separated from the animal by a simple piece of woven fabric. Our nakedness is hidden from view, and we become something new, something individual, something of ourselves.

The fact that Charlotte's receiver no longer exists to stand testament to that great moment does little to diminish its power or the part that it played in her all too fleeting life. In fact, the same is true for *all* those garments that she wore throughout infancy and childhood that have not survived – for most have not. Though no longer present, these things still warmed her, protected her, shaped her perceptions through their touch, taste and smell and helped her to find her place in the world. Though they are no longer physically here, they still transformed her body into a symbol, a conversation and 'made salient' what might otherwise have remained hidden.[5] They still connected her firmly to the time and the place in which she lived, to the siblings who had worn them before her and to those who would wear them after, to the friends and relatives who had gifted them and to the people and machines that had made them.

Their absence should come as no surprise. After all, how many of our own childhood clothes have survived? Beyond those one or two sentimental pieces, perhaps the lovingly chosen outfit in which we are first brought home or that which we wore the day that we turned two, the rest has been lost to the clear-outs, the wear-outs, the house moves and the pass-me-downs.

In Charlotte's case, her childhood wardrobe would have been formed of items inherited from her older sisters Maria (b. 1814) and Elizabeth (b. 1815), meaning most were second or even third hand before she even wore them. After she had herself outgrown them, some would have been passed on to her younger brother Branwell (b. 1817) and, if there were life still left to give, would then have been worn by Emily (b. 1818) or finally by Anne (1820), the sixth Brontë to be born in little more than seven years.[6]

Furthermore, in the early to mid-nineteenth century, laundering was hard on all clothes, and particularly on those white cotton or linen garments worn by infants and young children, which were subjected to boil washes, bleaching, harsh scrubbing, mangling and drying out of doors in the wind and sun. Even though this process was ruinous to fabric, by the early 1800s cleanliness had been enshrined as *the* social virtue and a key signifier of class, and thus could not be avoided.[7] And nor could the normal rough and tumble of childhood play, which would have inevitably resulted in ripped-seams and torn petticoats.[8]

Those everyday garments that *did* survive the rigours of Brontë family life would not have been allowed to languish unused. Serviceable items would have been passed on to a needy parishioner and even those items beyond wear would have been put to good use, for in the early nineteenth century fabric itself had intrinsic value, so much so that it was almost a currency in itself.[9] It could be used to make mends, quilts, dolls and dolls' clothes or remodelled into new garments.[10] And even rags had worth, employing at least one 'rag gatherer' in every local community.[11] Once these were collected and sold on, some were transformed into paper or bank notes, whilst wool or worsted fragments were cut and ground down before being manufactured into a coarse cloth called 'shoddy'.[12]

Of course, special items, such as christening gowns and caps, were not subject to the same fate. Consequently, it is these cherished garments that make up a disproportionately large percentage of the infant clothing found in museums and archives.[13] Charlotte Brontë's own christening bonnet, worn on 29 April 1816, is one such survivor.[14]

This tamboured muslin and lace bonnet, thought to have been stitched by Maria Brontë's close friend Elizabeth Firth, who mentions making a 'Baby's Cap' for Charlotte in her diary on 2 March, is ingenious in its design.[15] It

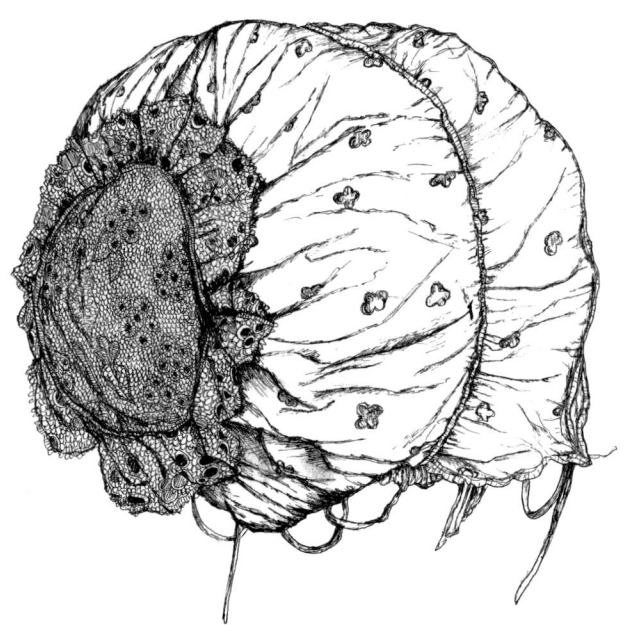

2.1 *Charlotte Brontë's christening bonnet, 1816*

features three rows of fine drawstrings that can be pulled tight through the minute hand-stitched cotton channels, or loosened to accommodate an infant's fast-growing head. As only small quantities of fabric were required to make a baby's cap, it was, in all likelihood, made from scraps of fabric and lace leftover from the making of an adult cap or gown. In her accounts of 1815, the year before Charlotte's birth, Elizabeth Firth notes the purchase of '4 yds tambour'd muslin', a fine woven cotton embroidered with chain-stitch like designs, and '2 yds of lace'.[16] It is likely that surplus pieces were turned to good use and that Firth, using patterns passed on to her by a friend or relative, pieced together the charming little cap that survives to this day.[17]

Charlotte's bonnet was not the only one of her garments to have been so lovingly hand made. Much of her infant wardrobe would have been crafted by her mother using well-honed sewing and embroidery skills that she had perfected since childhood and from patterns included in the countless parenting manuals and advice books that were now so popular.[18] Indeed, many of the infant Charlotte's outer garments would have been meticulously embellished with lace, broderie anglaise, hand embroidery and, most particularly, Hollie point (originally known as Holy point) – a whitework technique used to decorate baby hats, gowns and blankets and into which were often set initials or significant emblems or motifs.[19] For, ultimately, the production of baby clothes was an act of love, of maternal care, familial acceptance. It could also be an opportunity to highlight a family's social position as, where purely practical garments demonstrated due care and preparedness, highly embellished pieces deliberately drew attention to the fact that the child's mother, or those with whom she was associated, had the leisure time to create such ornamental objects.

However, by the early-nineteenth century, some ready-made items were also available. 'Childbed linen and baby clothes' were stocked in many of the new shops and warehouses that had sprung up in larger towns and cities and might also be purchased from a hawker, pedlar or market-seller, who brought drapery, haberdashery and a small range of ready-made garments into more rural areas.[20] Maria might have made the trip to Bradford, just four miles away, or sent away to more distant Leeds, where Jane Booth's well-known warehouse stocked a wide range of 'baby linen' and a selection of 'children's caps' and other off-the-peg items.[21] These white garments and infant accessories, often made from linen manufactured by Marshall's of Leeds, the largest and most successful mechanized flax spinning firm in Britain and Ireland, would have been sewn in cottage industries close to the Brontë family's first home in Thornton.[22]

During the first three months of life, Charlotte and her many siblings, regardless of their gender, would have been dressed in long gowns or 'frocks', shirts and petticoats, close-fitting caps and little knitted socks.[23] Linen or cotton nappies, called 'clouts' or 'napkins', triangular in shape and tied on with cotton tapes that threaded through a loop, were worn beneath, together with a flannel outer nappy known as a 'pilche' or 'pilcher' that was designed to save the clothes from troublesome leaks or explosions.[24] Long, straight pins were still sometimes used (safety pins were not invented until 1849), though their adoption was generally discouraged and particularly after William Cadogan, the 'Father of Childcare', published the story of an infant being inadvertently killed by an errant pin that had 'penetrated several inches into the body' 'causing convulsion-fits'.[25] One can only imagine just how many thousands of napkins Maria and the family nursemaids, Nancy and Sarah Garr, changed between the years 1814 and 1822.[26] If one sticks to the conservative estimate of 5,000 per child in the first eighteen months of life, then at least 30,000 were changed, washed, boiled and dried during that busy period in the Brontë household.

On reaching five or six months old, Charlotte's clothing was altered to reflect her need to move about more freely. The long, flowing frocks which she had worn as an infant were replaced by much shorter gowns, that featured a square-cut neckline, a waisted bodice and a skirt that finished well above the ankle. These simple garments would have allowed her to crawl, walk and eventually run and play, relatively unencumbered.

Until the last quarter of the eighteenth century, upper- and middle-class children had not enjoyed unfettered freedom in their dress and, as babies, had been swaddled tightly in cloths and were later bound by restrictive stays and garments that closely mirrored those worn by their parents. However, a new and radical philosophy, with roots stretching back to the work of British theorist and physician John Locke and echoed and expanded by

2.2 *Clothing of a young girl c. 1820*

others, most notably Jean-Jacques Rousseau and William Buchan, had sparked a revolution in juvenile dress.[27] By the time Charlotte was born in 1816, children's clothes were distinct from those of adults, and constrictive garments had been exchanged for loose and agile clothes that allowed for far greater freedom of movement, comfort and exploration. Charlotte and her siblings were fortunate to enjoy such sartorial liberty. By 1830, fashions would fly to the 'opposite extreme' and children's clothing once again featured tight bodices, more restrictive sleeves and full, cumbersome skirts overburdened with embellishment.[28]

As Charlotte moved from toddlerhood to childhood, she would have worn short-sleeved, high-waisted gowns with drawstring necks and bodices that often fastened at the back. These were coupled with cotton pantalettes or drawers to provide modesty and to add extra warmth to otherwise insubstantial outfits.[29] High-crowned bonnets, traditionally worn by young girls, were often composed of nankeen, beaver or straw.[30] For outdoor wear, long silk or cloth pelisses or short spencers were worn and on very cold days these were supplemented with warm woollen shawls and thick, white stockings.[31] Yet these measures were not always enough to keep out the cold. Phebe Lucas, born the same year as Charlotte, later recalled, 'even in winter, I never had long sleeves to my frocks tho' I suffered very much from chapped hands and arms, but it was not the custom to leave off short sleeves to our frocks until we were twelve or thirteen years old'.[32]

Printed cottons were often worn for ordinary daywear as cotton and its derivatives had overtaken silk in popularity.[33] Inexpensive and easy to wash, sew, repair and dry, it also came in an increasingly vast array of patterns. For, although roller printing had been utilized since 1790, it had only been possible to make small, monochrome patterns which often ran in stripes, but new innovations in printing ensured that by 1815, wider, more colourful designs could be produced at a low cost. White muslin was typically worn for Sunday best, but more robust cotton gowns in ditsy prints and ginghams, with tucks and hems added to allow for growth, made for a sensible choice for everyday use.[34] Yet, as Patrick Brontë himself made clear, the adoption of cotton was not without its hazards. In 1843, he wrote to the *Leeds Mercury* stating that he had buried between ninety and a hundred children whose cotton clothes had caught alight and consequently advocated for the wearing of less flammable silk and wool. But, as numerous cotton articles still remain at the parsonage, it seems that, for reasons of frugality and practicality, Patrick chose to exercise 'parental caution' rather than outright prohibition.[35]

The boots worn by upper- and middle-class children were made from strong cotton or leather, or a combination of the two. These came in a huge range of colours, and, though black was common for older children, red was popular for toddlers. Smarter occasions often called for silk or soft leather pumps, and these too came in a wide variety of hues, though black and white were most prevalent. Neither boots nor pumps were robust enough to protect the feet against the harshest Yorkshire weather, so pattens were often worn. These unyielding, oval irons were strapped to the underside of the shoe and lifted the wearer up and out of the mud.[36] Both adults and children also wore clogs or flat overshoes or mules. Indeed, the Brontë sisters are remembered as having worn 'strong, low-fitting shoes and various hued stockings'.[37] A small pair of thick leather-soled mules, just 20cm in length, have survived and, though research is ongoing, might well have been worn by Charlotte or one of her sisters.[38]

By 1820, the number of young Brontës living in the small house in Thornton had swelled considerably. The consequences were manifold. What had begun as a modest but manageable income when the Reverend and Mrs Brontë had arrived in the parish of Thornton in 1815 with one baby daughter, was now, with five more children and two maidservants to care for, considerably stretched. Although Maria's £50 per annum annuity, left to her by her father on his death in 1808, made all the difference, by January 1820, the family were really beginning to feel the pinch. Patrick's clerical salary of £127 per year did not go far, and, as he wrote in a letter to the Queen Anne's Bounty, a charity

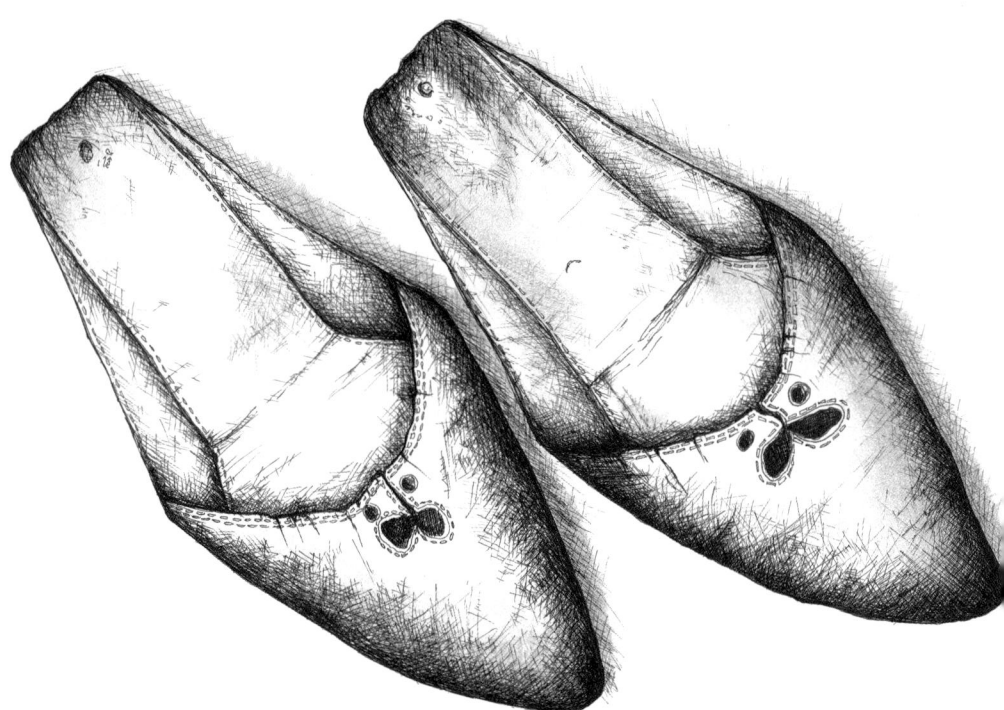

2.3 *Child's leather mules, c. 1820s, 2004.33.1*

which supplemented the salaries of poorly paid clergymen, even with 'the most rigorous economy', it was now almost impossible 'to uphold in appearance the due degree of Clerical respectability'.[39]

Patrick had been offered a higher paying ministerial position in the village of Haworth, just six miles north-west of Thornton, but political wranglings had ground all proceedings to a halt. He had long given up hope that the job would ever be his and, in consequence, had appealed to the Archbishop of York for his support in the application for a grant. Preferring to find a more permanent solution to the problem facing the Brontës, the Archbishop stepped in to intervene. Just four days later, the Reverend Patrick Brontë was formally offered the position as perpetual curate for the Church of St Michael and All Angels in Haworth. It came with a larger house, a larger salary and a larger parish. Little did they know then, just how much this place would come to change and shape them all.[40]

In the spring of 1820, the Brontës prepared to leave Thornton for the last time. There is little doubt that with six children and four adults to consider, it was a big move and one that would have entailed considerable planning and organization. Pots and pans, clothes and crockery, books and bedlinen were piled high onto seven horse-drawn carts, loaned for the occasion by local wool-stapler and farmer Stephen Taylor of Stanbury.[41] Whatever else came with them, once thing is certain, that as Charlotte travelled the six miles along rugged Pennine roads, passing through obdurate moorland and steep river valleys, so too did that ever-changing barometer of her life – her wardrobe.

If Thornton was, as Mrs Gaskell would later attest, 'desolate and wild', the moors around Haworth were far more so. Surrounded by hills so imperious, so immense, that they appeared to 'girdle the world like the great Norse serpent', the place that the Brontës arrived in was bleak and unforgiving, devoid of all hedgerows, empty of trees, with a sky as vast and tumultuous as any ocean.[42] On the outlying limb of the Pennine range, it was a landscape of silver, auburn and sage, where the wind blew cold and even the houses, solid as they were, stood dour on the rugged hillside.[43]

Yet, isolated, austere and rural as it all appeared, 1820s Haworth was also a place of great industry. Within reach of the fast-growing towns of Bradford, Halifax and Burnley, and served by the River Worth and other tributaries, by the time the Brontës arrived, numerous textile mills had sprung up along

2.4 *Haworth Parsonage*

the riverbanks, with at least eighteen within the wider parish and three in the centre of Haworth itself.[44] These factories, each involved in the manufacture of a dizzying array of worsteds and wool-based products, between them employed a high percentage of the men, women and children who lived in Haworth and its sprawling, outlying areas. Beyond the mills themselves, in cottages and farms dotted around the parish, were countless other workers – hand-loom weavers, woolcombers, yeomen, staplers, shuttle-makers, wool-sorters, spinners and farmers – all of whom added to the smoke and steam and smog and smells that filled the valley each day.

High up above Haworth there were quarries too, and from these was extracted the sandstone used in the many buildings being thrown up at speed throughout the West Riding of Yorkshire and beyond. The majority of the brooding, blackened houses that loomed over the village had been built from locally mined stone, including the impressive, large windowed, Georgian parsonage that would be Charlotte's home for the rest of her life. As almost the last house in Haworth, it sat at the very top of the village, looking out over the eighteenth-century church, St Michael and All Angels, on to Main Street below and then on to the windswept moorland beyond.

The village itself was a busy and bustling place, with eleven grocers, five butcher's shops, two confectioners and no fewer than six public houses, two of which could be seen from the Parsonage's front windows.[45] With many of the mills already lit with gas when the Brontës arrived in 1820, the deafening whack, crack and rattle of looms was the soundtrack of the village from early in the morning until late at night. To this was added the noise of pigs, sheep and cows, as local farmers and smallholders drove livestock up and down Main Street on their way to market or pasture.

It was to this place – parochial and revolutionary in equal measure – that the Brontës came to live and to serve their new community. After all the packing, unpacking and uncertainty, it must have been heartening for the family to find themselves finally settled in their new home. No doubt the children were delighted with their new-found freedom, with a garden back and front, and an endless expanse of moorland to explore. But, though there was much to be hopeful about, much to look forward to as summer approached, dark clouds were already gathering over the Haworth Parsonage.

Almost from the moment he had arrived, Patrick had thrown himself headlong into his duties, christening babies, marrying young couples, presiding over services, and visiting the needy and the sick. His characteristic enthusiasm did not abate, even as the months passed, and his wife Maria's strength began to falter. Yet, by the end of January 1821, her health had deteriorated to such an extent that those around her feared that it was an illness from which she was unlikely to recover.

The much loved and much heralded Haworth surgeon, Thomas Andrew, was swiftly brought in to offer his help and advice, but it was soon clear that there was nothing that could be done to slow her decline. It is now widely thought that uterine cancer was the likely cause of Maria's immense suffering, though, on reviewing the case, one renowned gynaecologist and obstetrician has argued that pelvic sepsis and anaemia could also have been to blame.[46] Patrick, and presumably the other physicians whom he called to the parsonage, certainly appear to have attributed Maria's symptoms to a malignant tumour. In consequence, the word cancer must have hung dark and heavy over that place, just as it has in many homes before and since.

In spite of the unfolding tragedy, Patrick's ministerial duties did not diminish and nor, apparently, did his desire to fulfil them. Although always a fierce advocate for his parishioners, he also knew that if he did not work, he did not earn and, with six children and an increasing number of medical bills to pay, Patrick was left with no choice but to juggle it all. To make matters worse still, as Maria's illness progressed, so too did her need for round the clock care. This came at considerable cost and, finding himself no longer able to cope alone, Patrick employed a nurse. The local woman, Martha Wright, tended to the patient in the day, but it was Maria's faithful husband who continued to do so at night – getting up at all hours to meet his wife's needs.[47]

Additional support was soon forthcoming. In May 1821, four months after the onset of the more acute stage of Maria's illness, Elizabeth Firth, that friend who had so lovingly made a bonnet for Charlotte, arrived to take the two eldest children, Maria and Elizabeth, back with her to Thornton for a month-long holiday. This kindness was only exceeded by the welcome arrival of Maria's sister Elizabeth, known to the children, and others besides, as Aunt Branwell.

Maria's grave illness was reason enough for Aunt Branwell to make the long journey from Cornwall, but the arrival of an even more prolific illness had hastened her arrival. Scarlet fever, one of the greatest child killers of the nineteenth century, had reached Haworth. Indeed, by the time that she had arrived, the characteristic rash, the sore throat, the fever, the bold inflammation of lymph nodes and abscessing of the throat and tonsils had already declared their presence at the parsonage, where coughs and sneezes were liberally shared.[48] The little Brontës, who were now aged between seven and one, were soon desperately ill. All their poor father and mother could do was watch and wait as the deadly bacterial infection swept through the house at astonishing speed – an experience that, in a post-pandemic world, we now understand more keenly. The weeks that followed saw Patrick shoulder 'the greatest load of sorrows that [had] ever pressed on [him]' as he faced the imminent loss of not just his wife but potentially that of his six children too.[49]

Just as all hope seemed lost, like some Florence Nightingale, Aunt Branwell swept in. Where her tender ministrations could do little to help Maria, her confident nursing could benefit her sister's poor, sick, soon-to-be motherless children. Slowly but surely the young Maria, Elizabeth, Charlotte, Branwell,

Emily and Anne all recovered, defying the odds that had been so severely stacked against them.[50] The illness would undoubtedly weaken them in the longer term, but for now at least they were well. Aunt Branwell's presence had transformed the atmosphere of the house. The irksome nurse, who had once enjoyed a good relationship with the Brontës, was, much to her annoyance, swiftly removed, and for the last dreadful days of Maria Brontë's life, familial love, mingled with practical efficiency, reigned supreme in the Haworth Parsonage.[51]

Thirty-eight-year-old Maria Brontë, née Branwell, died on 15 September 1821 surrounded by her husband, her sister and her six small children. Her middle daughter, Charlotte, was just five and a half years old. Anne, the youngest, not yet two. The tiny, scholarly, loving wife and mother was buried just seven days later in the vault near the altar. As was common practice in the early to mid-nineteenth century, Maria, Elizabeth, Charlotte, Branwell, Emily and even little Anne would have attended the service dressed in suitable mourning clothes of black silk, stuff or bombazine or, alternatively, in white with black ribbons.[52] Though no reference to their funeral dress survives, Aunt Branwell, as the children's new loco parentis, would not have allowed them to wear anything that reflected badly upon her recently departed sister, upon her brother-in-law or, perhaps more importantly, upon her own staunch self.

Maria's early death inevitably had long-term bearing on all the children that she left behind, and on Charlotte in particular. But, though the mother they loved had gone, in the short term at least, the day-to-day rhythm of their lives was little altered by her loss. She had, after all, been terminally ill for many months, or, as it no doubt seemed to them, for an eternity. Their father remained as constant and attentive as he had always been and watched 'over his bereaved flock with truly paternal solicitude and affection'.[53] His presence was a stabilizing force – as a much loving father as guardian and protector.[54] His good efforts were bolstered by the presence of Aunt Branwell, who according to Patrick was not only in constant attendance, but also acted as 'an affectionate mother' to the bevy of little Brontës. Young nursemaids Nancy and Sarah Garr were also unceasing in their care and kindness, and, though not a great deal older than the children whom they attended, proved themselves loyal and loving, even long after the children had grown.[55]

For Charlotte, any remaining gap, maternal or otherwise, was filled by her older sisters Maria and Elizabeth. Warm-hearted and intelligent, the two girls led their younger siblings out of grief and sorrow, first distracting and then engaging them with games and stories and invented plays. After morning lessons with Patrick, time was spent cooking with Sarah or sewing with Aunt Branwell. It was during this time that the Brontë sisters stitched small, square samplers. Six-year-old Charlotte's, which was originally made using red thread that has now faded to brown, features neat rows of letters, numbers and Proverbs 22:4, which reads, 'By humility and the fear of the Lord, are riches, honour and life'.[56]

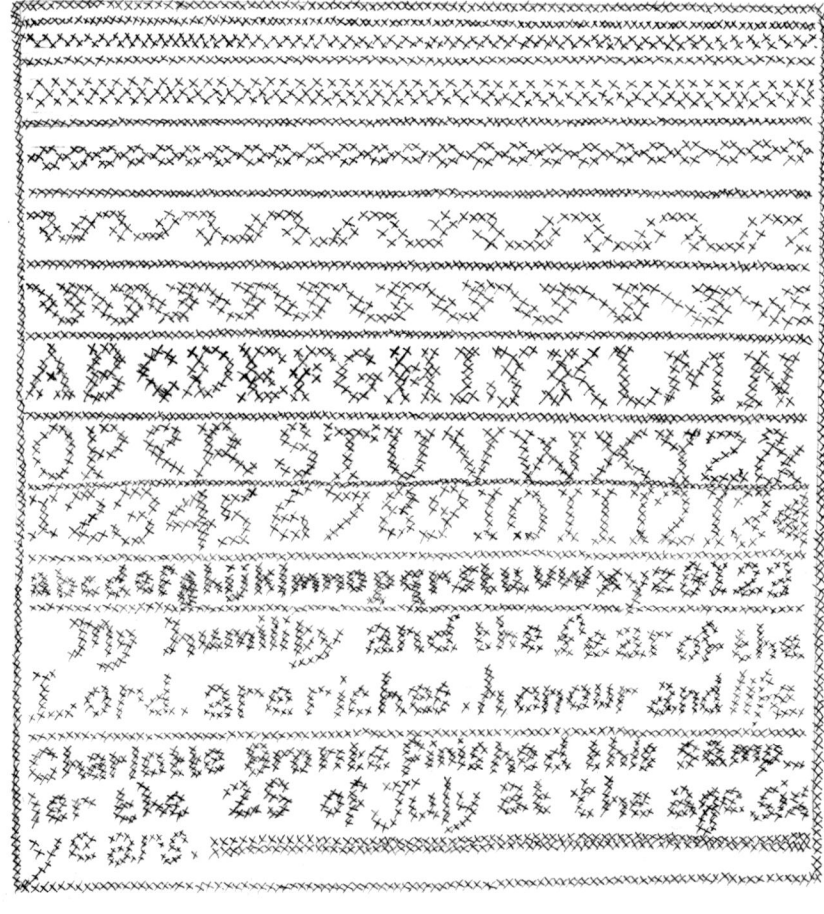

2.5 *Charlotte Brontë's sampler, July 1822, S15*

In the afternoons, the children poured out onto the moor, where 'they sallied forth, each neatly and comfortably clad' and enjoyed 'a game of romps and played with zest'. When together, 'their fun new no bounds' and they 'expressed it wildly ... with many a merry burst of laughter'.[57] Unbeknownst to Charlotte, through their resilience and determined joie de vivre, her older sisters were teaching her important lessons in leadership – the results of which she would have to put to use far more quickly than she could ever imagine.

In the months and then years that had lapsed since his wife's death, Patrick had taken the academic instruction of his children extremely seriously. As his friend William Dearden would later recall, 'He had too high an appreciation of the value of education to neglect his duty in that particular'.[58] Patrick knew its worth first-hand. It had been education that had changed the course of his own life and opened up a world of possibility far beyond the expected bounds set for him as the eldest of ten children born to a farmer in Drumballyroney, Ireland. Entirely because of the opportunities his learning had afforded him, against all odds, he had gained a place to study theology at St John's College, Cambridge and fulfilled his long-held dream to become a Church of England minister, gaining a living and pulpit of his own. Yet, despite how far he had come, he knew that the life he had built was precarious, and especially so for his children. For, with no money spare to save, and a house and income dependent on his post, at his death they would have nothing left upon which to live. And death, as he now knew, could be an all too unexpected and unwelcome visitor.

As a learned man, Patrick was well equipped to tutor his children in traditional academic subjects, but, where these, together with some functional skills, would be the main focus of his son Branwell's education, his daughters' requirements were very different. Contemporary society dictated that, alongside a basic education, emphasis should be placed on the perfection of feminine accomplishments such as singing, dancing, music, Italian, French, German, drawing and fine sewing. These, it was hoped, would prepare them for marriage to a man of substance (though with poor connections this was unlikely), or, failing that, for a life spent as a teacher or governess. Where Patrick could teach history or classical literature with ease, these more feminine refinements were beyond his capabilities. And, with his sister-in-law now beginning to consider her return to Penzance and Nancy and Sarah Garr less accomplished than the girls that they would teach, he had no choice but to send his older daughters away to school.

Maria and Elizabeth were the first to make the journey to the Clergy Daughters' School in the hamlet of Cowan Bridge, Lancashire. When they arrived in July 1824, the school was newly opened, with only sixteen other pupils already in residence. As its name suggests, it was a charitable establishment, formed specifically for the education of the daughters of poor, evangelical clergymen – just like the Brontë girls. Supported by the generous patronage of many good and wealthy benefactors, the school aimed to meet both the educational and spiritual needs of its pupils, and at a dramatically reduced cost to their parents. For Patrick, the school appeared to be an answer to prayer. Two daughters could receive a 'plain and useful education' for the same price that he would have paid for just one to attend a typical fee-paying school. And yet, as the prospectus promised, it would still 'fit them for the different stations of life [to which] Providence might call them.'[59]

It must have been hard for Charlotte to see her two older sisters leave home without her, but, challenging as their separation must have been, they did not have many weeks to wait until they were once again reunited. By August 1824, eight-year-old Charlotte had joined Maria and Elizabeth at the Clergy Daughters' School and by late November of the same year, so had little Emily.

In those countries where it is commonly worn, the moment we are clothed in our first school uniform is a significant one. Not only does it mark the beginning of a new life, separate from our parents, but it is also one of the first occasions in which we are materially conditioned by forces outside the family. This clothing does not reflect our individuality, or even the taste of those who have brought us up.[60] And, whilst it might have been chosen for reasons of practicality or to engender community, these prescribed shirts and ties, hats and coats can also be used to reinforce the idealized aims and identities of the school itself and project these onto the wearer for everyone to see. Therefore, though the wearing of uniform might seem inconsequential to some, to the sensitive, proud young Charlotte, this forced donning of 'borrow'd robes' proved extremely challenging and shaped her relationship with dress for years to come.[61]

From morning until night, Charlotte and her classmates' clothing was predetermined. The school prospectus stipulated that 'girls will all appear in the same dress'.[62] By day, all pupils wore a cotton shift, a pair of stays, wool and

2.6 Girl wearing winter uniform of the Clergy Daughters' School, Cowan Bridge

flannel petticoats, a pair of pockets, white cotton or black wool stockings, a brown pinafore, and, if cold, a nankeen spencer.[63] 'For the sake of uniformity' these items, which were made and brought from home, were accompanied by two frocks, a pelisse, a bonnet, tippet and frills.[64] These were provided by the school at the not insignificant cost of three pounds per child. During the summer, Charlotte was required to wear a plain, straw cottage bonnet, a nankeen cotton frock for working days and a white frock for church on Sunday. In the winter these lighter weight garments were exchanged for more substantial purple, stuff frocks and purple cloaks or pelisses. At night too, a strict uniform was observed, with the girls putting on plain white nightcaps and shifts or nightgowns.

The choice of purple as the school's representative colour, and particularly in those outer garments worn at church and when in public, is unexpected. Materials can now be printed or dyed almost any colour under the sun, but this was not the case in the early nineteenth century. Then, fabric manufacturers had only natural dyes at their disposal, and these varied drastically in cost, meaning not all colours were created equal. Purple dyestuffs were amongst the most expensive to produce and consequently the colour had long been associated with royalty, imperiality, authority and power.[65] So strong were its symbolic connotations that the Emperor Nero severely restricted the use of purple dyes, and Elizabethan sumptuary laws in England dictated that only Queen Elizabeth I and specific members of her wider family were permitted to wear it.[66] Though, by the nineteenth century, other, more cost-effective purple dyestuffs such as *orcein* (derived from various tree lichens) or imported logwood had been identified, it remained an expensive, though highly fashionable colour to produce. The material used to create Charlotte's purple spencers and pelisses would have been coloured using one of these alternative dyestuffs, but purple was still a surprising choice, especially as it would have increased the cost borne by the girls' parents.

We cannot know for certain why purple was chosen by the board of the Clergy Daughters' School. It might have been selected to draw attention to the generosity of the many eminent benefactors. Alternatively, purple may have been picked to make a subtle yet material distinction between *their* girls, the daughters of Church of England ministers, and the orphaned or poverty-stricken children who attended typical charity schools. By the early nineteenth century the uniforms worn by these charity school children had become iconic. Uniforms had been adopted in such educational institutions since the mid-sixteenth century, but, by the eighteenth, these often bright blue uniforms were used as a means of stamping a school's authority and values upon its pupils.[67] So synonymous did they become with the education of the poor, that small, blue-coated statues, sat high on buildings, in London's Hatton Garden for example, still mark many of the sites of former charity schools to this day.[68]

Blue or grey cloth was commonly chosen and largely for reasons of economy. All uniforms were necessarily provided by the charitable institutions themselves, meaning cost was a constant consideration. Woad or *Isatis tinctoria* is easily cultivated and inexpensive to produce. It yields a strong and long-lasting blue colour, especially on wool, making it the ideal dyestuff for coats and jackets. Grey, brown or drab-coloured garments were even cheaper to produce as they were created by simply interweaving the cream, grey and black fibres taken from undyed fleeces.

Aside from the obvious benefits of education, the provision of garments was one of the main reasons that impoverished parents chose to send their children to school.[69] Yet, it has been argued that the distinctive styles of the uniform were also designed to highlight the pupils' lowly status and tangibly remind them, and those around them, that they were in receipt of charity.[70] By the time Charlotte went to the Clergy Daughters' School in 1824, it was considered essential that a proper sense of humility was developed in the poor from an early age, so as to better prepare them for their future lives of subordination and servitude.[71]

In the light of all of this, it is not difficult to comprehend why Charlotte, young as she was, perceived her school uniform to be a badge of dishonour. Indeed, her visceral fears are given voice in the early chapters of her semi-autobiographical novel *Jane Eyre* (1847) where her protagonist attends 'Lowood', an establishment similar to the Clergy Daughters' School in Cowan Bridge, where fees were supplemented by subscription. Like Charlotte, Jane Eyre asks anxiously, 'Why do they call us charity-children?'[72]

The girls at Lowood are clothed in 'brown dresses, made high and surrounded by a narrow tucker about the throat', 'woollen stockings and country made shoes'.[73] Though hard-wearing and practical, the clothing does not engender pride in the school or unity amongst the girls. In fact, its affects are wholly negative. Charlotte describes the 'quaint assemblage' of pupils sitting 'motionless and erect' in their uniforms, which gave 'an air of oddity even to the prettiest'.[74]

Here at Lowood, and presumably at the Clergy Daughters' School, all individuality is deliberately 'cut off' with even 'curled hair' considered a 'vanity'.[75] It is the school's intention, or more accurately, Mr Brocklehurst's, the superintendent's intention, to 'mortify in these girls the lusts of the flesh, to teach them to clothe themselves with shamefacedness and sobriety, not with braided hair and costly apparel'.[76] For he believes that the girls' inferior position deems them undeserving of individuality or fashionable dress, but not so his own wife and daughters who are introduced to us 'splendidly attired' in 'velvet, silk and furs', their 'gray beaver hats … shaded with ostrich plumes' and placed on top of 'a profusion of light tresses, elaborately curled'.[77] Higher in social status (though it must be added only marginally), they are allowed sartorial freedoms that Jane, and by default the young Charlotte, are to be taught they are not.

Of course, we cannot view Charlotte's descriptions of Lowood as an unflinchingly accurate account of her own experiences at the Clergy Daughters' School – truth here is mingled with fiction. But her later struggles with prescriptive clothing, and particularly during her years of paid work, when a kind of uniform was once again expected, confirm that there exists an all too poignant truth at its heart.

The lasting impact of Charlotte's time in Cowan Bridge was in no way limited to issues of dress. The food served to the girls was, according to Brontë, as scanty as it was inedible, leading to irreparable physical and emotional damage. Charlotte, who often left her food rather than eat it, placed blame at the door of the 'dirty carelessness of the cook' who 'boiled the puddings in unclean water' and 'too often sent up the porridge, not merely burnt, but with offensive fragments of other substances discoverable in it'.[78] Though some contemporaries, and particularly former staff members, sought to challenge Charlotte's later assertions, others vehemently lent their support. One of her classmates argued that the 'food was almost always badly cooked, and besides that we certainly had not enough of it whatever may be said to the contrary'. She even recalled one harrowing incident in which, 'having once been sent for a cup of tea for a teacher who was ill in bed, and no teaspoon being at hand, the housekeeper stirred the tea with her finger, she being engaged in cutting raw meat at the time'.[79]

Given Charlotte's natural sensitivity, it is not surprising that both her appetite and her ongoing relationship with food were severely affected by her time at Cowan Bridge. Even five years after she had left the school and moved on to another, her friend Ellen Nussey remembered her 'exceeding thinness and want of complexion'.[80] Mary Taylor, another fellow pupil, observed Charlotte's physical weakness and remarked that she could rarely be persuaded to eat anything more substantial than vegetables as her main meal.

Throughout her life, Brontë continued to endure an uneasy relationship with food and, as her surviving clothes attest, remained notably thin.[81] In her letters she frequently speaks of being unable to eat before and after her travels to London, Brussels or following any challenging journey. Her lack of appetite was also apparent after the deaths of each of her siblings and during periods of cold weather. Phrases such as I 'had no appetite to eat',[82] 'it was impossible to eat a morsel',[83] and 'I always feel under awkward constraint at table' are commonly found in her letters, suggesting a negative association between the act of eating and excess emotion.[84] This connection was not limited to her personal life, Charlotte's complex relationship with food also made its way into her novels where the malnourished body often appears.[85] Here, just like Charlotte, her protagonists desire food but learn to repress their hunger, often in an effort to manage emotional chaos.[86]

Considering the lasting impact the poor food at Cowan Bridge had upon Charlotte, it is hard to believe that it did not also contribute to all the pupils' poor health. Certainly, Brontë believed the 'accommodation, diet, the discipline, the system of tuition' as well as the school's unhealthy geographical position, were responsible for the frequent outbreaks of typhus, scrofula and consumption that plagued the students.[87] Elizabeth Gaskell claimed that the school's poor conditions were directly responsible for Charlotte's 'stunted' growth and for the later deaths of her two sisters.[88] The degree to which blame can be placed upon the school was, and remains, a hotly disputed topic.[89] Yet, fifteen pupils died of either typhus fever or tuberculosis between the years 1825 and 1831 and two of that number were Charlotte's own beloved sisters, Maria and Elizabeth.[90]

The onset of her sister Maria's illness appears to have been gradual. When Emily arrived at the school in November, Patrick does not seem to have noticed a drastic change in the health of his eldest daughter. It could be that tuberculosis had not fully taken hold, or rather, that like Helen Burns of *Jane Eyre*, Maria bore her illness with an unnatural fortitude.[91] Whichever it was, by December, her consumptive state was apparent to all. Doctors were called, treatments administered, but perhaps because staff at the school hoped they could get her through the worst, her father was not informed. Three months passed before he was told, by which time it was too late. On receipt of the school's letter, a desperate Patrick immediately left for Cowan Bridge. On finding Maria critically unwell he instantly made the decision to bring her home to Haworth where he hoped the loving presence of her family would encourage her to rally. But, deep as his care and affection for his daughter was, it was not enough to save her. The second Maria Brontë died on Friday 6 May 1825, aged just eleven. Terrible as it was for all those at the parsonage, one can only imagine how the three eldest living Brontë daughters, Elizabeth, Charlotte and Emily, away at school and unable to properly mourn their sister, must have clung together on receiving the devasting news.

The loss of such a young life was not to be an isolated event in the Brontë household. Not long after Maria's death, Charlotte's remaining older sister, Elizabeth, also became gravely ill with tuberculosis. Once again, by the time she had returned from school to Haworth, there was little that could be done. Patrick immediately fetched Charlotte and Emily from the Clergy Daughters' School, in part to lessen their risk of becoming unwell, but also, presumably, to allow them to bid a proper farewell to their dying sister. On Tuesday 15 June 1825, just six weeks after Maria's death, Elizabeth passed away. She was ten years old.

Although their loss was felt keenly by the entire Brontë family, it was Charlotte who was most affected. Where, following her mother's death, she had been protected by her older sisters, she now experienced the full impact of bereavement. Companions, comforters, upholders, defenders, Maria and Elizabeth had proved themselves both sisters and substitute mothers since Maria Brontë's death in 1821. But in this, the very darkest period of Charlotte's young life, there was little time to grieve for herself, for now the eldest, she was required to pick up her sisters' fallen mantle. From this point on, it would be her job to nurture and protect Branwell, Emily and Anne in the same way that she herself had been four years before. And this unnatural responsibility would weigh heavily on her shoulders for much of the rest of her life.

3

Romance and Reality

Life in the Brontë household would never be the same again, and yet, as is so often the case after catastrophe, in many ways it was. Charlotte did not return to the Clergy Daughters' School, but she did resume lessons at the dining room table alongside her brother and sisters. Just as they had always done, the children poured out onto the moor in all weathers, trampling through the heather, running through ferns, climbing rocky outcrops or sheltering from the rain under their father's capacious brown umbrella.[1]

Although the children mourned their sisters and the life they'd shared before, writing stories and inventing plays had also become increasingly fundamental to their happiness. The world outside had proved itself a harsh and cruel place filled with danger, misery and loss. Yet here, safe behind the solid stone walls of the parsonage, Charlotte and her remaining siblings could withdraw to fantastical places of their own making – controllable spaces where only that which they allowed could ever happen. Thus, these imaginative kingdoms were exclusive, inviolable, closed to all but their tiny troupe.[2]

Their father Patrick might not have joined in his children's games, yet that does not mean he was not influential. His own enthusiasm for military history, politics, classics, poetry and literature can be discerned in the children's stories and early writings.[3] His library was always open to them, and, in what was highly unusual for the period, he placed almost no constraints upon their reading. Instead, he encouraged visits to circulating and subscription libraries and purchased books whenever funds allowed. He borrowed copies of *Blackwood's Magazine* and *John Bull* from his friend, Jonas Driver, who lived in the village. He himself also subscribed to *Fraser's*, a strongly conservative general and literary journal, to the *Leeds Mercury* and the *Leeds Intelligencer*. These the children scoured for news – local, national and international – military manoeuvres, political debate and discussion of pressing topical issues.[4]

It was not only Patrick's interests that influenced the Brontë children. They all, and especially the romantically inclined young Charlotte, returned to their mother's surviving library again and again. Largely composed of early editions of the *Lady's Magazine*, amassed by Maria during her youth and early adult years, the collection's unusual history only added to its allure. For, as the brine-stained periodicals attested, they had, quite literally, been saved from the stormy sea. In the winter of 1812, just before her marriage to Patrick, Maria had shipped her precious copies, along with some of her other more cumbersome belongings, from her family home in Penzance, Cornwall, to her new address in Yorkshire. Most of the items never arrived. The ship carrying Maria's trunk was wrecked off the coast of Devon, and all but Robert Southey's book, *The Remains of Henry Kirke White*, and the volumes of the *Lady's Magazine* were swallowed up by the waves.[5]

Like some forbidden fruit, Charlotte devoured the contents of these highly gendered magazines 'on holiday afternoons or by stealth when [she] should have been minding [her] lessons'. 'Never', she claimed years later in a letter to Hartley Coleridge, the eldest son of poet Samuel Taylor Coleridge, had she ever seen 'anything which [would] interest [her] so much again'.[6] Bursting with articles on fiction, poetry, art, fashion, music and society, it is not hard to understand why Charlotte was so drawn to the pages of the *Lady's Magazine*.[7] Though very outdated by the time she was old enough to read them, these volumes not only informed her stories, but also her artworks and her imaginative play.

Aunt Branwell shared her niece's interest in the *Lady's Magazine* and, unlike her brother-in-law, Patrick, was not alarmed by Charlotte's preoccupation with its 'foolish love-stories'.[8] Growing up in the lively port town of Penzance – a key artery that connected Britain with the rest of the world through a constant and dynamic flow of things, she and her ten siblings had been used to a much more cosmopolitan world than had Patrick.[9] Elizabeth and Maria's father, Thomas Branwell, was a well-known merchant and importer of foreign goods, who also owned numerous properties in the coastal town, including a busy grocer's shop, a brewery and several inns. As a successful businessman with strong connections within the thriving Methodist community, he wielded considerable power in the local area and Elizabeth, Maria and their brothers and sisters had enjoyed all associated benefits – including the latest imports of silks, tea and all manner of other goods, as well as access to endless social events and activities to which the great and good of all Penzance society were invited.[10] Accordingly, Elizabeth Branwell well understood the magnetic draw of the *Lady's Magazine*, for it must have brought her own youth to life once again.

There is little doubt that this broad spectrum of printed matter had profound impact upon Charlotte, Branwell, Emily and Anne's childish games and writings. Yet, in the end, the catalyst for their creative energies came not in book form, but rather in the shape of twelve painted wooden soldiers, given to Branwell by Patrick on 5 June 1826 on his return from a clerical conference in Leeds.[11] This unexpected gift would prove the stimulus for the creation of a whole new visionary kingdom that would dominate the children's creative lives for years to come. For, in the minds of the young Brontës, these simple toy soldiers would quickly become the 'Twelves' or the 'Young Men', veterans of the protracted Peninsular War who, at the end of their triumphant campaign had embarked on a daring voyage to Africa where they had set up camp in the kingdom of Ashantee.[12] The soldiers would go on to form the 'Glass Town Confederacy', a collection of states at the very centre of which sat The Great Glass Town – a towering, glittering metropolis of magnificent proportions.

From this point on, their writing and much of their art centred around this new, imagined kingdom. Together, the children invented complex histories, geographies and wars and outworked romances and alliances. They wrote and performed plays which only they would see, produced magazines, complete with advertising, and books of stories so small that they could only be read with a magnifying glass. Over time, a huge body of paradoxically tiny work was generated, some of which has survived and can still be seen in museums and archives across the world.[13]

As the years passed, the four young Brontës did not lose their enthusiasm for the inhabitants of Glass Town or its derivatives. Though they had, by 1829, begun to pair off, Charlotte with Branwell and Emily with Anne, they continued to spend many contented hours each day inhabiting their imaginary realms. But, though it seemed to them as if the cocoon they had created would protect them forever, in the summer of 1830, something happened to challenge this conviction. Their father Patrick, normally fit and healthy, was struck down by a severe inflammation of the lungs.[14] Busy as always with his family and with his never-ending duties within the parish, he did not, at first, grant his affliction due attention. By the middle of June he was confined to his bed, gravely ill. For three long weeks there was no improvement and, in what was a shocking departure for both Patrick and the community he served, his ministerial duties were temporarily passed to Thomas Plummer, headmaster of the nearby Keighley Free Grammar School.[15]

The children, and especially Charlotte, were deeply shaken by their father's sudden illness. To them he had always been a giant of a man – strong, brave, impenetrable, but his hacking cough and weakened lungs had laid his mortality bare. Suddenly, the horrors that Charlotte had pushed away to the recesses of her mind had found a way back in, and Patrick was well aware of them too. An uncertain future loomed ahead of them all. With his eldest daughter already fourteen, he knew the time had come for her to face the world. A single year of formal education was not enough to equip her for the road that circumstances required her to tread.

After the horrors of the Clergy Daughters' School, Patrick approached the choosing of a new educational establishment for his sensitive daughter with some trepidation. His final decision appears to have been dictated by a number of factors. Not only did Roe Head School have an excellent reputation, but it was also situated in a place with which Patrick was very familiar. The village of Mirfield was just half a mile from the church at Hartshead, where he had worked as curate in 1811. And, though some eighteen miles from Haworth, Charlotte's godparents, the Reverend Thomas and Frances Atkinson, lived less than a mile from the school, and the Reverend James Clarke Franks and his wife Elizabeth Franks (née Firth) just four or five miles further away. Charlotte would, he knew, be well looked after and, this time, should any problem arise, he was sure that he would be quickly informed.

His choice proved to be a good and sensible one. Roe Head could not have been more different from the Clergy Daughters' School. It was a genteel place, run by five genteel women – Miss Margaret Wooler and her sisters, Catherine, Susan, Marianne and Eliza. The building which housed the school was large, the rooms capacious. Surrounded by elegant grounds and woods through which the girls could safely walk, it was a kind of sanctuary. And, where the pupils at Cowan Bridge were all poor clergymen's daughters with limited expectations, here they were the offspring of the leading manufacturing families of the region – wealthy, polished, with prospects.

Roe Head was not a large school. No more than ten girls appear to have boarded at any one time. Most, like Charlotte, were thirteen or fourteen when they arrived, though the length of time they remained depended on the academic abilities of the individual and the particular requirements of their parents. Lessons were very much adapted to best suit the needs of each child and, though collective instruction was the norm, all new girls benefitted from one-to-one lessons with Miss Wooler before they joined the rest of the class.[16] Attention was focused on those then believed to be the more feminine subjects, namely history, geography, English literature and language, French, music, drawing and painting. Fine sewing was also taught and all with the aim of producing educated young women perfectly fit for a life of quiet gentility and marriage or, in Charlotte's particular case, for a future as governess or teacher.

Though the next few years would bring no challenges as great or as difficult as those she had faced at the Clergy Daughters' School, Charlotte's experiences at Roe Head were far from straightforward. For the first time in nearly five years she was to be separated from her siblings and from the games they played together. But more significantly still, she was to be confronted with realities she had not yet fully had to face – and almost as soon as she stepped down from the cart that had brought her across the moors from Haworth.

At home with her family, appearance had not mattered, nor should it have done. But the truth was, Charlotte Brontë was plain. In fact, as many others would come to attest, she was very plain indeed. Pre-fame portraits,[17] self-portraits and the descriptions of those who knew her, reveal that Charlotte had an unusually large head and a broad, square face.[18] Her chin jutted forward, and her forehead was bulbous, her nose disproportionately big.[19] Her mouth was broad, her lips uneven, her skin 'marred by a poor complexion' and, by the time she reached adulthood, many of her teeth were gone and the symmetry of her face had been altered.[20] Her hair, though not copious, was a pretty mid- to dark brown, and her eyes, despite her extreme short-sightedness, were large and unusually expressive.[21] But, even in spite of these good points, Elizabeth Gaskell still pronounced Charlotte to be 'thin', 'undeveloped', 'very little and very plain' – a description corroborated by countless others, including Matthew Arnold, George Henry Lewes, George Smith and William Makepeace Thackeray who declared her to be a 'homely-faced creature' 'without a penny worth of good looks'.[22]

But, if the young Charlotte had been aware of her appearance before her arrival at Roe Head, it was not something that she had dwelt upon for long. She was simply creative, sensitive, domineering, intelligent Charlotte – the leader of the family troupe, the co-creator of Glass Town and of Angria and the beloved, eldest surviving daughter of the Reverend Patrick Brontë. In the kingdoms that she had fashioned, neither her real face, plain as it was, nor her real clothes, practical and pragmatic as they were, were important, for there she and her protagonists could appear just as she chose or imagined. Yet, on her arrival at Roe Head, the fourteen-year-old Charlotte was to find that real life outside the Haworth Parsonage was neither so compliant, nor so uncritical. Here, unfair as it was, appearance mattered.

It was 17 January 1831 when Charlotte first stood on the drive of the 'cheerful, roomy, country house' in Mirfield with her father.[23] No doubt excited by the prospect of a new classmate, some of the girls had gathered at the window to witness her arrival. Their first impressions were not favourable. One pupil, Mary Taylor, described seeing what seemed to be a 'little old woman' dressed in 'very old-fashioned clothes, and looking very cold and miserable' stepping down from the 'covered cart'.[24] Another, Ellen Nussey, later recalled noticing Charlotte's 'dry, frizzy-looking hair, screwed up in tight little curls' and features made 'all the plainer from her exceeding thinness and want of complexion'. Like Mary, she believed that the 'dark rusty green stuff dress of old-fashioned make detracted still more from [Charlotte's] appearance.'[25]

These impressions were not improved upon meeting the new girl in person, for though Charlotte had changed her dress for another, this was 'just as old' as the last, and quite as outmoded.[26] Clearly, what had passed in Haworth as neat, functional and wholly appropriate for a country clergyman's daughter, drew comment in Roe Head. Here, young ladies wore gowns that reflected the latest styles and, unlike Charlotte, knew how to dress their hair according to the fashions depicted in the women's newspapers, magazines and journals of the day. As the daughters' of mill-owners and merchants, they not only had money to spend on such luxuries but also understood their importance. With only her aunt and father to guide and clothe her, and particularly an aunt whose own clothes were respectable but no longer vogueish, and her mother's thirty-year-old magazines for reference, Charlotte had arrived at her new school both ill-prepared and ill-dressed.

It would be all too easy to pass over the criticisms levelled at Charlotte by her new peers, to categorize them as not atypical 'mean girl' behaviours. This would not be an unreasonable assumption. But, when considered in the light of prevalent, contemporary beliefs around the expectations and place of young women within society, beliefs that the Roe Head girls were being specifically brought up to embody and embrace, their reproachments take on new meaning.

By the early nineteenth century, changing attitudes to marriage, and therefore to a woman's role in society, had placed an even greater emphasis upon outward appearance. For, where the upper and middle classes had historically based their matrimonial decisions on wealth and status, now 'companionate marriage', or unions founded on love and free choice, had become the norm.[27] As individualism increased its grip on society, the young and the eligible played a bigger part in deciding their own destinies and, consequently, sexual attraction, compatibility and character were given much greater weight.[28] But, as convention dictated that upper- and middle-class men and women only met under controlled situations where conversation was largely restricted to 'gossip of art, musical and pictorial, the party politics of the day and the chit chat of society', it is not surprising that a woman was often 'chosen for her face' rather than 'her passion, intellect or moral activity'.[29] And 'chosen' the woman was, for though both parties had more agency than they had ever done before, ultimately, the power still lay with the man, for it was he who asked the question.

With young women now being selected for their appearance rather than their status, increasing emphasis began to be placed on the attainment of beauty. In time, beauty actually began to be viewed as a woman's responsibility, prompting the author of the 1856 text, *The Science of Dress*, to declare, 'it is the duty of the fair sex to cultivate their personal attractions, as these are chief ornaments of a household and stand in the same important relations to a woman as mental endowments do to a man.'[30] Beauty was now deemed an essential asset – and not just when securing a husband. By the mid-nineteenth century, it was also considered a necessary attribute of the good and proper wife and the good and proper mother.[31]

The Industrial Revolution wrought other changes too, for with new technology and new practices came the proliferation of mass-produced visual imagery in the form of prints, engravings and even pottery figurines.[32] For the first time, there existed books on beauty and lady's magazines and journals filled with images and descriptions of beautiful and fashionable women. The increasing reproducibility of images and the consequent reduction in price, meant that such items soon entered the homes of even the lower and middle ranks of society.[33]

As the sheer number of images increased, beauty standards were both more diverse (in that many more artists were producing images) and more influential. Of course, beauty trends had been apparent before, but where portrait artists had previously been chosen for their style, their fame or to suit individual tastes, as multiple copies of images began to be produced and disseminated, general rather than particular perceptions of beauty and of current fashions became both more firmly established and more widespread.

By the 1770s printed, painted, carved or moulded images of the feminine ideal were, just like many of the media images that surround us today, not exact depictions of real women, but rather artists' impressions.[34] However, in order to advertise to, advise or entertain the public, it was essential that drawn or painted physical and sartorial details were in line with contemporary expectations. Less than perfect features were not included in most images. These were then, in effect, perfected versions of reality. Ordinary women were now comparing themselves to largely unobtainable, flawless models of beauty.

In response to these many and varied societal changes, the education of middle- and upper-class girls began to be increasingly centred on learning how to keep up with appearances – on how to look and dress, but also to act as a lady should. This formal education in 'true womanhood' was supported by novels, poems, short stories, etiquette manuals and women's magazines, very often, though not always, written by men.[35] These promoted housewifely skills, spiritual and moral fortitude, the latest beauty treatments and stylish dress. And so young women, like those that Charlotte met as she climbed down from the cart, were taught not only to view their bodies as objects to be displayed, but also how to restrain and regulate them through specific activities, fashionable clothing and social behaviours.[36]

The constant absorption of beauty ideals had another consequence too. With women now pitted against their fellow women as they sought to compete for male attention, they began to scrutinize not only their own appearance, but also each other's, far more critically.[37] It is therefore not surprising that the girls that Charlotte met at Roe Head, who had and were being brought up to exemplify all these new feminine ideals, were shocked to find a fellow pupil who did not.

To make matters worse still, the criticisms levelled at Charlotte were to be in no way limited to her clothes and personal appearance. Her unconventional education set her apart too. Under Patrick's enlightened tutelage she had gained an unusually broad education and consequently could 'confound' the other girls 'by knowing things that were out of [their] range altogether'.[38] Yet his system of instruction had been far from orthodox and when compared to her fellow pupils, though she exceeded them in many areas, there were obvious gaps in her knowledge. As Mary Taylor later revealed, 'we thought her exceedingly ignorant for she had never learned grammar at all and very little geography'.[39]

It would be easy to presume that Charlotte was unaware of all these personal observations – that the discussions that took place between the other girls were carried out behind her back and that she remained largely oblivious. Yet this was not the case. Charlotte was made all too aware of what others thought of her. Not only, in what seemed to her to be a slight upon her intelligence, did Miss Wooler suggest that she join the class of younger or less academic girls until she caught up, but she was also directly informed by fellow pupil Mary Taylor that she 'was very ugly'.[40] Now forced to see herself through the eyes of others, this new self-consciousness was only compounded by exposure to the beauty of her peers. For, by some fate, the plain Charlotte was required to use the 'very pretty' Amelia Walker as her life model in art class.[41] In these early days of enforced self-assessment, to be made, for some considerable length of time, to focus on the ordered, classical features of her wealthy school-fellow, can only have been additionally detrimental to a self-esteem already battered by repeated challenges. And, if things were not already bad enough, after noting the disparity between her clothes and those worn by the other Roe Head girls, her father's friends in the locality sent her 'a frock and muslin' and a shawl.[42] This must have rubbed salt into Charlotte's already gaping wound, for, though very kindly meant, their gifts only served to highlight her sartorial inadequacies and her deepening feelings of inferiority.[43]

In what would become her default, Brontë's response to these many and varied affronts was simply to remove herself. What had begun as a not atypical exclusion of the new girl had morphed into elective separation. When not at lessons, Charlotte would now sit or 'stand under the trees in the playground, saying it was pleasanter' and demonstrated a sustained and 'pliable indifference' towards the other girls.[44] But, hidden behind this seeming insouciance, this apparent self-sufficiency, the poor girl was miserable. So much so that a little more than a week after her arrival, fellow pupil, Ellen Nussey, found a 'silent, weeping, dark little figure in the large bay window'.[45]

Following these experiences, Charlotte's perception of self, and most particularly of her appearance, would never be the same again. It was as if the scales had fallen from her eyes. Like her later protagonist, Jane Eyre, when she was confronted with a vision of her true self in the looking glass of the Red Room, Charlotte now felt herself forced to look in the mirror and 'involuntarily explor[e] the depth it revealed'.[46] What she saw now, she did not like.

Many of us can still recollect harsh or unfeeling things said to us in youth and have experienced their lingering impact. Charlotte, already made vulnerable by her deeply sensitive nature, the loss of her mother and sisters and her experiences at the Clergy Daughters' School, was particularly susceptible to the damaging consequences of peer criticism and comparison. Indeed, a clear link has now been established between childhood adversity and low self-concept clarity – self-concept clarity being the extent to which an individual's beliefs about themselves are clearly defined and remain consistent and stable over time.[47] It has now been suggested that young people with low self-concept

3.1 *Sand, orange, red and green paisley wool shawl, D64*

clarity, when exposed to societal standards of attractiveness or shamed on account of their appearance, are more likely to unfavourably compare themselves to others and to become increasingly dissatisfied with their bodies.[48] Charlotte was in her early teenage years when she was first made aware that neither her clothing nor her physical appearance met the expectations of her peers and, significantly, many social psychologists now pinpoint adolescence as being a vitally important period of development.[49] During puberty, self-consciousness is heightened and adolescents begin to give added weight to the opinions and perceptions of others as their understanding of themselves, as both as individuals and social objects, grows.[50] In consequence, beliefs formed by a teenager about their own appearance during this key period of development can have a disproportionate impact on their overall self-worth, especially when their self-esteem becomes dependent on meeting sometimes unobtainable standards of beauty.[51] In the light of this, it is not surprising that Mary Taylor's forthright statement, 'you are very ugly', as well as other covert and overt criticism aimed at her appearance and spoken out by her peers in those early weeks of school, had profound and lasting impact on Charlotte's relationship with her body.[52] Negative or derisive comments about her dress were equally damaging, leaving Charlotte with a deep sense of insecurity about her clothing but also about its ability to lay her open to unwanted scrutiny.

Though these early weeks and months were very difficult for Charlotte, Roe Head did not remain a place of misery forever. As time passed, she grew more used to her new environs and to the girls with whom she now lived and worked, and they, in turn, grew more used to her. New connections began to form, green shoots appeared. In what was a returning to skills learned in adversity, Charlotte used her imaginative gifts and prodigious intelligence to draw others to her. This time, her tales and games were shared not with her siblings around the fire in the parsonage, but after school hours with her classmates, in the dormitory. Slowly, incrementally, relationships were forged and though still shy and socially awkward, Charlotte began to carve out a space for herself in which she could flourish. The outspoken Mary Taylor and refined Ellen Nussey, won over by her spine-chilling ghost stories and unexpected sense of fun, morphed from seeming villains to close allies and friends.[53] In a sign of change, Charlotte started to be invited to their homes for weekends and short holidays. She organized group performances and shared, for the first time with those outside her immediate family, all the latest news from Angria and Glass Town. Before many months had passed, Charlotte had become as integral to life at Roe Head as Miss Wooler or the grounds in which they played.

Though the lasting pain of her earlier experiences still lingered, Charlotte had uncovered a vital truth – that what she lacked in beauty and innate stylishness, she more than made up for in imagination, hard work and intelligence. From this point on, these attributes would prove persistent consolations to her. Charlotte's new friends also enriched her life considerably, improved her social skills and exposed her to divergent views and opinions. They aroused in her a new awareness of the Romantic, of the feminine, of clothing and fabric. Under their influence she morphed and changed. It was a kind of awakening, a blossoming of mind and spirit.

Academic studies stretched her too. Despite her slow start, Charlotte soon caught up with her peers and then surpassed them all, spurred on by the desire to triumph, but also to learn all that she could in the short time available to her. For never did the knowledge of her looming future leave her. Unlike the others, she could not be 'out and out a school-girl'.[54] Rather, it was her responsibility to gain an education quickly and so, as Ellen Nussey later wrote, 'she chose in many things to do double lessons [and …] when her companions were merry round the fire … she would be kneeling close to the window, busy with her studies'.[55]

Time at Roe Head passed quickly. In June 1832, after discussion with her father, Charlotte announced to her headmistress, Miss Wooler, that she would not be returning after the summer holidays. The same duty and expectation that had focussed her mind at school had now called her home and, having exceeded both the curriculum and her father's available funds, the time had come for her to leave. Reluctantly, though shrouded in the glory of academic attainment and cherished friendships, sixteen-year-old Charlotte travelled the twenty miles home to Haworth to continue her own studies and to release her father from the tutelage of her younger sisters, Emily and Anne.[56]

She arrived home much changed. She was, as Patrick had always planned, now well prepared to teach other young girls all that she had learned. Though it had been a considerable investment, the eighteen months that Charlotte had spent at Roe Head had equipped her for life. Now, if she did not marry, her father could rest easy knowing that self-sufficiency was within her grasp. In this sense, Roe Head had been an inordinate success. But what no one had factored in, what no one had considered, was how, after having had her eyes opened to the existence of a more traditionally feminine, more affluent world, Charlotte would fit back into life at Haworth. For though she had altered, life inside the parsonage had not.

Just over a month after she had arrived home, she wrote to her friend, Ellen Nussey:

> You ask me to give you a description of the manner in which I have passed every day since I left School: this is soon done as an account of one day is an account of all. In the Morning from nine o'clock till half past twelve – I instruct my Sisters & draw, then we walk till dinner after dinner I sew till tea-time, and after tea I read, write, do a little fancy work or draw, as I please.[57]

Having learned at Roe Head that a middle-class woman was distinguished as much by how she spent her leisure time as she was by her conversation and education, Charlotte's emphasis upon ladylike pursuits is telling.[58] For though she was, in fact, tied up for much of the day in teaching her sisters and in household tasks – work which was not typically carried out by genteel women – by emphasizing her more acceptable activities, she was signalling to Ellen that she was still very much one of them.

Of course, because of Patrick's liberal attitudes towards education, Charlotte had always spent time reading, writing and drawing, but the fact that her first, surviving, post-Roe Head pencil drawing features a young lady wearing a highly fashionable early 1830s dropped-shoulder, puff-sleeved, high-waisted gown, shows just how much she had been influenced by the other girls. Where her earlier depictions had drawn inspiration from her mother's old magazines, she now showed a new awareness of the very latest fashions – adding up-to-the-minute lace shoulder embellishments and decorative features.[59] But fashion conscious as it was, her art did not, in this case at least, imitate life. For Charlotte was now firmly back under the auspices of her aunt and her father, whose first priorities in matters of dress were respectability and economy. As Branwell Brontë's now famous 1834 *Pillar Portrait* attests, any newly formed, grandiose tastes were not to be realized in her actual garments. Parental

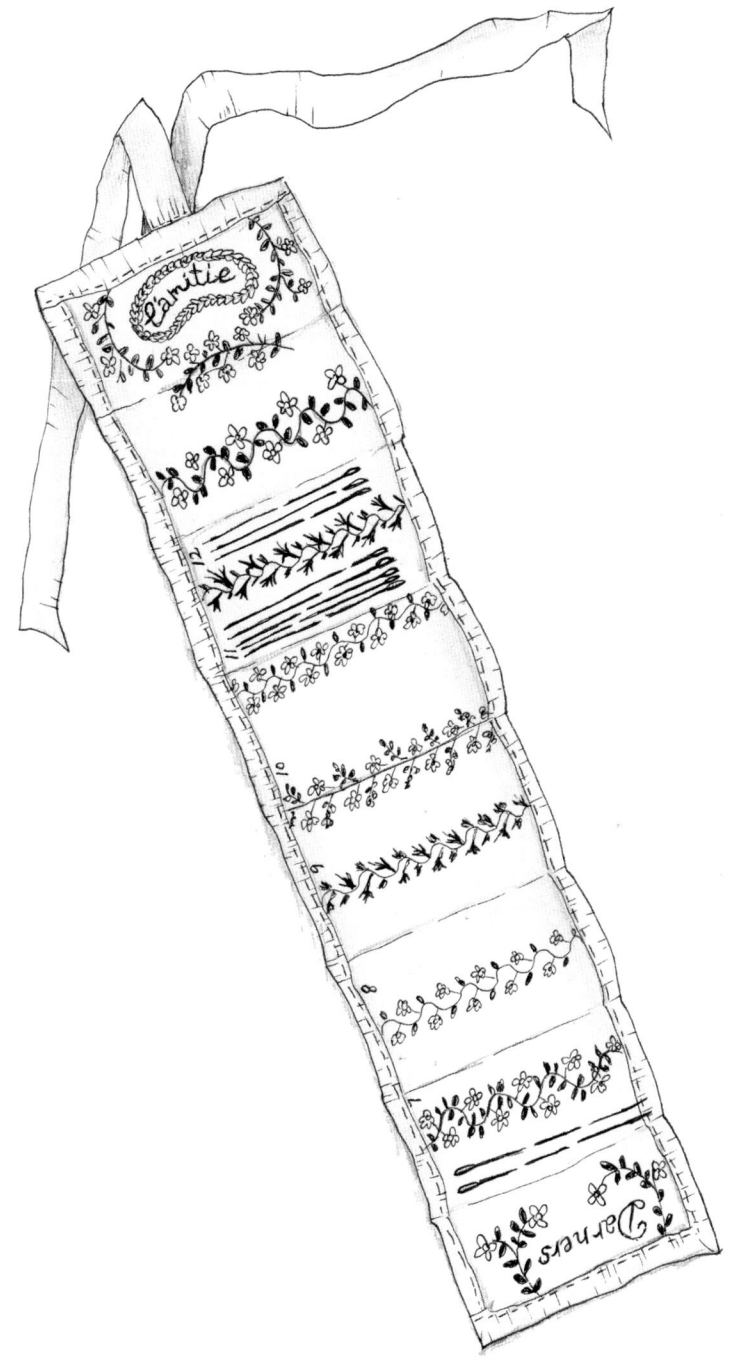

3.2 *Charlotte Brontë's hand-sewn needlecase, D154*

3.3 *Patrick Branwell Brontë, 'The Brontë Sisters', c. 1834. Oil on canvas, 35½ × 29⅜ inches. Located in the National Portrait Gallery, London, England, UK. Recently restored. (Photo by VCG Wilson/Corbis via Getty Images)*

influence is apparent in the sisters' heightened necklines and large lawn collars which cover décolletage as well as modesty.[60]

It is present too in their lacklustre sleeves, which, though expansive by our own modern standards, lack the exuberance (and internal scaffolding) of their peers.[61] And, though the dark, drab coloured silks might have been chosen to better suit Branwell's distinctive, sombre aesthetic,[62] the prominent lack of embellishment in their gowns, something which is not present in his surviving portraits of other female subjects, suggests that Charlotte, Emily and Anne's gowns were, at this time, largely devoid of decoration.[63]

Today, Branwell's painting can be found on permanent display at the National Portrait Gallery and is generally viewed as symbolic of both the huge literary achievement of the three Brontë sisters, but also of the personal tragedy that surrounded them. It is now impossible to separate the image from our (albeit sometimes constructed) knowledge of the sisters' isolated upbringing beneath the glowering Yorkshire moors, from their persistent attempts to become authors in an overbearing, patriarchal world, from the terrible but humiliating demise of their drug and drink dependent brother and, of course, from their untimely deaths as young adults.[64] It is perhaps because of this often paradoxical subtext that it has come to be viewed as one of the most iconic images of the Romantic period, and one that continues to draw countless visitors to London each year.

Because it has survived, Branwell's portrait has disproportionately shaped our views of the Brontës' and specifically of Charlotte's appearance and clothing ever since. *This* drably dressed Charlotte has haunted us through the years – has fixed our opinions, cemented our beliefs. She obscures a hankering for colour and for pattern, for sumptuous fabrics and rich embellishment. Though some of these would, when funds and freedoms allowed, be reflected in her later wardrobe, they were already apparent in the writing and drawing that was becoming, once again, central to her daily life. For whilst her days as pupil were now long behind her, her desire for beauty and for romance had in no way diminished with the passing of time.

Like many girls her own age, Charlotte found herself drawn like a moth to the idealistic novels and verse of Sir Walter Scott. His inspiration became paramount in her own works, with characters, wild landscapes and even key storylines being lifted and modified to suit her own Verdopolitan tales and tastes.[65] In an audacious but predictable move for the country parson's daughter, she turned too towards the poetry of the most scandalous and controversial of the major English Romantic poets – Lord Byron. Byron's aristocratic background and unconventional life story captured her imagination almost as much as did his progressive literature, from which she quoted freely. She did not stick, as she encouraged her friend Ellen to do, to what she called the purer 'Hebrew Melodies', but salaciously consumed the 'invariably revolting' *Don Juan* and *Cain*.[66] As a direct result of his influence, Charlotte began to develop a sexual and psychological intensity that would later become a hallmark of her work.

The dual influence of reading and Roe Head is apparent in Charlotte's novelette *The Green Dwarf: A Tale of Perfect Tense*.[67] This blatantly quixotic tale, written by an excitable seventeen-year-old, is crammed full of knightly figures in green mantles, hags in woodland castles and disguised lovers.[68] It tells the story of the beautiful Lady Emily Charlesworth who is faced with an unenviable choice – to marry Colonel Percy, a decorated war hero who believes himself entitled to her love, or to elope with Leslie, the brilliant but low-born artist who has stolen her heart. Though it centres around Emily's beguiling beauty – her 'soft and delicate' features, 'complexion transparently fair' and 'eyes, dark, bright and full of animation' – fabrics, textures, clothes and colours feature strongly. It is an assault on the senses; a teenage fantasy; an exploration of sensation and emotion.[69] This, like the many other stories and novelettes that Charlotte would write during this period of experiment, is removed from reality. There are few plain faces here, and even fewer ill-fitting or pragmatic garments made or adapted by a well-meaning aunt or family servant. This is life as she wished it could be, not life as it really was.

Realism is equally absent in Charlotte's drawings of this period, where the influence of Byron, the poet revolutionary, can once again be clearly discerned. Byronic-style heads replete with dark, curly locks and chiselled features are commonplace and so too are images of the women with whom the 'mad – bad – and dangerous to know' poet was in some way associated.[70] Cleverly adapted from existing engravings found in books like Edward Francis Finden, William Brockedon and William Finden, *Finden's Illustrations of the Life and Works of*

Lord Byron, Thomas Moore, *The Letters and Journals of Lord Byron* or Alaric A. Watts, *The Literary Souvenir*, Charlotte lifts these handsome women and takes them as her own. The famed society beauty and patroness, Marguerite Gardiner, Countess of Blessington is, with the turn of a pencil, morphed into Zenobia Marchioness Ellrington.[71] The delicate, ethereal figure of Ianthe, of Byron's *Childe Harold's Pilgrimage* fame, becomes Mary Henrietta Percy, Duchess of Zamorna and Queen of Angria.[72] Additional jewels, even more elaborate hairstyles or extra embellishments were often added, for there was, it seemed, no such thing as too much wealth or too much beauty. Other drawings, of similarly fashionable women, take their inspiration from *Heath's Book of Beauty* edited by the Countess of Blessington, copies of which were held at the parsonage, where emphasis is placed upon stylish gowns, symmetrical features and magnificence far beyond Charlotte's own reach.[73]

Despite Charlotte's increasing absorption in the characters who lived in the gleaming Glass Town Confederacy and later its derivation, Angria, harsh realities could not be pushed away forever. The Brontës were still, in relative terms at least, poor. Their existence was just as precarious as it had always been – and Charlotte had done almost all she could for her sisters. It was time for them to go through the refining fire of Roe Head for themselves.

As the four remaining children grew, so did the family's expected expenditure. With Branwell now intent on becoming a professional artist – a career that promised little future stability and no small amount of investment – it was time for the realities of life to be faced head on once again. Thus, in a letter to Ellen written in July 1835, Charlotte boldly announced that she was to become a schoolteacher. 'The last determination', she claimed, 'I formed myself, knowing that I should have to take the step sometime … and knowing also that Papa would have enough to do with his limited income should Branwell be placed at the Royal Academy, and Emily at Roe Head.'[74]

Charlotte's new teaching appointment had come at the bequest of Miss Wooler, her past headteacher. On paper, the arrangement made perfect sense. Though she would miss her family at home, and particularly her writing and sparring partner, Branwell, she would not be entirely alone; Emily would be with her. She would also be returning to the school that she had grown to love, to the place that had helped to shape and mould her. She would face, or so she believed, no unknown challenges there, for she had, over the course of the eighteen months that she had lived at Roe Head, faced them all before.

On 29 July 1835, nineteen-year-old Charlotte and seventeen-year-old Emily arrived at Roe Head School in Mirfield. Aware that their ages made them vulnerable to 'temptation' and unsuitable attachments, Patrick sent a letter ahead of them asking his old friend, Elizabeth Firth Franks, to watch over them in his absence. After all, they were, without chaperone, to enter what he called a 'delusive and insnaring world'.[75] Whether Charlotte's obsession with Romance was the root cause of his unease we cannot know. Certainly, Patrick had been concerned enough by Charlotte's behaviour to throw his wife's precious *Lady's Magazines* onto the fire, on account of her persistent reading of the 'foolish love-stories' contained within them.[76]

In the end, though, it was Emily, not Charlotte, whose wellbeing was most endangered by her departure from Haworth. Lacking, as had always been her tendency, a certain resilience, and increasingly homesick, she soon withered to a shadow of her former self. Like Charlotte, her connection with her own created worlds, in her case with Gondal, was central to her being. There was now no time to spend engrossed in personal writing and, forced to constantly be in the company of unfamiliar faces, she struggled to cope. Her mental and physical decline was so great and so fast that Charlotte 'felt in [her] heart that she would die if she did not go home, and with this conviction, obtained her recall'.[77]

Almost as soon as Emily had been returned to Haworth, Patrick brought Anne to Roe Head to fill her place. As Charlotte's teaching covered a significant proportion of the fees, it was too good an opportunity to miss. Like her older sister, Anne also found school life challenging, but, with characteristic grit, she set about making the best of the opportunity that she had been given, for unlike Emily she was fully appreciative of the sacrifices being made on her behalf.

As Anne settled in as pupil, Charlotte grappled with her new role as teacher. It was not an easy transition. Though there were other staff, Charlotte was responsible for a considerable percentage of the girls' education and also for their many and varied extracurricular activities. She worked long days and, alongside her teaching, was expected to care for Miss Wooler's infant niece, nephew and elderly mother, as well as attend to the never-ending piles of sewing and mending.

Teaching itself did not prove pleasurable either. Her previous pupils, Emily and Anne, had been both intelligent and compliant but, in stark contrast, she found her new students stupid and vacuous, slow to learn and unwilling to change. On 11 August 1836, she wrote despairingly, 'Am I to spend all the best part of my life in this wretched bondage, forcibly suppressing my rage at the idleness, the apathy and the hyperbolical & most asinine stupidity of those fat-headed oafs and compulsion assuming an air of kindness, patience and assiduity?'[78]

It was not long before the relentless responsibility, unremitting timetable and consequent, involuntary separation from her imaginary realms, proved overpowering. Like many addicts, Charlotte, and arguably even those around her, had underestimated her reliance on her drug. The places and people that she and Branwell had created were now integral to her being, but what had begun as a game was now impinging upon her life.

Charlotte's extraordinary connectedness to Glass Town and to Angria might be, to some, difficult to understand. Yet, the parallels between this and video game addiction – something that we are more familiar with in modern times – are striking. It is now thought that as many as 60 million people worldwide (3–4 per cent of all video gamers) suffer from internet gaming disorder, a condition characterized by an individual's inability to control their desire to escape to virtual worlds – something that Charlotte clearly struggled to do.[79] In fact, as her longing to withdraw from life grew, as her need to cognitively and emotionally leave behind reality increased, the less able she was to resist Angria's power.[80] In her journal she recalled:

> … while I watched the fluttering of his white shirt ruffles starting through the half-unbuttoned waistcoat and beheld the expression of his Arabian countenance, savagely exalting even in sleep – Quamina, triumphant Lord in the halls of Zamorna! in the bower of Zamorna's lady! – while this apparition was before me, the dining-room door opened and Miss Wooler came in, with a plate of butter in her hand. 'A very stormy night, my dear!' 'It is ma'am' said I.[81]

However immediately satisfying her reveries, truths remained. 'Arabian countenances', 'white shirt ruffles' and 'half-unbuttoned waistcoats' or their female equivalent, had no place in Miss Wooler's entirely practical sphere – a sphere which Fate had dictated was the likely and appropriate destiny for Miss Charlotte Brontë and where the only ruffles she would come across were those she was forced to mend.

She could never truly embody these clothes, any more than she could embody the characters that wore them. After all, the chasm between the real person of Charlotte and the beautiful, richly dressed protagonists that she had created was too great for her to leap, however much she tried. She need only look in the glass to see the disparity. Thus, whilst her 'exquisite' heroine, the Queen of Angria, surrounded herself with mirrors so that she could see 'if her loveliness and her adornments were quite perfect', Charlotte's own reflection brought 'a jar of discord, a pang of regret'.[82]

But, however hard it was to countenance, however hard to accept, deep down she knew that it was time to be the heroine of her own story. So, when Branwell introduced the dissolute Henry Hastings into the Angrian Kingdom, Charlotte finally summoned up the requisite courage and began the work of fashioning a female protagonist more akin to herself. Unlike her more glamorous predecessors, governess Elizabeth Hastings is 'plain and undersized', 'not handsome', with a 'fair rather wan complexion' and wearing 'a costume unpretending but not unladylike'. Though all too often overlooked by others, she is, however, ineffably clever, with not 'a single equal to herself in mind'.[83] Here in the development of this character are the stirrings of Jane Eyre and Lucy Snowe. Here, in fact, outworked in now brown ink across the yellowed pages of her manuscript, is Charlotte Brontë herself.

That this new, more mature authorial voice was discovered not in Mirfield, nor in Dewsbury where the school had since moved, but back within the solid stone walls of the parsonage, should come as no surprise. Charlotte's unhappy relationship with her work and place at Roe Head had increased exponentially over many months, resulting in what she described as 'mental and bodily anguish'.[84] In late 1838, having reached the limit of her endurance, she made the contentious decision to give up her post as teacher and return home to the bleak but beautiful moors of Haworth.

3.4 *Regency man's shirt*

Given the emphasis that she had so often placed upon duty, Charlotte's sudden removal from Roe Head was, if not unexpected, most untimely. Though always stretched to their limits, the Brontë family finances had been placed under particular strain by a change in parish boundaries which threatened to reduce her father's income by a fifth. Yet, having followed her impulse and packed up her bags, Charlotte exhibited a remarkably positive and unswerving frame of mind. This dramatic change in mood had dual attribution: her temporary release from what she termed 'wretched bondage' and her newfound creative direction.[85] Now, Charlotte had endless time to devote to the introduction of her new heroine.

However, despite Brontë's new willingness to explore the feelings that her appearance engendered, her Romantic obsessions continued to exert power. In setting her 'new' character in her 'old' world of Angria, Charlotte was still operating within familiar paradigms. The governess Elizabeth Hastings, plain, poor and diminutive though she was, is therefore shown to excite an unlikely, reckless passion in the aristocratic Sir William Percy, causing him to declare that he loved her 'more than at this moment than I do any other woman in the world'.[86] One cannot help but imagine that these ardent, illicit declarations, offered to a plain teacher by a handsome nobleman who sees appearance as no obstacle to love, are what Charlotte herself hoped one day to hear.

As fate would have it, it was not long before an unexpected offer of marriage, if not a protestation of devoted love, was forthcoming for Charlotte. Ellen Nussey's sensible but passionless, clergyman brother, Henry, had set about the task of selecting a wife with customary rationale and sobriety. Having already approached one young woman, whose father had rejected him, the Reverend had immediately looked about for another suitable candidate. Charlotte Brontë struck him as a fitting and appropriate choice.

As might be expected from such a staid and serious man, Henry Nussey's proposal was devoid of all passion. Needless to say, it did not appeal to a girlish heart fed on a perpetual diet of idealistic, romantic tales of love and lust.[87] Thus, to Ellen she wrote, 'I had not, and never could have that intense attachment that would make me willing to die for him.'[88]

Charlotte's letter of rejection to Henry is wholly revealing. Writing boldly and underlining key words for emphasis, she argued that she was not in possession of the "personal attractions" sufficient to please [his] eye and gratify [his] just pride'.[89] Brontë's plainness, though evidently not viewed as a significant barrier to Henry Nussey, was clearly an insurmountable obstacle to Charlotte. Here, she gave voice to her persistent fear, that over time her appearance would come to be the cause of repulsion and shame to her husband – particularly when not regarded through the lens of love.

Charlotte's disappointing offer of marriage would be followed quickly by another. For, just a few months after Henry's uninspiring proposition, Charlotte was asked for her hand in marriage yet again. This proposal was even more unexpected than the last. The Reverend David Pryce had met Charlotte on one single occasion and had immediately followed his visit with a written proposal. Charlotte's rejection was carried out with equal rapidity and David Pryce died six months later, still a bachelor.

There were, of course, inevitable consequences to Charlotte's decision to reject two serious offers from respectable and financially stable suitors.[90] In doing so, she had taken a bold step, one that could result in 'the stigma of [becoming] an old maid'.[91] In a letter to Ellen, she declared, 'I am tolerably well convinced that I shall never marry at all. Reason tells me so, and I am not so utterly the slave of feeling but that I can occasionally hear her voice.'[92] 'Reason' must also have told her that in rejecting marriage, or unromantic marriage at least, she must resign herself to work and to a life largely outside the traditional domestic sphere. In the words of her similarly plain and financially insecure protagonist, Jane Eyre, Charlotte must accept that she was 'formed for labour not for love'.[93]

4.1 *Charlotte Brontë's 'Governess Dress', back view, D11'*

4

The 'Governess Dress'

Charlotte was not the only Brontë to come home to Haworth that year. By early 1839 all the fledglings were back in the nest. Anne had been at the parsonage since Christmas 1837, having been sent home from Roe Head suffering from nervous collapse. Branwell, who had been following his ambition to become a professional painter, had reappeared in the early spring under something of a cloud. He had tried and failed to make his living as an artist and, now certain that neither monetary success nor artistic renown were within his reach, gave up his rooms and traded the companionship of his artist friends for that of his three siblings.

Emily's return from her teaching post was just as unexpected. Almost from the outset, she had found life as teacher at Law Hill School every bit as challenging as Roe Head. After enduring six months of 'slavery', apparently working from 'six in the morning until near eleven at night with only one half hour of exercise in between', she arrived home that spring in a poor state of health.[1] Traumatized by her experiences, she determined never to leave all her family for an extended period again. With characteristic resolve, and some might even say egotism, she never did. The 'stern Mistresses' of 'Duty' and 'Necessity' could never be so severe as to change Emily's mind once made up.[2]

Patrick cannot fail to have been distressed by the return of all four of his now adult children. With almost all of them still struggling beneath the weight of mental or physical fatigue, he must have feared for the future – how could he continue to support them all? What hope was there for the years to come? Yet, however deep his anxiety, there is no evidence to suggest that he urgently pushed any of his children towards paid employment. Still fractured from the loss of his wife and daughters, his desire to keep his remaining children safe and well was no doubt stronger than his wish to secure the family's financial future. Nevertheless, Charlotte and Anne, sensing their father's anxieties, and more affected by a looming sense of responsibility than their other siblings, began to search for work once again.

Little time had passed before nineteen-year-old Anne was ensconced with the wealthy Ingham family of Blake Hall, near Mirfield, where she would remain until the end of the year. Charlotte, spurred on by her sister's proactivity, soon followed suit and secured a temporary job as private governess with the Sidgwick family of Stonegappe, Lothersdale. On paper, this should have been a pleasant, albeit short post – her employers were wealthy and of some considerable standing, the house in which she would live was large and elegant, and the grounds 'divine'.[3] She was responsible for the education of just two young children, seven-year-old Mathilda and four-year-old John Benson, and would be residing less than ten miles from her home in Haworth. From the outset, however, Charlotte found Mrs Sidgwick haughty and the children 'pampered spoilt and turbulent', 'perverse [and] unmanageable'.[4] Any attempts to thwart them were met with 'black looks' from their mother, for they were able 'to do as they like[d]'.[5] To make matters worse, and much to Charlotte's disgust, she was also expected to take care of her young charges' every need. This included everything from tying their shoes, to wiping their 'smutty noses', fetching their pinafores or overseeing their mealtimes.[6] As far as Charlotte was concerned, teaching was one thing – childcare was quite another.

This first position as governess was always meant to be temporary, but Charlotte's appointment did not prove successful for either party. Mrs Sidgwick claimed that 'Miss Brontë often went to bed all day and left her to look after the children', and a relation of the family later recalled how the governess had 'no gifts for the management of children and was also in a very morbid condition the whole time'.[7] Needless to say, Charlotte left Stonegappe that July with a very dim view of 'governessing', and an even dimmer view of Mrs Sidgwick and her 'riotous' offspring.[8]

Charlotte did not take up another post as governess for a year and eight months.[9] Given her straitened circumstances, it is a little surprising that more than five weeks of this period of unemployment were spent with Ellen Nussey on a seaside holiday in Bridlington, East Yorkshire. Buoyed up by her first taste of sea air, she arrived home in excellent health and even claimed, employing no small amount of hyperbole, that she had grown 'very fat' from all the good food and seaside merriment.[10]

Her excessively cheery state did not last for long. The Brontës' much loved and faithful servant, Tabby Ackroyd, had become temporarily too unwell to work. With only an eleven-year-old servant girl now left to help their aunt, most of the heavy domestic chores fell to Charlotte and Emily. Charlotte made much of her new domestic role, but the truth is, her desire to earn her living had waned. When not absorbed by household tasks, she was, once again, engrossed in reading and in writing. The arrival of a new and handsome curate to the parish proved another distraction. Twenty-six-year-old William Weightman had appeared fresh from university in the late summer of 1839 and had got straight to work baptizing babies and burying bodies.[11] Amiable, intelligent and funny, his presence in Haworth did little to persuade Charlotte to step up her search for work – even when his attentions sometimes strayed to other young women within the parish. Some feeble attempts were made to secure a new position, but she quickly allowed the burden of job-searching to fall upon her old employer, Miss Wooler, who had offered to help her.

It was not until the end of February 1841 that Charlotte finally accepted a position as governess for the White family of Upper House, Rawdon. The post constituted 'a large sacrifice in salary', but she hoped that it was a cost worth paying for a 'society of cheerful faces, and hearts not dug out of a lead mine'.[12] For the Whites were, according to Charlotte, a 'good sort of people', whose children, though 'wild and unbroken' were 'not such devils incarnate as the Sedge[wi]cks'. Indeed she even declared that Sarah, aged eight and Jasper, aged six, were 'well disposed'.[13]

It seemed as though Charlotte had at last found a job that suited her, but her optimism was not to last. Just days after commencing her new post, she wrote despairingly to Ellen, 'no one but myself is aware how utterly averse my whole mind and nature are to my employment'.[14] On 24 December 1841, less than ten months after her arrival in Rawdon, she resigned her situation and returned to Haworth once again.

Numerous letters from this seminal period of Charlotte Brontë's life have survived. These have helped countless biographers, literary scholars and historians to chart the time that she spent as governess and to better understand how these experiences impacted her later writing. This large body of evidence is invaluable, but there is also another rich resource that had never been examined before – a vital, loquacious material witness to Charlotte's foray into the demanding world of work that her financial circumstances and even her plainness had forced her to inhabit.

An unassuming, now brown, silk dress has long resided at the Brontë Parsonage Museum in Haworth. It has always been attributed to Charlotte – not because a verified connection had been established with the author, for it had not, but rather because it was precisely the type of garment that one might have expected the creator of *Jane Eyre* to have worn.[15]

Uncovering the history of any individual garment is a slow and time-consuming business, but with enough work and sufficient tenacity, a paper trail can sometimes be followed, and a unique and fascinating record established (or disestablished, as the case may be). When it comes to the clothing of the Brontë family, there are unique processes and challenges that both help and hinder this search.

Ever since the Brontë Society was founded in 1893, Brontë-related artefacts and manuscripts have been carefully amassed and stored. In order to be accepted as part of the collection, items were generally required to have *some* association with at least one of the Brontës, even if this link has later been found to be unreliable. Museum systems have radically changed over time, but historically, and even when little was known about an artefact when it first arrived, the date and a description was entered into a stock book before it was assigned an identifying number. Items that arrived together were given consecutive numbers and any other supporting paperwork documented and cross-referenced before being stored in numbered object files. This cataloguing process has become more sophisticated over time, but the fundamentals have remained unchanged.

In the case of the brown silk dress (known at the Parsonage as D11), there is no such information in the stock books or dossier files and there are no allusions to its arrival.[16] In fact, despite careful and persistent searches, no references to the dress could be found anywhere in the museum at all.

Whilst creating a very detailed inventory of all the garments and accessories held at the Brontë Parsonage Museum, it became clear that only three other main garments, a striped silk dress, two patterned, woollen cloaks and a bonnet, lacked documentation of any kind. Each of these, which I have now dated to the period in which the Brontës were alive, remain largely unaltered. This is unusual and suggests that these garments are unlikely to have been passed down or sold to subsequent owners. The museum number assigned to the bonnet suggests that it was probably part of a donation of multiple bonnets (all with very similar identifying numbers) that came to the Parsonage via a single donor in the 1950s, but the four larger garments have no known donor associations and yet have been at the parsonage for as long as curatorial memory extends.[17] This strange anomaly obviously warranted further investigation, especially as the brown silk dress was among its number.

Thomas Carlyle once said, 'History is the distillation of rumour.'[18] In the case of the silk dress, this adage has proven true, for a tale had long circulated amongst past and present museum staff that, many years before, some Brontë dresses had been found 'blocked up in a wall'. Little more was known, but a short passage found within the 1977 book, *Haworth Parsonage: The Home of the Brontës* by Jocelyn Kellett, shed some further light.[19] Kellett wrote:

> The room across the landing over the kitchen on the left as you ascend the second flight of stairs contains the window blocked up by Mr. Brontë. A large cupboard had been secured to the wall covering the blocked-up window, and in this cupboard was a box containing dresses which had belonged to the sisters.[20]

To find a concrete reference to this event, and more importantly to the aforementioned 'box of dresses', was exciting, but it did not offer explanation as to how, where or when their discovery took place or, more specifically, what exactly was inside the box. But a careful piecing together of the facts allowed a likely timeline of events to be established.

After the death of Patrick Brontë in 1861, the Rev. John Wade, a serious man of the cloth, moved into the Haworth Parsonage. Unlike Patrick, who had warmly welcomed Charlotte's fans to his door, Wade had absolutely no interest in the lives or works of any of the Brontës and had no desire to encourage the constant flow of curious visitors 'who poured into the rectory garden and even wormed their way into his private sanctum'.[21] In 1871, Wade (sometimes known as Vandal Wade due to the extensive changes he made to the church and parsonage during his tenure) undertook largescale alterations – constructing a sizeable extension at the side and rear of the building to better accommodate the wife, sister-in-law, four young children and two servants who appeared on the census that year.[22] As part of these modifications, he added a staircase and a bathroom to what was previously Branwell's bedroom and, though we cannot know for sure, it is highly probable that it was at this time that an existing cupboard (which was noted on the original plans), together with its contents, was boxed into the new construction.[23] Given Wade's potent antipathy towards the Brontës and their lingering ability to disrupt his peace, it is not surprising that even had he known about the box and its contents, he took no trouble to save them for posterity – even though, in a strange twist of fate, that is exactly what he did.[24] For some sixty-five years later, eight years after the Brontë Society had purchased the parsonage, further alterations were made to the building to allow an exhibition space and custodian's apartment to be created. To make more room for these changes, the Rev. Wade's bathroom and staircase were removed, presumably revealing the concealed cupboard and the mysterious 'box of dresses' that had once 'belonged to the sisters'.[25]

Though Jocelyn Kellett cannot have been present in 1936 when the box was found, she, as later president of the Brontë Society, would have known members who were in Haworth at the time of the discovery. Her use of the collective term 'box of dresses' must refer to several, sizeable garments, at least some of which were dresses. As all the other gowns contained within the collection are accounted for and their provenance known, this only leaves a blue-and-cream striped silk dress (whose captivating story will be uncovered in Chapter 7), and the brown silk dress as likely candidates.

Little was known about the dresses when they were found and the phrase 'belonged to the sisters' could simply be attributed to the presence of the two surviving dresses which, it might have been assumed, had belonged to more than one of the Brontë sisters. But it is also possible that the two woollen cloaks, which also lack attribution and that were contained within the box alongside the dresses, were, due to their similarity of style, thought to have belonged to two separate sisters. In any case, given the building work taking

4.2 Charlotte Brontë's 'Governess Dress', front view, D11

place at the time that the box was uncovered, it is certainly possible that in the commotion these were not logged in the normal manner. Had this been the case, their history would have remained entirely undocumented, for with no donor there was no reason why one should be listed, for these garments had never left the parsonage.

With a Brontë connection now established beyond reasonable doubt, it was time to determine which of the three Brontë sisters had originally owned the dress. Thankfully, this question proved much easier to answer than had those that had come before it. At approximately four foot eight or nine inches tall, Charlotte was notably diminutive and, as Branwell's *Pillar Portrait* attests, was considerably smaller than either Emily or Anne. Indeed, she was so small that the writer Harriet Martineau stated that Charlotte was 'the smallest creature [she] had ever seen (except at a fair)'.[26] Allowing for differences in style and the number and thickness of the petticoats worn beneath, the silk gown is very similar in size to other surviving dresses known to have been worn by Charlotte.[27] Certainly, the silk gown was worn by a woman of small stature. All the evidence now pointed towards that woman having been Charlotte Brontë.

Knowing who made, owned and wore a garment changes everything. All of a sudden, the item that lies before you, on layers of tissue, transitions from object to personal possession, from artefact to participant in an individual's life story. But, before any item can really speak, before it can offer insight into that person's life, you must first find it out when it was worn, for then the secrets it reveals can be contextualized, can be better understood. As Charlotte's silk gown has not been subject to significant alteration, those stylistic details that remain are original and could be compared to other, existing garments, to fashion plates and to descriptions found in contemporary literature with relative ease.[28] As in any given period one or two fashionable features tend to dominate, identifying these can often prove helpful in dating a garment.

In this case, it is the sleeves that hold the key, for their leg of mutton shape is almost iconic.[29] The lowered shoulder and voluminous mid-sleeve, that narrows towards the cuff, indicates that the gown was designed and made in the late 1830s. For though the Regency period had seen sleeves swell to unnatural, outlandish, even ridiculous sizes, by 1835, like an expiring balloon, they had slowly begun to deflate.[30] The next few years saw a reduction in the width and breadth of the sleeve. By 1842 or 1843, the fullness around the elbow had been reduced, suggesting that Charlotte's gown was designed and made sometime between 1837 and 1841, after the decline of the late Regency period, and before the fitted shape of the early to mid-1840s.[31]

It was in May 1839 that Charlotte took up her first post as governess and it is no coincidence that this date perfectly coincides with the silk gown's likely date of production. After all, it is only natural that prior to taking up a new position she saw fit to expand her wardrobe. Some of her existing gowns could, of course, still have been worn, but she would also have needed new

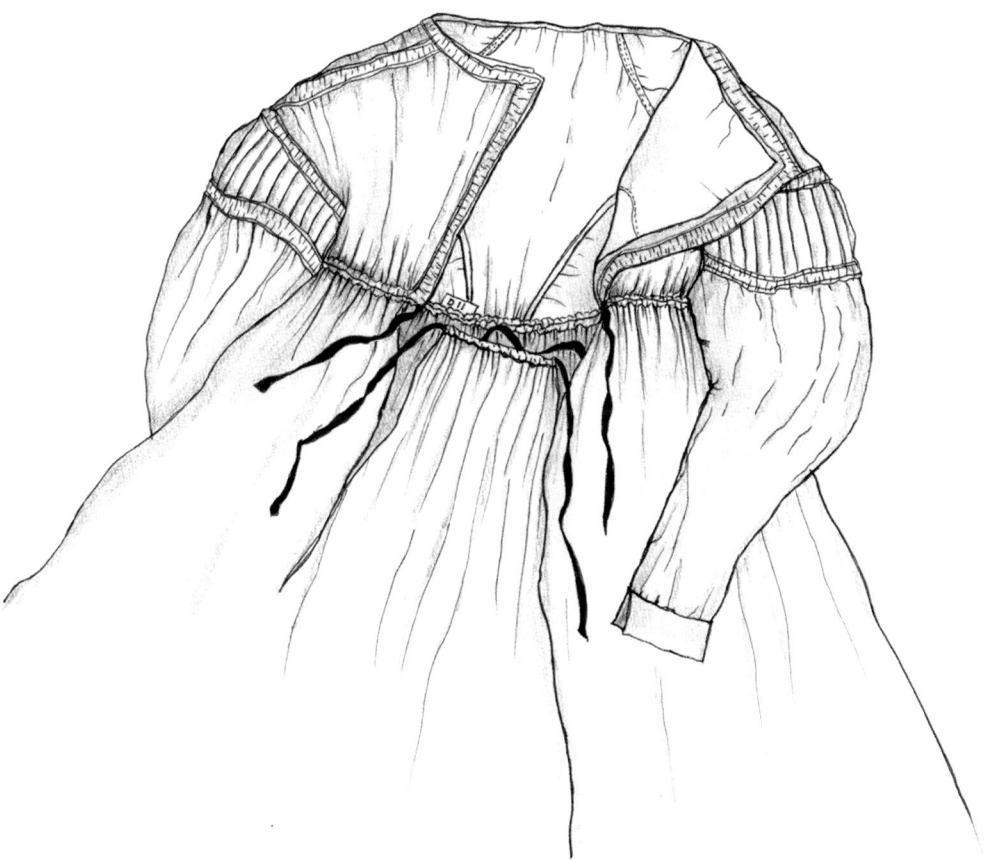

4.3 *Inside of Charlotte Brontë's 'Governess Dress', D11*

garments that were specifically designed to aid her in her new work – work that presented distinct challenges that she would be forced to negotiate.

Having worked as a teacher at Roe Head, Charlotte already had some knowledge of the sartorial requirements of the working woman, yet the role of live-in governess placed additional, often paradoxical demands upon the 'unmarried female members of the small merchant's family ... or the fortuneless daughter of the highly connected clergyman'.[32] With few existing guidelines from which to work, Charlotte, and the other women like her, had no choice but to write the rule book for themselves. In the creation of *Jane Eyre*, Brontë herself would play an important part in the forging of these 'rules'. But, until the 1840s, when an overabundance of manuals, etiquette books and novels filled shelves and constructed stereotypes, the challenges (sartorial and otherwise) of the schoolroom were navigated by individuals, like Charlotte, operating in relative isolation.

Though it is hard for the modern reader to fully grasp, one of the hardest things that Charlotte would face was having to work at all. In many ways, she was right to worry. By the mid-nineteenth century, access to education, when coupled with hard work and opportunity, had made it possible for men from the middle-classes to maintain or aspire to the status of a gentleman whilst working within a wide variety of professions. But the same was not true for women. Highly educated, middle-class ladies like Charlotte Brontë, who due to widowhood, singleness or financial insecurity were required to work for their livings, risked all – for as Lady Duff Gordon asserted, to admit to being a working woman 'was only one shade better than going in for crime'.[33] Author and social commentator Sarah Stickney Ellis drew attention to the extent of this gender inequality in her 1839 conduct manual, *The Women of England* when she wrote, 'Gentlemen may employ their hours of business in almost any degrading occupation and, if they have the means of supporting a respectable establishment at home, may be gentleman still; while, if a lady but touch any article, no matter how delicate, in a way of trade, she loses caste and ceases to be a lady'.[34]

Although a career as governess or teacher was deemed more respectable than other forms of occupation, loss of 'caste', now a wholly divisive term, was nonetheless inevitable.[35] The governess held a strange, lonely place in the house. She was 'neither fish [n]or flesh, lady or servant' – too low to socialize with her employers in the drawing room, but too high to find company in the servants' hall.[36]

Since medieval times, educated but poor women had been employed by the aristocracy to teach their daughters, however it was not until the late eighteenth century that the middle-classes began to appropriate the governess as their own. Manufacturers, merchants, millowners and bankers who had become rich as a result of the Industrial Revolution, sought to ascend the ranks, to mix more freely with the aristocracy, meaning those with the capital to do so, began to mimic the practices of the ruling classes.[37] The governess was perceived as central to the process of gentrification, and it was not long before more and more up and coming families looked to acquire one so as to signal to the world that they had 'made it'. In theory, these changes were positive. In practice, things were less simple, for these women were now being employed by those from a similar or sometimes even inferior social or educational background to their own. And, just as in Charlotte's case, deep resentments inevitably grew with 'the one … struggling up, the other drifting down'.[38]

For both parties, the governess's clothing was a surprisingly powerful tool in this fight for status. For Charlotte, and the many women like her, the garments she wore could help to stabilize her otherwise uncertain place in society. In adhering to the rules of dress and wearing clothes that underscored her respectability, she could emphasize her own middle-class status and go some way to mitigate the stigma that surrounded the woman forced, by circumstance or the ill-management of her male relatives, to support herself.[39] She could also differentiate herself from the other domestic staff who worked in the house – a point of particular importance given Charlotte's scarring experiences of enforced uniform at the Clergy Daughters' School.

But a governess's clothing had another role to play too, for in dressing like a lady she was also highlighting her employers' ability to secure a highly educated, refined governess for their children. Properly dressed, she was, if you will, a walking status symbol, proof of their elevated position within the community. For all these reasons, as *The Guide to Service* of 1844 informs, it was vital that Charlotte's working wardrobe was 'of the same general character as that of other ladies'.[40] Therefore, in line with all middle- and upper-class women, governesses were obliged to change their clothing several times a day. Jane Eyre, when arriving at Thornfield, was dressed in a 'black merino cloak and beaver bonnet', but was soon encouraged by the housekeeper to 'dress for the evening' and to replace her 'black stuff gown' with 'one of black silk'.[41] Later, when the house was filled with Edward Rochester's guests, Jane was compelled to change once again, this time into her 'best dress (the silver gray one purchased for Miss Temple's wedding and never worn since)', in order to be fitting company for her excited young student at the evening festivities.[42]

Such demands came at a heavy cost – one that most governesses' salaries were not sufficient to meet.[43] In her second post, Charlotte Brontë was promised just £20 per annum, a sum that would be further diminished by the deduction of £4 for her laundry. Even by contemporary standards this was a small income for a full-time post, especially when one considers the added strain that caring for small children would have put upon Charlotte's clothing.

On such a meagre salary, a governess could afford to own only a limited number of gowns, so any garments that she had made before taking up her post needed to be both versatile and durable. Jane Eyre speaks of possessing just three main garments. Each of these she adapted using just a few key accessories – a shawl, locket, brooch, ring, slippers, shoes, boots, cloak and either a straw or beaver bonnet. In effect, these items formed a capsule wardrobe that it was hoped would equip her for every possible social eventuality.

Charlotte's 'Governess Dress' was then, as might be expected, a pragmatic choice. Elegant, unobtrusive and simple in design, this day gown was formed from dark silk – a fabric more typically the preserve of the upper- and middle-classes. But, though at first glance, it is entirely unremarkable, closer inspection reveals that there is much more to it than initially meets the eye.

To begin with, unlike most gowns of the late 1830s and early 1840s, the gown fastens at the front rather than the back. As governesses were typically given their own room near to the nursery or schoolroom, most did not have a servant readily available to help them dress. Though Charlotte would still have required assistance with putting on her corset in the morning, in wearing front-fastening dresses, she would have been able to dress and undress without help for the rest of the day. As her unrelenting schedule gave her little time to herself, this extra autonomy, this added privacy, would have been welcome, for Charlotte's long-term insecurities meant that she would have avoided such exposure at all costs.

The bodice and skirt are equally serviceable. Though joined at the back to form one piece, unusually, both are closed at the front and sides using a series of ties and drawstrings. This system of closure was popular in gowns of the early nineteenth century and before, but by the time Charlotte made the 'Governess Dress', it had largely fallen out of use and was only commonly adopted in maternity wear (to allow a gown to grow in size).[44] However, the design did have two main benefits. First, it would have been relatively quick to put on and off and, second, both the bodice and the skirt could easily be drawn in to form a neat waistline – the strung waistband being covered by an apron or pinafore.[45] The draw strung, drop-down front panel of the skirt (which remains unstitched 29 cm down from the waist) also ensured there was easy access to the large, independent pockets that Charlotte would have worn tied on a string around her waist and hanging down beneath her skirts.

Though the inclusion of plackets (an opening in a garment for access or to cover fastenings), was not uncommon, their prominence here is unusual,

4.4 *Embroidered pockets, early nineteenth century*

suggesting that pockets were a key feature of the ensemble. By the 1830s, as *The Workwoman's Guide* of 1838 states, most 'pockets [were] worn either tied around the waist, fastened into the petticoat or buttoned upon the stays'.[46] These separate pockets were both strong and capacious – necessary qualities for the self-sufficient, working woman who was required to carry around essential items that she would need in her day-to-day life.[47] In Charlotte's own 1853 novel *Villette*, teacher Lucy Snowe's dress pocket was found to contain a 'purse full of money', 'a memorandum book … with a small plaited lock of Miss Marchmont's grey hair' and a 'bunch of three keys' for her 'trunk, desk and workbox'.[48] Worn close to the body, pockets were not merely a practical requirement for the teacher or governess, they also offered some protection for her few, personal possessions away from the prying eyes of her employer.[49] Charlotte presents the pocket as fundamental to the independence of her female protagonists, as, following Rochester's fateful revelation that he was already married to the woman in the attic, it is to her pocket that Jane Eyre entrusts her most precious worldly possession – a 'purse containing twenty shillings'.[50] These few coins are all that stand between the fleeing Jane and starvation on the moor.[51]

Though clearly important, functionality was not Charlotte's only concern when planning and making her 'Governess Dress'. Consideration was also given to the style and design of the gown and the underlying messages it conveyed. For her ambiguous status forced her to walk a sartorial tightrope. Maintaining her own and her employer's status was imperative, but it was also vital that her clothing did not compete with that of her mistress – not only to avoid offence, but also to safeguard her own propriety.

By the time Charlotte took up her first post in 1839, a domestic storm was brewing. Troubling stories of beautiful and overly fashionable governesses using their well-honed feminine wiles to seduce sons or husbands had become commonplace. This so-called 'temptress', well-educated, single and genteel as she might be, began to be viewed with fear by wives and mothers everywhere. And, as collective social anxiety grew, so too did the number of artistic references in novels, newspaper articles and ladies' magazines, all of which stoked the fires of fear. Governess Becky Sharp dominates Thackeray's *Vanity Fair* with her 'taste [in dress] as [good as] any milliner in Europe' and complexion that 'could bear any sunshine'. Employing her beauty, wit and captivating style, Miss Sharp achieves her aim of entrapping the affections of both the handsome Captain Rawdon and his recently bereaved father, Sir Pitt Crawley.[52] Even the more benign and docile Clara Copperfield, mother of the eponymous David, had some success in improving her lot. In the opening chapter of Dickens' *David Copperfield* Clara recounted, 'I was nursery governess in a family when Mr. Copperfield came to visit, he was very kind to me and took a great deal of notice of me and paid me a great deal of attention, and at last proposed to me.'[53] Whilst in the 1857 novel, *John Halifax*, Mrs Halifax, whose sons had both fallen in love with Miss Silver, a pretty, French governess, bitterly exclaims, 'Would to Heaven she had never entered [the house]!'[54]

So great was this societal preoccupation, that the plain-faced governess began to gain advantage over her beautiful competitors.[55] Thackeray, ever the social barometer of his time, alludes to this unexpected bias in *Vanity Fair* when deciding between two potential candidates to fill the post of governess to the children of Sir Huddleston Fuddleston. Whilst both were 'perfectly qualified to instruct in Greek, Latin and the rudiments of Hebrew', it was Miss Leticia Hawkley, 'whose face is much pitted with the smallpox … has a halt in her gait, red hair and a trifling obliquity of vision' who was deemed less 'objectionable' than the 'eighteen-year-old' Miss Tuffin 'of exceedingly pleasing personal appearance'.[56] As Thackeray makes so clear, governessing was one profession in which being in possession of a plain face was an advantage. This fact would not have been lost on Charlotte Brontë, whose own struggle with her appearance continued, unabated.

To help to evade these well-publicized concerns, governesses often chose to dress in dark, unobtrusive clothing. Real-life governess Nelly Weeton deliberately selected a gown that allowed her to 'pass unnoticed; a dark print'.[57] Jane Eyre also aims to 'pass unnoticed'.[58] After the fire, when the whole household is assembled on the landing, and despite her significant role in saving Thornfield Hall from certain devastation, Jane wishes only to retreat, 'unnoticed, as unnoticed as [she] had left it'.[59] The sombre colour of Charlotte's own, now brown, silk dress could also be attributed to her desire to remain camouflaged and hide in the shadows. Few dyes of any type stand up to light or other environmental factors without changing or fading over time, but nineteenth-century, black and brown dyed silks are particularly vulnerable, so it is likely that the colour we now see is quite different to the gown's original shade. Naturally procured black dyes (most notably logwood) often fade to a dark purple-brown, and it is therefore probable that Charlotte's gown was once black. This comes as no surprise, for invisibility was the safest option for the socially vulnerable governess and, ever fearful of criticism, even more so for Charlotte after her painful early weeks at Roe Head School.

With all these complex issues to consider, it is understandable that Charlotte might have looked about for a template to help her. This she found, not amongst the novels or fashion books of the day, so many of which were written for the upper- and middle-class woman operating firmly within the confines of the domestic sphere (as daughter or wife and mother in the home), but rather in the wholly respectable clothing of the Quaker woman. Though never uniform, the wardrobe of these hard-working, pious, and compassionate members of society was distinctive. During the day, it often took the form of a dark or drab silk gown that closed at the centre-front bodice and on either side of the skirt at the waist.[60] This was a development of the apron or fall-front gown of the 1820s and 1830s and was typically fastened using a system of ties, just like those found inside Charlotte's own gown.[61] A full or half apron, neckerchief, shawl, cap and bonnet completed the ensemble.

Certainly, there is evidence to suggest that Charlotte would have come into close contact with members of the Quaker faith. There was a long history of Quakers in the West Riding of Yorkshire. As early as 1669 a monthly meeting was formally established in Brighouse (13.6 miles from Haworth). The Quaker community grew in number and by 1851 meetings were taking place in Keighley (just 4.2 miles away), Skipton, Bradford, Leeds and Bingley. It is likely that Brontë had personal encounters with these worshippers and was aware of the impact that they had upon the local community. For example, John Hustler (1715–90) had been a prominent Quaker and had revolutionized Bradford, transforming it from a small town to a prosperous city. Thus, there is little doubt that Charlotte would have had the opportunity to consider Quaker practices and beliefs at close quarters.

The Quaker woman was a well-established figure of nineteenth-century society. George Fox, the founder of the movement, believed that all of mankind was equal before God.[62] In comparison to the vast majority of their sex, Quaker women were afforded much liberty and their reputation for good works and for social reform preceded them as they went. As William Howitt, prolific writer and social critic, asserted in the *Sheffield Iris* of February 1835, the Quakeress, '… on her missions of moral and religious business, goes to various parts of the world, and to different scenes of life with no protection but her purpose and her purity – secure in her common sense and right feeling, and her power of appeal to these in others'.[63]

Their visual image conveyed a reassuring, virtuous authority.[64] And, as it became increasingly synonymous with altruism, it began to offer some protection for the Quaker woman called to work in some of the most degenerate or dangerous places that a woman could go – prisons, workhouses, hospitals and slums.[65] For even when surrounded by depravation and horror, when up to her arms in dirt and grime, the Quakeress's distinctive clothing marked her out as being *in* these worlds but not *of* them. She could arrive with 'purpose and purity' and could go home each day with her reputation intact.[66] In fact, as essayist Charles Lamb pointed out, it was as if her clothing, and by default her virtue, was 'incapable of receiving soil'.[67]

To our modern eyes, nineteenth-century Quaker dress seems restrictive and prudish when compared with the more flamboyant gowns seen in fashion plates, newspapers and magazines of the period. However, plain Quaker dress was modest, but it was also appealing. It covered and enveloped the figure whilst still revealing its womanly shape.[68] Though plain, these gowns were alluring in much the same way as well-tailored, female business suits might be considered today. Indeed, the distinctive qualities of Quaker dress were almost liberational for those who adopted it. Dressed in this way, women could retain all the positive attributes of the feminine sphere, yet remain able to venture safely beyond it, into previously forbidden and masculine territory. In other words, Quaker-like clothing was quietly reformative.[69]

Middle-class, respectable, practical and yet profound – the model fulfilled all key criteria, especially for a clever parson's daughter forced by circumstance into the world of work. In the light of Charlotte's own clothing choices, her later persistent use of the term 'Quaker' when describing the clothing of Jane Eyre and Lucy Snowe is suddenly comprehensible.[70] Of the four references to the term 'Quaker' in *Jane Eyre*, three refer to the clothing of the governess herself. Jane willingly identifies herself as a 'plain, Quakerish governess' and describes her own dress, 'Quaker-like as it was'. Later, she depicts herself as being 'in my usual Quaker trim, where there was nothing to retouch – all being too close and plain, braided locks included, to admit disarrangement'. In each case, the term 'Quaker' is deliberately used to convey connotations of purity, modesty, goodness, neatness, cleanliness and chastity.[71] The association is deliberate. Charlotte wishes to establish Jane as a character who is as trustworthy, moral and good – she is no Becky Sharp. Ironically, though Jane breaches conventional, even acceptable lines in marrying her rich, high-status employer, Edward Rochester, it was her dark, Quakerish silhouette that helped to form the enduring stereotype of the nineteenth-century governess. In putting on similar dress to that worn by the Quaker women she saw at work, both Charlotte and her protagonist, Jane Eyre, were seeking benefit by association. Their plain gowns adhere to many of the complex codes and conventions of their station whilst, at the same time, proclaiming, just as Jane herself did, that 'no net ensnares' them for they are 'free human being[s] with an independent will'.[72]

This proclamation of independence and individuality is further reinforced in Brontë's surviving, dark silk dress, where delicate details on the sleeves and the back of the bodice demonstrate both an awareness of current fashions and an appreciation of aesthetics. The small, uniform pleats and tucks that ornament it are quietly extravagant. This is no parsimonious design. Extra fabric and long hours of labour have been worked into the very body of this gown. The dress might be subdued, but it is clear that its owner refused to be vanquished, and especially by her need to work.

Charlotte tried hard to withstand the subjugation that she felt so keenly in her role as governess, but, ultimately, she found she could not continue. The White family were not unkind to her, in fact they were quite the reverse, but Charlotte could not settle to her work. It had become clear that, though she begrudgingly accepted her financial obligations to both herself and to her family, she intensely disliked any role that placed her in a subordinate position to those of her own class, or to those whom she considered her intellectual inferiors (in other words, almost everyone). It was these complex, driving emotions that would lead her to the conclusion that if she must teach, self-employment was the only solution.

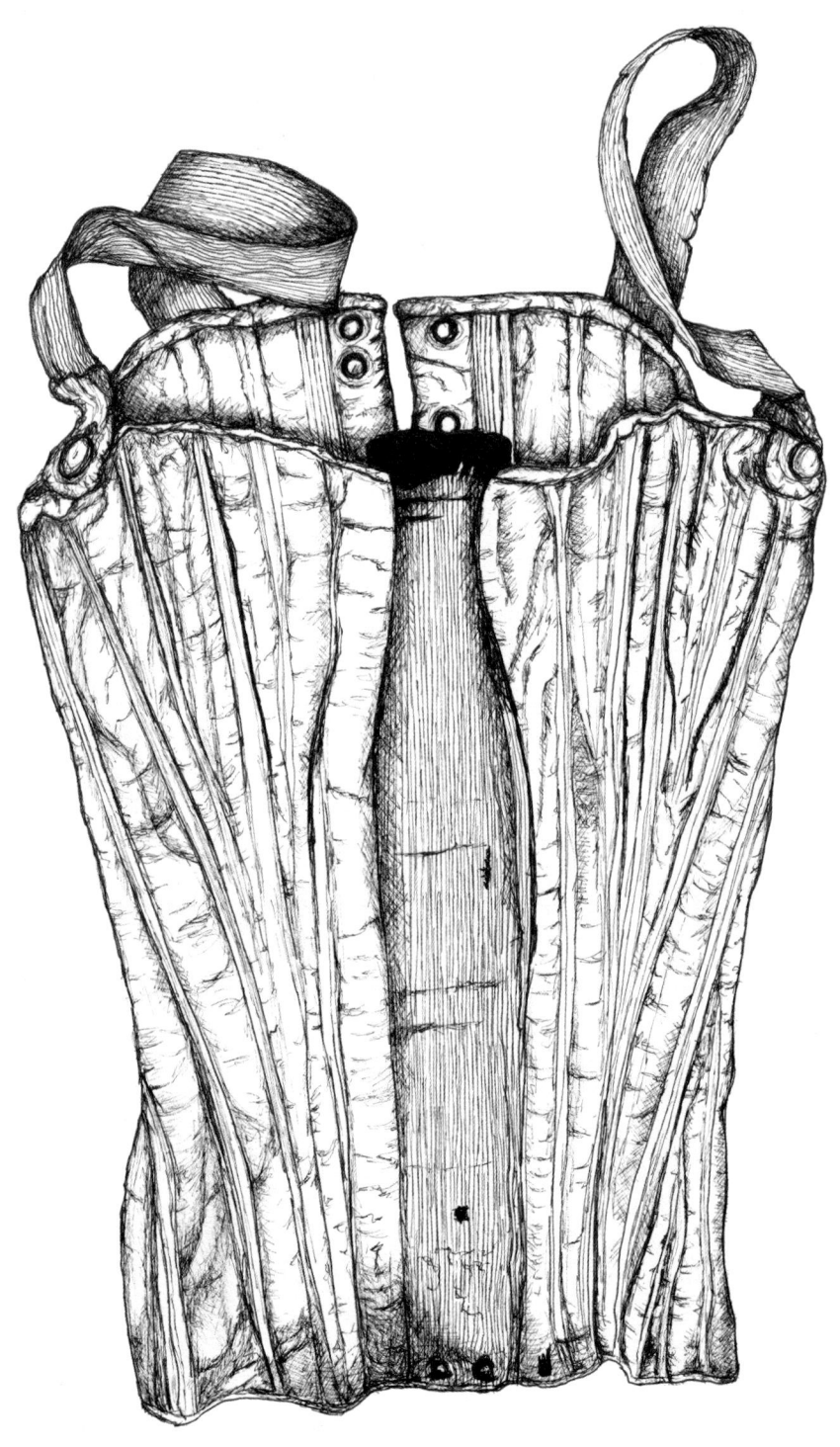

5.1 *Charlotte Brontë's corset, c. 1842, D116*

5

The Corset

Charlotte had not even handed in her notice to the Whites before she had begun to throw herself with uncharacteristic enthusiasm towards a new venture – one that she believed would offer both herself and her sisters all the financial advantages of employment without having to degrade themselves by wiping the noses of other people's children. It was with palpable excitement that she wrote to Ellen: 'There is a project hatching in this house … The project is yet in its infancy – hardly peeping from its shell … To come to the point – Papa and Aunt talk … of our – id est – Emily, Anne and myself commencing a School!'[1]

It could be viewed as serendipitous that just as Charlotte, Emily and Anne had decided to open a school of their own, Margaret Wooler, headmistress of Roe Head, should announce the closure of her own. Believing it to be the answer to all their problems, she immediately offered the Dewsbury Moor premises and its contents to the Brontë sisters in exchange for the promise of continued bed and board for herself. Just eighteen miles from their beloved Haworth and from their father, it was a ready-made opportunity for the young women. The school was already successful, already acclaimed and all ready to go. But, despite this apparently providential proposition, and perhaps because the harsh realities of work were once again scratching at her door, Charlotte made the daring decision not to accept Miss Wooler's offer. In a letter to Ellen she wrote, 'I am not going to Dewsbury-Moor – at least as far as I can see at the present … it is a poisoned place to me – besides I burn to go somewhere else.'[2]

Charlotte's sudden wanderlust might have had its roots in procrastination, but the travel exploits of her friends Mary and Martha Taylor were also a stimulus. Following their father's death in December 1840, the two sisters had bravely set off on a continental tour, taking in 'pictures the most exquisite – & cathedrals the most venerable'.[3] Their letters, which were filled with descriptions of far-flung places (by mid-nineteenth-century standards at least), appear to have awakened something deep in Charlotte's soul. Suddenly, atypically, Charlotte was stifling 'a strong wish for wings – wings such as wealth can furnish – such an urgent thirst to see – to know – to learn'.[4] And when Mary and Martha settled at the Château de Koekelberg, a finishing school in Brussels, Charlotte made up her mind to follow her friends' example and to, as she so extravagantly termed it, allow herself to 'expand boldly'.[5]

Before any such expansion could take place, Charlotte knew that funds must be secured, for her own meagre savings would not allow her to travel far. Her Aunt Branwell had already been persuaded to lend her nieces the money for their grand school project, but it was now Charlotte's hope that some of those funds might be used to make this new dream of travel a reality. Summoning her most convincing arguments, she wrote to her aunt: 'My friends recommend me to spend … time in some school on the Continent. They say schools in England are so numerous, competitions so great, that without some such step towards attaining superiority we shall probably have a very hard struggle and may fail in the end.'[6]

Incredibly, Charlotte's plan worked. The same stiff but strangely enlightened aunt, who had allowed her teenage niece to immerse herself in the magical world of the *Lady's Magazine*, would be instrumental in helping her to fulfil another, very different fantasy – for now, in the spring of 1842 Charlotte would go to Brussels. It was decided, though, that she could not undertake this 'wild and ambitious scheme' alone.[7] Emily, who had vowed never to leave Haworth under any circumstances, who had become homesick to the point of breakdown, had been prevailed upon to accompany her sister across the Channel. One can only wonder at the heated discussions that must have passed between Charlotte and Emily in the months before they commenced their trip. Anne would surely have made a more willing companion, but, as she was still working, the loss of her salary could not be justified. And, as Patrick would not have permitted Charlotte to reside in an alien country by herself, Emily was most reluctantly forced to submit to her sister's demands.

So, after months of planning and scheming, on 8 February 1842, Charlotte, together with Emily and Patrick, set off for Brussels with a trunk almost large enough to house them all. At Leeds they were joined by Mary Taylor and her brother Joe, who were by this time themselves seasoned travellers. The journey to London took eleven hours, but they arrived safely and moved to the Chapter Coffee House in Paternoster Row, where Patrick had stayed on previous trips – a 'convenient … quiet, sombre, clerical house', that would soon afterwards be frequented by Anthony Trollope's Mr Septimus Harding in *The Warden*.[8]

They arrived late in the evening, tired but excited to explore the capital city that they had read so much about. The next three days were spent exploring the sights and fitting in all manner of galleries, churches and landmarks before finally collecting their belongings and catching the steam packet to Oostende. From here, they made the long journey to Brussels, eventually arriving to find the city pitch-black due to the lateness of the hour.

The Pensionnat Heger, a 'Maison d'éducation pour les jeunes Demoiselles', was situated in Rue d'Isabelle, in the ancient quarter of Brussels.[9] It was a grey, unprepossessing building which sat long and low, like some regimental barracks.[10] But, if the Brontës were disappointed by the uniform exterior, they would find that what the Pensionnat lacked in external beauty, it more than made up for in hidden charm. Its garden was verdant and secluded, filled with 'gravelled walks' and, at the height of summer, 'sun-bright nasturtiums … orchard giants … jasmine and ivy'.[11]

Inside, the schoolrooms were large and bright, and the dormitory, which slept twenty, clean and well appointed. The school was run by a formidable couple, the authoritarian directrice, Madame Claire Heger, and her irascible but gifted husband, Monsieur Constantin Heger. Though less expensive than the Château de Koekelberg attended by Mary and Martha, it was still a relatively exclusive establishment, with costs amounting to 650 francs per pupil, per year, for basic board and education. There were considerable extras too, meaning the total price for the two Brontë girls was 1,055 francs or forty-two pounds each.[12] Though the money lent to them by their Aunt Branwell would cover this sum, there would be little left over for contingency.

Patrick remained in Brussels for about a week before embarking on an adventure of his own. Fully satisfied that his two daughters were established in their new, temporary home, he travelled south of Brussels to Waterloo – the site of the final defeat of Napoleon I by Patrick's hero, the Duke of Wellington. From there he visited Lille, Dunkirk and Calais, before returning home to Haworth via London.

Though Patrick had been reassured by the strict and ordered atmosphere of the Pensionnat and the emphasis that would be placed upon his daughters' education, Charlotte and Emily did not settle as quickly as he might have hoped. They would soon find that there was much to set them apart from the other girls in the school. Their age, their nationality, their Protestantism and even their very English clothing would prove hindrances to integration and, as Charlotte wrote in a letter home, formed a 'broad line of demarcation' between the Brontë sisters and their Belgian schoolfellows, leaving them feeling 'isolated in the midst of numbers'.[13] But, although Charlotte might have complained about the warmth of their welcome to Ellen, the truth was that neither she nor Emily made much effort to cultivate friendships with the natives or venture far from their new home. Instead, they stuck determinedly to those English friends who now lived nearby or, as they had done so many times before, shut out that which they did not like and turned to each other for succour.

Had it not been that the girls could look forward to uninterrupted time to read and write, study and think, and all beneath the guise of self-betterment, Charlotte might well have cut their trip short, but she could not pass up such an opportunity to focus solely upon herself. For the first portion of her time in Belgium, this prospect dwarfed all other considerations – even loneliness, issues of difference and separation from those she loved. Six long months of freedom stretched before her, during which she need not worry about work, be frustrated by reprobate pupils or weighed down by responsibility. At last, she was freed from it all.

Charlotte was to find, however, that she would not be allowed to sit on her laurels. Constantin Heger proved himself an hard taskmaster. He quickly perceived the unusual abilities of his two English pupils and, in a break from his typical methods of instruction, devised a system that aimed to drastically improve not only their grasp of the language, but also their understanding of structure, of style, of tone and of nuance. Both Charlotte and Emily were assigned carefully chosen passages from literature to study before being asked to compose their own responses in a similar style. Having to order and constrain their thoughts and bind their natural verbosity was an entirely novel experience, but this new, disciplined way of reading and of writing had a profound effect upon them both. However, where Emily simply enjoyed the introspection, Charlotte found the heady mix of intellectual stimulation and personal, male attention wholly intoxicating. For pugnacious and punctilious as Heger was, he gave her time in a way that no one had before. The small, plain, overlooked Charlotte had finally been given notice, and masculine notice at that.

The Brontës' six-month stay passed quickly, and Charlotte felt little incentive to return home. She set about persuading Madame Heger to allow them both to stay for another six months, this time not as pupils but as teachers. They could, she argued, teach a range of subjects, and all for the price of board and lodging. With an intake of English girls due to arrive, Madame Heger readily agreed. Charlotte and Emily began teaching in the hot summer of 1842 – a period in which no rain fell across Europe for many months. They were both, for the first eight weeks at least, quite happy. But, as the season began to change and the leaves of the great plane trees that lined the streets turned from green to brown, so too did their fortune.

The 2 November brought news from Haworth – serious news about their Aunt's failing state of health. The following day brought worse intelligence still; Aunt Branwell, their aunt-mother, the family stalwart, was dead. If this were not terrible and unexpected enough, so too, they found, was William Weightman, their father's much-loved, much-relied upon twenty-eight-year-old curate.[14]

This double blow left the girls with no choice but to return home to mourn alongside the rest of their family. They arrived at the parsonage early on Tuesday 8 November, carrying with them the news from Brussels of yet another unexpected death. Martha Taylor, the vibrant, younger sister of Charlotte's close friend, Mary, had passed away from cholera. Enveloped by such gloom and despair, and with the figure of Death hemming them in on all sides, it must have been hard for Charlotte and Emily to board the ship from Antwerp and make the long and tiring journey back to Yorkshire, not knowing if they would ever return again.

The Haworth Parsonage was a melancholy place that autumn. Aunt Branwell's loss was felt keenly by all, but especially by Branwell and by Anne, who had 'lost the guide and director of all the happy days connected with [their] childhood'.[15] They all missed William Weightman too, for his warmth and good humour had made him an integral part of not only the parish, but also of the tight-knit Brontë household. Emily moved to fill the practical void left by their aunt and took on the daily running of the household, but Patrick would not find so able a curate for some time to come.

By early January, Charlotte's grief had turned to restlessness. She missed her aunt and mourned her loss, but with Emily now holding the household together – a role she had come to enjoy – Charlotte saw no reason to stay. Grief had taught her that life was short, but perhaps, more truthfully, it was her attachment to Heger that drove her back. Either way, on 27 January 1843, less than two months after she had left Belgium, she caught the early morning train from Leeds to London. In a reckless move, one that highlights her father's distracted state, Charlotte embarked on the long journey to Brussels entirely alone. She and her trunk arrived at the Pensionnat Heger late the following day, having circumnavigated errant watermen, rough waters, late-night steamers and petrifying darkness. It was a portentous voyage. For though Charlotte would arrive at the pensionnat in a state of hope, even ecstasy, she would not leave that way. This time, things would be very different. This time, there would be no breakthrough to happiness. In fact, in the coming months Charlotte would pass through a refining fire so hot, so deeply personal, that it would burn through the dross of youth and reveal the mature woman hidden deep within.

It is strangely apposite that this seminal period should be so vividly brought to life by a now greying corset that was worn so close to Charlotte's body that it took the form of a second skin. Though once a deeply intimate garment, seen and touched only by those closest to her, it is now one of the few surviving witnesses to this painful, private but wholly formative chapter of Brontë's story. And what a witness it is, for though each and every surviving artefact held within the clothing collection has something important to impart, there is no more compelling and vociferous chronicler.

The garment has a straightforward provenance and, consequently, there is no doubt as to its owner. After Charlotte's death in 1855, the corset was left to the Brontë family's long-standing servant, Martha Brown, before being passed to relatives at her death. Some years later, it was sold to an American Brontë enthusiast, before finally being acquired by the Brontë Society in 1916 at a Sotheby's sale, after which it was awarded the functional but unprepossessing moniker of D116.

Considering that most women wore some form of corset, relatively few from the early to mid-nineteenth century have survived. This is because such personal, made-to-measure garments were frequently disposed of rather than bequeathed, remodelled or repurposed. In fact, in order to spare her ghostly blushes, Charlotte's own corset almost met such a fate.[16] Yet, though far fewer examples than might be expected have survived, the corset was an integral part of the Victorian woman's wardrobe.

By the early 1840s, when Charlotte's corset is now known to have been made, these garments had undergone something of a revolution. From the late sixteenth century until the late eighteenth century, fully boned, laced bodices known as 'stays' had been worn by the vast majority of women. These transformed a woman's upper body into an upright, inverted, conical shape.[17] By the 1770s, fashionable women adopted what would eventually become known as the 'corset', a much less rigid garment often made from quilted linen or cotton that favoured a looser, more natural form. In 1810 a new type of corset appeared and, though more structured than what had come before, placed emphasis not on rigidity but on gently curving lines that flowed out from a slender waist.[18] It was from this point on that corsets began to be formed from cut and pieced white, cream or buff-coloured fabric panels that followed the contours of the body. Each individual pattern was slightly different as it was cut in accordance with each woman's particular size and shape. Though no longer brightly coloured, they were often embellished with same colour, decorative stitching or ornamental cording.[19]

On first examination, this corset appears to be similar in design to others from the early to mid-nineteenth century. It is composed of tough cotton and would have extended from the middle of Charlotte's breastbone all the way

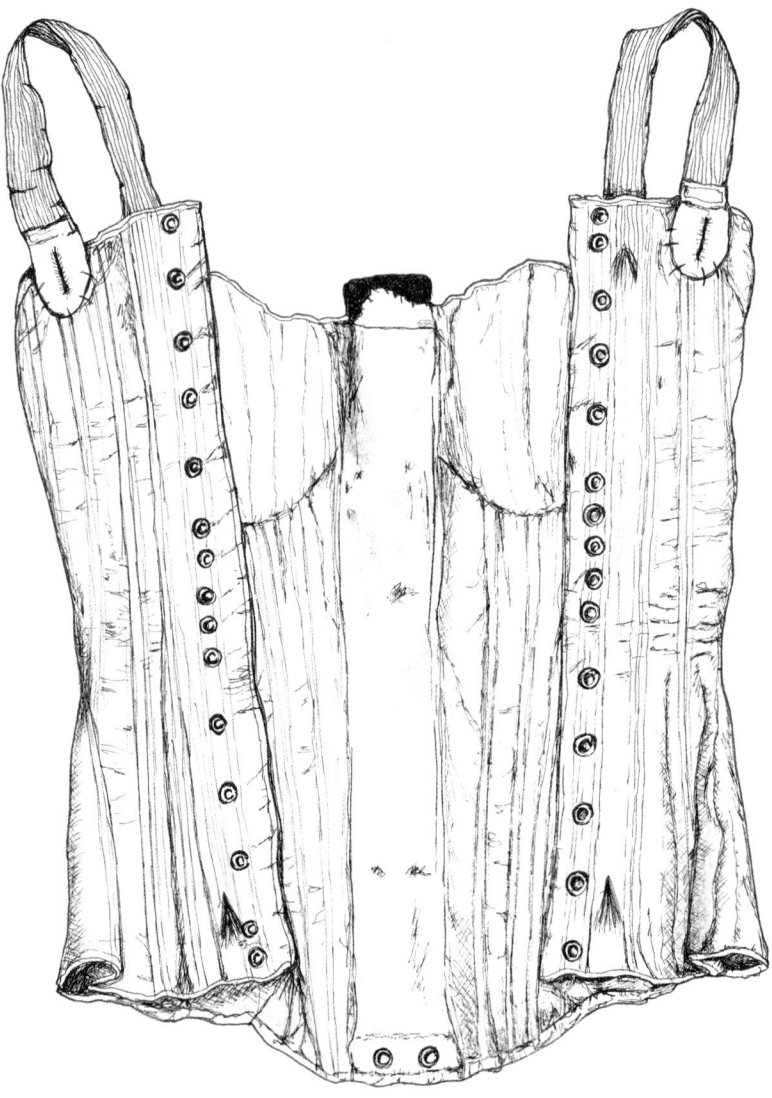

5.2 *Inside view of Charlotte Brontë's corset showing bust enhancers and metal eyelets*

down over her hips. The corset fastens at the back using round metal eyelets through which a ribbon or lace would have been threaded. It is held in place by thick, detachable shoulder straps that could be removed to accommodate the off-the-shoulder evening gowns so popular in the early years of Queen

Victoria's reign. An impenetrable, central metal busk runs from the top to bottom of the garment and this, together with the numerous whalebones that have been inserted into channels at the front, sides and rear, would have moulded Charlotte's body into the desired shape.

Several of these key features proved helpful in dating the corset, not least the metal eyelets, of which there are thirty-two – fifteen on each side and two at the base of the busk. For though metal eyelets were patented in 1823, stamped eyelets, like those seen in Brontë's corset, were not invented until 1828, confirming that the garment must have been made after this date.[20] The unusual placement of the eyelets also hints at a later date.[21] The grommets have been set asymmetrically according to the single lace method – one in which one end of a cord or lace is anchored to the corset and then the other threaded down through the eyelets before being tied off. Though this is more commonly seen in corsets of the earlier Regency period, in this case, at the waist some of the grommets have been placed at closer intervals. This unusual feature, an innovation of the early 1840s, allowed the corset to be tightened more firmly in this specific area.[22] This placement is more commonly seen in corsets closed by the use of a technique known as *à la paresseuse* or the 'lazy-lacing system', first introduced in 1843. This system, which typically employed two laces, when combined with other innovations such as the split iron busk and stud fastenings, allowed the wearer to dress without assistance and to tighten the garment by pulling the two long loops that were formed at waist level.[23] Charlotte's corset does not have these other features, but its uncommon lacing arrangement suggests it was a precursor to this new lazy-lacing system and can therefore be dated to the very early 1840s. This is further corroborated by the corset's longer length and the presence of shoulder straps which, by the mid-1840s had largely been removed to accommodate the lower necklines of eveningwear and some daywear.[24]

To those who have not studied dress before, it can be hard to convey just how long it can take to uncover the history of a garment or to find out how, why, from what and by whom it was manufactured. Many hundreds of hours went into the mapping of this particular corset's story, but it is alarming to think just how easily its peculiar history might have been missed.[25] This is because, though it curved and undulated in accordance with other gusseted designs of the period, on closer inspection, it was radically different. For Charlotte Brontë's corset was seamless, and, rather than being composed of cut and shaped pieces that had been sewn together to form a whole, had been woven in one, single, continuous piece, with integral channels included for bones and busk.[26] It was a rare and entirely unexpected revelation; it was a feat of engineering; it was a masterpiece of mid-nineteenth-century technological advancement and it elevated Charlotte Brontë's corset far above its already lofty status as celebrity curio.

Very few woven corsets are known to have survived.[27] Of those that have, most date from 1860 onwards, and the majority from 1880. It is possible, indeed likely, that other examples exist in archives throughout Europe and beyond, but that due to the close examination required and the time it takes to study them, these have not been identified. Charlotte's 1840s undergarment can therefore be viewed as an early and significant specimen.

The first woven corset was, in fact, produced ten years earlier on an especially adapted jacquard loom designed and built by a young and ambitious Swiss-born inventor, Jean Werly of Bar-le-Duc, France. Spurred on by the hope that he could begin to mass-produce corsets – a garment that he knew most Western women wore but currently had to have measured and made to order – in 1832 he took out a patent for a loom that could produce a woven material referred to as 'rondes bosses' [in the round/three-dimensional]. This term was initially used in classical sculpture to describe the practice of carving a three-dimensional figure that could be viewed from all angles. In much the same way, Werly's fabric, once woven, was moulded to a three-dimensional body using steam and then boned and bound to form a corset 'sans coutures' [without seams].[28] By making only a slight adaptation to the looms, Werly found that corsets of differing sizes could be manufactured quickly and in large numbers.

Encouraged by his own progress, Werly set about fabricating not only looms, but also other forms of corset-making apparatus. Yet so distracted did he become by his efforts to dominate the market and build his business, that he failed to notice that the patent protection he had taken out in 1832 would only safeguard his inventions for a period of five years. His competitors wasted no time, by late 1837 both his innovative corset designs and his pioneering machinery had been copied. Now, woven corsets were being produced in factories across Europe and not only by Monsieur Werly.

Despite Werly's early domination, Charlotte's corset was not made in Bar-le-Duc. Nor, indeed, was it made or purchased in Britain – for woven corsets were not widely available in England until 1846 and do not appear to have been manufactured here until the early 1850s.[29] Given the distinct shape and design of Charlotte's corset, it is highly probable that it was acquired whilst she was living in Brussels and, consequently, that it enveloped her body as she battled through one of the most turbulent and formative periods of her short life.

Just three manufacturers of woven corsets are known to have existed in Belgium.[30] Of these, only two were producing corsets in the early 1840s, when Charlotte was staying at the Pensionnat Heger. Both of these put forward their 'corsets san coutures' for evaluation in the 1841 exhibition of manufactured products held in Brussels that year. Madame Van Beneden, née Bruers of Bruxelles, was highly commended for her seamless corsets, and, along with her husband Mathieu, would later go on to be included in the Great Exhibition held at Crystal Palace, London in 1851.[31] Here, and ironically alongside products made by Robert and Jean Werly of Bar-le-Duc, from whom the original technology for the making of woven corsets had been stolen, they would be awarded medals for the 'excellent manufacture', 'unexceptionable shape' and 'excellent workmanship'.[32]

Monsieur J.B. Van Beneden-Bruers, also of Brussels and presumably a relative of the aforementioned van Beneden family, was also a manufacturer of woven corsets 'sans coutures'.[33] His products were sold all across Belgium, but particularly in Ghent, where surviving porcelain trading cards suggest that they could be purchased from retailers Vve. Verberckmoes and Virginie Van Caneghem.

Both Monsieur and Madame Mathieu Van Beneden and Monsieur J.B. Van Beneden-Bruers' offices were located in the central St Joose-ten-Noode area of Brussels. Given the number of times that these names were linked in exhibition catalogues and exhibition reviews, it is clear that the two manufacturers were once very closely connected.[34] In the 1838 copy of *Almanach Royal et du Commerce de Belgique*, under the heading 'Brevets d'invention' or 'Patents' is written 'Van Beneden, frères, à Bruxelles – B. perf., 10 ans. Perfectionnements aux corsets sans couture de Werly'.[35]

These few short lines, hidden amidst a 568-page volume, are important. Not only do they confirm that there was a family association between the two firms, later broken by rift, but also the Van Beneden/Werly connection. Evidently, just months after Werly's five-year, 1832 patent had lapsed, the inventor's Belgian counterparts had brazenly taken out patents of their own, effectively squeezing Werly out of the very market that he had created. Brontë's surviving woven corset then, ugly and utilitarian as it is, is evidence of pirating and industrial espionage, of dirty dealings, of betrayal and of corruption. It reminds, if such a reminder were needed, that however bold, however inventive, however entrepreneurial the individual, in business, perhaps as in all things, administration is king.[36]

Whether Charlotte purchased her corset from Madame van Benenden's shop in Rue de Paroissiens or direct from van Benenden-Bruer's factory in Le Marché aux Bois (now known as Houtmarkt), she would not have had far to walk.[37] Rue d'Isabelle, the street in which the Pensionnat Heger was situated, was demolished in 1909 to make way for the Palais des Beaux Arts, now in central Brussels, but study of contemporary maps suggest that Heger's house was less than a third of a mile away from either establishment. Perhaps she caught a glimpse of the innovative design, not yet available in Britain, as she wandered past the shop window on her way home from an afternoon walk. Perhaps its versatile, removable straps enticed her inside, or perhaps, its greatest attraction was the ease by which it could be purchased. An individual need enter a shop armed only with a waist measurement – a fact unlikely to be lost on a young woman in a foreign land, with a notably poor body image. There would be no need to stand in nothing but a chemise as the seamstress pinned and prodded, tucked and basted. This corset could be bought off the peg. Yet, innovation and ease of acquisition were not the only reasons that Charlotte was drawn to this plain, functional garment. Its greatest attraction was something far more meaningful, far more impactful.

The evidence suggests that it was this corset's strength; its ability to mould and to constrain, to shrink and to confine that most attracted her to it. For Charlotte's corset has an unusually heavy structure. It is composed from nine 0.5 cm wide 'bones' on each side of an impenetrable central busk. These outer 'bones' are made from baleen – a keratinous material found in the upper jaws of the baleen whale. Similar in composition to the human fingernail, it is strong and flexible, yet softens slightly when warmed by the body. In contrast, the central busk is harsh and unyielding. Made from iron, it is 36.5 cm in length, 4.5 cm wide and 1.5 mm in depth.[38] Covered on both sides by a thin strip of fine kid leather, it is not, as many busks were, aesthetically pleasing.[39] Indeed, this is no engraved token of love, no hand-carved beauty. It adds an almost punitive quality to the corset – not only is it cumbersome but it is also entirely utilitarian. And no more so than when worn by the diminutive Charlotte.[40] Though long on any wearer, on her small frame, the busk would have run from her sternum, down between her breasts and well beyond her pelvis, meaning that when she wore it she would have had no choice but to perch on the extreme edge of her chair as she sat.

The corset's waist dimension is markedly small when compared with other mid-nineteenth-century, surviving corsets. Until the 1870s, middle- and upper-class women wore their corsets relatively loose. They were worn to control posture, for modesty and to gently shape the body, not to reduce the size of the waist. The majority of corsets, according to research, measure between 52 and 67 cm when closed and an additional 5 to 10 cm can be added to each of these measurements because, as *Godey's Lady's Book* of 1857

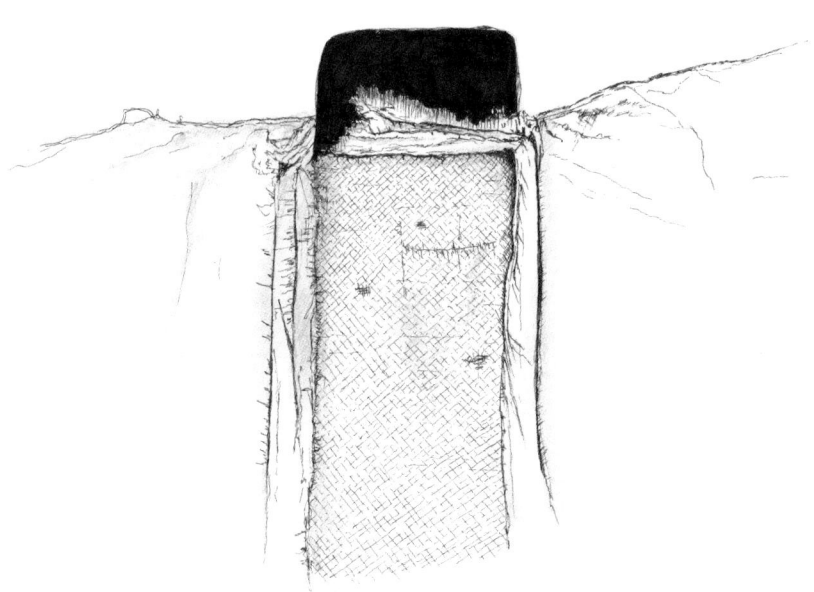

5.3 *Impenetrable busk of Charlotte Brontë's corset*

asserts 'stays ought NOT TO MEET when they are laced on'.[41] Yet Charlotte's corset measures just 48 cm/18.5 inches across and is a true reflection of the dimension of her corseted waist. For not only do her existing corset covers and dresses verify this small measurement, but there is both written and physical evidence to suggest that she defied contemporary cultural practice and wore her corset tightly laced.[42]

Charlotte did not meet the man who would publish her books until 1848, but both during and after her life, George Smith expressed concern that she had far 'too small a waist' and later went so far as to declare that though it 'shocks the respect for a fine genius to say it, [he had] no doubt that tight-lacing shortened Charlotte's life'.[43] Nearly forty years after her death, still impacted by what he had seen, Smith told his friend, the novelist George Gissing, that Charlotte was 'very vain of her narrow waist ... and laced herself so tight as to injure herself'.[44]

Charlotte's corset was purchased five or six years before she met Smith, but the garment itself is testimony of her practice of tight-lacing. Conspicuous, horizontal creases run across the corset at the waist and even over the busk. On the inside of the corset, where Charlotte's body was pressed up close against the metal busk, her sweat has caused rust to form. And, despite the impenetrability of the iron structure, even the fabric that surrounds it has deteriorated under the tension. Around the eyelets there are also clear signs of distortion, and marks on the outer edges of the fastening area suggest that, against common practice, these have been pulled so hard that they overlapped. Due to the constriction and consequent flattening of her breasts, a small pad has been hand-stitched inside each cup to increase bust size and artificially attain the womanly silhouette. These appear to have been added by Charlotte herself as they are composed of a very different fabric and only tacked in place, presumably for easy removal.

Unlike many of her other surviving garments, the corset was not worn by anyone other than Charlotte. Not only was her waist unusually small, but with the new emphasis that had been placed on hygiene in the early to mid-nineteenth century, it is unlikely that her corset was worn by anyone else after her death.[45] Therefore, all areas of obvious strain and deterioration can be attributed to Charlotte herself.

It would be easy to presume that it is common to find such evidence of tight lacing on other nineteenth-century corsets, but this is simply not the case. Eleri Lynn, costume curator at the Victoria and Albert Museum writes, 'though the idea of the hand span waist is popularly associated with Victorian corsetry, objects at the V&A and other museums suggest that very tight-lacing was uncommon'.[46] Valerie Steele, author of *The Corset: A Cultural History* has done much to challenge the prevailing view that 'most women in the past had "wasp-waists"'. She rightly argues that 'though many women did reduce their waists ... accounts of tight-lacing to extreme tenuity usually represent fantasies'.[47] Paintings and surviving early photographs or daguerreotypes of corseted women of the 1840s, made close to the time that Brontë's corset was manufactured, support Steele's assertion. On close inspection, the majority depict the gentle shaping of the body rather than a harsh, unnatural whittling. Large skirts and sleeves do help to make women's waists appear smaller but, though there are exceptions, corsets themselves did not tend to be excessively constrictive.[48]

Where tight lacing was practised, it was generally looked upon unfavourably, with most writers and social commentators finding the custom abhorrent. Catharine Esther Beecher in her book, *A Treatise on Domestic Economy for the Use of Young Ladies at Home, and at School*, summed up contemporary feeling when she wrote of the 'evils of tight dressing' in which corsets 'are made to hold up the body, so that those muscles, which are designed for this purpose, are released from duty, and grow weak; so that, after this has continued for some time, leaving off the unnatural support produces a feeling of weakness'.[49] In her opinion, tight lacing also restricted 'the office of the lungs' and thus prevented 'the full purification of the blood'.[50] Her advice to 'all sensible women' was to 'oppose any resistance' and to choose a corset that allowed freedom of movement 'when engaged in common employments' like 'sewing, reading or study'. Such views were only reinforced by the medical profession which produced articles highlighting the dangers for that small number of women who chose to tight lace.[51]

George Smith's recollections and Charlotte's own surviving corset reveal that she belonged to that minority of women who carried corset lacing to an extreme. In other words, Charlotte's decision to tight lace – and it was a decision – must be viewed as significant. Why then did Charlotte Brontë feel the need to lace her corset with such force, and to whittle her waist to so small a size? Inevitably, this question has multiple, complex answers. In order to understand why she chose to challenge the norm; it is necessary to first determine why women at this time wore corsets at all.

It could be argued that the act of corseting was a direct consequence of patriarchy; that it was a nineteenth-century construction of a 'masochistic', 'submissive' feminine ideal.[52] Though such arguments are not entirely unfounded, Brontë's relationship with her own corset demonstrates that corsetry in the mid-nineteenth century cannot be viewed as one, undeviating, uniform experience to which all women were subjected before finally being 'liberated by feminism'.[53] Indeed, as will be explored, there were many reasons why women wore corsets during the 1840s when Brontë acquired and wore her own.

Beauty was a fundamental concern. After all, it was the nineteenth-century woman's duty to be beautiful, and a compact, elegant waist sat at the very centre of this beauty imperative.[54] Unlike the muscular masculine figure, which was triangular in form, the ideal female body in the years 1830 to 1860 was much like an egg timer, with a narrow middle and a rounded top and bottom.[55] This curvaceousness, this desired voluptuousness, was difficult to achieve alongside a small waist, so some form of external bodily manipulation, usually a corset, was needed to meet beauty standards and to ease criticism.[56]

But adherence to a preordained concept of beauty was not the only reason that Charlotte and her contemporaries chose to wear corsets – ironically, good health was also a motivating factor. As English corsetiere Madame Caplin declared, it was deemed important that women 'maintain the uprightness of the superior regions of the body' in case of collapse.[57] It had long been believed that a woman's internal organs and frame required proper support and, in consequence, from the seventeenth century onward, young girls were corseted to 'prevent deformities of the skeleton' and to 'procure an agreeable waist and a well-positioned bust'.[58] This early discipline, which was continued into adulthood, soon became intrinsically linked to the idea of physical self-control and courtly display, to stiffness and restraint – attributes which, in the seventeenth and eighteenth centuries, would become strongly correlated with high social position and with power.[59]

This connection between physical straightness, morality and status continued into the nineteenth century as the corset, or rather the corseted waist, became an increasingly important signifier of class. This is because, though most women wore corsets, in practical terms, it was difficult for working women (meaning those who worked in factories, fields or in domestic service) to wear corsets that restricted their movements.[60] It is not hard to see how difficult it would have been for women to move freely enough to work machines or carry out heavy domestic tasks in the impenetrable metal busk and heavy structure of Brontë's corset. Therefore, adaptations were often made, leaving the more constrained, slender waist the preserve of the upper- and middle-classes and, accordingly, an indication of refinement. But even those women who undertook manual labour made some concession as, in the nineteenth century, morality was determined as much by dress as it was by action. A flabby waist connoted indolence and ill-discipline at best and at worst a life of ill repute. Conversely, a firm, upright posture achieved by the use of corset or stays conveyed moral fortitude and respectability – hence the double meaning of the adjective 'strait-laced'.[61]

Given this prevailing belief, there is distinct irony in the fact that the corset was also an object of overt sensuality.[62] Not only could this inherently paradoxical undergarment sculpt the body into a highly feminized shape, but it was also one of the last garments to be exposed as the wearer transitioned from fully clothed to fully naked. The corset worked by both concealing and revealing the body and existing in that dangerous, ambiguous state where the body ends and clothing begins.[63] Even though often made from plain woven cotton rather than satin or silk, the corset was, in itself, erotic, for it obscured some of the most intimate parts of the female body, and even moulded itself in their image. In it, women could be sexually provocative, but in a manner that was still deemed ladylike.[64]

Charlotte may not have been fully aware of these motivating factors when purchasing her own corset, but they would have had influenced her, nonetheless. Similar forces still impact us today, and yet, unless unpacked, unless considered, these psychological and societal pressures often go unnoticed. For Charlotte, the issue of her appearance was, like a shadow, always present. She might have hoped to leave it behind her as she crossed

5.4 *Charlotte Brontë, 'Self portrait' within 'Letter to Ellen Nussey, 6 March 1843', 1843, ink on paper (BS50.4), © Brontë Society, BPM, Haworth*

the Channel from London to Oostende, but her self-hatred followed. Her acute, often dysmorphic awareness of her own plainness soon showed itself in letters home to Yorkshire. In a self-portrait, scrawled at the bottom of a missive to Ellen, Charlotte depicts herself as a markedly stunted, hooked nosed, big chinned but small waisted woman. A wide sea separates her from the opposite shore and a steamboat, a mid-nineteenth-century signifier of the English Channel and of the physical distance that existed between Charlotte and her friends and family, can be seen on the horizon. Across the water, there stands an elegantly dressed woman wearing a fashionable 1840s gown. Where Ellen is depicted as tall, stylish and accompanied by a dashing gentleman, the quintessence of a hopeful young woman with excellent prospects, Charlotte is a lone figure with gnarled features, an enormous head and a tiny body.[65]

This *is* a caricature, yet this does not mean that the real person of Charlotte Brontë does not lurk beneath. As art historian Amelia Faye Rauser states, 'caricature's operation is fascinatingly paradoxical. Caricature deforms the exterior features of a person, selecting and exaggerating certain notable features ... yet this exaggeration and deformation paradoxically makes a more-like likeness, a truer portrait.'[66]

Brontë's caricature then, though at once deliberately humorous and self-deprecating, can also be viewed as a true depiction of herself. Her most distinctive features have been exaggerated to make her recognizable,[67] but so have those of which she was proud, namely her corseted waist and tiny feet – details corroborated by George Smith's comment that Charlotte had always been 'very vain of her narrow waist and small foot.'[68]

Given the emphasis placed on the neat waist by mid-nineteenth society, it is not surprising that Charlotte sought to emphasize this part of her body. Where she had little control over the rest of her appearance, and hated almost every part, through the use of a corset she could ensure that her already small waist was made even smaller – that she did not just adhere to this beauty standard, but radically adhered to it in the hope that it would mitigate criticism of those features in which she believed herself lacking. It was then a type of armour, a shield against that which she dreaded most – public censure.

Censure took many forms, and its flaming arrows came at her from many directions. As an unmarried, Protestant woman, alone in a foreign country and forced to work for her living, Charlotte was extremely vulnerable to criticism. She was, once again, stepping outside the expected safe, domestic sphere, 'outside the cage'.[69] As pupil alongside Emily, her clothes, her religion and her points of difference had been subject to scrutiny, but her fee-paying status and the presence of her sister had offered some protection. On her return to the Pensionnat Heger in January 1843, Charlotte had come 'with an ulterior view of instructing others', of supporting herself as teacher.[70] Though she arrived full of hope that this time it would be different, once again she would be forced to inhabit the very hinterlands of polite society. To live on the outside, looking in.

With her respectable status as a middle-class woman in jeopardy, and her place within the domestic sphere once again under threat, it could be argued that in putting on her corset and pulling it so tight that creases became integral to its very being, Charlotte was deliberately and blatantly exhibiting her femininity. She was signposting to all who would look at her that, though she worked, though she must support herself, she was, without doubt, a woman. This display of 'hyper-femininity' – an exaggerated observance of a contemporary, stereotypical, gendered practice – was only amplified by the addition of her handmade 'chicken-fillets' or bust enhancers that enabled her to adhere, even more exaggeratedly, to societal body ideals.[71]

Charlotte was not only an unhappy outlaw of the feminine sphere, but also of class. Therefore, just as she had done when wearing her silk 'Governess Dress', she used her outward appearance to signal her position to the world. This time the garment was hidden, but the aims were the same – to visibly separate herself from the servants with whom she shared her environs. In pulling her laces tight, Brontë was assertively disassociating her own body from those lower-class bodies 'bent by hardship and toil'.[72]

The appearance of moral fortitude would have been another key factor in Charlotte's decision to tight lace and most particularly when living in Brussels. For whilst there, as a daughter of a Protestant, evangelical clergyman surrounded by Catholics, her core belief systems were open to question.[73] As Charlotte wrote to Ellen 'the Belgians hate the English – their <moral> external morality is more rigid than ours'.[74] This observation explains why the 'unworthy heretic', Lucy Snowe of *Villette*, was constantly subjected to pious lectures from her Catholic colleagues and reveals the kind of criticism to which Brontë herself was exposed whilst in Brussels.[75] The harsh words of the little pensionnaire to her Protestant teacher in *Villette* also ring too true to be based entirely in fiction:

> 'Mademoiselle, what a pity you are a Protestant!'
> 'Why Isabelle?'
> 'Parceque, quand vous serez morte – vous brûlerez tout de suite l'Enfer!'
> 'Croyez vous?'
> 'Certainement que j'y crois: tout le monde le sait: et d'ailleurs le prêtre me l'a dit.'[76]

With those around her believing her soul to be destined for hell, it is easy to see why Charlotte felt the need to tight lace, to become the physical embodiment of *utterly* irreproachable mid-Victorian propriety. Yet again, her corset was a shield that not only protected her from criticism, but also actively repelled such accusations. With her corset pulled so tight, how could she be anything but honourable?

These varied and complex criticisms were not all that Charlotte had to contend with when far away from home. One danger remained that opened her up to far greater scrutiny – her status as a single woman. Apparently 'formed for labour not for love', it would be easy to assume that Charlotte's job, and the largely female dominated world in which she lived, would work to protect her, but this was not the case.[77] Not only was she in greater physical danger, as her uncomfortable journey from the notorious London wharf had proved, but she was also open, as she wrote to Ellen, to what she termed the 'stigma of husband-seeking'.[78] Constantly scanned for immodest or flirtatious behaviour, Charlotte believed herself held to a higher account, forced to 'act and look like marble or clay'.[79] Straight-backed and strait-laced, she had come to understand that a controlled appearance, one that offensively displayed the strength of her morality and her chastity, could help to safeguard herself against criticism.

Little did Charlotte know when she first arrived back in Belgium after her to return to Haworth, just how important these nuances and, by default, her corset, would become. It was only as her feelings for Constantin Heger morphed from intellectual respect to something more akin to love – even passionate obsession, that the appearance of morality and of chastity, if not entirely representative of truth, would become all the more important.

Since the publication of the letters that relate to Charlotte's relationship with Heger, there has been much debate about the nature of their liaison.[80] Given the strong moral stance that Charlotte would later take in *Jane Eyre*, it seems unlikely that their union was ever physical, but the relationship was far from platonic. Heger deliberately 'made much of her, drew her out, petted her and won her love'; 'he was a worshipper of intellect and he worshipped Charlotte Brontë'.[81] Like Charlotte, he was a man of passion. A man who had suffered repeated loss; a man whose past still haunted him. Brontë had arrived in Belgium desperate to experience life outside the confines in intellectual, emotional, psychological, even, sexual terms. She was, in effect, ripe for the picking and Heger wasted no time in exploiting the teacher/student relationship. It was not the first time he had done so. 'I only have to think of you to see you', he told a former pupil, 'smoking my cigar, and with a heavy will I evoke your image – and you come.'[82]

Heger's natural authority, his latent sexuality, his praise, proactively encouraged dependency, even worship.[83] And, as a third child forced by grief and by circumstance to hold the dominant position of firstborn, Charlotte submitted, relieved to relinquish power and surrender herself mentally, morally, if not physically, for perhaps the first time since childhood.[84] She wrote to Ellen:

> I was twenty-six a week or so since; and at this ripe time of life I am a school-girl … It felt very strange to submit to authority instead of exercising it—to obey orders instead of giving them; but I like that state of things. I returned to it with the same avidity that a cow, that has long been kept on dry thatch, returns to fresh grass. Don't laugh at my simile. It is natural to me to submit and very unnatural to command.[85]

Charlotte's desire to be conquered, dominated, subdued did not diminish. Nor, it must be said, did her yearning for Heger's notice. As a self-confessed plain woman, Charlotte had long feared that she would always remain overlooked by any man who evoked an equal or greater passion within her and, consequently, she revelled in his attentiveness and yearned for more.

Few months had passed following her return before Heger's heated interest had begun to wane, or, more accurately, had been redirected by his all too perceptive wife. Madame Heger, well used to her husband's weakness for intelligent, fawning women, knew what must be done. In May 1843, Charlotte wrote to her brother Branwell, 'I rarely speak to Monsieur now, for not being a pupil I have little or nothing to do with him. From time to time he shows his kindheartednesses by loading me with books, so that I am still indebted to him for all the pleasure and amusement I have.'[86]

As Charlotte became increasingly separated from the man she had grown to love, upon whom her obsession had focused, so her sense of isolation and misery multiplied. Her pupils, whom she had previously enjoyed teaching, now caused her to 'get red in the face with impatience at their stupidity'.[87] As the days passed, and her desperation grew, she became more and more unamiable, more and more 'Robinson-Crusoe-like'.[88] She refused to socialize with her fellow teachers outside of class and, as the time she could spend with Heger diminished, so too did her relationship with his wife, whom she blamed for Constantin's otherwise unfathomable distance. 'Mde Heger ... never comes near me', she wrote to Ellen. 'I try to read, I try to write but in vain I then wander about from room to room – but the silence and loneliness of the house weigh down one's spirits like lead.'[89]

Though, in her letters home, she concealed her guilt with anger and a burning sense of injustice, calling Madame Heger 'a rosy sugar-plum' that she knew 'to be a coloured chalk', Charlotte was all too well aware why her employer had so grown cold towards her.[90] She knew that her feelings for Constantin had not gone unnoticed. As the daughter of an Anglican clergyman with a professed faith of her own, her obsession with a married man was nothing short of reprehensible. Her conscience burned.[91] Trapped in the chasm that exists between passion and propriety, and with no friend to talk to, Charlotte found herself 'perishing for a word of advice or an accent of comfort' and struggling beneath 'the pressure of affliction on my mind of which it would hardly any longer endure the weight.'[92]

The true extent of Charlotte's inner struggle is revealed in a poignant self-portrait, found sketched onto the back of a map of Australia in thick, lead pencil.[93] The image, drawn as she whiled away tormented hours, makes up part of a series of other scribbles, calculations, doodles and lists dotted throughout the atlas. Yet this image of a young woman, who sits with her chin resting on her tiny hand, is its most significant treasure.[94] Here, just as in her earlier self-portrait, she draws attention to her own distinctive features – to her disproportionately large head, to her dominant brow, expansive forehead and jutting nose and chin. But, where the other self-derogatory image was sketched for the amusement of a friend, this was made for Charlotte alone. An inherent intimacy is apparent, for with no audience to play to, the emphasis has changed. Comedy has been replaced by harsh self-reflection, self-criticism. As biographer Claire Harman suggests, the position of the body and the angle of the head indicate that the drawing has been composed with the use of mirrors and that, surrounded on all sides by her reflection, Charlotte has momentarily forced herself to confront reality.[95] It proved an experience that she would not forget. Indeed, she later compels her own heroine, Jane

5.5 *J.C. Russell*, Russell's General Atlas of Modern Geography, *unnumbered page, sketch of an unnamed girl.* The Morgan Library & Museum. PML 129886. Bequest of Helen Safford Bonnell, 1969

Eyre, to undergo the same brutal practice as she struggles with *her love* for her employer Edward Rochester who 'cannot possibly intend to marry her'.[96] Increasingly desperate, Jane too tells herself that this forbidden love can only lead 'into miry wilds whence there is no extrication'. In an effort to subjugate her romantic longings, she cries out, 'Listen, then, Jane Eyre, to your sentence: tomorrow, place the glass before you, and draw in chalk your own picture, faithfully, without softening one defect; omit no harsh line, smooth away no displeasing irregularity; write under it, 'Portrait of a Governess, disconnected, poor, and plain.''[97]

Teetering once again on the verge of mental collapse and still struggling with conflicting forces, Charlotte's corset, with its unyielding form must, at times, have been all that held up her upright. For the connection that exists between mind and body is as impenetrable as the iron busk that ran from her hip to her sternum. We are now so used to the prevailing narrative that corsets were always a form of cruelty, of imposed restraint, that we do not give space to consider how such constraint could be, for some women at least, comforting and enabling.[98] Clothing has the power to alter posture, gait, action, even emotional states of being. Clothes are not passive, inert, torpid. They have the ability to work upon us, to change us, to fashion our beings. But in the case of a corset, a garment so assertive that it moulds the body and holds it upright, this effect is intensified. The height of an individual can quite literally be increased, the waist moulded and compressed, the ribs thrust upward, the pelvis downwards and the spine stretched to its full capacity – all of which enables the wearer to stand straight, tall, elongated.[99] These inherent benefits, only strengthened by Charlotte's tight lacing, turned her aesthetically unappealing, utilitarian corset into a protective device; a form of armour that shielded and fortified, that defended those parts of her most susceptible to pain.

By October 1843, Charlotte's broken-heartedness had reached new proportions. She had little desire to return to the life of a governess, or even to set up a school of her own, but loneliness, obsession and homesickness proved a wretched mix. 'I should like uncommonly to be in the dining room … ', she cried, in a letter to Emily 'yet … I cannot go home', 'without fixed prospect when I get there; and this prospect must not be a situation; that would be jumping out of the frying-pan into the fire'.[100] In the end, it was Mary Taylor, that friend who so often saw past Charlotte's protestations and assertions to the real, visceral anxieties and emotions that lay beneath, who ordered her home to Haworth. With Monsieur Heger a largely abstract concept and almost all of her English friends gone, there was nothing but misery for her now in Brussels. 'I have taken my determination', she wrote to Emily. 'I hope to be home the day after New Year's Day.'[101]

Charlotte's much anticipated trip to Europe, which she had hoped would expand her beyond measure, had ended in misery. Now her corset, which had upheld her throughout her darkest feelings of rejection and abandonment, had yet more work to do as she embarked on the long and lonely 437-mile journey back to Haworth, far away from the man whom she had grown to love. By the time she had reached home, every ounce of power had been extracted from the woven garment, but as each line, each crease, each distortion still makes so clear, every ounce of power had been needed.

6.1 Front view of feasible design of Charlotte Brontë's 'Muslin Print Dress'

6

In Print

Nearly ten years had elapsed since Branwell had immortalized his sisters in paint. Yet, though eternally united on canvas, Charlotte's siblings were no longer all in all to her. Life had crept into the crevices and eased them apart. That which working alone as teacher and governess had begun, her experiences in Belgium had finished. She had returned to Haworth that winter a mature woman, one who knew what it was to love and what it was to lose. Neither Emily nor Anne could comprehend what she had suffered in Brussels, nor could they fathom the depths of her despair. They did not read her frenzied letters written to Heger, each more desperate, more overwrought than the last. They did not perceive her sorrow as she faced the prospect of a loveless future. Charlotte kept these things hidden in her heart, and her sisters, preoccupied with their own lives, did not appreciate how much she had changed.

But in the summer of 1845, nearly eighteen months after Charlotte's return to Haworth, a dramatic event took place that 'stung them to life'.[1] Branwell, who had been working as tutor to a young boy at Thorp Green, in the same house as Anne had been working as governess, received a letter of immediate dismissal. The girls' rascal brother had been found by the gardener, in a boathouse, midassignation with Mrs Lydia Robinson, his employer's wife.[2] The consequences of this revelation were as serious as they were immediate: Anne left her post, Patrick was near prostrate with ignominy, Charlotte was furious, gossip was rife, and Branwell, barred from seeing the woman he claimed to love, took to drink.[3]

Branwell's relationship with Mrs Robinson was shocking in itself, but it also had opened an old wound for Charlotte. Whilst in Belgium, she could convince herself that she was working towards a more secure financial future, one over which she had some control. But, though she had made some small attempt to fulfil her earlier promise to open a school, her efforts had ultimately proved futile. Advertisements had been placed, flyers distributed, but no pupils for 'The Misses Brontë's Establishment' had been forthcoming. With the school plan now abandoned and Branwell's career prospects severely limited by his increasingly unstable psychological state, the Brontë family's future looked more precarious than it ever had done before.

If all this were not bad enough, Patrick, the one constant and reliable breadwinner, was beginning to falter. Since Charlotte had left for Brussels, his already troublesome eyesight had worsened, rendering him largely unable to carry out his parochial duties without significant assistance. Though there was some slight hope that his sight could be improved through innovative surgical intervention, success was in no way guaranteed. Suddenly, he upon whom they had all relied, he who had always supported and provided, was reliant upon them for help with even the simplest of tasks. For Charlotte, and probably for them all, it seemed a foretaste of the future. Patrick was getting old. That which they had always feared was becoming a reality. Another source of income, Charlotte knew, must be found, and speedily too.

It is ironic that it was Branwell, Charlotte's 'unhappy brother', who first gave her the idea of becoming a published author, but writing was all that could distract him that summer of discontent.[4] Perhaps because of heartbreak, perhaps because of rancour, poems and stories flowed from him with unprecedented speed. By September 1845, he had begun work on a new project for which he had bold ambitions for publication. He would not live long enough to finish this novel about faith and forbidden love, but writing had become his salvation and, for now at least, it was all.

Given the amount of time that she had spent writing, it is certainly strange that Charlotte had not actively pursued publication before, yet the idea, now planted, quickly took root. And then, along came serendipity. 'One day, in the autumn of 1845', wrote Charlotte in a biographical notice some five years later, 'I accidentally lighted on a MS. volume of verse in my sister Emily's handwriting … I looked it over and something more than surprise seized me, – a deep conviction that these were not common effusions … I thought them condensed and terse, vigorous and genuine. To my ear they had also a peculiar music – wild, melancholy and elevating.'[5]

If Charlotte was astonished by the quality of her sister's work, she was to be yet more so by the fury that followed its discovery. Emily was blazing with anger. To learn that her elder sister had rifled through her personal belongings was bad enough, but that Charlotte should have taken it upon herself to read works considered private was indefensible. Only Anne, close ally, co-creator of Gondal and long-time writing partner, was permitted access, but no such privilege was, or had ever been, extended to Charlotte. It was only Anne's quiet presentation of her own secret poems, probably in an attempt to pour oil on troubled waters, that finally lessened Emily's wrath.[6] But, despite Emily's reluctance to consider publication, reading these only served to bolster Charlotte's resolve – she was now certain. It was decided. All three would seek to earn their livings by their pens.

Over the coming months, the Brontë sisters worked hard to compose and compile a volume of their collected verse. At Emily's fierce insistence, they adopted strict pseudonyms and any overt references to the private world of Gondal were removed. By early January 1846, Currer, Ellis and Acton Bell's manuscript was ready for despatch. Charlotte identified suitable publishing houses in London and then in Edinburgh and as soon the contents of the package were rejected by one, she sent it off to the next. It was a brutal process but, with the bit now firmly between her teeth, and relieved to have a new life plan that did not involve teaching, she persisted.

After countless disappointments, Charlotte wrote to the small publishing house and stationers, Aylott and Jones of London, in the hope that, if they did not feel that they themselves could 'undertake the publication of a Collection', they might see fit to 'undertake it on the Author's account'.[7] Given the vast amount of money that the three Brontë sisters would have to part with in order to realize their dream, it is not surprising that Aylott and Jones did indeed see fit to allow Currer, Ellis and Acton Bell to publish their own work. On 3 March, less than five weeks after she had first reached out to them, Charlotte sent a banker's draft for the colossal sum of £31 10s – extracted from that left to them by their Aunt Branwell.[8] Printing began almost as soon as the money had cleared, and, within one week, sample proof sheets had arrived at the parsonage. On 7 May 1846, the first copies of *Poems* were delivered – three neatly printed and bound volumes, one for each of them.

Had enthusiasm alone been enough to ensure success, the Brontë sisters' book of poems would have been an instant hit, but the volume was not granted the praise it deserved, nor was it widely circulated amongst the public. Yet, seeing her name, or rather her pseudonym, in print proved wildly encouraging to Charlotte. Though she had learnt the hard way that sinking vast sums into publication might not produce the results that she craved, she was in no way deterred and in no way downcast. As she later wrote, 'ill-success failed to crush [us]: the mere effort to succ[eed] had given a wonderful zest to existence: it must be pursued'.[9]

Now focused on her goal of becoming a properly published and recognized author, Charlotte lost no time. By 6 April she had written to Aylott and Jones once again, 'C. E. & A. Bell are now preparing for the Press a work of fiction – consisting of three distinct and unconnected tales'.[10] This was no exaggeration, for little more than three months later, her first novel, *The Professor*, was complete and ready for despatch. So too were Emily's *Wuthering Heights* and Anne's *Agnes Grey*.

The three sisters, still bound by their desire to succeed, had worked without ceasing. Each evening, the newly formed triumvirate ensconced themselves in the dining room and read the latest paragraphs of their novels aloud to one another as they paced round and round the table. As they walked and talked, argued and defended, they ironed out problems with plot, grappled with grammar, crafted their characters and educed their settings. It was a sort of refining fire, a panning for gold and, for two of the sisters at least, this intense, co-operative practice produced immediate results – *Wuthering Heights* and *Agnes Grey* are worthy representatives of their hard-working creators. But for Charlotte, who was returning to the writing of fiction after such a scarring experience and so long a gap, creative fulfilment was more elusive. Rather than boldly implementing all that she had learned, and all that life had taught her since she had lived in the hyperbolic world of Angria, Charlotte, in her insecurity, looked backwards. To ease herself into the writing of *The Professor* she drew heavily on earlier tales written in youth with or by Branwell and, in an act of unwitting self-destruction, resurrected the male narrator, thereby muting her own voice and limiting her involvement in a story which was, essentially, her own. Set in a school in Brussels and centred on a tale of complicated love, this should have been *her* story, but trapped by the past, it never really was.

The three manuscripts were packed off to London publishers early in July. Much time would pass before news of an encouraging nature would reach their ears. Yet, though the waiting was agonizing, there was much to occupy them. Life did not stop merely because the Misses Brontë had composed what they hoped were masterpieces.

To start, there was the continuing problem of their father's failing sight. As the eldest, much of his care now fell to Charlotte, who, aided by the newly appointed and ever obliging curate, Arthur Bell Nicholls, often worked as amanuensis and guide. When not employed as carer, much of Charlotte's time was taken up with domestic chores, for though the elderly Tabby Ackroyd had by this time returned to the parsonage and was now assisted by eighteen-year-old Martha Brown, there was still much to be done at home and in the wider parish. Beyond cooking, which was largely Emily's domain, and tending to the house and garden, the production, cleaning and care of clothing was greedy of time.

Washing, ironing, marking and mending were, without the technology of today, long-winded and laborious processes. Wash day, which typically happened monthly, was nothing short of disruptive.[11] As many cotton or linen items looked alike, each was initialled in thread or labelled using a kind of indelible ink, often made from a combination of lunar caustic and gall.[12] This natural ink was surprisingly resilient to persistent boiling and many of Charlotte's surviving stockings or linen goods still bear marks written in a neat, cursive hand.[13]

Vast quantities of water were required to properly wash and rinse laundry and as much as twenty gallons per wash had to be collected and heated on the fire or fireside boiler in the kitchen.[14] In this, the Brontës were fortunate. Thanks to an adjacent spring, the parsonage was one of only two buildings with its own clean water supply, but most other families were required to transport water from one of the eleven pumps dotted throughout the village.[15]

Once the water was hot, garments were rubbed and scrubbed in tubs in the back kitchen and all stains removed. Plain whites were then rinsed in 'stone blue' (small lumps of indigo and starch that were placed in the rinsing water) and all items wrung out or mangled, before being hung out to dry on worsted or flaxen washing lines in the back garden that faced the gorse speckled moor.[16] As soon as they were dry enough to press, different types of irons were employed – an exotically named 'Italian iron' for frills, a sleeve iron for, well, sleeves, and a goffering iron for ruffles, caps and collars.[17] Great skill was needed to iron well, and as a teenager, Charlotte had excited her 'Aunt's wrath very much the first time [she] attempted to Iron'. Despite references to occasional mistakes of burning, by the time she had reached adulthood, however, she was far more proficient and often alluded to hours spent ironing in her letters to Ellen.[18]

Though many of the heavier duties were consigned to Martha and Tabby, as an able needleworker, Charlotte often undertook the making of new clothes and undergarments for herself, for family members and even for friends. Patrick and Branwell's shirts, collars and nightshirts were made at home by the Brontë sisters and there was often a flurry of activity prior to an important trip away, when the manufacture of new shirts or undergarments 'fully occup[ied] their time.'[19] Such plain sewing was time-consuming work, but though ready-made clothing, particularly in the form of caps, handkerchiefs and chemises, was available to buy by this time, it was far cheaper and arguably more fitting for the daughter of a clergyman to make her family's and her own.[20] After all, not only was plain sewing a means by which Charlotte could practically contribute to the family economy, upon which she remained dependent, but it was also firmly believed that a 'thrifty disposition' could not be 'too highly prized' or too 'diligently cultivated', for the result was not merely prudent but also 'moral'.[21]

The production of such mundane garments, though expected, must have been tiresome.[22] Certainly, Charlotte complained on being compelled to hem 'yards of cambric' when working as governess for the Sidgwicks and, in those moments, might very well have agreed with Mary Wollstonecraft's assertion that 'Englishwomen whose time is spent making caps, bonnets and the whole mischief of trimmings … [and other trifling] employments, have rendered woman a trifler.'[23] But, when making things for herself or even for others, Charlotte, just like Jane Austen, who claimed to have 'ruined herself' 'putting in plain doubt plaits' and 'proper pearl edges', took great pains to inject artistry into each and every item – even those that would not be seen by others.[24] Charlotte's chemise, a plain cotton undergarment worn beneath her gown, has been embellished with a perfectly stitched broderie anglaise trim; her corset cover, worn to stop the bones of her corset from snagging on her gown, has been finished with a pretty fluted lace at neck and cuff, whilst her large, cambric handkerchief features rows of deftly executed tucks and has her name embroidered in the corner.[25]

Charlotte's skills were not limited to the production of undies and nightwear, collars, caps and petticoats. The making of gifts to send to friends was considered an important part of female friendship and much time was given over to it. The things made were, quite literally, a labour of love and Charlotte sent a great number of gifts to Mary Taylor and Ellen Nussey and many others from her teenage years onwards and received many in return.[26] Handmade cuffs, collars, wrist warmers and pen-wipers were particularly popular, but sometimes larger items were undertaken. When living in Belgium in 1842, Charlotte took great pains to meticulously hand stitch a Berlin wool work bag for Elizabeth Wheelwright, mother of Laetitia, Emily, Frances, Sarah Ann and Julia, the young girls that she and Emily had tutored when working at the Pensionnat Heger in Brussels.[27] Throughout the middle decades of the nineteenth century, Berlin wool work was the height of sophistication and a popular pursuit of the day for upper- and middle-class women keen to emphasize their refinement. The pattern for Charlotte's geometric, navy and turquoise bag will have been purchased as a printed single sheet or copied from a lady's newspaper or magazine. By 1840, more than 14,000 'point' paper patterns had been imported into Britain from Berlin and a wide variety of patterns soon began to be included in women's publications such as *The Lady's Newspaper* or *The Ladies' Companion*.[28]

As well as the production of mundane garments and hand-sewn gifts, there was another hugely time-consuming activity to which Charlotte was required to attend – the design and manufacture of outer garments like gowns, cloaks and bonnets. Her sisters and servants no doubt helped with the cutting out

and piecing of gowns, but no seamstress was employed until November 1849.[29] Charlotte's letters to Ellen are peppered with references to the purchase or arrival of fabrics or to the making of dresses – after all, to embark on the production of a new gown was an event in itself. Her budget would have allowed for the creation of only a few new dresses per year, for with each requiring around eight yards of main fabric and at least two of lining, the cost was substantial. But, though the price of material was always a consideration, sometimes causing her to waver between the 5 or 3 shillings a yard silks, one benefit of living in the West Riding of Yorkshire, at the very epicentre of textile manufacture, was that Charlotte had access to the very newest and most innovative fabrics and prints.[30] And, contrary to popular belief, she did not stick solely to drab shades, but instead availed herself of the endless and exciting array of patterns, textures and colours that dominated 1840s designs.

Charlotte's muslin 'Paisley Dress', dated to the early 1840s, challenges our preconceptions of the author. Bold and bright, the four-colour print from which the gown is formed was inspired by the complex patterns found on the many thousands of shawls that were being imported from central Asia.[31] Still now, it is shockingly modern in its striking using of angular lines juxtaposed with flowing, almost painterly paisleys, but with printing processes now more accurate, more controllable, such intricate designs were not only possible, but were much in demand.[32]

Muslin is synonymous with the earlier Regency period, but it remained a firm favourite amongst the upper and middle classes all throughout the early and mid-nineteenth century and even beyond.[33] Though not quite as hard wearing as more substantial cotton fabrics, its ethereal qualities ensured an elegant drape for summer. The fabric of the 'Paisley Dress' has a relatively dense weave (by muslin standards at least) and fine white stripes have been woven into the ground for additional interest and to give added body. Similar stripes are present in another of Charlotte's muslin dresses, though of this only a fragment now remains. Here, the woven stripes are narrower still, but the printed pattern is every bit as arresting as the last. Stylized flowers and foliage in shades of sunshine yellow, carnation pink, sap green and deep Windsor

6.2 *Charlotte Brontë's Berlin wool work bag, D31*

6.3 *Front view of Charlotte Brontë's 'Paisley Dress', D8*

red fill the fragment, offering a tantalizing glimpse of what must have been a surprisingly audacious gown.[34]

Eyewitness accounts suggest that Charlotte's espousal of print was in no way confined to muslin and nor was she the only Brontë sister to partake of a pretty pattern. In fact, there remains at the parsonage a large patchwork quilt, thought to have been made by Charlotte, Emily and Anne, and probably composed of scraps of leftover silk, cotton and velvet fabrics from all manner of projects or garments collected over their lifetimes. Though now faded, it was once full to bursting with colour, pattern and texture and includes a particularly vibrant pink tartan of a type popular in the late 1830s and 1840s.[35]

One of Patrick's parishioners, who often saw Charlotte and her sisters as they walked the cobbled streets of Haworth on their way to the butcher or baker, or filed into their pew each Sunday, later recalled, 'I can see them as plain to my mind's eye as if they were here. They wore light coloured dresses all print … I don't know that I ever saw them in owt but print – I've heard it said they were pinched – but it was a nice print … They looked grand.'[36]

The old lady's emphasis on 'nice print', on the Brontë sisters' preference for quality fabrics, is certainly borne out in their wardrobes. The two short cloaks, highly likely to have been found in the box holed up in the wall along with Charlotte's 'Governess Dress' and her striped silk gown, have been formed from extremely hard-wearing, patterned, expertly woven cloth.[37] Both have been made according to the same simple pattern – one found in a sewing manual or acquired from a friend. Full-scale, commercial patterns were not readily available until the 1860s, so the sharing of self-drafted or copied patterns was important in any community, but particularly in more rural areas where clothing was often influenced as much by pragmatism as it was by fashion.

Unlike those grander permutations of the humble cloak depicted in the fashion plates of the period, the Brontë cloaks have no frills or tucks, no holes for the arms, no pockets nor embellishments.[38] Mid-length at the rear and cut back at the front so as to leave the forearms free to move, each is fastened neatly at the neck by the use of a single hook and eye. Their very simplicity suggests that inspiration has been taken, not from the magazines or lengthy descriptions of the latest Parisian fashions, but from the traditional country garments that Charlotte, Emily and Anne would have seen about them since

6.4 *Fragment of floral muslin worn by Charlotte Brontë, D148*

childhood. These are the younger relation of the widely worn, ever practical scarlet cloak of Little Red Riding Hood fame which, though period dramas rarely feature it, instead dressing the rural masses in endless muddy shades, had become synonymous with English countrywomen throughout the eighteenth and early nineteenth centuries.[39] Though many were long and featured a hood for added warmth, a great number finished at the waist or mid-thigh.[40] This more practical alternative was not only more economical in its use of cloth, but also allowed the wearer greater freedom of movement because, as any full-length cloak wearer will tell you, you can't *do* anything in such a cloak.[41]

The Brontë cloaks are formed from highly patterned, rather than plain, woollen cloth, but that did not mean that they were not just as hard-wearing or just as weatherproof as their blood-red predecessors. Both the Burberry-like tartan and the tan, sky-blue, bottle-green and purple striped cloth have been densely woven and heavily milled, meaning they could withstand even the most penetrating rain as the sisters trudged across the moor or dashed into the village for provisions. Given the complexity of their designs, it is likely that both cloths were woven quite close to Haworth, and potentially even on a Hattersley loom, a machine designed and developed in Keighley just a few miles from the Brontës' home.[42] If they were not manufactured in Haworth itself, they would certainly have been produced in one of the many, many woollen mills situated at every convenient fall of water in and around Leeds and Bradford.[43] These factories produced the vast majority of British woollen and worsted goods, and as the Industrial Revolution progressed, all manner of inventions made even the most intricate weaves increasingly possible.

Though many more hard-wearing cloaks were formed from plain cloth, there was plenty of precedent for pattern. All throughout the Regency period, tartan cloaks had been adopted for walking or for travelling.[44] These were popular, not only because of the high-profile espousal of tartan by Queen Victoria, but also because the close pattern conveniently hid mud and dirt, creases and tears.[45] Perhaps inspired by her own chequered garment, Charlotte dresses her beloved Miss Temple in a simple 'plaid cloak', 'which the frosty wind fluttered' as she walked along an 'exposed and hilly road' as the 'bitter winter wind blowing over a range of snowy summits to the north, almost flayed the skin from [her] face'.[46] If nothing else, the cheery mantle is shown to

6.5 *Heavy woollen cloaks belonging to the Brontë sisters, D16, D17*

play its part in lifting the battered spirits of the little pupils who accompanied their kind-hearted teacher on the long journey home to Lowood.

In the nineteenth century, sarapes and other similar woven garments became popular among ranchers and traders in the South-west, blending with Native American weaving traditions. Some regional variations emerged, influenced by Pueblo, Navajo, and other Indigenous textile styles. The bright, geometric patterns and durable wool fabrics made them practical as both clothing and blankets.[47] Though this might seem surprising, the West Riding of Yorkshire had a long trading association with the United States, Mexico and South America and exported vast quantities of blankets made specifically to suit these markets.[48] One such mill, based in Dewsbury Moor, a small hamlet with long textile associations, situated on a loop of the River Calder where Charlotte had worked as a teacher and Anne had lived as pupil, was making a vast array of colourful and brightly striped goods for export as early as 1826 and worked hard to match samples sent to them by their American contacts.[49] It is therefore entirely feasible that the Brontës' striped cloak has some strong aesthetic connection to the arid deserts and red rock landscapes of the Southwestern states – for, as this simple garment makes so clear, globalization had already begun its steady march.[50]

If the two cloaks are a reminder of just how embedded the sisters were in their local community, of how their clothing was impacted by the often harsh and obstinate West Yorkshire weather, by relative rurality, by parochiality, by globalization, but also by what the rugged landscape that surrounded them could produce, Charlotte's attitude to fashionable dress tells us something of her relationship with contemporary culture. The number of garments owned during this period of her life was in no way excessive, but what has survived is of high quality and, though not fashion-forward, certainly shows signs of fashion consciousness. Her 'Paisley Dress' features the tiered, bell-shaped sleeves so popular in day dresses of the early to mid-1840s and her fawn silk, beribboned bonnet mirrors exactly the prevailing silhouette of the period.[51] But though, by this time, Charlotte was clearly mindful of the general fashions and was gently swayed by their undulations, her Belgian experience continued to have bearing. After residing on the Continent for more than a year, she now found herself drawn to the simpler, more streamlined shape often favoured by the women that she had seen on the streets of Brussels. Consequently, in spite of the general excitement over flounces that was sweeping through Britain, Charlotte would have none of it – as far as she was concerned, such swaggers were strictly off limits.

Her attitude to the continued care of her existing garments is also telling. There is no sense that 'old' gowns should be cast aside, rather, it is clear that the repairing or remaking of existing gowns and garments was a constant in her life. Nearly all of her surviving dresses feature neatly executed mends, replaced panels or restored hems, after all, sustainability was then a way of life.[52]

6.6 Front view of D102

A brown silk dress with a wide velvet hem and elaborately ruched sleeves, known at the parsonage as D102 and potentially worn by one or all of the Brontë sisters, appears to have been constructed from an old gown, indicated by unnecessary darts in now inappropriate places on the bodice.[53] Certainly, it has been made as economically as possible. The piping silk has not been cut on the bias (a practice which uses considerably more silk), the selvedge edge has been incorporated into the design of the bodice, meaning every scrap was put to use, the sleeves have been made up of numerous, misshaped fragments and the skirt panels are of notably different widths. At the time of construction, dress shields have been added beneath the arms, suggesting that, even at the outset, thought was given to ensuring the garment's long-term survival. There are also indications of later, extensive mending, with patches of neat darning around the eyelets and mends to the front of the skirt. It is then, in essence, indicative of the Brontës' frugality and practicality.

Clothing of all sorts was expensive, and with the family finances persistently constrained, efforts were made to make do and mend. There is no doubt that as a clergyman's daughter Charlotte was aware of the dangers of materialism, but in any case, except for those of high wealth and status, used or heavily mended garments made up a large proportion of almost every individual's wardrobe.[54] As the brown silk and velvet gown demonstrates, alterations could be far more radical than simply fixing tears or mending frayed edges. Clothes could be re-dyed, shortened, lengthened, let down, let out or even entirely deconstructed and remade to better reflect the newest styles.[55] Though much was done at home, local industries, like dyeworks, sprung up to aid these transformations. In this case, garments were unpicked at home before being sent off to be metamorphosed into what would be presented (to nosy parishioners or neighbours at least) as entirely new and exciting. Surviving letters reveal that Anne's figured silk dress and, later, even Charlotte's dining room curtains were sent off to Keighley to be dyed in this way, thus injecting new life into otherwise tired-looking textiles.[56]

The manufacture, care and rejuvenation of clothing undoubtedly absorbed much of Charlotte's, and indeed most middle-class women's, time, but as the speedy production of *The Professor* makes clear, she could, and did, make time to write. Once focused, Charlotte was nothing if not tenacious. Even the

6.7 *Inside view of D102 showing pieced sleeves*

continued trauma of her father's deteriorating eyesight did little to deter her from the new and exciting literary project that she had undertaken. A new manuscript, the beginnings of *Jane Eyre*, accompanied her as she travelled with Patrick to Manchester to see renowned surgeon William James Wilson in a last-ditch attempt to restore his sight. On this she worked for much of August and September 1846 as she juggled writing with the post-operative care of her temporarily fragile father who could himself do nothing but wait, with the blinds pulled down to keep out the light, in the desperate hope that he might see again.

Patrick's vision did not return all at once, but slowly, incrementally, the world became brighter, more defined. Metaphorically, much the same could be said for Charlotte's new novel. In a sense, it was a book that she had been writing since youth, but it was only now, with age and experience to help and guide her, that she begin to see it take shape in her mind's eye – that she could begin to make use of the darkness and of the light that she had encountered. Suddenly, that which she had struggled against, battled through, could be brought to the fore, explored and expanded for the benefit of others. It was as if Charlotte had finally realized that to omit these things was to deny herself, to enervate her influence.

Given the depth of Charlotte's very personal experience, the issue of appearance was central to *Jane Eyre*. Before her pen had even touched the page, she had announced to her sisters and thus, in effect, to the world: 'I will show you a heroine as plain and small as myself, who shall be as interesting as any of yours'.[57] In this new book, Brontë deliberately set out to disprove the prevailing paradigm that all heroines should be beautiful and that it was 'impossible to make a heroine interesting on any other terms'.[58] Rather, she felt it an obligation to create a protagonist as brave, strong and passionate as any traditional male counterpart – one judged by actions and not by appearance or even by dress. To do so had become an imperative, indeed, Charlotte Brontë was righting a prejudice she believed to be 'morally wrong'.[59]

By essentializing the issue of appearance and boldly placing it front and centre, Brontë was signalling her readiness to publicly confront the issue. The path to such admission had been a slow and excruciatingly painful one but her continued grappling with harsh and far-reaching realities had forced her to form strong opinions. Now aged twenty-nine, in creating her plain heroine she was not merely dipping her toe into (largely) uncharted waters.[60] Rather, she was consciously challenging society's treatment of the plain woman, as well as the plain woman's treatment of herself. Accordingly, *Jane Eyre* was not only a new type of novel with a new type of heroine but was also an outworking of Charlotte's own radical manifesto – one that would be carried on and developed in all that she would go on to write.

But this was not the only contentious societal issue that Brontë would confront. Jane Eyre is presented as a young woman forced to operate within a society that will not recognize either her intelligence or her agency. As a poor, plain, orphaned child she is unwanted, mistreated, maligned. As governess she is, to all but Edward Rochester and Adèle, the child for whom she is responsible, wholly invisible. Made to dwell in the uneasy, liminal space that exists between servant and employer, Jane is socially redundant. And yet, the reader sees something in her – moral courage or a special kind of genius? She is, in the end, awarded unbridled, passionate love, status, intellectual independence and money of her own. Though Charlotte could not be sure of such recompense for past and future pains in her own life, no one could stop her from 'writing' the wrongs done to her doppelganger.

Charlotte's attention might have shifted to her new work, but that did not mean that *The Professor*, *Wuthering Heights* and *Agnes Grey* were not still doing the rounds. The original manuscripts were getting increasingly battered from constant return, but, although becoming inured to disappointment, she did not give up all hope. The writing of *Jane Eyre* was proving strangely cathartic – at last she had found an outlet for the emotions that she had concealed from those around her for so long.[61]

No longer set on publishing the books as a trio, Charlotte sent off *The Professor* to Smith, Elder and Company, a small publishing house on Cornhill, London. It was an eleventh-hour act, a last-ditch attempt. Little did she know, as she crossed off the address of the previous publisher to whom it had been sent and then summarily rejected, that this time things would be different.[62] This time, although *The Professor* would not be published on account of its 'want of variation' or 'striking character', Smith and Elder assured her that, such was the quality of her writing, that 'a work in three volumes would meet with careful attention'.[63]

Charlotte needed no further encouragement. Just two weeks later, having worked around the clock to finish the novel into which she had poured her heart, she packaged up the fair copy of *Jane Eyre* and set it off on the long journey to London. Two more anxious weeks would pass before the hopeful author received news of its fate. On 12 September 1847, with a formal offer of one hundred pounds for copyright and first refusal of Currer Bell's next two books at last in her hands, she finally found herself in the position to write a long-awaited letter of acceptance.[64] *Jane Eyre* would be brought to life in print and unlike her sisters, whose works had been accepted on terms more akin to *Poems*, she need not part with a bean.

The package containing the tightly bound, cloth-covered, three-volume novel arrived at the parsonage early on the morning of Tuesday 19 October 1847. Its appearance wrought great excitement but also feelings of profound trepidation. That which Charlotte alone had owned, that which she had created, no longer belonged solely to her. Unprotected, *Jane Eyre* was to be sent into the world. 'You have given the work every advantage which good paper, clear type and a seemly outside can supply', she wrote to Smith, Elder and Company, 'if it fails – the fault will lie with the author – you are exempt. I now await the judgement of the press and the public.'[65]

Charlotte's deep-seated fears did not prove baseless. Early reviews were far from effusive. Currer Bell's critical portrayal of religious sentiment, the bold promotion of romance between the lowly Jane Eyre and high-ranking (already married) Edward Rochester and the elevation of 'coarseness', individualism and excessive emotion raised many a critic's eyebrow. Elizabeth Rigby of the *Quarterly Review*, who would later become famed socialite Lady Eastlake, was *Jane Eyre*'s most vocal and scornful opponent. It was the morality of the novel which most perturbed her, for she perceived that its 'tone of mind and thought' overthrew all societal authority and 'violated every code human and divine'. Misreading the righteous anger of the poor, plain, single, working woman, Rigby bitingly pronounced:

> Jane Eyre is throughout the personification of an unregenerate and undisciplined spirit ... altogether an anti-Christian composition ... the impression she leaves on our mind is that of a decidedly vulgar-minded woman--one whom we should not care for as an acquaintance, whom we

should not desire for a relation, and whom we should scrupulously avoid for a governess.[66]

As Charlotte's later, fierce rebuttal made clear, such bold criticism of her personal morality hit hard. But this and other chastising reviews did little to dampen book sales. Rather, intrigued readers soon flocked to purchase the book that had set 'the literary world of that day vibrating'.[67] In no small part *because* it was a 'naughty book', 'an extraordinary book', *Jane Eyre* was soon deemed 'decidedly the best novel of the season'; 'a story of surpassing interest'; 'a very clever book'.[68] Charlotte, who had made every effort to rein in her expectations after years of unrelenting disappointment, was wholly surprised by the constant stream of glowing appraisals sent to her by her publishers. Positive newspaper and journal reviews came in thick and fast, but it was the commendations sent by her peers, literary giants like William Makepeace Thackeray, Leigh Hunt and George Henry Lewes, that moved her most. For 'one good word' from such was, as she breathlessly confessed in a letter to publisher William Smith Williams, 'worth pages of praise from ordinary judges'.[69]

Jane Eyre's success quickly surpassed the expectations of everyone – even those of her publisher who, on first reading the manuscript, had found himself so captivated that he had stayed up into the small hours to finish it. The first edition of 2,500 copies sold out within three short months, and even despite some overtly aggressive and well publicized critiques, two more editions were published in January and April 1848, ensuring *Jane Eyre* was amongst the fastest-selling books of the period.[70]

The mysterious name of Currer Bell seemed to hang in the air that year, but despite *his* renown, despite *his* popularity, Charlotte Brontë's daily life remained largely unchanged.[71] To all but Emily and Anne, in whom she fully confided, and later her father and Mary Taylor, she was still just Charlotte – the local parson's eldest, motherless, spinster daughter.

It must have been strange to carry such a secret about her as she purchased needles from the haberdasher or sausages from the butcher, as she listened to her father's lengthy sermons or ironed her brother's shirts. Perhaps some hidden part of her sought some praise for herself; wished she could renege on her promise of anonymity to Emily and introduce 'life and light' to what she called her 'torpid retirement where we live like dormice'.[72] Yet, whatever she might have felt, Charlotte did not willingly reveal herself as the real author of *Jane Eyre*. In the end, her mask was lowered, not as a result of journalistic investigation or a careless slip of her own pen, but rather by the deliberate dishonesty of her sister's publisher.

Like Charlotte, Anne had embarked on her second book soon after she had finished the first. *The Tenant of Wildfell Hall* was published by Thomas Cautley Newby in the last week of June 1848.[73] Yet, what should have been a happy event, one filled with joy at the culmination of months of work, was quite the reverse. For, in an effort to exploit Acton Bell's known connections with the markedly successful Currer Bell, Anne's unscrupulous publisher had taken it upon himself to sell the first sheets of *The Tenant of Wildfell Hall* to an American publisher and did so on the false premise that the novel was the latest work of the pseudonymous author of *Jane Eyre*. Newby, knowing full well that he was conveying an untruth, then declared that 'to the best of his belief' '"Jane Eyre" "Wuthering Heights "Agnes Grey" – and "The Tenant of Wildfell Hall" (the new work) were all the production of one writer'.[74]

Newby's 'dishonest move' might have been cast off as a minor annoyance had it not been for the fact that Charlotte's own publishers, Smith, Elder and Company, had already made an agreement with an American publishing house, Harper and Brothers, that they could have exclusive rights to publish any and all of Currer Bell's subsequent works.[75] Therefore, when George Smith's American agent, Sampson Low, was made aware of Newby's widespread assertions, he immediately notified Smith, Elder and Company as to this serious and potentially damaging breach of contract. No doubt anxious that Charlotte had found another publisher for *The Professor*, Smith and Elder dispatched a note to Haworth at once, leaving Charlotte with little choice but to reveal the truth.[76]

Just a few hours later, Charlotte, accompanied by the ever-compliant Anne, boarded the night train to London. No amount of pleading could persuade Emily to join them, despite Charlotte's firm insistence that Currer, Ellis and Acton Bell should reveal themselves to George Smith en masse and thereby prove, once and for all, that they were indeed three separate authors. So anxious was she to get there that little thought was given to what she would wear or how she should present herself. A few clothes, just enough for two nights away, were thrown into a 'small box' which was sent down to the railway station at Keighley ahead of them.[77]

The two intrepid women made their way across the sprawling, unfamiliar city to the Chapter Coffee House in Paternoster Row. It was the same guest house in which Charlotte had stayed when on her way to Belgium and was the only place in London with which she was familiar. After dropping off their luggage, breakfasting and tidying themselves after the long journey and a poor night of sleep, Charlotte and Anne set off, maps in hand, towards 65, Cornhill, the offices of Smith, Elder and Company.

Dwarfed by their surroundings, the two 'quaintly dressed little ladies' arrived, 'pale faced and anxious looking' and, after presenting themselves to the clerk, were ushered into an anteroom by an astonished George Smith who promptly left in search of William Smith Williams.[78] It is hard to know which of the two parties was more overcome – Charlotte's publishers by the sudden appearance of the mysterious author of *Jane Eyre*, or the two women, finally confronted by the magnitude of what they had done in travelling the 210 miles to London to present themselves to strangers. But though it was a meeting of some significance for all present, the righting of wrongs was not a drawn-out affair. The wicked Mr Newby was 'anathematized' with a vehemence that Charlotte later regretted and Currer and Acton Bell were materially proven as distinct and separate entities.[79] Their mission complete, Charlotte and Anne got up to leave. But Smith, now certain that the writer of his new bestseller was, in fact, a respectable, well-schooled young woman and not the ill-bred fellow that London gossip, and a few harsh critics, had sometimes supposed, only grew more and more excited. 'How long do you stay in Town?' he asked enthusiastically. 'You must make the most of the time – tonight you must go to the Italian opera – you must see the Exhibition – Mr Thackeray would be pleased to see you – If Mr Lewes knew you were in town – he would have to be shut up.'[80]

Had it not been for Charlotte's firm cessation of Smith's barrage of suggestions, it might have continued, but on the issue of continued anonymity, she was unbending – on no account could her identity be revealed to the public. No doubt her promise to Emily was foremost in her mind, but though she had sometimes been tempted by aspects of fame, Charlotte also had her own reasons for retaining her invisibility.

The success of *Jane Eyre* had taken everyone by surprise, and not least Charlotte herself, who had written the novel without daring to hope that it could be a runaway success, without thinking what publication would mean for her family or even for herself. She was now faced with the very real fear that, if her identity was revealed, those characters that she had drawn from life would become instantly recognizable, and not least the real-life, local figure of William Carus Wilson, on whom she had based her now infamous malefactor, Mr Brocklehurst.[81] As a woman with a latent and persistent fear of public scrutiny, scandal was something she wished to avoid at all costs. But it was not only unwanted coverage that Charlotte feared. As the Brontë sisters had known when picking deliberately androgynous pseudonyms, the publishing world was a traditionally male domain. In joining the ranks of the literati, Charlotte would be publicly and provocatively stepping outside the domestic sphere. And where, before her time as governess, she had not known what it was to inhabit the hinterlands, she was now only too aware of their inherent dangers. To safeguard herself from accusations of impropriety, of unfemininity, she remained firm in the belief that all issues concerning the promotion and retailing of her book should fall under the remit of her (male) publishers.

What Charlotte had not fully grasped as she sat in that small anteroom with Anne and the men responsible for bringing *Jane Eyre* into being, as she listened with growing anxiety to George Smith's plans to reveal her to the world, was that in the increasingly mercurial publishing world of the mid-nineteenth century, as celebrity and authorship were converged, complete obscurity was no longer feasible.[82] Still clinging to the belief that her responsibility as novelist began and ended with her pen – that it was the quality of her writing, not her public persona, that determined the number of books sold, she did not understand that to sustain her position the real Charlotte Brontë must step forward.

The two women left the offices of Smith, Elder and Company only marginally less anxious than they had entered it. In righting Newby's wrongs they had achieved all that they had set out to accomplish. But, having exposed herself to a world she had not fully known existed, it felt to Charlotte as if Pandora's box had been prized open. She was not yet sure if she liked what was inside. She arrived back at the Chapterhouse much agitated and with a 'thundering headache & harassing sickness'.[83]

The Brontë sisters spent the remainder of the day resting after their ordeal, but were not much rejuvenated when a knock was heard at the door to their room. Expecting no visitors, Charlotte and Anne were much agitated to find Smith and Smith Williams both 'dressed in evening costume white gloves &c.', accompanied by 'two elegant young ladies in full dress' standing before them with expectant looks upon their faces. It seemed the impresario in George Smith could not be quashed. Despite Charlotte's earlier protestations, he would not take no for an answer – the Misses Brontë *would* accompany them to the Royal Opera House to enjoy Rossini's *Barber of Seville*.[84]

For two shy, socially awkward people to be forced, without warning, to attend an event of such magnitude was horrible to contemplate, but for Charlotte and Anne the situation was more terrible still. For as it no doubt dawned on them as they argued with Mr Smith, the 'small box' that they had sent ahead of them to Keighley Station the night before contained no gowns befitting of the opera.[85] Indeed, as they well knew, the box contained no finery at all.

One can only imagine the panic that filled the room as George Smith's party made their way back down to the carriage to wait for Charlotte and Anne to join them. Though we cannot know what had been brought in the box from Haworth, it can be assumed that the contents reflected their expectations. On leaving for London, they had anticipated that their stay would last no longer than two nights and that after their meeting with Smith and Elder, their time would be spent staring at vaulted ceilings or walking along the Thames. Therefore, beyond the necessary nightgowns and undergarments, hairbrushes, and combs, the Brontës would have packed little more than an extra day gown, a spare shawl and a change of shoes apiece. But the truth is, even had they known that such a grand invite would be forthcoming, they still would not have been much better prepared, for as Charlotte later declared, 'we had no fine, elegant dresses either with us, or in the world'.[86]

And so it was that Charlotte and Anne entered the red and gold velvet splendour of London's finest opera house dressed in the 'plain, high-made country garments' that they had shoe-horned into their luggage before rushing off to catch the train. As they climbed the stairs towards their box, they were passed by gentlemen dressed in fine evening attire and ladies clothed in low-necked gowns of silk, velvet or satin. The Brontë sisters, keenly aware of their sartorial deficiencies, were filled with abject humiliation.[87] Even some months later, still smarting from the embarrassment of the occasion, Charlotte recalled how she and Anne had appeared 'queer, quizzical looking beings' and had found themselves forced to suffer the ignominy of 'supercilious glances … quite warranted in the circumstances'.[88]

The next day, in a desperate attempt to mitigate any further embarrassment and fully aware that Smith had yet more plans which they could not avoid,

6.8 *Charlotte Brontë's paisley parasol, D133*

Charlotte and Anne rushed to a nearby ladies' outfitters to purchase accessories that might bolster their inadequate wardrobe. Charlotte's cash book of 1848/9 suggests that here they acquired two pairs of gloves and two parasols at the phenomenal cost of five and sixteen shillings respectively.[89] Whilst we do not know which, if any, of the many of parasols that remain in the Brontë collection were bought on this occasion, the cost suggests that the two women threw caution to the wind and purchased highly embellished parasols of a kind popular in the late 1840s. It is certainly feasible that it was here that Charlotte

6.9 *Charlotte Brontë's black-and-white silk parasol, D106*

purchased her printed wool parasol with its hinged handle, gold fringing and complex paisley pattern of greens, pinks, gold and burgundy.[90] Alternatively, that July day, she might have acquired the elegant, black and white striped silk parasol with decorative frayed edges, black tassels and contrasting black trim that remains at the parsonage to this day.[91]

Though Charlotte would venture to London on many more occasions in the years ahead, both these parasols are uncharacteristically conspicuous in their grandeur and when compared to the others in the collection, look very much like dressy items bought in an attempt to distract the eye from other, less prepossessing garments.

Over the course of the next three days, Charlotte and Anne were treated to many more extraordinary experiences. They heard the famed poet, novelist and historian Dr George Croly speak; they dined with George Smith and his mother at their Bayswater home on more than one occasion; they took in exhibitions at the Royal Academy and the National Gallery and took tea with William Smith Williams, where they were introduced to the daughter of essayist and poet, Leigh Hunt. For the two Brontë sisters it was a whirlwind of a week. But, if George Smith and William Smith Williams had hoped to use the glitz and glamour of London society to persuade Charlotte to give up her pseudonym and reveal herself as the author of *Jane Eyre*, they were not successful. Unused to such sustained activity, she returned to Haworth much 'excited', but much changed.[92] She later wrote that the unrelenting social exertions had left her a self-proclaimed 'jaded wretch', with a face that looked 'grey and old with strange deep lines ploughed in it', eyes that 'stared unnaturally', and a body 'weak and restless.'[93]

That Charlotte's response to these new social exposures was to suffer not only extreme emotional and bodily exhaustion, but also an even deeper awareness of her own physical inadequacies, is significant. For those four crowded days, she had been exposed to persistent scrutiny. She had always been acutely, even disproportionally, attuned to the perceptions of others but, in this instance at least, she had discerned correctly – her appearance, and her own attitude to it, *had* been under evaluation. Years later, George Smith would write of those first days spent with Charlotte, the author that he had waited for so many months to meet:

> I must confess that my first impression of Charlotte Brontë's personal appearance was that it was interesting rather than attractive. She was very small and had a quaint old-fashioned look. Her head seemed too large for her body. She had fine eyes, but her face was marred by the shape of the mouth and by the complexion. There was but little feminine charm about her; and of this fact she was uneasily and perpetually conscious. It may seem strange that the possession of genius did not lift her above the weakness of an excessive anxiety about her personal appearance. But I believe that she would have given all her genius and her fame to have been beautiful. Perhaps few women ever existed more anxious to be pretty than she, or more angrily conscious of the circumstance that she was not pretty.[94]

To a modern reader, Smith's published assertions make for uncomfortable reading. Yet, in many ways they offer unprecedented insight into the challenges Charlotte was soon to face. For, what Smith had voiced was merely the prevailing attitude of his age (and arguably still of our own) – that all women should be beautiful and celebrated women yet more so. Without beauty, without easy charm and with a crippling awareness of her lack, Charlotte's relationship with the fame that was to come, would, George Smith knew even then, prove even more challenging.

7

Mourning

It was not only Charlotte who felt the winds of change that summer of 1848. The world was teetering on the edge of cataclysmic change.[1] Revolution was in the air and Britain was not immune from its contagion. The Irish potato famine had wrought mass death, displacement and malcontent and, following the news of revolt on the streets of Paris, the Chartists had gained momentum once again, raising the risk of serious uprising and threatening the stability of the Crown. Fear gripped the nation. Fear gripped the parsonage. And fear made its way into Charlotte's new novel, *Shirley*. But political turbulence was not all that would have a hand in the shaping of this third book, for trouble of a very different, much more personal kind was to have an even greater influence on both the work and its maker.

Charlotte's literary success had in no way eclipsed the problem of Branwell. There were now only a few hours each day when he was not drunk or hungover, drugged or pleading for money to cover his debts. He was but a shadow of his former self, a shell of a man. Yet, though no one knew it, addiction was not all that now gripped Branwell's pitiable body. This enemy signalled its presence in shortness of breath and rapid weight loss, fainting fits and frequent bouts of delirium. Having breached the strong stone walls of the Haworth Parsonage once again, tuberculosis had found an easy victim.[2]

Not even the doctor had predicted how quickly the illness would take him. Patrick Branwell Brontë died at nine o'clock in the morning 'after 20 minutes struggle' on Sunday 24 September 1848, supported by his father and his three remaining sisters.[3] He was just thirty-one years old. 'I do not weep from a sense of bereavement', wrote Charlotte to William Smith Williams in the dark days after her brother's death. 'There is no prop withdrawn, no consolation torn away, no dear companion lost – but for the wreck of talent lost, the ruin of promise, the untimely dreary extinction of what might have been a burning and a shining light … I trust time will allay these feelings.'[4]

Time would, in the end, allay these difficult feelings, but not before Charlotte had lived many more days in the valley of the shadow of death. This first real glimpse of what she called 'the awe and trouble of the death-scene', 'the speculation of the pale corpse', had induced 'more acute, more bitter pain than [she] could have imagined'.[5] Though there was much to do, Charlotte took immediately to her bed, beaten into submission by headache, nausea and overwhelm, leaving the practicalities of death and mourning to her more pragmatic sisters.

The most urgent task for Emily and Anne was the laying out of Branwell's body – the closing of his jaw, the shutting of his eyelids, the straightening of his wasted legs, the washing and packing of his body and the burning of the bedclothes in which he had died.[6] These were sacred duties, typically carried out in silence, in solemnity, with the help, no doubt, of faithful servants Tabby and Martha. They were final acts of love and of closure, but so too were the many bureaucratic matters that Emily and Anne attended to in that quiet, forlorn period between expiry and burial. The death was registered, the funeral tea arranged, the mourning stationery purchased and the commemorative cards printed and sent out to all who those who had known Branwell in his too short life. If the visceral act of preparing their brother's body for eternity had not helped them to assimilate the painful truth that the boy that they had loved was gone, the sight of these grave, black-edged, memorial cards embossed with a classical rendering of a sarcophagus draped in cloth, can only have persuaded them.[7]

With Charlotte still largely confined to her room, the organization of the family's mourning attire also fell to her sisters. The traditional black worn by close relatives would not have been adopted immediately after Branwell's death. It was normal for ordinary clothes to be worn until proper mourning garments could be made or acquired – something which could take some days.

Patrick's mourning dress would have been relatively easy to obtain, for as a male mourner and a clergyman, his day-to-day dress would not have been substantially altered. A black mourning cloak, black gloves and a silk or crape hatband would have been worn in public, but all of these items could be purchased ready-made or even hired from larger stores in Leeds or Bradford.[8] As Patrick routinely officiated at funerals and it was traditional to give gloves, hat bands and scarves to the presiding clergyman, he was, in all likelihood, already well equipped.[9] For the three sisters, the amassing of mourning wear was a far more complex affair. As siblings of the deceased, they were required to visibly mourn for their brother for six, long months. All the main classifications of dress were impacted – both those worn in private and those worn out in public.[10] Matte black fabrics such as bombazine, Paramatta, Coburg, barège and crape were most commonly used for full mourning gowns as their non-reflective qualities were said to convey the true depth of the griever's gloom and sorrow. As the months passed, gowns of shinier black silk could be adopted, and some subtle trimmings added to gowns, cloaks or bonnets. But, even with these slight modifications, the overall effect was consciously sombre and continued to be so until the socially prescribed period had ended.[11]

The Brontë sisters did not yet move within the higher echelons of society, where the rules of mourning dress were even more prescriptive, but the cost to the family would still have been considerable. Even the servants were expected to wear black and though some existing garments could be dyed or adapted, gowns, gloves, capes and bonnets would have been required and probably in time for the funeral itself, which took place just four days after Branwell's death.[12] Some specialist shops offered a speedy service and endeavoured to produce mourning garments at short notice, but it was also possible to manufacture gowns quickly at home – especially if help was drafted in from local needlewomen from the village.[13] Becky Sharp of Thackeray's *Vanity Fair* resourcefully pulled together a mourning outfit quite promptly by 'cutting, ripping, stripping and tearing all sorts of black stuffs available for the melancholy occasion'.[14] Whilst within the space of just two days, young seamstress Margaret Jennings of Elizabeth Gaskell's *Mary Barton* succeeded in cutting out and finishing four worsted mourning gowns for Mrs Ogden, a greengrocer's wife, and her three daughters.[15] Though she stayed up most of the night to complete them, her hard work ensured that they were ready in time for the family to wear at the funeral.

Charlotte was too unwell to help with any sewing in those days immediately after Branwell's death, but her references to mourning dress in *Jane Eyre* demonstrate both her understanding of the conventions and the benefits of embracing them. Having recently lost their father, Mary and Diana Rivers are, on first meeting, dressed in the 'somber garb' of 'deep mourning' in 'crape and bombasin'.[16] Their black clothes are the silent herald of their suffering – Jane, and the reader with her, immediately grasp that, in their grief, the two women are inhabiting that purgatory-like place that exists between the world of the living and the world of the dead.[17] Their clothes ask for kindness and for sympathy. They signal that, for the duration of their mourning, they are released from socialization, from conviviality. For Charlotte, this metaphorical wall of bombazine and crape is more than mere fabric, it protects, excuses and explains, comforts, reminds, and memorializes.

Perhaps these deep and varied meanings were at the forefront of Charlotte's mind as she stepped into her dark gown on the morning of Branwell's funeral; as she pulled on her black silk stockings, boots, mantle and bonnet and went downstairs to join her father and sisters. Little did she know then that such garments would enshroud her for far longer than six months. Even as the remaining members of the Brontë family made the unhappy journey towards the church behind Branwell's coffin, the enemy was circling. It would only be a matter of weeks before the White Plague would notify them of its presence once again.[18]

Shirley was far from finished. The story of the Luddite uprisings was still in skeletal form, but Charlotte found she could not write. Fear for her sisters' health was growing exponentially. What had begun as a series of typical, seasonal illnesses was morphing into something far more malign. Emily was the worst affected, but, with characteristic stubbornness, shunned all medical help or sympathy. Patrick was quick to grasp the gravity of his daughter's situation whilst Charlotte, desperate not to accept the loss of yet another sibling, this time one whom she loved without complication, swung like a pendulum between unrealistic hope and abject hopelessness. By late November, Emily's physical decline was so apparent that even Charlotte was forced to fully acknowledge the inevitable.

On the morning of 19 December 1848, Emily rose at seven, dragged her weary and emaciated body into the black gown in remembrance of Branwell and made her way, unassisted, downstairs to the parlour.[19] Here she picked up her sewing and began to work, fighting to hold her body upright as she dragged her needle up and down through the fabric. By midday, she could keep up the pretence no longer. 'If you will send for a doctor', she uttered breathlessly, 'I will see him now.'[20]

Thirty-year-old Emily Jane Brontë died at two o'clock that same afternoon. She lived the last moments of her life just as she had always done – boldly, fiercely, individualistically. 'Tuesday night and morning', wrote Charlotte to William Smith Williams on black-edged paper, 'saw the last hours, the last agonies, proudly endured to the end … it is incomprehensible as yet to mortal intelligence. The last three months … seem to us like a long, terrible dream.' The 'galloping consumption had merited its name'.[21] Charlotte's beloved sister was lost, and now only Anne was left.

There could be no retreat from responsibility for Charlotte this time; Anne was too sick to be left to manage the arrangements alone. Joseph Fox, the confectioner from Keighley, was called in to supply the funeral refreshments, as well as the simple, black-bordered memorial cards that were sent out to friends and family.[22] The sisters placed obituary notices in the *Leeds Mercury*, the *Bradford Observer*, the *Leeds Intelligencer* and the *Halifax Guardian* and, as was traditional when mourning a young, unmarried woman, purchased white gloves, and probably white scarves too, to give to the mourners as tokens.[23] Two pairs of these knitted, silk gloves have survived and offer an all too poignant link to that sad day on 22 December 1848, when Patrick, accompanied by Emily's beloved mastiff, Keeper, walked the short distance to the church with Charlotte and Anne, Tabby and Martha following close behind.

The two surviving Brontë sisters were still shrouded in black for Branwell, but Emily's death now ensured that they would remain so on into the summer months. Additional garments and accessories, made from lighter, though still socially acceptable, fabrics were now needed to supplement their wardrobes. Though we cannot know exactly what the sisters bought, a half-ripped page in Charlotte's cash book for 1848/9 suggests that visits were made to a Miss

M. Young of 14, Park Row, Leeds, seller of 'an elegant Assortment of Millinery and Dresses &c.' and also to a Miss Atkinson of 30, Portland Crescent, Leeds.[24] Here, Charlotte is likely to have acquired black-dyed leghorn straw or silk-covered chip bonnets and black silk parasols in preparation for the warmer spring weather.[25]

It was perhaps whilst visiting the milliner in Leeds that she called upon a 'Fancy Hair Worker', taking with her lengths of Emily's long brown hair, lovingly cut from her sister's head in the hours after her death. Whether she visited Thomas Harrison, 'Hair Cutter, Wigmaker, Perfumer and Toy Dealer' of Lowerhead Row, Leeds, or J. Naismith's of 14 or 15, Albion Court, Bradford, or indeed sent the tresses by post to famed hair workers, William and Walter Winspear (later inventors of the 'celebrated hair lotion for restoring human hair') of York, Charlotte had Emily's hair fashioned into pieces of jewellery – items that she could wear close to her own body as an intimate, tangible reminder of a much-beloved sister and confidante.[26]

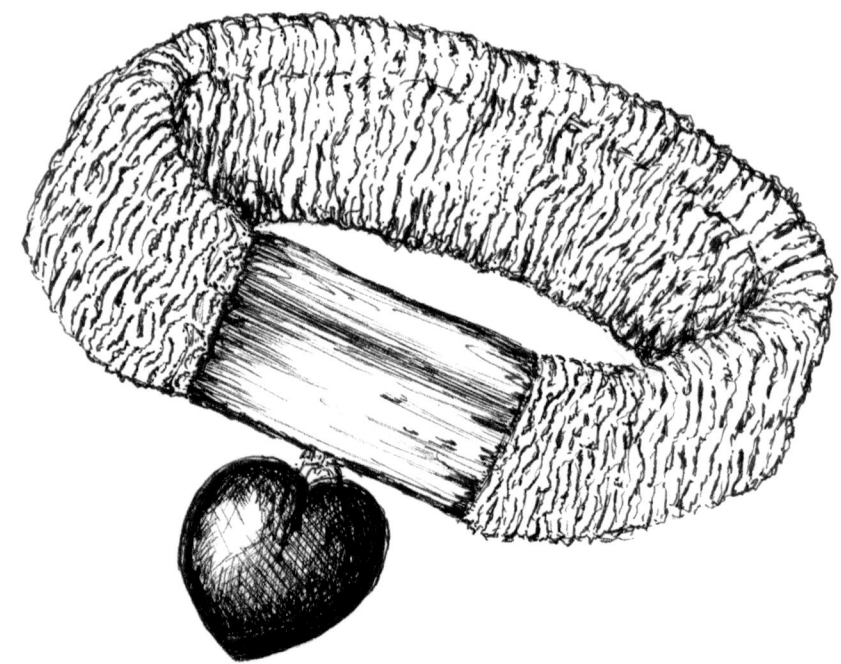

7.1 *Charlotte Brontë's hair and brass bracelet made from Emily Brontë's hair, J13*

Some smart jewellers also offered hairworking services and combined hair elements with gold or silver or even semi-precious jewels.[27] Whilst this might now seem to us a macabre or even distasteful practice, hairwork was a highly fashionable art form all throughout the nineteenth century – one carried out by professional artistes or skilled amateurs alike.

As a medium, hair is remarkably versatile, but in the nineteenth century it was viewed, as Emily wrote in her poem 'Long Neglect Has Worn Away', as a kind of memory, as a way of bringing the dead back to life in the mind:

But that lock of silky hair,
Still beneath the picture twined,
Tells what once those features were,
Paints their image on the mind.[28]

It could be plaited or sewn, woven or knotted to make three-dimensional structures such as bracelets, rings, earrings or necklaces.[29] But though Charlotte partook in this fashionable, evocative demonstration of memory and of sentiment, it was not the only form of jewellery that she acquired during this difficult time.[30] Two matching bracelets, embellished with carved bows and surprisingly reminiscent of the now iconic Bakelite designs of the 1930s and 1940s, have survived and remain at the parsonage.[31] These matte black accessories, presumably bought by or for Charlotte and Anne, are made from jet, a black mineraloid formed over 180 million years.[32]

Jet has strong links to Yorkshire and, though it is found all throughout the world, the best hard jet in England is found on its north-east coast, close to Whitby. It was here that the Brontës' bracelets would have been manufactured by skilled craftsmen who cut, carved and finished a huge range of pieces by hand. By the middle of the nineteenth century, an enormous industry had built up around the town, based in no small part on the Victorian cult of mourning, but also boosted by the growth of the railways and the consequent development of the souvenir industry.[33]

Though jet is always black or dark brown, it is a surprisingly versatile material. Unpolished it has a sombre, velvety appearance but it can also be buffed to a high shine. In the nineteenth century, dull pieces could be worn as soon as the most acute period of mourning was over, but as the months passed, more polished items, like Charlotte's own shiny, faceted necklace, were permitted.[34] These pieces glinted and gleamed, offering metaphorical flickers of hope to the wearer that the very worst, most painful days had now passed. But if Charlotte yearned for a time when she too might feel such hope, she yearned in vain.[35] Anne was declining quickly. Charlotte had noticed 'the gradual approaches of decay … the little cough, the small appetite, the tendency to take cold at every variation of atmosphere'. In January 1849 she wrote to William Smith Williams 'when we lost Emily I thought that we had drained the very dregs of our cup of trial but now when I hear Anne cough as Emily coughed, I tremble lest there should be exquisite bitterness yet to taste.'[36]

Though doctors were called and Anne, aware of the pain Emily's lack of compliance had caused her father and sister, yielded to their varied and often unpleasant ministrations, nothing appeared to help. There was little to be done but wait. In a desperate attempt to distract herself from what lay both behind and before her, Charlotte turned her attentions to *Shirley*. Yet she was soon to find that Currer Bell could not be roused. Unable to move her story on, she set about drawing up a fair copy of the first volume, all that she had written so far. 'If I shew it to you', she pronounced to Smith Williams in a letter soon after she had finished, 'it is on two conditions. The first that you give me a faithful opinion … the second that you speak of it to <u>none</u> but Smith.'[37]

The manuscript arrived in London soon afterwards, but a number of weeks passed before Charlotte received a response from Smith and Elder. Their answer had proved hard to formulate, for keenly aware of Charlotte's mental and physical fragility and the gargantuan efforts that she had made to continue to work in spite of her circumstances, they did not know how best to convey the truth – that this new book did not compare favourably with *Jane Eyre*. Their notes were gentle but did make some tentative effort to steer and to shape, particularly that first part of the novel that centred on the only loosely disguised past and present curates of her parish. Yet, intractable as ever, Charlotte did not heed their advice, and chose instead to leave the first volume largely unchanged.

By the end of March, it was becoming clear that Anne's breathing was worsening. In a characteristic attempt to make the situation less traumatic for both her father and sister, Anne devised a plan to take a trip to the seaside, accompanied not by Charlotte, but by the always faithful Ellen Nussey. Charlotte would not even consider such a move, but Patrick, eager to fulfil what he knew could be his youngest daughter's final wishes, pushed all fears aside. Anne, he pronounced, could go to the sea and breathe in the curative, briny air, but only on one condition – that both Charlotte and Ellen accompany her, leaving him in the capable hands of Tabby and Martha.

It cannot have been an easy decision for Patrick. Having already lost four of his children, as well as countless parishioners, to the same deadly disease that was now devouring Anne, he must have known that she might not return to the parsonage alive. He must also have realized that if Anne were to die whilst far away from home, Charlotte, his then only remaining, sensitive and emotionally fragile daughter would have to carry a terrible burden. With all this in his mind, their parting on Thursday 24 May can only have been distressing. If tears did not fall as he, Tabby and Martha stood outside the parsonage, watching and waving as Charlotte, Anne and Ellen were carried off to Keighley Station to pick up their first train to Leeds, then surely they did as he went back inside to sit alone in his study.

Despite Charlotte's 'heavy heart' and all too natural anxiety, the three women's journey to York, where they had planned to spend their first evening, went remarkably smoothly.[38] Assistance was found 'wherever [they] needed it' and, much to Charlotte's relief, there 'was always an arm ready' to lift Anne 'in and out of carriages' or 'carry her across the line'.[39] From the station they travelled to their hotel, where, after resting for a short time, Charlotte and Ellen arranged a bathchair for Anne and together they set off into the city in search of supplies.

Though still shrouded in black in honour of Emily (their official mourning for Branwell having ended in February), Charlotte and Anne were keen to equip themselves for their seaside holiday and also to momentarily forget the inevitable challenges still to come. In the cash book that Charlotte had carried with her that year, she wrote a list of their requirements:

To be bought
Bonnets
Corsets
Stockings black silk

Dress
Gloves
Ribbon for neck

Famed for its numerous, high-quality shops and stores, York was the perfect place to fulfil such a list, but, though the three set off with some gusto, it was soon clear that Anne's body could not keep up with her desire for normality. Not physically strong enough to traipse from shop to shop or even stand in line for service, it was soon apparent that some items would have to be sacrificed. In the end, Anne only had strength to pick out bonnets, gloves and dresses (probably loose, informal, morning wrappers which could be bought ready-made). These were presumably all in black, black and white or grey, though, as the end of their formal mourning for Emily was now within sight, they were now in a position to choose something slightly less sombre, something that defied the solemn reality that still faced them both.[40] Whatever they selected, they returned to their hotel soon after, so that the worn-out Anne might rest quietly until morning.

Charlotte, Ellen and Anne arrived in Scarborough the next day, after visiting York Minster in the morning at Anne's particular request. Their lodgings at No. 2 The Cliff were modest but 'pleasant' and with a wide and sweeping view that looked down across the bay. Buoyed by the fresh air and cheering sights, Anne lost little time, and, despite her weakened state, 'insisted on going to the baths' before 'driving out in a donkey carriage' across the sands and taking in the views later that afternoon.[41]

Though the weather was fine, Charlotte might well have taken the opportunity to wear her wind bonnet or 'ugly' over her the brim of her straw bonnet to help protect it from the winds that so famously whip across Scarborough's sandy bay.

The date of its purchase is not known, but whether it was spotted in a shop on Charlotte's first trip to London, or in a smart shop in York, despite its strange shape, the vivid blue, collapsible bonnet was the height of fashion between the years 1848 and 1864.[42] The ugly bonnet had evolved from the popular late eighteenth-century folding hood known as a calash.[43] But, where the calash covered the whole head and indeed, rose high above it so as to accommodate

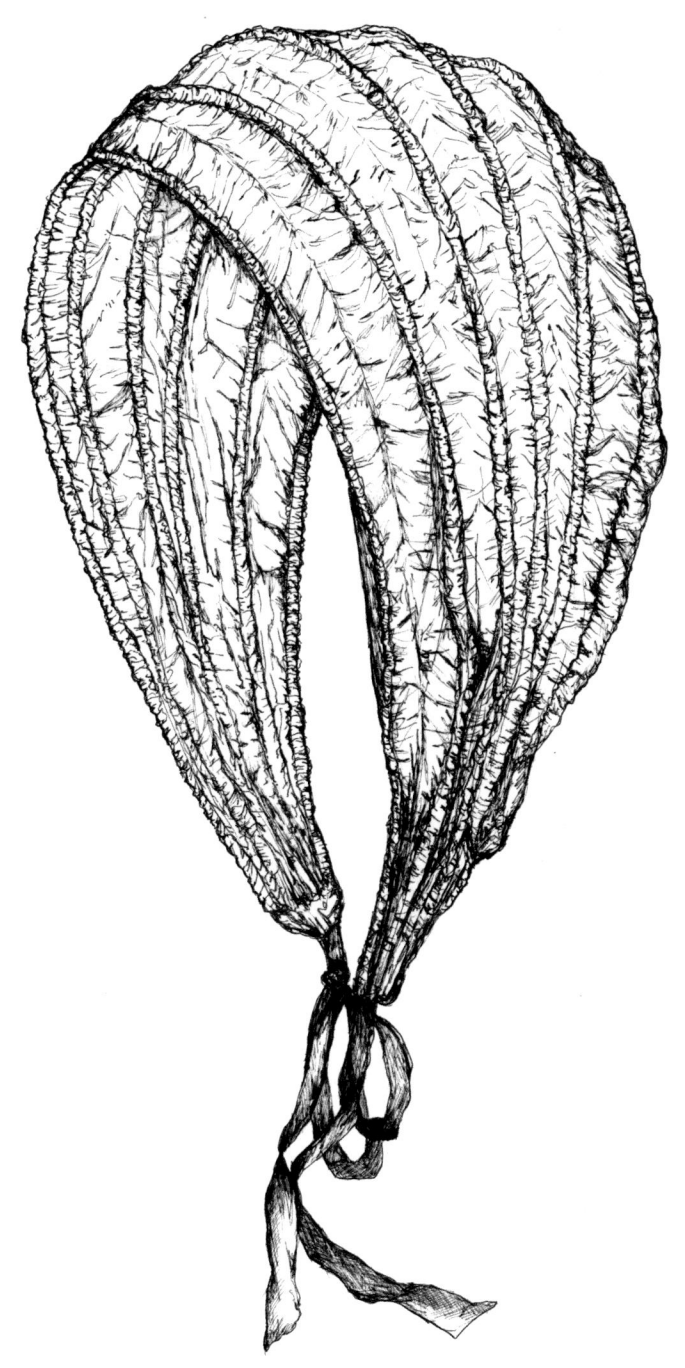

7.2 *Charlotte Brontë's blue silk ugly bonnet, D21*

the towering hairstyles of fashionable ladies, the ugly was worn around the front of the bonnet brim to help protect the wearer's face from the wind or sun. Made from fine strips of reed sewn into channels of silk, their design was clever, as they could be concertinaed down and popped into a trunk for easy packing. The oil painting, *Ramsgate Sands* (1851–4), by William Powell Frith, which depicts a sea of women sat on the sand, their heads shaded by their fine, straw bonnets and overlaid, silk uglies, highlights the popularity of these hands-free parasols.[44] And, though ugly bonnets would not become commonplace in more provincial places, like Haworth, for some years to come, by the summer of 1849, they would already have been a familiar sight in fashionable Scarborough. Had Charlotte acquired her ugly by then, she would have looked very much the part and saved her brim in the process.

Given the gravity of Anne's condition, clothing was no doubt far from Charlotte's mind, for after that first happy day she deteriorated quickly. By Monday morning, it was clear to them all that death was near and that a return to Haworth was now impossible. As she had always done, Anne did her best to support her sister in their final hours together, but at around two o'clock on the afternoon of 28 May 1849, Anne Brontë died. It was a valiant death, a good death, one which would have offered some comfort to her grief-stricken father. 'My poor sister is taken quietly home at last', wrote Charlotte to William Smith Williams two days later. 'With almost her last breath she said she was happy—and thanked God that Death was come, and come so gently. I did not think it would be so soon.'[45]

The storm of grief crashed over Charlotte almost as soon as Anne's eyes had closed for the final time. Thus, it was Ellen who registered Anne's death, Ellen who reached out for help to the faithful Miss Wooler, who mercifully now lived in the seaside town, and Ellen who arranged that an obituary notice be placed in the papers.[46] In the midst of her own grief for Anne, she led Charlotte calmly and quietly through the corpus of consignments that death always leaves in its wake. She did all but write to inform Patrick, for that terrible task could only fall to Charlotte herself.[47]

The decision was made to bury Anne's body in Scarborough, far away from Haworth and the family who had loved her. It was a choice that would haunt Charlotte for many years to come, but one made in an effort 'to save [her]

Papa the anguish of the return and a third funeral'.⁴⁸ In consequence, there was only Charlotte and Ellen to follow the coffin, but they were met in the church by Miss Wooler, who came to honour Anne's life and to stand alongside her friend in the depths of her grief. Seventy miles away, at the parsonage in Haworth, Patrick could do nothing but weep for his lost daughter and pray for the continued sustenance of Charlotte, as she carried out her mourning duties on behalf of them both.

The sartorial elements of mourning had long ceased to be a consideration for Charlotte – she was now well acquainted with the dress of death and possessed all its accoutrements. But, as she prepared to exchange the all too cheerful town of Scarborough for the quieter, more contemplative resort of Filey a few miles down the coast, she was left with the wretched task of packing up Anne's clothes – the items she that had loved and cherished, perhaps even those garments in which she had died. These she could not lock away in a cupboard or hide until strong enough to look at them. Instead, she was compelled to fold them, smooth them, feel their touch, breathe in their essence. And, through their very tangibility, Charlotte was forced to acknowledge Anne's intangibility and thus to face a reality that she inherently wished to reject.⁴⁹

Having arranged for all excess luggage to be picked up by a courier and taken home to Haworth ahead of her, Charlotte packed up some of her own clothes and belongings too – things that she would not need in Filey. Into one box went a pair of beaded, deerskin Iroquois moccasins with a velvet vamp and ankle cuffs, made by Mohawks at the Kahnawake reserve, on the south shore of the St Lawrence river.⁵⁰ She had worn these unlikely shoes as slippers as she had nursed Emily through her fatal illness, as she had written the first chapters of *Shirley* and had sat with Anne in her final hours. Though made many thousands of miles away, by a team of skilled native women, in what Charlotte perceived to be the endless, untamed wilderness of North America, these culturally unfamiliar objects had offered unexpected warmth and comfort, even inspiration. But these, together with a shawl of Anne's, another pair of slippers, a beaded bag and a number of other objects, never made it home to Haworth.⁵¹ Despite her careful arrangements and letters home to Martha to prepare her for its arrival, the box containing the moccasins was never sent on from Scarborough. Charlotte, who was too caught up in grief to notice in

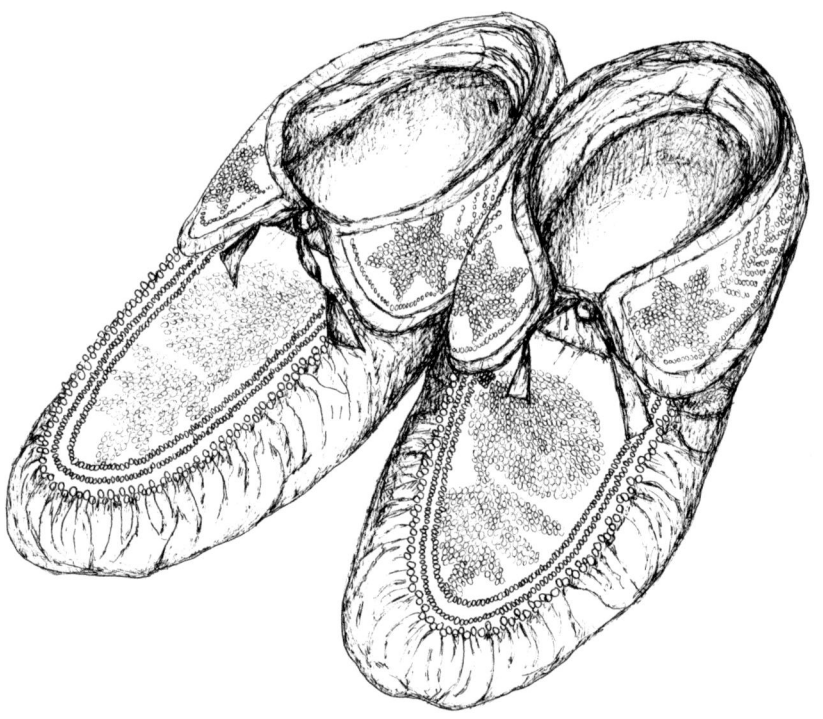

7.3 *Charlotte Brontë's Iroquois moccasins, D124*

time or to organize its later return, never saw her moccasins again – except that is in the shadowy world of her imagination, on the pages of *Shirley*.[52] The leather shoes themselves did, however, finally return to the parsonage in 1983 and have remained there ever since.[53]

Against all odds, Charlotte found relative peace in Filey. It was, as she wrote to her father, 'a quieter and more lonely place than Scar[borough]' with a wild sea, 'a black, desolate reef of rocks' and 'sea-birds on the beach and about the cliffs'.[54] Had it not been for Ellen, she would have embraced its solitary nature for longer, but keen to have her own spirits lifted by the presence of others, her friend encouraged a move to Easton Farm on the 'great brewing tub of Bridlington Bay', where they had stayed together ten years before.[55]

Charlotte and Ellen stayed in Bridlington for a little under a week before making the decision to return home to Haworth. No longer able to find comfort in the unruly sea, Charlotte knew that the time had come to reunite with her father and finally face the sorrow that awaited her in every empty room of the parsonage. The journey home was long and slow as the pair did not break their journey at York, but instead continued on to their respective homes, ensuring Charlotte did not arrive back in Haworth until eight in the evening.

The days after were every bit as hard as Charlotte had anticipated. Her 'home was not the home it [had] used to be'.[56] Almost as soon as she re-entered the parsonage, 'desolation and bitterness took possession of [her]' and the 'agony that <u>was to be undergone</u>—and <u>was not</u> to be avoided came on'. The loss seemed more potent here; it was as if the very walls of the place cried out for those it too had lost. For Charlotte, the pain reached a crescendo in the evenings, for those hours which had once been filled with literary discussion and laughter, books and games, were now darkened by the 'burden of solitude' and by intrusive memories of the now five siblings 'who had gone like dreams'.[57]

Each new dawn brought 'some strength to fight the battle of life', but often only because there was much yet to be done.[58] Though the majority of the heavy domestic work was still carried out by Tabby and by Martha, Charlotte was now solely responsible for both the running of the house and for the daily care of her father. There was too, of course, the matter of her half-written novel. *Shirley* had not been much attended to since Anne's sickness and death or since she had received the notes from Smith and Elder, but although creativity cannot have flowed easily from such a battered soul, Charlotte worked hard to finish what she had begun. She hoped, no doubt, that hard work would prove 'a radical cure for rooted Sorrow', and that her efforts would, in time at least, lift her out 'of the dark and desolate reality to an unreal but happier region'.[59]

Against all odds, this they did. Nothing could replace what she had lost, and she keenly missed those whose influence and consultation she had always sought, but there was something seductively familiar about inhabiting a world of her own creation once again. Here she could find safety, retreat. For though pain and sorrow could not be kept out altogether, in the land of *Shirley*, they could be outworked, ruled over, kept within the bounds that they had escaped in life. To live here was cathartic and, spurred on by instinct and a deepening will to live, Charlotte found the hidden strength to stand.

The completed manuscript was picked up by James Taylor of Smith, Elder and Company on the 8 September 1849. Some revisions were quickly requested, but, for the most part, Charlotte would make none of them. 'I cannot alter now', she replied. 'It sounds absurd but so it is.'[60] On one point, however, her publishers would not be moved. The preface to the book, which had been written in direct response to Elizabeth Rigby's wounding review of *Jane Eyre*, they deemed far too treacherous to print.[61] Whilst they agreed that Rigby's anonymous critique had been unnecessarily provocative with regards to the question of her sex, they feared that Charlotte, and indeed Smith and Elder themselves, would come to regret what would follow such a passionate and public outburst. And as it was, they were right, for Brontë's second book caused quite enough of a furore as it was.

'People are mystified about "Currer Bell"', wrote one critic soon after the publication of the new novel in October 1849, 'some think it is a man who rejoices in that name, others a woman.'[62] Speculation was rife, yet a general consensus soon emerged. 'We have hesitated to speak of the writer of *Jane Eyre* as a woman', argued the *Literary Examiner*, 'but the internal evidence of *Shirley* places the matter beyond all doubt.'[63] With the number of published, female writers being so few, Smith, Elder and Company knew that it was only a matter of time before Charlotte's mask would start to slip.

If anonymity were still important to her, in this, she had not helped her own case. Where only those with a detailed knowledge of Charlotte's early life could have guessed her connection with *Jane Eyre*, the characters contained within *Shirley* made her much easier to identify. Her comedic references to recent Haworth curates were extraordinarily accurate and these, together with her allusions to local geography, and her own frequent trips to nearby post offices laden with manuscript-shaped parcels destined for London, soon ensured that local readers of *Shirley* recognized not only the setting of the novel, their friends and their acquaintances but even, on occasion, the author herself. With all these dots joined, and excitement levels almost at breaking point, it was only a matter of days before her publishers were fielding enquiries, with the name 'Charlotte Brontë' being constantly mooted.

Charlotte was the last to grasp that she could 'no longer walk invisible' and, despite repeated requests from her publishers to finally admit to the world that she was Currer Bell, she clung on to her secret with a vice-like grip.[64] Still submerged in her grief, her promise to the sisters that she had lost remained paramount, but this was not the only reason she so persistently 'maintained an incognito'.[65] As she admitted in a pseudonymous letter to Elizabeth Gaskell, she also harboured a deep fear that 'if she relinquished it, strength and courage would leave her, and she should ever after shrink – from writing the plain truth'.[66]

Evidently, the name of Currer Bell was a safety blanket that the serially bereaved Charlotte was not yet ready to throw off, but that did not mean that she was not keen to locate pleasure where she could. Since her first visit to London in June the previous year, George Smith had invited Charlotte to come and stay with him and his family at their Paddington home on more than one occasion, but preoccupied with the illnesses and deaths of Branwell, Emily and Anne, she had persistently declined. By November 1849, having garnered some strength from the generally positive reviews of *Shirley*, she at last felt robust enough to face both the long journey and the gruelling social calendar that Smith and his mother would surely arrange.

This decision to once again 'set foot in the strange, busy world of the Strand and Cornhill' had serious, sartorial consequences.[67] Charlotte had not forgotten the deep embarrassment wrought by her wardrobe on her first visit to London and would not, on any account, allow herself to be caught short again. Accordingly, she quickly set about making the necessary arrangements – even going so far as to employ a dressmaker to aid her in her efforts and ensure she was properly prepared to step foot into society. The clothes and accessories that she chose were all made up in the dark hue of mourning, because, though six months had passed since Anne had died, she did not yet feel ready to lose the protective qualities of her 'weeds' or indeed to so overtly signal her formal reintegration into society.

Having been in mourning for more than a year, Charlotte was already in possession of a range of gowns suitable for her life in Haworth – for her quiet, domestic day-to-day existence, for church on Sunday or for visits to friends in the locality. After some rejuvenation, potentially by the use of Dr Winn's 'True Anticardium Paris Black Reviver', famously designed to revitalize mourning garments, the smarter of these, those she had worn when visiting Ellen, or when shopping in Leeds or York, she could take with her to London to wear on those mornings spent at home with Mrs Smith or for more informal activities.[68] But, as her earlier trip to the capital had made so clear, Charlotte's wardrobe was, and indeed had always been, decidedly lacking when it came to more conspicuous day and evening garments – those deemed appropriate for the theatre, the opera, for formal dinners, or even when visiting art galleries or exhibitions accompanied by George Smith or William Smith Williams. She had, quite simply, never needed such gowns and so, despite insisting that 'the dresses [be] made up quite plainly', these she left to the dressmaker whom she reluctantly invited to Haworth on 16 November, not yet knowing whether she was 'a good hand'.[69] Charlotte need not have worried, the newly made garments arrived just ten days later and she was forced to admit that they had been executed 'pretty well'.[70]

As Charlotte's mad dash to purchase parasols and gloves when last in London had proved, smart day and evening accessories were also obligatory when out in society. Her black velvet, fingerless mittens were probably acquired in the days leading up to her departure and might even have been made by Charlotte herself, as numerous patterns for 'mitts' could be found in ladies' magazines, companions and newspapers.[71] She would have worn these hand seed-beaded, silk-lined mitts, or her gossamer thin, black netted lace pair, in the evening, when she attended dinner with George Smith and 'five critics' or was taken to see the famed tragic actor William Macready in his farewell performances of *Macbeth* and *Othello* at the Haymarket Theatre.[72]

Three very different pieces of elegant black lace, designed to be worn as bonnet veils, draped over the shoulders or even, as the novelist George Eliot wore hers, in the Spanish style, over a tortoiseshell comb at the back of the head, might also have been acquired during Charlotte's period of mourning, and very possibly in time for her trip to London.[73] Though black lace was not normally worn during the early stages of mourning, it was commonly adopted in the later phases and added a quiet opulence to an evening or very smart day ensemble and, as Lucy Snowe found in Charlotte's later book, *Villette*, could afterwards be worn to soften and subdue a brightly coloured dress.[74] However, even by the late 1840s, there was some concern around wearing black lace close to the face, as dark dyes could transfer, leaving a ghastly bluish tint on the cheekbones or forehead or worse still, if the colourants used were particularly noxious, 'burning the skin an intense black'.[75]

7.4 *Charlotte Brontë's black lace veil, D169*

Charlotte's black sateen, ribbon-laced pumps, with rosette flourishes, might also have been bought in the days or weeks before her departure for Smith's house in Westbourne Place.[76] Such slippers, as they were sometimes known, were an essential part of formal wear and, depending on the nature of the event, could be worn with either black or white silk stockings.[77] Though Charlotte's slippers feature the squared toe and throat so popular in the 1840s, they are unusual in one key respect. To ward off chilblains during that cold December trip, the little shoes, which privileged form over function, and measure just 23 cm in length, have been lined with soft white fur that still bears the imprint of her tiny feet.[78] The same cannot be said for her two pairs of dark, square-toed, low-heeled cloth boots.[79] Like most ladies' footwear dated to the late 1840s and early 1850s, the inners are made from simple calico and have little padding, making them hard underfoot and subject to the cold and the damp.[80] In fact, Charlotte struggled so much with icy feet that, on her return journey from London, George Smith's sister, Eliza, made her some 'little boots' which she later deemed 'a perfect treasure of comfort'.[81]

Charlotte arrived in Paddington on Thursday 29 November with the new clothes and accessories that she had purchased especially for the trip packed up carefully in numerous boxes and bags. Mrs Elizabeth Smith and her daughters welcomed their guest warmly, for having finally been let into the secret that they were harbouring <u>the</u> Currer Bell, there was all the more reason to be attentive. 'I had a fire in my bedroom evening and morning – two wax candles &c.', wrote Charlotte to Ellen a few days after her arrival. 'Mrs S … treats me as if she liked me and I begin to like her very much.'[82]

Two weeks passed quickly. Barely a minute was left vacant, with her days consumed by sightseeing excursions, afternoon teas with Smith and Smith Williams and visits to galleries, her evenings with lively dinners, theatre trips and informal meetings with fellow authors or socialites. Highlights included 'a beautiful exhibition of Turner's paintings' and a late evening visit to writer and social theorist Harriet Martineau and her cousin Lucy, who later wrote of meeting 'the neat little woman, a <u>very</u> little sprite of a creature nicely dressed' in her 'deep mourning dress'.[83] Charlotte's most memorable experience, however, that which took up the most space in her letters home to her father and to Ellen, was her meeting with her long-time hero, William Makepeace Thackeray. Such was her excitement that on first setting eyes on him, she felt herself in a dream, 'I was only certain it was true', she wrote, 'because I became miserably destitute of self-possession … I spoke stupidly.'[84] But even in spite of her excessive nervousness, even in spite of her embarrassment, the literary star did not disappoint. She found Thackeray 'very ugly indeed' but wholly fascinating – 'kind', 'satirical' and 'stern' in equal measure.[85]

Charlotte returned home to Haworth on the afternoon of Saturday 15 December, physically and emotionally exhausted, but with her mind vivified by the sights and sounds and smells of London. The trip had been a great success. A process of expansion had begun in her. She could sense a way out, and, though the anniversary of Emily's death was looming, and it was a date that she greatly feared, there were now days in which the darkness did not feel as black. A light could be perceived at the end of the tunnel of grief and Charlotte could feel herself moving towards it. Yet, as anyone who has survived loss will know, though her visit to London had propelled her forward, that did not mean her grief was over. Her recovery, or rather, her reconstruction, would prove a slow and painful process – in no way straight and in no way smooth. Charlotte's wardrobe, ever the barometer of change, would mark these oscillations – be they socially prescribed or much more personal.

Charlotte had already chosen to remain in full mourning dress and to send letters edged in black for longer than polite society demanded, but then there were no clear guidelines for repeated bereavement and so, not for the first time, she was forced to write the rule book for herself. Whether it was her recent trip to London that triggered the change, or she simply felt the time had come to lighten the heavy burden of black, it was during these winter months that Charlotte began to modify her dress once again – to begin to shed the sombre skin of mourning.

Charlotte's large-sleeved, whitework blouse of fine, white cotton, with black, oak-leaf trim, might well have been worn during this 'new' period.[86] The blouse's enormous, highly decorative sleeves and embellished front suggest it was worn beneath a gown with an open corsage and wide, 'half long sleeves' that finished at mid-forearm.[87] This dress style was hugely popular in the early 1850s and would have been made up in black or dark-grey silk in accordance with the tradition of half-mourning. On other occasions, this same open-fronted gown would have been worn with a much plainer, white chemisette and her silk, black-and-white fringed, chequered neckerchief tied neatly at the neck.[88]

7.5 *Charlotte Brontë's whitework blouse with black trim, D171*

Though black and grey, punctuated by white, continued to dominate, Charlotte did slowly inject some colour and pattern into her wardrobe. Purple shades, ranging from deep mauve to pansy, heliotrope to lavender, had long been associated with mourning and by the nineteenth century had been tentatively incorporated into half-mourning. Her lavender, grey, white and black plaid, fringed barège shawl, recently acquired by the Brontë Parsonage Museum as part of the Blavatnik Honresfield Library Collection, is likely to have been worn during this period of transition.[89] For though this 'new' shawl seems inappropriate – it is, to us, bold and bright – her contemporaries would have deemed it entirely acceptable.[90] The same was true of the two plum, silk-covered dress buttons that were found nestled, along with a spool of matching plum thread, deep in Charlotte's work basket – or rather, so too was the silk garment to which they first belonged.[91] Purple shades were still 'expressive of gravity, sorrow and sadness', yet, as they could also fashionably be worn outside of the mourning period, gowns and accessories made up in these rich hues were long-sighted purchases.[92]

The colour purple might have marked the beginning of the end of Charlotte's official time of mourning but, as she began to prepare to cast off all external manifestations of grief, that did not mean that all sartorial challenges were behind her. Emily and Anne's clothing, those items that they had lived in, those things that had held them, had absorbed their sweat, their stains, their shape, remained.[93] Her sisters had gone, but the clothes that had worn them were still present; lifeless, atrophied and yet strangely alive.[94] Material reminders, the shawls, slippers, bonnets, gloves and trinkets left behind, 'brought back to life realities that [she had] long thought decayed, dissolved and mixed in with grave mould'.[95] But what should she do with these portals to the past? These relics of the dead?

The intrinsic value of the things themselves made a difference. All memories aside, they were, quite simply, too valuable to throw away. Clothing had monetary worth, in part because fabric, and especially good fabric, was expensive, but also, as Charlotte well knew, because they took time to design, to cut, to make and to finish. They were, therefore, rich in effort, in what Marx would that same year call 'wage labour'.[96] More importantly to Charlotte, they were rich in Emily and Anne's effort – something that took on new meaning now that they had laid down their young lives 'like a burden'.[97]

Charlotte's own body was smaller than that of her sisters, but many everyday items she could wear or use without alteration. Handkerchiefs and stockings marked for Emily and Anne were saved, not always for reasons of sentiment but because they were useful.[98] The same was true for chemises, collars, cuffs and chemisettes. Even at her own death, a great number of these remained, suggesting Emily and Anne's items were pragmatically embraced as her own. All these could now be washed without care for whom they belonged, for there was now only Charlotte left to wear them.

7.6 *Charlotte Brontë's printed wool shawl, D12*

Those garments too large, or on account of Emily's peculiar taste, too singular for Charlotte to wear in public, were no doubt altered or given away to servants, friends or those in need. But all the things that mattered were kept. Strange things sometimes – clothes that reminded, garments that had witnessed happy days, bravery, suffering, love. There was Emily's small brown, striped silk bodice – only large enough for a child of seven or eight.[99] This was childhood; innocence and experience shared. There was the wide, tortoiseshell comb which had held up Emily's dark hair in the Spanish style when they went out shopping together in Bradford.[100] There was even Anne's blood-specked handkerchief – gross in itself, but an emblem of a last battle bravely fought and lost. What they held within them was painful certainly, sometimes excruciatingly so, but also beautiful, also good.[101]

7.7 Charlotte Brontë's tortoiseshell comb, J73

There were shawls too, an amorphous mass of shawls, left to her by the women who had loved her – her mother, her aunt, her poor, departed sisters.[102] These she saved to wrap around herself, perhaps because she wished to be caressed by the dead – to have them haunt her, envelop her, protect her.[103] It was, after all, the closest she could get to them now. For as these bits of wreckage so potently reminded, Charlotte was now almost alone.

8

Fame

On Friday 7 March 1850 Sir James Kay Shuttleworth, politician, educationist and first baronet of Gawthorpe Hall and his wife Lady Janet made their way up the stone path towards the Haworth Parsonage. County borders had been crossed in their pursuit of Currer Bell, or rather, as they now knew her better, Miss Charlotte Brontë. It was not the first time that they had tried to introduce themselves, but now, at last, the 'courtly mannered' baronet and his 'rather handsome' wife had succeeded in arranging a private meeting with the famed author of *Jane Eyre* and her elderly father.[1]

If either Charlotte or the much-excited Patrick were in any doubt that the proverbial cat was now out of the bag, that Charlotte's secret had been at last been widely uncovered, then the arrival of the enthusiastic baronet and his lady wife on their doorstop can only have convinced them. Few such personages had ever had call to visit the parsonage, but now that Currer Bell was all but dead, it seemed that the world was clambering to meet his successor.

Little more than a week later, at the earnest bequest of Sir James, Charlotte found herself ensconced in the magnificent 'antique oak-panelled drawing room' of Gawthorpe Hall, 'a three centuries old, grey, stately and picturesque' house set in forty acres of woodland near Burnley, East Lancashire.[2] It can only have felt 'utterly strange', alien even, for the provincial, plain, oft-overlooked clergyman's daughter to be sat in such grand surroundings, not in her capacity as teacher or governess, but as celebrated author, honoured guest.[3] Her 'quiet life' was changing faster than she cared to admit and, having already been dramatically undermined by repeated loss, there was no small amount of nervousness at what the future held and whether she felt strong enough to sustain it.⁴ 'The worst of it is', wrote Charlotte to William Smith Williams on her return from Gawthorpe Hall, 'is there is now some menace hanging over my head of an invitation to go to them in London during the season – this, which would doubtless be a great enjoyment to some people is a perfect terror to me. I should highly prize the advantages to be gained in an extended range of observation – but I tremble at the thought of the price I must necessarily pay in mental distress and physical wear and tear.'⁵

This tug of war between Charlotte's deep desire to enjoy first hand all the 'éclât and bustle which an open declaration of authorship ... certainly entail[ed]' and her latent fear of strangers would continue to personify her relationship with fame.⁶ And fame it now was, for from this point on Charlotte's life would never be quite the same again. Letters of appreciation and invitations to lunches, dinners, lectures, exhibitions, parties and grand openings from enthusiasts, influencers and 'literary coteries' alike, flowed in with surprising frequency. She was invited to stay with Harriet Martineau at her country home in Ambleside and with Elizabeth Gaskell. She was asked to contribute to magazines and periodicals; her real name appeared in newspapers up and down the land and even Patrick received a standing ovation after speaking at the Haworth Mechanics' Institute, purely on account of being the father of the distinguished Miss Brontë. The uncovering of her identity had begun to have real impact, just as Emily had always anticipated it would.

This new phase of Charlotte's life – what biographer and critic Sir Sidney Lee would later christen her 'feast of fame' – was no more straightforward than any that had come before it.⁷ There were triumphs, some great, some even, for Charlotte at least, spectacular, but there were also trials; trials that would, in the end, lead her to step away from the spotlight and slink back to relative obscurity once again. Two gowns, each worn during this transformative period of Charlotte's life, offer unprecedented insight into her paradoxical relationship with fame. Different as night and day, they elucidate two sides of this changed life – those parts that she came to love and those parts that she came to loathe.

The first witness to the stand takes the form of a blue-and-white, printed skirt and bodice with a mandarin collar of soft, brown velvet and brass and mother-of-pearl buttons. Its provenance is strong, for the 'Thackeray Dress', as it has colloquially come to be known, was bequeathed to Martha

8.1 *Charlotte Brontë's 'Thackeray Dress', D129*

Brown soon after Charlotte's death.⁸ It was later given to Martha's niece, Eleanor Ratcliffe, who brought the dress up to date with some extensive alterations. It was Eleanor who placed the piece of brown velvet over the original collar.⁹ She also removed at least a panel and a half from the skirt, cut off the lower part of the bodice and moved the waistband. She is also thought to have been responsible for cutting slits in the cotton lining of the bodice, presumably to make space for her more expansive bust. Having been purchased by a tenacious collector, the gown was finally donated to the Brontë Society in 1928 and has been placed on display in the museum many times since.

In testament to both the quality of the fabric and the original gown's strong connection to Charlotte, those pieces that were removed were not thrown away but instead went on to have lives of their own.¹⁰ A detached skirt panel, after having, for a time, been in the possession of Charlotte's biographer, Ellis Chadwick, was sold by Martha Brown's nephew, William Binns, to a Brontë enthusiast for one pound five shillings in 1916. It was later returned to the parsonage, where it has since remained. Far more dramatically, the portion removed from Charlotte's bodice has recently been found nearly three and a half thousand miles away from where the gown was first made, hidden in a small, wooden slide box, along with some snippets of Charlotte's other gowns.¹¹ It is not yet known how the fragment and its companions made their way to the United States of America, but its survival helps us to essentially turn back time and reimagine the gown as it was in the early summer of 1850, when a surprisingly audacious Charlotte Brontë wore it to meet her literary hero, William Makepeace Thackeray.

Even in spite of Eleanor's changes, the 'Thackeray Dress', which was intended to be worn as a smart day gown, was always relatively simple in its design. Charlotte's original skirt would have been more voluminous than it is now, in keeping with late 1840s designs. The separate bodice, which is currently cut straight across at the waist, would previously have been finished at a low v, with the loose pleats that start at the shoulders continuing down to a rounded point. The original collar, though now covered in brown velvet, can still be seen beneath, suggesting Charlotte's gown also featured a similar neckline.

8.2 Front view of Charlotte Brontë's 'Thackeray Dress'

Many of Eleanor's alterations, and particularly those made to the skirt, have been carried out by the use of a sewing machine, as evidenced by the perfectly uniform stitches that run from waistband to hem. Yet, though when viewed through a magnifying glass slight differences are apparent, the original seams are so impeccable that it is sometimes hard to believe that they were hand stitched by Charlotte and Martha, in the parlour of the parsonage.[12]

It is not known exactly when the pair worked together to make the gown, but, though Charlotte certainly wore it on her trip to London in early June 1850, the distinctive shape of the sleeves suggests that it was manufactured a couple of years before, soon after her 1848 trip to London, but in the days or months before Branwell died and the Brontë household entered their extended period of mourning. For, by 1850, narrow sleeves, which had been popular for the latter part of the 1840s, were slowly being replaced by much more voluminous designs. The low-shouldered, tight-fitting sleeves of Charlotte's 'Thackeray Dress' were still being worn in 1850, indeed, they can still occasionally be seen in fashion plates, but had the dress been made especially for her 1850 trip to London, it is likely that she would made the dress in the newer style, just as she had done with other gowns made for this or other occasions.[13]

After the tumult of the past few years, many of us can relate to Charlotte's decision not to waste her gown merely because it no longer reflected the very newest fashions. Just like the still-labelled work suits, wedding outfits or satin evening gowns rendered redundant during the dark months of 2020/1 and left to hang unworn in wardrobes across the world, Charlotte's 'Thackeray Dress' had become a casualty of war. That did not mean, however, that it could not be worn once the immediate battle was over. Indeed, there was something special about this vibrant blue dress – something that recent, state of the art experiments have now proved made it far too good to discard.

The scientific analysis of Charlotte's 'Thackeray Dress' was initially undertaken for quite a different reason. The continued vibrancy of the dyes had long caused consternation. How, after nearly 170 years, had the blue dyes remained so vital? Which colourants had been used to produce the magnetic, cerulean shades? Why had repeated washing and ironing had so little bearing on the vibrancy of the pattern? A chance meeting over a dry, university vol-au-vent, saw a collaboration form with Professor Andrea Russell and her PhD students Danai Panagoulia and Alexander Keeler.[14] We could, it seemed, through the use of Raman spectroscopy on a fragment of fabric not much larger than a pea, reveal the secrets of the gown's eternal youth. Raman spectroscopy is a spectroscopic technique in which the difference in frequency (colour) between the light shone on the fabric, and that scattered off its surface, allows the molecules that make up the fabric to be identified.[15]

A hushed silence fell over the museum library at the moment of extraction. It was a surprisingly low-tech process involving nail scissors, a pair of tweezers and the panel of Charlotte's skirt that Eleanor Ratcliffe had removed to alter its shape. But, never has a pair of scissors hovered more nervously over a piece of fabric. Never has there been more anxious a snip. Never has so minute a piece of material been so guarded on its long journey from Yorkshire, all the way to the Hampshire coast.

8.3 *Microscope images of D129 taken using Nikon Eclipse LV100ND microscope, x2 objective. Images taken by Danai Panagoulia, Alex Keeler and Eleanor Houghton, University of Southampton*

Once in the laboratory, things moved fast, and earlier hypotheses, established using more traditional techniques, were quickly challenged. It soon became clear that the fabric of the dress was composed of two separate fibres. However, though a cotton warp was quickly identified by the use of an exceptionally strong microscope, that could take images at x2 and x10 objectives, the weft remained something of a mystery. Raman spectroscopy was therefore employed, and spectra taken from both the fibres. Chemical wizardry soon established that fine alpaca fleece and not sheep wool, as had previously been supposed, had been used to create the soft, lustrous fabric. This finding was not only wholly unexpected but also hugely important, for the unusual discovery made identifying the likely manufacturer of the fabric far more feasible.

Peruvian Indians had long made blankets and cloth from the fleeces of the alpaca, which were indigenous to South America, but it was not until the late 1830s that alpaca fleece began to be used in large-scale textile production in Britain.[16] Titus Salt was the first to see the potential of the soft fibres. He had already set up as a worsted manufacturer in Bradford and mastered the process of spinning the exceptionally coarse Russian Donskoi wool into usable yarn, but became excited when he came across a large stack of abandoned bales of alpaca fleece in the shipping warehouse of Hagan and Co., Liverpool.[17] Ever the entrepreneur, Salt set to work and, against the advice of fellow worsted manufacturers who had already deemed alpaca impracticable for large-scale use, spent more than eighteen months adapting his existing machinery to better cope with the ultra-fine fleece. After much trial and error, he found that he was able to spin a fine, even thread that, when woven with stronger cotton or silk threads, formed a soft, luxurious, but surprisingly hard-wearing cloth. The manufacture of these mixed-fibre fabrics would prove the *magnus opus* of his career and the basis of his tremendous fame and fortune – even prompting Charles Dickens to immortalize Salt's story in his 1853 article for *Household Words*, enticingly entitled, 'The Great Yorkshire Llama Drama'.[18] By 1839, Salt was importing 2,186,480 lbs of alpaca fleece per year and by 1863 he was operating more than 1,200 alpaca adapted power looms. To the wealthy, his alpaca mix fabrics came to be considered worthy rivals to silk and, by the mid-nineteenth century, their popularity had soared. Indeed, by the time Charlotte bought the blue-and-white *Alpaca Orleans* fabric for her new gown in or around 1848, she was buying *the* fabric of the moment.[19] Far more meaningfully, she was also buying local.

For many years Titus Salt, whose mills were based in Bradford just over nine miles from Haworth, and later in a vast and ultra-efficient textile factory built at the centre of the new industrial metropolis of Saltaire, just over eight miles from Brontë's home, monopolized the production of alpaca-based fabrics. Together with G. and J. Turner of Great Horton (nine miles from Haworth), Fosters and Sons of Queensbury (eight miles) and the Mitchell Brothers of Bradford (eight miles), he arranged the purchase of all alpaca fleeces that entered the country from Peru, thereby ensuring the continued domination of the market.[20] But, though other manufacturers in the Bradford area did begin to make alpaca mix fabrics, Salts Mill was by far the largest manufacturer of foreign fibres, making this the mill that is most likely to have produced the fabric used in Charlotte's gown. In any case, it could now be judiciously stated that Brontë's *Alpaca Orleans* cloth was woven within a nine-mile radius of her home, making it a truly local product and one of which she could be proud.

Having determined where the fabric for the 'Thackeray Dress' was woven, the team set about identifying the vibrant dyes used in the printing of the fabric, which would have been carried out just over the border in Lancashire, and probably in Accrington, where a great number of printing works were located.[21] It was clear that the flowers, leaves and tendrils had been created using a darker blue for the outlines and a lighter blue for the infill. The stylized pattern, very similar to others from the period, suggested that the fabric had been printed in the late 1840s or early 1850s and therefore at a time in which both indigo and Prussian blue dyes were in constant use.[22] These dyes were often used in combination on mixed fibre fabrics like *Alpaca Orleans,* so as to ensure a uniform appearance on both the wool/silk/alpaca fleece and cotton fibres, which tend to absorb colourants very differently.[23]

It had previously proved impossible to determine whether the two-tone pattern had been printed using one dye of varying strengths or two entirely different dyes.[24] Raman spectra were therefore obtained from both the light- and dark-blue fibres of the dress fragment. The results suggested that both shades had been obtained by the use of different concentrations of the same dye or mixture of dyes, rather than by the use of two distinct dyes.[25] Mordants, chemical substances which eat away the surface of the fibres so that the colourant better penetrates them, might also have been used to encourage the dye to take more intensely, but sadly, as these were rinsed away after the printing process was completed and were further removed through laundering, none could now be detected.[26] In this case, sulphate of zinc or nitrate of iron are the mordants most likely to have been used, but as printing and dyeing were key aspects of fabric production, chemists, like Frederick Steiner and Frederick Gatty of Broad Oak Print Works in Accrington, were working on new possibilities all the time, ensuring Britain remained leaders in the field.[27]

To help identify the dyes used in the gown, Raman spectra of the dyed dress fibres were compared with others found in reliable scientific databases. A clear match was found between the spectrum taken from the stronger, dark-blue fibres and a reference spectrum taken from Prussian blue dye of the type used in the mid-nineteenth century.[28] Cheap and oft-used indigo sulphate was not detected, which means that the most advanced scientific innovations of the period must have been employed to ensure that both the alpaca and cotton fibres were evenly dyed by the Prussian blue. For, as late as 1849, prevailing manuals still advocated that both Prussian blue and indigo should be added to the vat when dyeing/printing mixed stuffs. The successful application of pioneering practices certainly played their part in ensuring that Charlotte's 'Thackeray Dress' remains every bit as vibrant as it was the day that she bought the fabric.[29]

It might seem as though these discoveries are unrelated to Brontë's all-important morning meeting with William Makepeace Thackeray in early June 1850, but, in fact, quite the reverse is true. There was real meaning in her decision to wear her Prussian blue, *Alpaca Orleans* dress that morning. The meeting was planned. On 6 June, Thackeray had sent word to George Smith's mother, with whom she was staying, informing her that he intended to call upon the famed Miss Brontë.[30] His arrival engendered excitement but also anxiety. Thackeray was formidable, gallant, but also irascible, bold, outspoken. A certain strength would be needed to face this literary rival and clothing, as Charlotte had learned first-hand, could prove a potent source. Though still held firm by her corset, this time she also looked to derive power from a very different place – from the lustrous, expertly woven alpaca fabric of her gown and, more importantly, from the tremendous regional pride that it engendered within her.

Charlotte's second book *Shirley*, the first to build a story around the Yorkshire textile trade, had laid bare her knowledge of the mighty hives of industry that had sprung up in her own little corner of the world – one in which many thousands of hands, and, later, machines of dizzying complexity and power, would come to produce superior products at a previously unimaginable rate.[31] In it she had shone a spotlight on the *people* at the heart of this fast-changing industry; those whose lives were entirely enmeshed with the complex manufacture of cloth and the wild, unyielding landscape that worked so hard to make it. This was the community that her father had given his life to serve. These were the people, and this was the place that generated in her what the workers she described called 'a pride of raight mak', a 'Yorkshire clean pride'.[32] For these things had played an active part in determining who she was and, as so much else had now fallen away, as so much else was lost, it was something upon which she could proudly stand.[33]

The *Alpaca Orleans* gown, composed as it was from fabric printed little more than twenty miles away from Haworth, woven less than ten miles from the parsonage, on machines designed and adapted in the West Riding of Yorkshire, from fibres made usable by the tenacity and ingenuity of locals, can only be viewed as symbolic of Charlotte's regional identity. Many women wore such fabrics, but not all women understood their significance. Not all women understood what it took to make cloth of such quality, innovation and distinction. Not all women knew from whence their cloth had come or just how many hands it had taken to create it. But Charlotte knew because, as the saying goes, she 'was Yorkshire to begin with and Yorkshire she would remain until the close'.[34]

And so it was that Charlotte entered George Smith's drawing room that June morning, clad in her 'high-made', blue-and-white printed, *Alpaca Orleans* gown, ready to meet the man to whom she had so enthusiastically dedicated the second edition of *Jane Eyre*. Normally shy and awkward with strangers, she was quite another person that day, for there was fire where fear should be. More than ten years later, Thackeray recalled being struck by the sheer force of character present in the 'austere little Joan of Arc'.[35] In this private setting, far away from the prying eyes of outsiders, her slight, four-foot-eight figure stood, unintimidated by her alien surroundings or, more importantly, even by the 'giant' size of her six-foot-tall opponent.[36]

'An impetuous honesty seemed to me to characterize the woman', wrote Thackeray of their interview. 'Twice I recollect she took me to task for what she held to be errors in doctrine … New to the London world, she entered it with an independent, indomitable spirit of her own; and judged of contemporaries, and especially spied out arrogance or affectation with extraordinary keenness of vision.'[37] This was a meeting of equals. Neither gender nor rank featured in Brontë's mind as she 'rebuked' Thackeray 'when [his] conduct or conversation fell below her ideal' or even as she tackled his 'shortcomings … one by one'.[38] Garbed in her newly monikered 'Thackeray Dress' and speaking, in seclusion, as one successful author to another, she was confident, vocal, assertive. This was the side of fame that Charlotte Brontë relished. It was the side of fame that she had always wished to attain.

One might think that Charlotte's great success would have marked a turning point in her turbulent relationship with fame. She had, after all, now sparred with one of the greatest writers of her age and had been accepted as a worthy opponent. But, though the 'Currer Bell' part of her had proved strong and courageous, beneath this assured exterior still lurked the other Charlotte – one that would appear all too clearly on that same trip to London in June 1850 and many, many times subsequently. Her deep-rooted insecurities over her appearance had not in any way diminished, nor had her fear of scrutiny. When with Thackeray, her love of literature and of debate had recalled in her the same passion that she had shared with her siblings, she had momentarily forgotten her anxieties and enjoyed a temporary reprieve from the negative thoughts that dominated when surrounded by any but her closest friends or family. Yet, this amnesty was to be short-lived, for a social engagement, ironically hosted by Thackeray himself, would stretch the other Charlotte almost to the limit.

It was early in the evening of Wednesday, 12 June 1850 that Charlotte arrived at William Makepeace Thackeray's Kensington home for the large, formal dinner party that he had arranged in her honour. Charlotte was not the only figure of note present that night, but there is little doubt that she was the focus.

Curiosity had brought numerous well-known celebrities to 16 Young Street to see 'the lioness of the hour'.³⁹ Though there had been no formal unveiling of Currer Bell, anyone who was anyone now knew that the 'tiny delicate, serious little lady, pale with fair straight hair and steady eyes' who stepped down from the carriage was indeed the writer of *Jane Eyre*.⁴⁰ But if this gathering of writers and socialites had come hoping to meet the passionate, provocative creator of Mrs Jane Rochester, they were to be disappointed. Gone was the David who had faced her Goliath. Met with a roomful of expectant strangers, she had been drained of all power.

Overwhelmed by the glare of the spotlight, Charlotte had no sparkling conversation. She was devoid of all anecdotes and offered no insights into her literary practices. Except for Miss Truelock, governess to Thackeray's children, she made no connection with any of the guests and, in consequence, the atmosphere of that great Kensington drawing-room 'grew dimmer and more dim'.⁴¹ The break for supper did nothing to improve the situation. Charlotte, who had asked to sit close to her host, soon proved herself equally uneasy at table. Overcome by her new friend's insalubrious consumption of potatoes, she broke her anxious silence only to 'clasp her hands' in horror as she sought to stop 'a fifth potato' from 'disappearing down his throat' with the piercing cry of 'Oh Mr. Thackeray! Don't!'⁴²

To all those who had gathered to meet her, Charlotte Brontë, the great writer, had proved a great disappointment. One guest later bitingly declared that the event had turned out to be 'one of the dullest evenings she had ever spent in her life'.⁴³ And, such was Thackeray's own embarrassment at having subjected his guests to so dreary a dinner, that as soon as the 'silent' and 'serious' Charlotte had been bundled off into her carriage, he deserted all those remaining and slunk, dejected, off to his club to enjoy the 'consolations of a cigar'.⁴⁴

The dinner took on iconic status after that. Many of those in attendance wrote or spoke of the evening in the years that followed and humorously recalled Charlotte's profound ability to 'chill a party' with her 'want of social gifts'.⁴⁵ Celebrated socialite Frances Brookfield went one step further, claiming that despite tremendous efforts on her own part, she had found Miss Brontë 'the most difficult woman to talk to that she had ever met'. She would often then recount the succinct conversation that they had shared on that fateful evening by way of evidence. 'I opened it by saying', began Mrs Brookfield with notable charm, 'I hope she enjoyed London; to which Charlotte Brontë replied curtly, "I do and I don't" … [and] that [was] all.'[46]

In the unfamiliar and highly critical environment to which she had been exposed that evening, Charlotte's newfound celebrity fitted her as ill as did the incongruous, false hairpiece that she had requested Ellen Nussey buy her in April 1850, in readiness for her visit to London.[47] Here, her dread of 'being made a show of' prevailed.[48] And, as the very public, post-dinner evaluation of her character makes clear, she had every reason to be fearful, for criticism was not only limited to her lack of social skills. Comments were also made about that which Charlotte feared more than almost anything – her appearance.

Though it had previously been thought that Charlotte had worn the 'Thackeray Dress' to this dinner and had thus committed a desperate faux pas, she had, in actuality, made some considerable effort to mitigate sartorial censure that evening.[49] She had chosen a 'little barège dress with a pattern of faint green moss' which she had paired with fingerless 'mittens', no doubt formed from cream, crocheted cotton, and a plaited silk hairpiece.[50] But despite her best endeavours, she was still found wanting. Thackeray's daughter, Anne, remarked some time afterwards that Charlotte had borne 'no curls or loops such as ladies wore then', 'frowned at [her] whenever [she] looked at her' and gave 'a general impression of chin about her face'.[51] Frances Brookfield, in her essay, 'A Party for Charlotte Brontë', instead described 'a timid little woman with a firm mouth' – one 'who did not possess a large enough quantity of hair to enable her to form a plait' and so, in an attempt to conceal her lack, 'wore a very obvious crown of brown silk.'[52]

Charlotte was not immune to such criticism. Whenever in London, her letters home were filled with references to sleepless nights when she nervously dissected the day's events.[53] Sensitivity to the opinions of others continued to prove both mentally and physically exhausting and was only heightened by the alien nature of her environment. For life in Haworth 'went like clockwork … where no one comes to the house; nothing disturbs the deep repose; hardly a voice is heard … everything fits into, and is in harmony with, the idea of a country Parsonage, possessed by people of very moderate means'.[54] In contrast, she found London 'a big Babylon'.[55] The capital was filled with new people, new sights and new codes of expected conduct. It was a scene of 'fickle and rapid shifts of impressions and alliances', where everyone fought to maintain their place and to keep everyone else in theirs.[56] Ruthlessly scanning for signs that betrayed social positions and flushing out, exposing and barring those ignorant of the rules, had become a compulsive preoccupation of the prevailing classes.[57] So much so that the dynamic, bustling, burgeoning city had become a hyper-critical environment that encouraged a much more intense awareness of one's own subjectivity than did the slower paced, more provincial life to which Charlotte was so used.[58]

In this city, culture, beauty, manners, conduct and the art of conversation were deemed essential to success. They were, in effect, vital assets that determined social existence.[59] Appropriate clothing was another crucial armament in the battle for wholehearted acceptance by London society, and arguably, in Brontë's case now that her identity had been uncovered, for sustained books sales. But the codes and conventions of dress were complex – especially for the middle-classes who did not have titles or high-status surnames to confirm their rightful position.[60] Consequently, strict sartorial rules were implemented which were specifically designed to protect the elite from imitators and interlopers. These helped to create space between the 'in-crowd' and those who presented a threat to their place in society. The rules of fashion were deliberately subtle, and meanings were located in the smallest, nuanced details – in the shape of a bonnet brim, the width of a ribbon or in the particular knot of a cravat.[61] For those, like Charlotte, who due to birth and constrained finances already inhabited the hinterlands of the middle-classes, confident adherence to these rules was even more important, but, arguably, even harder to achieve.

There is no doubt that Charlotte understood the vital importance of correct dress, or that she had grasped that one had to keep up with the latest styles in order, ironically, to remain unobtrusive. After her fateful first trip to London, she had made considerable efforts to adapt and dramatically extend her wardrobe to meet the new requirements of fame and its social consequences.[62] However, neither her awareness of the classifications of dress, nor the acquisition of more conspicuous clothing were enough for her to pass without criticism. This is because the art of dress was far more complicated than simply drawing together apparently acceptable options. Rather, it involved selecting gowns and accessories from a relatively narrow range in accordance with particular, often obscure rules which were different for each activity or time of day and changed from season to season.[63]

Navigating the subtleties of the deliberately fast-changing codes inevitably proved even more taxing than did understanding the basic precepts of acceptable dress. Consequently, when in the company of London's elite, the physically plain and socially awkward Charlotte 'usually felt as out of place as she looked'.[64] This inability, as London socialites Charles and Frances Brookfield observed, 'to fall in with the easy *badinage* of the well-bred people with whom she found herself surrounded' resulted in considerable anxiety.[65] She sought constant reassurance and before trips to London often called upon Ellen to 'look on [her dresses] and give a dictum'.[66] Far more trusting of the opinions of others than of her own, she often sent her long-suffering friend on shopping missions to purchase accessories like 'a boa and cuffs', 'lace cloaks' or 'brown satin ribbon' on her behalf.[67] But Ellen was not the only person she commandeered for help. Her new friend Elizabeth Gaskell, a woman far more used to navigating the choppy waters of London society, was also called upon for style advice.[68] She was, according to Charlotte's biographer Ellis Chadwick, 'of great assistance to … Brontë, who never enjoyed shopping, or choosing her own clothes.'[69]

One might hope that time and experience would alleviate Charlotte's insecurities; that the more she was exposed to London, the more comfortable she would become. But, despite her best efforts, quite the opposite was true. Self-doubt continued to flourish. In May 1851 after visiting Leeds, she wrote to Ellen:

> I had thought of telling you when I was going—and having your help and company in buying a bonnet etc. but then I reflected this would be merely making a selfish use of you–so I determined to manage or mismanage the matter alone—I went to Hunt and Hall's for the bonnet–and got one which seemed grave and quiet there amongst all the splendours–but now it looks infinitely too gay with its pink lining.[70]

Even before her arrival in Leeds, Charlotte had convinced herself that she was in danger of 'mismanaging' this all-important acquisition. Though, as she admits, she should be able to 'manage' alone it is clear that deep down she fears that she cannot. Her purchase is no mere frippery, it is an event demanding sober financial and sartorial consideration. And, though by 1851 Brontë was at the very height of her fame, her use of the word 'splendours' suggests that the procurement of such an object still feels unnatural. Unsurprisingly, she seeks safety in an inconspicuous and unremarkable choice. The fine, leghorn straw bonnet, lined with palest pink silk and conservatively trimmed with rose-pink jacquard ribbon is discreet when compared to the more ebullient, more heavily embellished examples found in fashion plates of the period.[71] But back in Haworth, where it still remains, even this more demure bonnet transforms into something 'infinitely too gay' for a clergyman's daughter of modest means.

Charlotte's persistent struggle with the complex demands of the mid-nineteenth-century fashionable world and indeed, with that side of celebrity that she found so difficult, is tangibly demonstrated in a striped silk gown trimmed with artificial flowers, bows and lace.[72] The gown, the second key witness to her fame years, has remained at the Brontë Parsonage Museum for as long as curatorial memory extends. Yet, it is so opulent, so lavish, that it was never considered Charlotte's; it was, quite simply, an anomaly. After finding it, tucked away in the Bonnell Store, administrative checks were made, yet no paperwork relating to the striped silk gown could be found, including any references to the arrival of the gown at the parsonage. No known history (mythical or otherwise) could be unearthed. Only one obvious conclusion remained – that if, when studied, the size of the dress proved comparable with others held within Charlotte's collection, then this gown, however incongruous its design, might also have been one of those found holed up in the wall during the museum renovations of 1936.

Until this new research was undertaken, the embellished silk gown had never been placed on show or given credence. It was a book that had been judged entirely by its cover. But its bewildering design was not reason enough to discount it as once having been owned by Charlotte. Perhaps it would prove to be the item that would challenge our preconceptions more than any other?

Similarities were soon found between the size of the striped silk and Brontë's 'Paisley Dress', worn in the early to mid-1840s and with excellent provenance.[73] The measurements suggest that, if allowances are made for the difference in

8.4 *Charlotte Brontë's blue-and-cream striped silk gown, early 1850s, D10*

the style and date, both gowns were worn by a small woman of similar height to Charlotte Brontë. The lack of any major alterations also points towards her ownership. Just like the 'Governess Dress', only small mends remain, suggesting that it did not pass through the hands of subsequent owners and had probably always remained at the parsonage.

In terms of design, Charlotte's gown has a collarless neckline with a lace-trimmed opening at the front, a full, floor-length skirt and bell-shaped sleeves that finish at mid-forearm. The main body of the dress has been made from a striped, woven 'changeant' silk. The nine-panelled skirt features panels of differing widths and has been lined using heavy, glazed cotton. All around the front of the gown to just beyond the hip on each side, 4 cm-wide knife pleats have been used to reduce the fabric at the waist. At the back of the skirt and on either side of the long placket, fine cartridge pleats have been incorporated to ensure an elegant drape at the rear.

At the front of the skirt, left of centre, is a large deep pocket which has been lined with the same glazed cotton as that used to line the bodice. These male-style, sewn-in pockets were present in female clothing as early as 1690 and were sometimes used instead of the ever popular, aforementioned tie-on pocket.[74] On the right-hand side of the skirt is another narrow but deep pocket that has been lined with the same striped silk as the gown. This would, in all likelihood, have held a watch, but the lack of so capacious a pocket in any of Charlotte's other surviving dresses, as well as the different style of stitching evident on the main seams, suggests that the silk gown was made by a dressmaker.[75]

The bell-shaped sleeves have been ornately trimmed in keeping with more opulent fashions of the very late 1840s and early 1850s, whilst the embellishments of the skirt are clustered 'en tablier', meaning the decorations were centred in a triangular formation down the front.[76] By the mid- to late 1840s, women's newspapers and journals were filled with images of gowns 'en tablier' and the custom continued to be popular until the early 1850s. The fashion was largely restricted to formal day or evening wear and therefore to garments worn by the upper- and middle-classes. The embellishments on Brontë's gown take the form of wide, bias-cut strips of the same blue-and-cream silk, bows of embossed, chiffon ribbon and large and small bouquets of waxed paper leaves and cotton lily-of-the-valley blooms.

8.5 *Ribbon and faux flower detail on lower bodice of D10*

Long, v-shaped bodices were often seen in formal day or demi-formal evening dresses of the 1840s and early 1850s – and particularly in gowns made from silk. In the case of the striped dress, and therefore in keeping with many dresses of the period, the pleats are soft and voluminous at the shoulder but become gradually narrower, closer together and more controlled as they reach the long 'v' at the centre front. Great skill has been employed to ensure that the stripes of the silk remain straight, despite the softness of the pleating.

The bodice has been lightly boned to add structure, with three bones fanning from the centre-front and side bones running up to the armpit. Hooks and eyes close the bodice at the back but the original hand-sewn eyes have been become strained with tension and a second row of eyes has been added.

This time, metal eyelets have been attached to a heavy-duty cotton tape to help protect the fragile silk.

The elaborate floral trimmings, ample skirt and sumptuous fabric immediately mark this gown as conspicuous attire, but aspects of its design raise some important questions that have great bearing on Charlotte's complex relationship with fame. The high neckline and demi-long sleeves suggest that it would have been worn to formal, public daytime events or to evening dinners that required conspicuous or demi-full dress. Yet, ornate, floral embellishments like those seen on the blue-and-cream striped silk were normally reserved for the most formal of evening events such as a ball or a visit to the opera, making this dress something of a conundrum.[77]

Throughout the years 1848–52 conspicuous day-dresses were normally made from coloured (sometimes patterned) silks and were trimmed with ribbons, braid or heavy fringing.[78] Either collared chemisettes or white cotton, lace or lawn collars were worn at the neck and cuffs were also added. There are many examples of such items in Brontë's surviving wardrobe, but the absence of pin or stitch marks at the neck and the unusual shape of the neckline suggest that the blue-and-cream dress was not worn with a collar.[79] The addition of flowers, which made laundering difficult, also indicates that the gown is likely to have been saved for occasional wear. However, to add to the confusion, the straining around the handsewn eyes and subsequent repair, demonstrates that the garment has been either well-used or, alternatively, that Charlotte's predilection for a tight fit at the waist caused some damage to the dress.

Formal dinner gowns were typically worn without collars and often feature a greater proliferation of passementerie (elaborate trimmings of fringing, braid or cord), lace or richly coloured or embroidered ribbons.[80] Charlotte's gown does comply with at least some of these classifications, and it is therefore feasible that it was worn to one of the many dinners to which she was invited when staying as the guest of Smith, Gaskell, Martineau or the Kay-Shuttleworths. It is equally possible that it was worn at an evening dinner party in 1850, attended by poet and cultural critic Matthew Arnold and the Prussian Ambassador, and held at the home of the historian Thomas Arnold.[81] The presence of floral adornments, customarily the reserve of full evening dress, suggest that the gown might well have been designed to wear at more formal events such as a ball or opera. Certainly, Brontë had need of full dress.

On her visit to London in 1850, she attended a ball at the Smith's house near Hyde Park, where she 'sat with' George Henry Lewes 'for a great part of the evening'.[82] In 1849 and then twice in 1851, Charlotte also joined the Smiths at the theatre. Her publisher also took her to a second opera and, though the exact performance remains unconfirmed, it is likely that they saw Meyerbeer's *Les Huguenots* at Covent Garden on 8 June 1850. Newspaper reports suggest that on that evening, the performance attracted a 'crowded house' and the 'Duke and Duchess of Cambridge, Prince George and Princess Mary of Cambridge occupied her Majesty's box'.[83]

Though Charlotte clearly had need for grand, evening wear, the floral adornments and bows on Charlotte's gown are the only obvious sign of full dress. Gowns worn to the opera or ball were typically low cut, off the shoulder, short-sleeved and generally made from plain, sumptuous fabrics and then heavily trimmed and embellished.[84] Therefore, if the striped gown, with its high neck and demi-full (or three-quarter length) sleeves was indeed worn to any one of the conspicuous, auspicious events to which Charlotte most certainly attended, she can only have appeared prudish and staid.[85]

This is not beyond the bounds of possibility. George Henry Lewes, after meeting Charlotte at the George Smith's ball in June 1850, an evening in which full dress would have been expected and worn by all, later described being faced by a 'little, plain, provincial, sickly-looking old maid'. Though we cannot know if the blue-and-cream gown influenced Lewes' appraisal on this occasion, whatever Charlotte wore that night clearly did nothing to convey youth and vitality.[86] No more did the 'pretty thing' that Charlotte and Ellen sent to their friend Mary Taylor in New Zealand. On pulling the accessory out of the box, Mary apparently cried, 'What veritable old maids you … must have grown if you really use such a thing … The staylace was particularly amusing. I have not seen such a thing in five years.'[87]

Charlotte's own modifications to what was expected of full dress, her deviations from the norm, could be attributed to what Elizabeth Gaskell termed the Reverend Patrick Brontë's 'ideas concerning the simplicity of attire befitting the wife and daughters of a country clergyman'.[88] As an evangelical Christian, Patrick, like many men of the cloth, had strong views about what constituted appropriate dress. Gaskell, in her biography of Charlotte, claimed that Patrick had once cut up one of his wife's dresses in a fit of rage 'because it was not according to his consistent notions of propriety'.[89] She also maintained that Patrick had destroyed his young children's coloured boots because they were 'too gay and luxurious ... and would foster [in them] a love of dress'. Both potentially scurrilous tales were hotly disputed by Nancy Garr, the family's nursemaid, though she did confirm that Patrick had removed the sleeves from his wife's dress on account of them being 'too expansive', before quickly replacing the damaged gown with the silk for a brand-new one, bought at nearby Keighley.[90]

Whatever the truth at the heart of these stories, Patrick had clearly instilled a deep sense of propriety in Charlotte – something that her plain, functional corset, and numerous, modesty enhancing chemisettes confirm. But the changes, or rather potential changes, that she made to typical full dress might have been made for other reasons too – namely a deep-seated desire to embrace frugality. Money had always been a consideration for the Brontës, mainly because it had always had to be. But the growth of materialism and Victorian society's increasing emphasis upon conspicuous consumption was also cause for concern and particularly for those, like Patrick, charged with maintaining the moral and spiritual standards of his community.[91] Again and again, when shopping or mulling over the purchase of an item of dress, Charlotte reveals that she is anxious. Prices are questioned, quality checked. She asks herself, does she need it? Is it worth the money?

Where she can double a garment's use, she does so – her surviving wardrobe is filled with bows, tassels and other embellishments that can be added to plainer styles to change or elevate their look on a shoestring.[92] Therefore, it is certainly feasible that, for reasons of economy, Charlotte's dress, with its high neckline and bountiful trimmings, represents her attempt to fulfil the requirements of both demi-full (smart evening wear) and full dress (the very grandest of evening attire) in one single garment. It is possible that the trimmings were added to the striped silk afterwards, in the admittedly vain hope that it might just pass muster.

Significantly, though, whether the silk gown was worn as a formal day dress, a demi-full dress or full-evening dress, it does not appear to reflect Brontë's usual taste. Certainly, it does not shout 'Charlotte'. But her fish out of water status in London was destabilizing. It confused. It discombobulated. Try as she might, it was not easy to adhere to the complex rules set by London Society –

8.6 *Jacquard ribbon tie, D184*

especially when further constrained by finances and moral considerations that did not affect the majority of those with whom she was now mixing.[93] Though she now had more money than she had ever had before, she still found herself unable to 'keep up with the Jones's'. And, try as she might, Charlotte was no fashionista. This begs the question – how did she end up with a dress like this? Had someone, presumably with more elaborate tastes than her own, helped her, goaded her, guided her?

In her 1853 novel, *Villette*, the last book that Charlotte would complete, she vividly recalls the moment that her protagonist, Lucy Snowe, is gifted a dress. The gown, just like Charlotte's own embellished, blue-and-cream, striped silk gown, is not of her own choosing. It is stylistically alien – it does not personify the Lucy that the reader has come to know in the first nineteen chapters of the novel. This bold scene has truth at it its heart for, like so many incidents included in the novel, it was drawn from Brontë's own experience.[94] Sidney Lee later stated that the 'incident, in all the minuteness of its detail', is true of an identical experience of Charlotte Brontë at Mrs Smith's Bayswater home.[95] George Smith, though he did not refer specifically to the gifting of the dress himself, agreed that '*Villette* is full of scenes which one can trace to incidents which occurred during Miss Brontë's visits to us ... my mother was Mrs Bretton; several of her expressions are given verbatim. I myself, as I discovered, stood for Dr. John.'[96]

It is in Chapter Twenty that the great dress event occurs. Whilst a guest at the Brettons, Lucy Snowe is extended an invitation to accompany Dr John and his mother, Mrs Bretton, to a 'concert', a 'grand affair' attended by the 'King, Queen and Prince of Labassecour'.[97] She recollects:

Mrs. Bretton, coming promptly into my room, desired me to open my drawers and show her my dresses; which I did, without a word.

'That will do,' said she, when she had turned them over. 'You must have a new one.'

She went out. She returned presently with a dressmaker. She had me measured. 'I mean,' said she, 'to follow my own taste, and to have my own way in this little matter.'

Two days after came home - a pink dress!

'That is not for me,' I said, hurriedly, feeling that I would almost as soon clothe myself in the costume of a Chinese lady of rank.

'We shall see whether it is for you or not,' rejoined my godmother, adding with her resistless decision: 'Mark my words. You will wear it this very evening.'

I thought I should not: I thought no human force should avail to put me into it. A pink dress! I knew it not. It knew not me. I had not proved it.

... About six, I was ushered upstairs. Without any force at all, I found myself led and influenced by another's will, unconsulted, unpersuaded, quietly overruled.[98]

Mrs Bretton's inspection of Lucy's 'drawers' is peremptory. Just like Charlotte's, Lucy's wardrobe is limited. According to Mrs Bretton, she does not own a gown suitable for such a 'grand affair', especially one at which royalty is present. The reader is informed that Mrs Bretton's actions are at the instigation of her son, who had insisted upon 'attention to costume' at this socially significant event. There is an overriding sense of urgency and determination. Both Mrs Bretton, and by default Mrs Smith, are in no doubt about the wardrobe deficiencies of their sons' protégée. They cannot allow their sons to be humiliated in front of their hosts. In consequence, decisive action, a direct fulfilment of their matriarchal role, is taken. Lucy, and thereby Charlotte, is taken in hand.

The gifted dress might not be to their taste, but as guest and giftee, they have no choice but to accept it, despite all reservations. Lucy is 'unconsulted', 'unpersuaded', 'overruled'. There is no physical pressure and yet she finds herself 'resistless'. Yet, whilst mindful of the obligations of her position, Lucy's principles and dread of scrutiny prompt her to seek some modification of design. The black 'lace mantle' that she pulls over her shoulders not only subdues the conspicuous attire, but also, and more importantly, shrouds her décolleté. Just like her creator, she professes a 'sense of shame and fear of ridicule' at the thought of 'decking [herself] out to draw attention'.[99] And, despite Mrs Bretton's attempt to dramatically alter Lucy's appearance, so as to make sure that she clearly adheres to the sartorial codes and conventions set by Brussels Society, she was not immune to her guest's reservations. Therefore, the resultant gown, though of 'light fabric and bright tint', was 'made with extreme simplicity, guiltless of flounce and furbelow'.[100] Consequently, Lucy's full dress, though much more appropriate than anything else she that had previously possessed, is still shaped by her reservations. Like Charlotte's own, it is a dress of compromise.

Whether or not the blue-and-cream silk is *the* dress alluded to in this passage, Mrs Smith's intervention must be viewed as a bold criticism of Charlotte's previous efforts to dress correctly in this new alien world. Clearly,

Elizabeth and George Smith had been embarrassed enough on previous occasions to now step in and act. Well used to navigating the critical, demanding and fast-changing sartorial rules of London society themselves, they understood, more fully than did Charlotte, that appropriate dress was essential for success – and not just for her, but for them too. Also, having got to know her, they now grasped just how acutely she felt the criticism of others and, seeing her grapple with the unrelenting demands of the new world into which she had been thrust, felt compelled to help.

One thing is certain, whether the blue-and-cream dress was worn to an opera, to the theatre or to one of the many private dinners that she was now expected to attend, in it, Charlotte would always have been an object of attention, a celebrity. But, as the dress itself has proved, to whichever event she wore it, she would have missed some subtle sartorial nuances, and this would not have gone unnoticed. Therefore, if the 'Thackeray Dress' represents the confident, assertive author at one with herself and enjoying the opportunities her authorship had brought her, the striped silk gown is symbolic of the famed Charlotte Brontë at her most vulnerable. It speaks of the 'other Charlotte' who found social interaction and public scrutiny 'disagreed with her both mentally and physically'.[101]

This constant pressure to adapt and conform only compounded Charlotte's already present and enduring insecurities with regards to her appearance. The unrelenting rounds of dinners, concerts and visits at which focus was often placed squarely upon her, took their toll. Famed socialite Monckton Milnes, on meeting Charlotte at a lecture in London in 1849, noted how 'the shy little person in a bonnet lined with pink silk ... had to endure the ordeal of being stared at through the lorgnettes of the fine people who crowded Willis's Rooms', and who later formed an 'avenue of eager and admiring faces' down which she had to pass to leave the lecture hall.[102] The impact of such experiences on a previously sheltered woman, already suffering from low self-esteem and body dysmorphia, was significant. Early in their relationship Gaskell discerned Charlotte's 'nervous dread of encountering strangers' and 'ascribed this to the idea of her personal ugliness, which had been strongly impressed upon her imagination early in life, and which she exaggerated to herself in a remarkable manner'.[103] After relaying an occasion

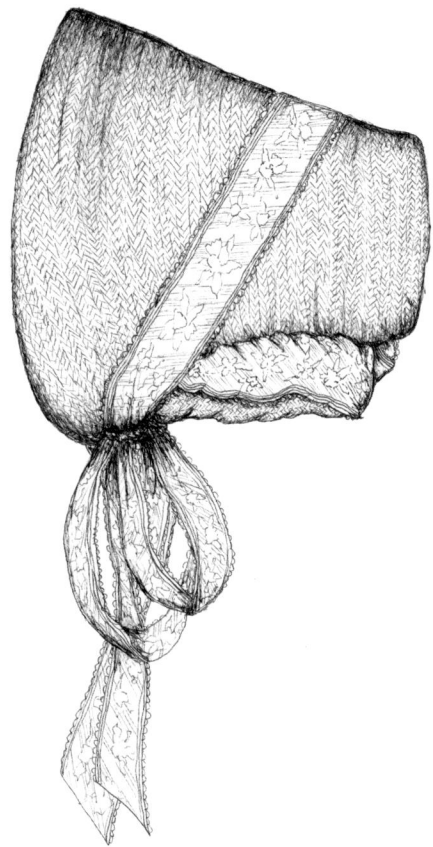

8.7 *Charlotte Brontë's pink-lined leghorn straw bonnet, D140*

where Brontë's 'courage had failed her' and she had found herself physically unable to enter a room and meet the sister of some friends, Gaskell recalled Charlotte's poignant proclamation that, 'after a stranger has once looked at [her] face, he is careful not to let his eyes wander to that part of the room again'.[104]

Elizabeth Gaskell was not the only person to notice Brontë's deep anxiety about her appearance. Fame, it seemed, had done little to either alleviate Charlotte's vulnerability or to teach her how to conceal it. George Smith, who also did not meet her until 1848, declared her 'uneasily and perpetually conscious' of the fact that 'there was little of the feminine charm about her'.[105]

Even forty-five years after Charlotte's death, he remained unbending in his belief that, 'the possession of genius did not lift her above the weakness of an excessive anxiety about her personal appearance'. From his patriarchal perspective, it is clear that he failed to fathom why Charlotte's rare 'genius' and her resultant, hard-won 'fame', were not enough to halt her persistent insecurity.

As a businessman preoccupied with producing bestselling books, in a sphere far more accepting of men than it ever was of women, Smith was blinkered. From his perspective, the uncommon literary success that she had so craved had been made a reality. Yet Charlotte, having got it, 'had found it was of no use'. According to Mary Taylor, 'her solitary life had disqualified her for society'.[106] Indeed, she had found to her detriment that:

Fame is a bee.
It has a song -
It has a sting -
Ah, too, it has a wing.[107]

Success, despite its many perks, had turned the act of writing into a 'literary tight-rope dancing machine for gold'.[108] It had become abundantly clear to Charlotte that in order to earn her living by her pen, public exposure was a necessary evil. She now comprehended that literary success was reliant not only upon her prodigious talent, but also upon her *being* a celebrity – on her feeding the insatiable appetites of the publishing industry and the reading public. Charlotte's first-hand experience of this demanding triumvirate led her to paint 'her impressions of London life in most forbidding colours', expressing a 'clear, cutting, intense distaste of it'.[109] She believed Thackeray had sold his soul 'to the Great Ladies',[110] had sacrificed his great mind to be 'pet and darling' of the duchesses and marchionesses who filled his coffers.[111] Entirely ill at ease in their presence, Charlotte Brontë had no desire to follow suit.

The pain inflicted by constant promotion and parading were only compounded by the constant expectation of production. The ever-present pressure to yield new work also began to weigh heavily on the increasingly tired Charlotte. Of her later manuscripts, Gaskell recalled Brontë's 'utter weariness' and frustration over 'the labour they had given her'.[112] In the late summer of 1850 Charlotte admitted that she 'had looked literary life full in the face and was contented to die in Haworth, rather than live like that'.[113]

But fame brought pleasure as well as pain. Charlotte continued to exchange letters with Smith and Smith Williams, with Gaskell and with Martineau. She acted as 'unofficial reviewer' for Smith, Elder and Company and, accordingly, helped to 'shape the literary tastes of the popular market'.[114] She was unceasing in her enjoyment of her meetings with Thackeray and found gratification in the intellectual stimulation of some of the lectures and exhibitions to which she was invited. She was awed by the Great Exhibition of 1851 and deeply moved by her arranged visits to Pentonville and Newgate prisons, Bethlehem Hospital and the Foundling Hospital.[115] Her earnings – though not enough upon which to rely – and her own and her father's apparent pride in her achievements were also of great import. Yet, despite all these things, Brontë's yearning to be 'forever known' had waned and, as the seasoned socialite Monckton Milnes observed, there was now 'a loneliness amid her fame' which 'touched [him] keenly'.[116]

9

The Wedding Dress

Although unaware of it at the time, Charlotte first met the man that she would later marry in the spring of 1845. The Reverend Arthur Bell Nicholls, a 'strong built, somewhat-hard-featured' twenty-six-year-old, had arrived at the parsonage on 18 May, fresh from ordination and ready to work.[1] This earnest, new curate from Killead, Country Antrim did not, it must be admitted, incite great passion in her – it was no love at first sight, he was too staid for that. 'He appears a respectable young man', wrote Charlotte stiffly soon after his arrival, 'he reads well, and I hope will give satisfaction.'[2]

Though he lacked her father's natural charm, he did give satisfaction and quickly proved himself an able, hard-working and solicitous new addition to the Haworth community. Much of the heavy burden of pastoral work was soon lifted from the increasingly frail Patrick's shoulders, freeing him to concentrate on other, less physically arduous aspects of parish work. The two men worked well together, meaning Arthur naturally spent a great deal of time at the parsonage. His visits, necessary and innocuous as they were, caused an inevitable frisson of excitement to ripple through the village – was 'Miss Brontë … going to be married to her papa's Curate?' Charlotte's response was characteristically acerbic, causing her to maintain that 'never was a rumour more unfounded … A cold, far-away sort of civility are the only terms on which I had ever been with Mr Nicholls'.[3]

In spite of her protestations and his dogmatism, Charlotte did eventually warm to Arthur. Humour proved a uniting force. She greatly enjoyed the fact that he often found their fellow parishioners so amusing that he would 'laugh out' at importune moments.[4] He, in return, had been so tickled by her thinly veiled descriptions of local curates in *Shirley* that he had given 'vent to roars of laughter' and clapped and stamped his feet on the floor in delight. He was even entertained by those refences to himself. Indeed, they were the cause of so much laughter that the sexton and his wife, with whom he lived, thought he had 'gone wrong in the head'.[5]

It is difficult to pinpoint exactly when Arthur's feelings for Charlotte transitioned from friend and colleague to something more like love. The turbulent events of his youth, which saw him, and his brother, removed to their uncle's house following the premature death of their father, had made him naturally reticent and slow to form attachments. But once he did so, as Charlotte herself perceived, they were 'close and deep – like an underground stream, running strong but in a narrow channel'.[6] Charlotte noted a marked change in his conduct towards her in the early summer of 1851. It was then that he changed from his usual argumentative and inflexible self, to 'extremely good – mild and uncontentious'.[7] Though she could not see a reason for his improved behaviour at the time, it was not long before she grasped its root cause. By the end of 1852 the penny had fully dropped, prompting Charlotte to write to Ellen, 'I have felt for some time – the meaning of his constant looks – and strange feverish restraint.'[8]

A 'statue-like' 'Mr. N' proposed on 13 December 1852. 'Shaking from head to foot, looking deadly pale, speaking low, vehemently yet with difficulty', he stuttered out his surprising offer of marriage, leaving Charlotte in a state of 'strange shock'. As his strong feelings for her were not at all reciprocated, she was not inclined to accept, but, aware of his unstable emotional state, did not reject his request outright, as she had done other offers before. Rather, she promised him 'a reply on the morrow' and, on seeing Arthur out, made her way along the corridor to talk over the matter with her father.[9]

Patrick's response was far removed from the calm, quiet and measured one that Charlotte might have anticipated. He was, quite simply, incandescent with rage. His astonished daughter later described how, on hearing the news, he had immediately 'worked himself into a state not to be trifled with – the veins on his temples started up like a whip-cord – and his eyes suddenly became blood-shot'. Clearly, he deemed Nicholls entirely unworthy of his famous, talented and now only daughter. To him, Arthur's seemingly lowly status, Puseyite views, Irish background and the underhand nature of his proposal, were an anathema. He would not, on any account, agree to the marriage. Frightened for her father's health, Charlotte quickly moved to offer Mr Nicholls her 'distinct refusal', leaving him in no doubt that all hope was lost.[10]

The cordial relationship between the two men was effectively severed from this point on. Arthur's misery was abject and Patrick's anger unrelenting. With no realistic prospect of a change, Nicholls began to make radical plans to leave Haworth. In a desperate attempt to distract himself, he wrote to the Society for the Propagation of the Gospel to offer himself as a missionary to the Australian Colonies of Sydney, Melbourne or Adelaide.[11] Distance, he now believed, was the only remedy for a broken heart. But when the time came, Nicholls did not board a ship bound for the other side of the world. He found he could not be so far away from Charlotte – somewhere deep within him, some hope still lingered after all.

His decision to stay in Yorkshire, albeit thirty-two miles away in Pontefract, did little to diminish his grief during the months in which he worked out his notice. He continued 'to struggle with his dejection' and according to onlookers, 'gave way to it in a manner to draw notice'.[12] He sat 'drearily in his rooms', sought 'no confidant', 'rejected his meals' and looked 'ill and miserable'.[13] No one could fail to notice Nicholls's conspicuous wretchedness, but, though concerned for his welfare, and disconcerted by his erratic behaviour, Charlotte's attention was necessarily diverted by other, more pressing matters.

On 28 January 1853, her new novel, *Villette*, was published. She had arrived in London in late December to finish her final edits under George Smith's roof. This trip was far quieter than those that had gone before it, but, though Charlotte's time was largely taken up with work, she did enjoy eye-opening visits to Pentonville and Newgate prisons, to the Bank of England, the Foundling Hospital and even to Bedlam – the infamous psychiatric hospital at St George's Field. Charlotte's interests had previously focused on the plight of the plain and on the miserable experiences of teachers and of governesses. But, with her latest book now finished, the pressure to find a new subject for her next novel was building. She had almost exhausted her own experience and, now with access to the very latest books, she cannot have failed to notice the new emphasis being placed on social issues. The time had come to expand her horizons and, as leading literary lights like Gaskell and Dickens had done before her, even consider those yet more unfortunate than herself.

Charlotte returned home to Haworth buoyed by an awakened imagination and generally excellent reviews of her latest work. Patrick, who was still seething over Nicholls, was also much cheered by the favourable assessments of *Villette* and openly revelled in his daughter's success. Arthur's dramatic dejection was the only thing to spoil Charlotte's good mood. His public moping and constant hangdog expression had begun to grate. With more than two months remaining before he was due to leave Haworth for Pontefract, Charlotte found she could stand it no longer and took the opportunity to accept a longstanding invitation to visit Mrs Gaskell in Manchester.

Charlotte had clearly been under the impression that her visit to Gaskell's house would be a quiet one, but on arrival she realized that it would be no such thing. She was immediately confronted with a houseful of strangers. As might be expected, her response was not a happy one. The insecurities that had dogged Charlotte since youth came flooding back. Unfortunately, her 'constrained' behaviour and her deep fear of being rejected by others because of her appearance, soon became very apparent to Mrs Gaskell and her guests.[14] The visit lasted a little less than a week, but for Gaskell, the stay felt far longer. However, having now grasped the true extent of her friend's vulnerability, her fondness for the 'piteous' Miss Brontë had only grown.[15]

Returning home to Haworth after her ordeal, Charlotte found Nicholls's spirits were lower than ever. In what was the last Sunday service over which he would preside as assistant curate at St Michael and All Angels, Charlotte reported to Ellen that 'he struggled – faltered – then lost command over himself – stood before my eyes and in sight of all the communicants white, shaking voiceless … and could only with difficulty whisper and falter through the service'. Such was the spectacle, that many of the female parishioners present sobbed in sympathy. Even Charlotte found she could not 'quite check her own tears'.[16]

Patrick's violently negative response had had the opposite effect to that which he had intended. Charlotte's feelings for Mr Nicholls had ricocheted back and forth since his proposal the previous December. She had found his conspicuous wretchedness arduous, but there was something about his passion, his near obsession with her, that was magnetic to the creator of Edward Rochester and Paul Emmanuel. Now that the time had actually come for him to leave, she felt herself pulled in two directions. 'I may be losing the purest gem', she wrote to Ellen anxiously, 'and to me far the most precious – life can give – genuine attachment – or I may be escaping the yoke of a morose temper'.[17] But whatever her own thoughts, whatever conclusion she might have come to if left to herself, her 'conscience [would] not suffer [her] to take one step in opposition to [her] Papa's will'.[18] Consequently, on 26 May 1853, a most dejected Arthur Bell Nicholls left Haworth, believing that he might never stand in the presence of the woman that he loved ever again.

The summer that followed brought many troubles to the parsonage. Charlotte's health deteriorated sharply. Influenza followed by a bout of constant headaches depleted her and then, just as she began to improve, Patrick suffered a serious 'stroke of paralysis' in which his sight was temporarily lost.[19] Aware that no one of any calibre had stepped in to help shoulder the burden of the parish and of the heavy load that had now landed squarely upon Charlotte, Arthur quickly rushed to extend letters of concern. His motivations, were not, it can safely be said, entirely selfless, but Charlotte could not fail to notice his kindness and was not unmoved by his attentions.

It was after the sixth, solicitous letter from Nicholls that she finally relented. And so began a clandestine correspondence in which they sought to share the minutiae of their lives via letter. For Charlotte, this communication marked the beginning of something new, something different. And as the weeks passed and the number of letters increased, her feelings for 'Mr N.' deepened. They did not constitute love, but as she was all too aware, he had passion enough for the both of them.

On discovering Charlotte's slow-changing position, her friends came down on either side. Ellen, concerned that Nicholls would steal her own place in Charlotte's heart, tried to discourage the relationship. The more broadminded Mary Taylor reasoned that Charlotte should 'consider her own pleasure' first and marry if that was her wish.[20] But, as those around her debated the situation behind her back, Charlotte took time to consider her position. Her father's health had not improved and, with her siblings gone, there was now no one left with whom she could share the load. Patrick would not, she knew, be there forever and once gone she would be alone. Fame had proved unsatisfying – worse, the consequent scrutiny had further stripped her of confidence. Literary success had given her some financial security, but there was no certainty that this source of income would continue. She knew now just what it took to maintain her position as a bestselling author. When all these things were squarely faced, marriage, even pragmatic marriage, to a man she respected but did not love, begun to look increasingly attractive.

These things all had undeniable bearing, but it was something else entirely that seems to have tipped the balance of Charlotte's mind. Almost from their first meeting, she had found herself attracted to George Smith. Rich, successful, handsome and eight years her junior, it is not hard to see what she saw in him. She had not vocalized her feelings; indeed, she was not even conscious of the true extent of them, but the hope of something had lingered on, nonetheless. She had read fondness in his letters. She had perceived affection in his kindness. Mrs Smith, with her mother's instincts attuned to the author's quiet ambitions, had done all she could to put Charlotte off. The socially-awkward former governess was, after all, no match for her ambitious, capable son. But though the issue was never directly broached, and though Smith had not done nearly as much as she believed to encourage her in her hopes, Brontë chose not to be dissuaded.

It is not known whether Charlotte arranged her own November 1853 trip to London with the express goal of discerning George's own feelings before finally deciding to raise Nicholls's hopes further or whether she did indeed, as she wrote to Mrs Gaskell, have 'business' to which she knew she must attend.[21] Smith had remained quiet since mid-summer so there were certainly outstanding issues yet to discuss. But before she had even left for London, the real reason for her editor's silence was made clear. It was not Smith who informed her of his happy news. This near impossible task fell to his mother. In answer to Charlotte's news-enquiring letter, she promptly wrote that her son was 'quite well and happy' and about to take 'a very important step in Life'. For having met Elizabeth Blakeway, a wealthy and beautiful wine merchant's daughter in April of that year, he had found himself besotted. Now, with the full blessing of his friends and family, he would soon be married.[22]

Only the draft has survived, but the fact there was a draft at all shows how difficult this letter proved to write. Mrs Smith's words are considered but they are fierce. Aware that finality was kinder than circumlocution, all doubts were, quite deliberately, quashed. Charlotte was left in no doubt – George Smith Esq. had been taken off the market. The consequences were severe. The London trip was cancelled. A huge box of borrowed books, accompanied by a terse note, were returned to Smith, Elder and Company and Smith's eventual letter, which detailed his engagement, was answered with a missive that, even after years of friendship, ran to just two lines. She wrote,

My dear Sir,
In great happiness, as in great grief – words of sympathy should be few.
Accept my meed of congratulation – and believe me
Sincerely yours,
C. Brontë[23]

Even George Smith cannot have failed to perceive her pique and pain. For Charlotte it was a deep severance – one from which the relationship could never recover. Though she knew she could not prove it, like the fictional Dr John, he had deceived her, he had rejected her, he had abandoned her. But Smith's loss would prove Arthur Bell Nicholls's gain. What could she now do but to turn to the one person who had shown her unwavering adoration? He, she knew, could be relied upon. He, she knew, desired her unequivocally. He, she knew, would love her unconditionally. And oh, how she needed love.

Six months had now passed since her surreptitious communications with Nicholls had first begun. But Charlotte was not in the habit of lying to her father and even though her recent disappointment had proved a distraction, the burden of her secret soon weighed heavily upon her conscience. As she wrote to Ellen, 'I grew very miserable in keeping it from Papa. At last sheer pain made me gather courage to break it – I told all.'[24] Boldly, determinedly, she set about changing her father's staunch position:

Father, I am not a young girl, not a young woman even – I never was pretty. I now am ugly. At your death I will have £300 besides the little I have earned myself—do you think there are many men who would serve seven years for me? ... I must marry a curate if I marry at all; not merely a curate but *your* curate; not merely *your* curate but he must live in the house with you, for I cannot leave you.[25]

That Charlotte's feelings of insecurity over her appearance should figure so heavily in her argument should come as no surprise. They had done so at almost every key moment in her life before. Fame had done little to lessen her acute awareness of her looks or to dilute her strong belief in their far-reaching power to repel. Her deeply romantic self had always longed for many 'Jacobs' willing to 'serve' seven years of labour in order to win her hand. Yet, as she grew older, she found herself even less able to identify with the 'shapely and beautiful' Rachel.[26] Ironically though, despite her fears that no one would ever love her enough to serve seven years, Arthur had already done so. And little did either of them know then, he would serve Patrick for many more – and the majority of them after Charlotte's death.

Patrick was not happy with Charlotte's decision, but even he could see that things could not go on as they had forever. Begrudgingly, he gave his consent, finally persuaded by the promise that Arthur would reside with them in the parsonage and take up his duties as his curate once again. The engagement announcements were restrained, much, it would seem, like Charlotte's feelings for 'Mr N.'. Many years before, she had advised Ellen, 'No young lady should fall in love till the offer has been made, accepted – the marriage ceremony performed, and the first half year of wedded life has passed away.'[27] Now, with her own nuptials looming, it was as if she were sticking to her own rule. Largely gone, it appeared, was the romantic girl who had fed herself on a diet of Byron, fine frocks and fiction, on imaginary worlds and passionate love affairs. Largely gone, it seemed, was the woman who had cried 'All my heart is yours, sir: it belongs to you; and with you it would remain, were fate to exile the rest of me from your presence forever.'[28] This time, though she had been moved by the passion of the man who loved her, her head was ruling her heart.

The clothes that Charlotte chose to wear for her wedding day – both those that have survived and those that have not – offer unprecedented insight into her conflicted state of mind as she approached her wedding day. More than mere fripperies, these highly communicative items have much to reveal

9.1 Annotated drawing of Charlotte Brontë's reconstructed wedding dress, 2003/17

about her role as bride, her relationship with her body, with her age, with her changing place in society, even with her future aspirations. Her careful choices show that Charlotte was acutely aware that the clothes that she wore on her wedding day would play a central role in this highly public performance.[29]

Like many brides, Charlotte approached the task of choosing her wedding attire with some trepidation. After all, there was much for her to consider. She was a mature actor in a play whose principal characters tended to be youthful. She was a remarkable woman marrying an unremarkable man. She was a woman of some means marrying a man of none.[30] She hated to be looked at but had long desired to be a bride. She naturally desired romance but in her choice of husband had been overcome with pragmatism. She longed to be beautiful but knew herself to be decidedly plain. Whether cognizant of these powerful contradictions, or of their influence, Charlotte's choice of dress must, she knew, meet both her own expectations and those of the other people present that June morning. A note, thought to have been written to Elizabeth Gaskell after Charlotte's trips to Leeds and Halifax to arrange her wedding trousseau, reveals her anxious state of mind:

> … my conscience is satisfied – a sort of fawn-coloured silk and a <?silver> drab barège with a little green spot in it – (I left them with the dress-maker at Halifax or you should have specimens-) Of the third – the wedding-dress – I wholly decline the responsibility. It must be charged upon a sort of friendly compulsion or over-persuasion. Nothing would satisfy some of my friends but white which I told you I would <u>not</u> wear. Accordingly, they dressed me in white by way of trial – vowed away their consciences that nothing had ever suited me so well – and white I had to buy and <u>did</u> buy to my own amazement – but I took care to get it in cheap material there were some insinuations about silk and tulle and I don't know what – but I stuck convulsively to muslin – plain book muslin with a tuck or two. Also the white veil – I took care should be a matter of 5s – being simply of tulle with little tucks. If I must make a fool of myself – it shall be on an economical plan. Now I have told you all.
>
> C.B.[31]

The language that Charlotte uses is enlightening. In the phrase 'my conscience is satisfied' she attempts to reassure herself (and Mrs Gaskell) that she has given full moral consideration to these important decisions whilst her use of the word 'the' before the phrase 'wedding-dress' replaces the possessive adjective 'my' that we might expect her to use.[32] This linguistic alteration suggests that Brontë viewed the symbolic garment (her wedding dress) as something from which she was disconnected, a fact reinforced by her subsequent declaration: 'I wholly decline the responsibility.'

The terms 'friendly compulsion' and 'over-persuasion' are also carefully chosen to implicate others. Charlotte (probably untruthfully) intimates that she has been overpowered by a group of 'friends' – an amorphous assembly of people whom she does not identify. Whether or not the coercive forces to which Charlotte alludes were as strong as she suggests, the letter implies that her mind was changed, and her choices reversed: 'Nothing would satisfy some of my friends but white which I told you I would *not* wear.'

Yet again, in her choice of dress, Charlotte has been, or more accurately, has allowed herself to be, influenced by others. But her own unconscious longing for the romantic obviously also had bearing. As she admitted to Elizabeth Gaskell, 'white [she] did buy to [her] own amazement'. In this audacious act, Charlotte has overturned her earlier decree that her purchases should be neither 'expensive or extensive' and that they should be practical enough to be 'turned to decent use and worn after the wedding-day'.[33]

Frugality, as one might expect from a clergyman's daughter and soon to be clergyman's wife, is also underscored. She vehemently claims, and with perhaps more vigour than is necessary, to have firmly resisted temptation and to have 'stuck convulsively' to cheaper muslin over silk. She chooses too, a tulle veil 'with little tucks' over more expensive lace, for if, as she claimed, she 'must make a fool of [herself] – it should be on an economical plan'.

Charlotte's note highlights her overt fear of criticism. Clearly, the bullying that she had faced as a teenager at Roe Head School because of her unfashionable clothing, and the sartorial mistakes that she had made in her early trips to London after the publication of *Jane Eyre*, had left their mark. But although she fully expects that her choice of bridalwear will see her deemed a 'fool', someone deficient of all sense, she still opts to wear a youthful, white bridal gown. When the actual moment of decision came, Brontë had chosen romance over practicality – something she had simply not done in her choice of husband.

Today, the fact that Charlotte wore white to her wedding at the age of thirty-seven raises little consternation. Most women marrying, at whatever age, do. In the year 2023, the average age of a British bride for a first marriage was 34, whilst at last count, 83% choose to wear white for their big day.[34] In 1854, the year that Charlotte married, the median age of a first-time bride living in the West Riding of Yorkshire was only 23.3 years old.[35] Moreover, the wearing of bridal white was a relatively new phenomenon. For though she was not the first bride to have worn it, it was not until Queen Victoria married Prince Albert on 10 February 1840 that the white wedding dress became cemented in tradition.[36] Where, previously, the white dress had been the preserve of the wealthy due to its post-wedding impracticality, it quickly became the popular choice for all strata of society. From 1840 onward, white bridalwear began to appear in fashion plates, magazines and novels, and white bridal fabrics were placed in shop windows and displayed at the Great Exhibition of 1851, which Charlotte visited on five separate occasions.

Despite the growth of this trend, older brides still commonly chose to wear coloured dresses to the altar. As etiquette expert Clara de Chatelain wrote in 1856, although it could not be 'fancied' that 'any young maiden be dressed otherwise than in white', it was believed that there was 'a modest propriety in [widows or the more mature] declining to play the bride'.[37] Yet, as the inscription upon William Mulready's 1846 painting *Choosing the Wedding Gown* attests, brides who opted 'not for a glossy surface but for such qualities as would wear well', still ensured 'the dress always conformed to the current fashion'.[38] The surviving wedding dress of Mary Brownfield, aged thirty-two, corroborates this trend, for at her marriage to silk manufacturer Ferdinando Jackson at Bethesda Chapel, Hanley, on 20 October 1842, she wore a grey corded silk and wool gown, figured with a twilled design and trimmed with pleated ribbon. In keeping with contemporary styles, the bodice was boned, the skirt full. Agnes Eleanor Hubbersty of Darley, North Yorkshire was thirty-one years old at the time of her 1843 marriage to forty-two-year-old magistrate, Nicholas Price

Wood. She sported a vibrant, red satin silk dress with detachable sleeves which would have later been worn as both smart day and fashionable evening wear.

Even many younger women of a similar social status to Charlotte opted for a coloured wedding dress that could be used on future occasions. Plain-coloured silk garments could be easily altered and did not date as quickly as did patterned cotton/muslin fabrics, though these were sometimes worn. Elizabeth Wright, aged twenty-eight, who married tailor James Powell in the village of Marden in 1839, chose a plain, plum-coloured satin to best convey her future aspirations as the wife of a successful artisan.[39] Ellen Whipp of Clitheroe wore a tartan check silk dress on the event of her marriage to master grocer William Hargreaves in 1849, whilst Mary Abigail Williams, aged twenty-one, elected for a pale lavender silk dress trimmed with cream lace and mauve, silk ribbon for her marriage to the Rev. William Edward Cousins in Oxford on 4 May 1865. Even Charlotte herself had previously declared that, should her friend Ellen Nussey ever marry, she would give her the choice of 'silver-grey and white' or 'dove-colour and pale pink' for her wedding gown, but that for Ellen's sister Ann, 'some shade of violet would be preferable'.[40]

There is nothing to suggest that Brontë's white, full-skirted muslin gown was worn again after her wedding, and it is not thought to have survived. However, much evidence about the dress remains and, as with many of her surviving garments, its story is captivating.

Following the author's death in March 1855, Charlotte's wedding dress, some flowers from the wedding bonnet, a stole, a pair of gloves and some handkerchiefs embroidered with the letters C.B.N. were safely stored away in a box labelled 'Rowntree's of Scarborough'[41] and/or in the bottom 'drawer'[42] of a 'press'[43] or 'tallboy'.[44] After Patrick's death in 1861, Nicholls returned home to Ireland. The wedding garments, amongst some other items that had been added later, accompanied him to Banagher, apparently in the same box in which they had originally been stored.[45] They remained at his farmhouse until Nicholls's death, when they were bequeathed to his niece, aptly named Charlotte Brontë Nicholls, on the condition that she agreed to burn the entire wedding ensemble before she died. It had always been presumed that, three years before her death, she had carried out Arthur's final wishes.[46] Indeed, according to Margaret Ross of Belfast, Charlotte Brontë Nicholls's own niece, the wedding dress *was* burnt, in Bath, in or around the year 1954. But another source (who has asked to remain anonymous) has since claimed that the gown was instead sent to the Belfast Museum after Charlotte Brontë Nicholls's death, or, more specifically, to the Ulster Museum Textile Collection. If this was the case, then the dress was, ironically, still engulfed in flames, though not for another twenty years or more. For in a fateful twist, in November 1976 a terrorist bomb that targeted Malone House, Belfast (the then headquarters of the National Trust in Ireland) caused a fire to rip through the building where the wedding dress would have been housed. The entire collection and all accompanying paperwork were lost. No record of the gown's arrival in 1954 could now be found, if, of course, it had ever even been there.

Whether the gown was reduced to ashes in 1954 or 1976, it did not do so before Frances Bell, a niece of Mr Nicholls's second wife, had been shown the dress and accessories.[47] Margaret Ross also saw the dress and, when still a child, was allowed to try it on.[48] She noted how small the dress was and also memorized its style, shape and design, as well as that of the other items that Charlotte apparently wore on her big day. In 1964, soon before she herself died, Ross described the wedding dress to Lisbon journalist, Elsie Ashe, and to the Irish Chapter of the Brontë Society. They arranged for sketches of the original dress to be drawn up, just as Ross remembered it.[49] Though these drawings have never resurfaced, in 1967 a replica of the dress, based upon them, was created by costumier Jean Agnew.

Photographs of the reconstructed dress were taken, and these have survived. After some considerable detective work, Agnew's actual gown was located in the parish church of Drumballyroney, County Down, Northern Ireland and the associated paperwork to Banbridge District Council. Since then, staff from the Brontë Parsonage Museum have been to visit it in the church. In fact, this replica can still be seen there, if the key to the church is first collected from the church warden who lives nearby.

Margaret Ross was a young girl when she saw and tried on the wedding dress but there are some aspects of her recollection that can confirmed with certainty – namely that the dress was made from white muslin. Of course, Charlotte herself speaks of the purchase of this finely woven fabric in her letter to Mrs Gaskell in the days leading up to her wedding. Gaskell was not present on the day itself, but later spoke to those who were there,[50] and confirmed Charlotte's choice, pronouncing that the dress was fashioned from 'white embroidered muslin'.[51] Arthur's niece, Frances Bell, also described the dress as being composed of 'white book muslin' – a fine, diaphanous material which was folded in a book-like manner when sold by the piece.

It is very likely that Charlotte purchased her bridal muslin whilst on a shopping trip to Halifax, probably at the same time as she bought for the fabrics for her 'Going Away Dress' and her 'Barège Dress', known to have been made up as part of her wedding trousseau.[52] Biographer Esther Chadwick refers to this trip and claimed that she later met the 'young man' who had 'served her' and had, for years after, boasted about how he 'had sold goods to the great author of *Jane Eyre*'.[53]

In her purchase of muslin, Charlotte's choice was fashionable but not nearly as expensive as silk or satin. An 1850 advertisement for the haberdashers, Beech and Berrall's of London states that 'Muslins' cost between 10½ d–1s 3½ d per yard', whilst satin cost between '2s 4½ d–2s 9½ d per yard'. 'Fancy Striped Silk' was selling at '2s 9½ d and 3s 6½ d per yard' and 'Glacé Silk', '9½ d–11½ d per yard.'[54]

There are several surviving examples of muslin wedding dresses dated to the early 1850s, and some of these bear striking similarity to Margaret Ross's description of Charlotte's original gown which had a large, full skirt, voluminous sleeves, a soft, pleated bodice and a high neck.[55] An 1851 muslin wedding gown from the Victoria and Albert Museum features very similar 'unstitched' pleats on the bodice. It was worn by the young Eliza Sabina Sneath from the West Riding of Yorkshire for her marriage to twenty-two-year-old brewer, Joseph Candlin in July 1851.[56] This dress, with its gently frilled hemline and bishop sleeves is comparably simple in its design, unlike other, more typical muslin gowns of the period which abound in embellishment. A general fashion for frills, flounces and ornamentation occurred following the wedding of the Empress Eugenie in March 1853.[57] Charlotte's dress eschews all these, and Bell and Ross's description of 'tucks' or 'horizontal bands' are very much in keeping with her known, more streamlined taste.

Brontë's white, diaphanous gown, though simple, certainly left an impression on the villagers who had excitedly assembled to witness her walk the 'fifty yards from the parsonage through the narrow lane to the entrance of the church', arm-in-arm with Margaret Wooler.[58] Evidently surprised to her see her garbed in bridal white, they later deployed a series of similes which, though not deliberately unkind, are certainly incongruous when applied to someone of Charlotte's age and status. One onlooker described her looking 'like a snowdrop', whilst a member of the sexton's family, 'who saw her leave the church', said that she looked like a 'girl of sixteen, coming from her first communion service' and that 'Mr Nicholls [who] was not a tall man' 'seemed almost like a giant with the girlish little bride on his arm'.[59]

That Brontë gave the impression of what Gaskell termed a 'pale, wintry flower' was in no small part to her large, effervescent wedding bonnet with its

9.2 *Charlotte Brontë's wedding bonnet, D2*

profusion of cream lace and artificial flowers.[60] For as much as her dress bucked contemporary bridal trends with its relative simplicity, her bonnet took the mid-1850 predilection for adornment to extremes. It was fashioned from a wire frame covered in cream satin binding, silk thread and lined with satin, whilst lengths of machine-made lace and cream satin have been stitched on the outside. Where the brim meets the crown, hand-crafted silk 'carnations' have been copiously applied. Cream silk roses and rosebuds, lily of the valley, an assortment of embossed green, paper leaves and curled, turkey biot feathers have been attached to the outside of the brim.[61] On the inside of the brim, where the bonnet frames the face, wax, silk and paper orange blossom blooms, buds and leaves have been stitched in place to form an arch. A single, now heavily faded pale-blue, beaded feather hangs down from the side of the brim, perhaps to ensure that Charlotte adhered to the adage, 'Something old, something, new, something borrowed, something blue.'[62] The earliest written reference to this poem has been traced to the May 1876 edition of the Oxford journal, *Notes and Queries*, but the inclusion of the otherwise incongruous feather found in Charlotte's bonnet suggests that the tradition might have been around far longer, in Yorkshire at very least.

The bonnet would have been tied beneath the chin with the long, wide, scallop-edged, cream ribbons that hang from the bottom of the bonnet brim. The blooms that adorn it were clearly once tinged pink but the whole headdress has become discoloured over time. Reports indicate that long before the bonnet came to the museum, it was owned by a member of Martha Brown's family, who had displayed it close to a coal fire. Over a period of many years, the bonnet became covered in soot and, though it has since been thoroughly dusted off and cleaned, sadly, the resultant grey tone remains.

After much time spent amongst the archives, it has now been determined that Charlotte bought her wedding bonnet at a millinery shop called Hunt and Hall, located at 42, Commercial Street, Leeds. Indeed, a 'Bradford correspondent' for the *Yorkshire Evening Post* recalled how her 'grandmother had worked as a milliner for the store in Commercial Street when Charlotte Brontë got her bonnet there.'[63] This turned out to be the very same shop from which she had so daringly bought the bonnet lined in pink silk that she later wore in London.[64]

Though the wedding bonnet might have been commissioned especially for the occasion, it is more likely that it was one of those brought over from France in the weeks preceding the wedding. According to a newspaper advertisement dated to 1 May 1854, and included in the *Leeds Intelligencer*, Mrs Hunt, owner and proprietor of Hunt and Hall, had returned from Paris with a 'New Supply of Novelties.'[65] As Charlotte's bonnet bears some similarity to surviving French designs and, as Patrick took the *Leeds Intelligencer*, it is feasible that she saw the front-page advertisement and subsequently attended the showroom. But whether or not it had been made in Paris, this wedding bonnet, with its heavy embellishment, was not a practical purchase.[66] In fact, it is highly unlikely that she ever wore it again after her wedding day.

Charlotte makes no mention of the acquisition of a bonnet in her letter to Gaskell. By 1854, the majority of newspapers and fashion plates favour brides attired in long veils and wreaths of orange blossom.[67] For, although bonnets were also habitually worn, as *The Etiquette of Courtship and Matrimony: With a Complete Guide to the Forms of a Wedding* of 1852 stated, for brides, 'it [was] considered more stylish to go without'.[68] The orange-blossom wreath, with its roots in Greek and Roman mythology, had risen in popularity following the wedding of Queen Victoria in 1840.[69] Rather than donning the expected diamond tiara, the monarch defied all by choosing to wear a wreath of fresh, waxy white blooms. To Queen Victoria, her headdress was highly symbolic – it signified that she would marry Prince Albert as a woman, not, as he feared, in her role as monarch.[70]

Such highly scented, hot-house flowers were prohibitively expensive for the majority of brides, so orange-blossom imitations were created as an alternative. Single, artificial stems were commonly bound together to form a bridal wreath or wound into the hair of the bride.[71] In adding these hyper-ritualized stems to her bonnet, Charlotte was not only highlighting an awareness of current trends, but also her desire to explicitly draw attention to her bridal status.[72] This was particularly significant given her age. As a rule, younger women simply dressed their hair, but older or second-time brides chose to wear a bonnet. However, in Charlotte's case, any matronly connotations were completely undermined by the addition of excessive ornamentation and impracticality.

Of course, there could have been additional reason for her choice. It is not uncommon for brides to choose to deliberately draw attention to those parts of their body they like, or to distract the eye from those they do not.[73] They often elevate qualities that evoke body confidence or conceal those which have, or which they fear might have, been the cause of censure in the past.[74] Charlotte had often chosen to draw attention to her 'fine eyes' and to detract attention from what numerous witnesses described as her 'thin' hair.[75] To the fearful and self-critical Brontë, her bridal bonnet would have offered refuge, yet would also have placed focus on those features upon which she could best rely. For, as *Blackwood's Magazine* of 1845 noted, the broad brim forced observers to 'look down a sort of semi-funnelled hollow' to 'where the ambiguous shade of [a woman's] countenance was illuminated only by the radiance of her eyes.'[76]

As was traditional for brides, Charlotte wore a short, embroidered tulle and lace bonnet veil to the ceremony. This has survived, but stands in stark contrast to the one that she described as having chosen in her letter of early June 1854,

9.3 *Charlotte Brontë's wedding bonnet veil, D97*

which was 'simply of tulle with little tucks' and cost a mere '5s'.[77] As previous Brontë Parsonage Museum curator Rachel Terry wrote, 'we can only conclude that there was a change of plan before the wedding day itself'.[78] Whether this can be attributed to a last-minute romantic gesture from Nicholls, or the temptation presented by a clever saleswoman recently returned from Paris, life would imitate art once again. Jane Eyre had also initially opted for a modest 'square of unembroidered blond' to cover her 'low-born head'.[79] Yet, 'rent in two' by the hand of the 'clothed hyena', Bertha Rochester, the simple square of tulle was replaced with Edward Rochester's gift. This took the form of a veil of 'princely extravagance' which 'mask[ed his] plebeian bride in the attributes of a peeress'.[80] Charlotte's final choice of veil would also, for very different reasons, far outshine the original.

Controversy also surrounds the other accessories that Charlotte wore as part of her wedding attire. Gaskell describes her as wearing 'a lace mantle' over her shoulders.[81] Bell recalled seeing a 'bertha with two long curls coming down at each side',[82] whilst Ross remembered 'a kind of stole' lying in the box.[83] Chadwick, who later spoke to locals, described Charlotte as having worn a 'white lace cape' and yet, a wool and silk, cream and pink striped shawl, which, according to the Binns' Sale Catalogue of 1886, was worn by Brontë to her wedding ceremony, also survives.[84] Of course, none of these sources are first hand, so none can be relied upon with any certainty. If a piece of lace was worn, it would have been a relatively costly acquisition. The same is true of the striped shawl, for though not as luxurious as a Kashmir, the rich, silk inserts suggest that this garment was quite an expensive accessory.[85]

Charlotte makes no reference to her choice of footwear, but several witnesses remember shoes having been placed alongside the wedding dress, some orange-blossom stems and a shawl or stole. Nicholls's second wife's niece, H. K. Bell, describes seeing 'sandalled shoes',[86] whilst Ross recalls shoes that had become 'cinnamon coloured with age'.[87] Frances Bell recollects seeing 'small black shoes with one elastic [that] wound around the ankle, low heels and square toes'.[88] However, wedding shoes of the period were typically cream, so it is unlikely that it was these that were worn to the ceremony itself. As other items were also stored alongside the wedding garments, it is not improbable that the black slippers, which have survived, had some other sentimental association for Nicholls.[89]

Flat-soled 'slipper' shoes were made in huge quantities between 1800 and 1850. Cream silk stained easily and consequently was kept for indoor wear, for evening dress or for special occasions.[90] Women from the upper- and middle-classes bought numerous pairs at once, and more cream shoes remain in museums than any other colour.[91] Cream kid leather was also sometimes used both for the upper and inner parts of the shoe, but as kid leather darkens over time, it is possible that Ross remembered correctly and that the wedding shoes placed in the container had originally been cream.

It is not known which items of jewellery from her collection Charlotte chose to wear to the ceremony. There is evidence to suggest that her hands were covered by 'a small pair of white gloves with one small pearl button at the wrist'.[92] A number of similar pairs remain at the parsonage.[93]

Collectively, Charlotte's wedding ensemble conveys a plethora of paradoxical messages. Her letter to Ellen, written in the weeks before her wedding, sets out her intention to acquire a sensible trousseau, one befitting a modest clergyman's wife with a limited future income. At that point, Charlotte, rather pragmatically, was preparing for the 'destiny' that 'Providence' had 'doubtless' deemed 'was best'.[94] Yet, in spite of her firm intentions, forces, that remained inexplicable to even Brontë herself, caused her to make unexpected acquisitions. Her white, muslin wedding dress evokes that of the secretly envied Paulina de Bassompierre of *Villette*. Her 'girlish' garment, 'in fashion close, though faultlessly neat, but in texture clear and white', revealed the 'grace and sweetness' of a life 'thus blessed' not that of one who has been forced to, like Charlotte herself, 'breast adverse winds'.[95] Her bonnet, with its overabundance of lace, flowers and feathers and probably of the latest Parisian fashion, is reminiscent of the fascinating and beautiful 'butterfly' Ginevra Fanshawe of the same novel.[96] Yet where Ginevra, who relied on her beauty to provide her with the finery she so craved, and is scathingly denounced as a 'jay in borrowed plumes', vitally, Charlotte's finery was bought with 'money which was [her] own' and moreover, money earned by her own creative genius.[97]

In the light of Charlotte's typically retiring nature, fear of scrutiny and her recent decision to largely eschew a public life, her choice of conspicuous, bridal white remains perplexing, until one considers that Brontë had already played a white-robed bride in her imagination. Her alter-ego, Frances Henri of *The Professor*, is typically dressed in the expected 'black or sad-coloured stuff' of a teacher. However, for her wedding she had chosen 'white of a most diaphanous texture … so clear full and floating' and a veil which 'shadowed her head and hung below her knee, a little wreath of pink flowers fastened it … and thence it fell softly on each side of her face'.[98] Similarly, Jane Eyre's 'pearl-coloured robe' was accompanied by an 'embroidered' 'vapoury veil that gave out a most ghostly shimmer'.[99] These wedding clothes made Jane 'so unlike [her] usual self that it seemed almost the image of a stranger'.[100] To both protagonists, such overt bridal adornment was alien yet, to Brontë, somehow deeply requisite for the occasion.

On Thursday 29 June 1854, Charlotte Brontë walked out of the parsonage and down the cobbled street towards St Michael's and All Angels church. Her friends Ellen Nussey and Miss Wooler, and not her father, accompanied her along the uneven path early that 'dim, quiet' summer morning. At the very last minute, when Charlotte's dress was 'laid out' ready, together with her flowers, Patrick had 'announced his intention to stop at home' and not attend the wedding. The night before he had pressed Miss Wooler into taking his place. Whether it was that he did not feel able to give away his last remaining daughter or whether he was, as he had claimed, not well enough to sit through the service, one can only guess. Patrick's decision must have been painful for Charlotte, but determined to go ahead with her plans, she forged on alone.

The service was short and the wedding party small, in line with Charlotte's stipulation that everything should be kept as small and quiet and simple as possible. Indeed, as local Haworth man, Mr John Robinson, later wrote, 'it was not known in the neighbourhood that the marriage was coming off" and so it was a surprise to all but those few attendees who made their way to the church early that morning.[101] Arthur's friend, Sutcliffe Sowden, the vicar from Hebden Bridge, officiated. Miss Wooler, the woman who had for so long proved a guiding force in Charlotte's life, accompanied the veiled bride down the aisle in her father's absence. The ever-present Ellen served as bridesmaid in a brown, fringed silk dress with patterned stripes and a rather jaunty, beribboned rust brown hat.[102] She no doubt carried out her ceremonial tasks assiduously – holding Charlotte's bouquet as she exchanged her vows with Arthur. She also carefully signed her name in the register that, to this day, remains open at the entry.

After the ceremony, the little group of friends made their way back up Church Lane to the parsonage, where Martha and Tabby had laid on an impressive wedding breakfast complete with 'boiled ham'.[103] At their own instigation, they had raided local gardens of summer blooms and foliage and consequently the house was filled with sweet-smelling bouquets and scattered petals.[104]

Though Charlotte had impressed upon everyone that the celebrations should be discreet and understated, she must have been touched by the considerable efforts to which her friends had gone to make the day memorable. After all, as her surprising wedding ensemble proves, a part of her had always longed to play the bride. And, reservations about her new husband aside, she had finally got her wish.

10.1 *Charlotte Brontë's 'Going Away Dress', D74*

10

The 'Going Away Dress'

A new and dramatically different era in Charlotte Brontë's life had begun. This fact cannot have been lost on her as she clambered out of her bridal clothes and into the striped silk bodice and skirt that she had commissioned especially for the occasion.[1] This ensemble, unlike the profusion of muslin and lace and faux flowers that she would leave on her bed as she left for her honeymoon, was neat, substantial, even stately. No expense had been spared in the making of the voluminously skirted, big-sleeved gown. This was a practical choice, designed to be 'turned to decent use and worn after the wedding-day'.[2] This was the wedding gown that might have been expected. Yet, though very different to her bridal attire, it is no less enlightening. Bought at a moment of great transition, like the two-headed Janus, it looks both backwards and forwards. It is representative of the Charlotte that had been, but also of the one still yet to come. For, whilst its fashion-conscious design bears witness to the seismic influence that fame had had upon her, its gentle grandeur tells us something of the life that she anticipated as a newly married woman with continued, though modified, literary ambitions.

The provenance of this now brown silk gown is unsurpassed. After Brontë's death in 1855, it was given to Martha Brown and later bequeathed to her sister Ann Binns. The dress was eventually passed to Binns' daughter Ellen, who sold it in 1907, together with a collection of other items, directly to the Brontë Society for £1.10.0.[3] As further confirmation of its attribution, several fragments of the dress fabric have also survived independently, and these also remain in the collection.[4] Two of these fragments have been attached to cards and both are annotated and refer to the portion/s as being from 'Miss

Charlotte Brontë's Travelling Dress' and worn on the 'day of her wedding'.[5] As the dress remains intact, the pieces must have been cut from leftover fabric, rather than from the dress itself.

Questions have long been raised as to the garment's original colour. In the letter to Gaskell written in early June 1854, Charlotte refers to the purchase of a 'sort of fawn-coloured silk'.[6] Chadwick claimed to have seen the dress when it was in the possession of the Binns (and therefore before 1907) and declared it composed of 'a neat striped silk, dove-coloured and brown'.[7] Clement Shorter in his 1896 biography, describes the 'Going Away Dress' as having been made from 'lilac silk',[8] whereas Lewis Hainsworth in his *Descriptive Catalogue of Objects in the Museum of the Brontë Society at Haworth* of the same year, pronounced the dress to be formed from 'shot silk, lavender ground with a fine horizontal stripe'.[9] In 1988, Brontë curator and librarian Juliet Barker specified that 'the original lavender and silver, finely striped silk has faded to a uniform silvery brown'[10] – an assertion corroborated by subsequent curators Jane Sellars[11] and Rachel Terry[12] and then later included in the online catalogue which now reads: 'finely striped shot silk with silvered background and dark mauve (originally lavender) stripes'.[13]

A variety of risks endanger historic textiles. One of the major challenges is their susceptibility to environmental changes.[14] Garments dyed using organic dyes, as the vast majority were prior to the year 1856, are the most vulnerable to change.[15] It was clear from the conflicting descriptions, written between c. 1907 and 2002, that the dress's now mink-brown shade does not reflect its original colour. The gown had inevitably been exposed to unstable environmental conditions since its manufacture in 1854, but until the fibres, dyes and mordants used were identified, it was not possible to determine the original shade of the silk.[16] Once again, chemist Professor Andrea Russell and her team and Renishaw plc offered their assistance as we sought to solve this complex mystery.[17]

Though it was already apparent that the gown was composed of silk, the hypothesis was confirmed by both scanning electron microscopy-energy dispersive X-ray analysis (hereafter SEM-EDX) and microscope images (taken using a Nikon Eclipse LV100ND microscope) of the fragments taken from the original.[18] To the naked eye, it appeared that the lighter silk ground had been

10.2 *Microscope images of D74 silk taken using Nikon Eclipse LV100ND microscope, x2 objective. Images taken by Danai Panagoulia, Alex Keeler and Eleanor Houghton, University of Southampton*

punctuated only by fine, brown silk woven stripes, but, when placed under the microscope it soon became clear that the fabric was actually comprised of three separate, coloured fibres – white, blue and brown. The brown, twisted fibres of silk make up the weft, whilst the blue and white fibres constitute the warp. The main stripe, which is actually blue, is composed of two blue warp strands which are juxtaposed to four white strands. Together, the three interwoven colours give an iridescence to the fabric that may, in part, account for some confusion in its description.

Using Raman spectroscopy and those same methods previously utilized to ascertain the dyes in the 'Thackeray Dress', single spectra from the brown, blue and white fibres were taken – this time from some leftover fragments held at the parsonage. Once again, it was established that the blue fibres had been dyed using Prussian blue.[19] The white fibres 'showed strong spectral similarities' to plain, undyed silk, suggesting that no dye had ever been applied.[20] The dye used in the brown fibres proved much more difficult to ascertain, yet, in order to establish the original colour of the garment, this was clearly the most important dye to identify.

A search was carried out to compare the spectrum of the brown fibres with spectra taken from a pigment database. No exact match was found, but a close link was identified between the brown fibre spectrum and lazurite – a mineral used as a pigment in painting and in the dyeing of cloth since the sixth century.[21] By the mid-nineteenth century, it was less commonly used in dyeing due to its excessive cost.[22] Taken from the parent mineral, lapis lazuli, it produces a deep ultra-marine blue dye that tends to darken over time.[23] Lazurite could not have produced the now visible, brown-like colour alone and so must have been mixed with other pigments. Throughout the nineteenth century, it was common practice to mix different dyes – even as early as 1808, William Nicholson in his book *A Dictionary of Practical and Theoretical Chemistry*, describes the practice of combining indigo with cochineal to produce 'beautiful violets on silk'.[24] So, to help ascertain which dyes might have been added to the vat to produce the now brown tint, a list was compiled of all the possible red/purple colourants commonly used at the time that the garment was manufactured. Over a period of weeks, the team took Raman spectra from each of the following dyes: manganese brown (which forms a range of colours from light fawn to deep brown), cochineal (pale pink to red to purple), logwood (violet to black), madder (red), lac (scarlet), brazilwood (red to purple) and brazilein (red).[25] No match was found between the spectra taken from madder root extract and the brown dress fibres. Cochineal and lac were also eliminated with relative ease. Logwood and brazilwood did not yield strong results – not because the dyes were not definitively present, but because the bark-based substances did not produce strong spectra and tended to fluoresce (emit a glow) when placed under the laser.[26] This is not uncommon but was only compounded by the fact that these organic colourants are highly tinting, which means that only a small quantity of pigment remains on the textile.

Orchil, a purple dye made from lichen, was also identified as a possible candidate.[27] The proximity of Halifax (where Charlotte purchased the fabric) to Leeds, where silk was routinely being dyed purple using the Bedfords' ancient recipe, and the 'substantive nature' of the dye itself, which was 'especially advantageous to silk' because 'no mordant was required', heightened the possibility that this was the dye used.[28] Orchil was sometimes mixed with other dyestuffs to produce a deeper shade of purple and may therefore have been used in conjunction with lazurite.[29] But, despite these indicators, no correlation was found between the spectra taken from the orchil dye and those taken from the gown's brown fibres.

As the majority of red producing dyes available in the mid-nineteenth century had been eliminated, brazilwood and logwood were identified as the two most likely colourants to have been used alongside lazurite. With scientific results proving inconclusive, efforts were once again focused upon traditional historical research. Logwood is a natural dye, capable of producing a range of colours such as red (when mixed with acids), violet (when mixed with tin), blue-grey (alum) and the best natural black (iron), depending on the mordant used.[30] To put it simply, logwood is reactive and produces roseate colours when exposed to acidic substances, and bluer shades when placed in more alkaline solutions.[31] A colourless crystal called haematoxylin is extracted from the bark of the logwood tree and from this, the colouring agent, haematein is produced. The wood, which is native to South America and the West Indies, had been introduced to Europe for dyeing purposes in the early sixteenth century, but trade peaked in the mid-nineteenth century when 100,000 tons were being exported annually. Much of this was imported to Britain where it was used in the dyeing of fabric and leather, in inks and art materials.[32] Logwood is frequently referenced in dyeing manuals of the early to mid-nineteenth century and was often used for the purposes of dyeing and weighting silks.[33] Had logwood been added to the dye mix used in Charlotte's gown, then depending on the mordant added, it is likely that the dress would have originally appeared much more purple in colour. If lazurite (ultramarine blue) had also been added to the vat, as the experiments carried out suggest, then the silk would have appeared violet, the blue mixing with the red/purple of the logwood.[34]

Though logwood remained feasible, brazilwood was also given consideration, not least because the dye was often mixed with logwood to produce a burgundy or deep red – the colour still apparent in the unfaded areas of the fine, needlecord cuffs, collar and hem of Brontë's gown.[35] Brazilwood is the name given to a genus of hard, brown-red trees that produce, depending on the mordants added, a wide range of red-based dyes. When the principal matter, brazilein, is mixed with tin it produces a rich pink, with aluminium, a deep red and with iron, brown.[36] It was a much-used dyestuff throughout the early to mid-nineteenth century but eventually waned in popularity because it is not lightfast[37] and fades to a 'lighter shade' and then to 'a yellow-brown colour' with relative speed.[38] This phenomenon could account for the mink-brown of the silk, but, in order to confirm its presence, more invasive microchemical experiments would be necessary and a larger fabric sample required.[39] Given the historic significance of Brontë's gown, such invasive experiments are not feasible.

Though it has not, as yet, proved possible to categorically ascertain the original colour of Brontë's dress, the presence of blue-based lazurite in the brown fibres, together with the confirmed existence of Prussian blue in the stripe, suggest that the garment is likely to have had a notable purple/violet appearance when first worn in 1854. Whether this purple was more red or more blue-based in tone depends largely on whether logwood and/or brazilwood dyes were also used. As all commonly used red dyes have been eliminated by scientific experiment and yet the fibres still appear reddish-brown under the microscope, it can be assumed that the current brown appearance can be attributed to one or both of these dyes having been used alongside lazurite/ultramarine blue. If this is the case, then it is likely this/these dyes have deteriorated over time, in large part due to atmospheric or chemical changes and that the dress does not now appear quite as it did when Charlotte Brontë wore it.[40] These findings are significant, not least because a purple silk gown, irrespective of shade, would have communicated very different messages than would a drab brown one. It seemed that, yet again, our preconceptions of Brontë were to be confronted, their legitimacy challenged.

Determining the original colour of the dress was important, but there were other revelations yet to uncover. Charlotte's letter, written to Ellen Nussey on 11 June 1854, indicates that, unlike the majority of her other gowns, the 'Going Away Dress' was made by a dressmaker from Halifax, one of the many listed in the 1851 census.[41] She wrote, 'I got my dresses from Halifax a day or two since – but have not yet had time to take the cord off the box – so don't know what they are like.'⁴²

In terms of style, the gown is composed of a separate bodice and skirt. The skirt has six panels and has been lined with cream tarlatan. An opening on the left-hand side of the skirt conceals a pocket with a silk and glazed cotton lining. The skirt opens at the right-hand seam and measures 343 cm at the hem, but the vast quantity of silk has been reduced at the waist by the use of organ pleating at the front and sides of the skirt and finer cartridge pleats at the very rear. There is a visible line at 97 cm from the waist, suggesting that a hem might have been let down, though there are no stitch marks or signs of added fading, so it is possible that this is simply a crease caused by display.

The hem of the skirt has been trimmed with the same fine needlecord used for the cuffs and collar, whilst the waistband has been made from a plain silk and had been attached to the skirt using backstitch. The skirt is closed by two pairs of hooks and eyes and the bodice of the gown fastens at the front and is lined in glazed calico. The main closures are attached not to the silk, but to the lining of the bodice, meaning the outer silk is closed only at the neck and waist. Similar in design to both the blue-and-cream striped gown and the 'Thackeray Dress', the soft, deep pleats run diagonally from the lowered shoulder towards the centre front. Where the bodice meets the waist, large Vandyke points have been added.⁴³ These triangular points, that drew inspiration from the seventeenth-century paintings of Anthony van Dyck, would have directed attention to Charlotte's small waist. Each of these has been trimmed with a fine silk fringing that is now pale gold but is likely to have faded over time. In some areas, a pink tinge is visible, but, once again, further scientific analysis would be necessary to determine the original colour. Such embellishments were common in conspicuous daywear, with the *Yorkshire Gazette* of November 1854 declaring, 'dresses are usually much trimmed with drawn ribbons, fancy braids, shaded plush, curled fringes, fur or plaits of every description'.⁴⁴

The collar is unusual for the period in that is stands upright – just as it does in her 'Thackeray Dress' and in her broderie anglaise blouse. This was obviously Charlotte's favoured style as the majority of conspicuous day dresses of the mid-1850s had high, round necklines to which a removable collar was then added.

The sleeves of the 'Going Away Dress' are exceptionally voluminous and very much in keeping with the high fashions of 1854, and particularly with other travelling gowns of the period.[45] But, even withstanding the gown's original violet/purple shade, it is still less flamboyant than the majority of other dresses of the same classification. Yet, where it might be deemed conservative when compared with the cutting-edge styles seen in contemporary paintings and

10.3 *'Fringed Silk Day Dress'*, 1854/6, (YORCM:BA3602), York Castle Museum, York

fashion-plates, for Charlotte, the gown was markedly more fashionable and more expensive than anything that she had ever owned pre-fame. 'Babylon' had changed her and whilst she might never fully understand the nuances of fashionable dress, nor wish to follow them to the nth degree, her 'Going Away Dress' proves the extent to which her eyes had been opened, her tastes had altered.

In her choice of design, Charlotte was not, it seems, the only individual to subtly modify the fashions of the day to suit a more subdued taste. Housed at the York Castle Museum is a dove-coloured, glacé silk Quaker wedding gown that bears an incredibly close resemblance to Charlotte's own.[46] Similarities are apparent in both the overall design and in its decorative features. Even the silvery-purple hue of the wedding gown is comparable to the original colour of Brontë's gown. Having said this, had the dyes been the same, then this too is likely to have been subject to atmospheric changes over time.

The one-piece dress is associated with Rachel Hannah Walker of Kirkby Malzeard near Harrogate and is thought to have been worn at her wedding to Thompson Walker, a 'mercantile clerk' and second son of a yeoman farmer from Rawdon.[47] The ceremony took place at the Quaker monthly meeting in York on 16 October 1856. In keeping with the general demands of mid-nineteenth-century Quakerism, the dress is not ostentatious, but no expense has been spared in the quantity or quality of fabric used and the silk covered antique-gold buttons are likely to have been costly. The circumference of the skirt measures a whopping 363 cm and the loose, deep pleats that make up the bodice are equally generous in their use of silk. In this liberality, the gown is arguably representative of Walker's newly cemented rank, but also of her aspirations – of the societal place that she and her new husband hoped to gain or to maintain.

Both Charlotte and Rachel's gowns would have been expensive, and each is likely to have been made by a dressmaker in Yorkshire and designed to reflect the prevalent fashions. However, where Walker's gown was intended to be worn in fashionable Harrogate, Brontë's would have been notably conspicuous in unsophisticated Haworth. This suggests that either fame had elevated Charlotte's sense of consequence when on home ground or that she was aware that her role as authoress might yet necessitate more formal dress when visiting London, Gawthorpe Hall or Ambleside.

Uncharacteristically, there is no evidence to suggest that Charlotte sought reassurance from others in the selection of this gown. She left her preferred fabric 'with the dress-maker in Halifax' and decided not to send 'samples' to Gaskell.[48] This unprecedented self-reliance can be attributed to several key factors, as on her return to the provincial community of Haworth, she was now amongst the most travelled, the most experienced and, as a direct result of her fame, amongst the most formidable of its inhabitants. Charlotte's numerous trips to 'Babylon', though painful, had forced her to confront and embrace a world in which a relationship with dressmakers was both necessary and normative. By 1854, shopping for fabric and accessories had become a more common occurrence for her, and, as a direct consequence of celebrity, she was now better able to afford them than she had been in her pre-fame life.[49]

If the blue-and-cream striped dress of her fame years can be said to be representative of the side of fame that Charlotte Brontë had come to despise, her choice of 'Going Away Dress' must be viewed as symbolic of a diluted fame in which she had more control over both her environment and her appearance. With the notable exception of her wedding ensemble, in the acquisition of her trousseau, of which her 'Going Away Dress' was part, she was choosing garments that would serve her in her new life.[50] One in which she believed she would be combining her more financially secure, socially acceptable status as a married woman, with a modified, selective role as successful author and celebrity. With her future secured by her union with Nicholls, Brontë was no longer *required* to exhibit herself, unless she chose to do so in order to further or maintain her position as a published writer. Marriage to Nicholls and her duties as wife would inevitably have some impact on her ability to write and to self-promote, but, beyond his influence, the amount of exposure to which she would be subjected remained in her own hands.

However, real life with Arthur differed considerably from that for which she had anticipated as she went about choosing her trousseau. From the very moment that she stepped into the carriage that would take her and her new husband to the railway station at Keighley, Charlotte's life began to change. Arthur had planned every detail of the honeymoon, from the tickets to the daily timetable, to the handling of the luggage.[51] For a woman who had taken such pains to manage the details of her own life, these changes must have seemed strange and disorientating. Yet Charlotte did as she was expected and boarded the train at the station at which she had so often stopped when travelling to and from London. From here, they travelled to North Wales to commence their honeymoon.

They arrived in the quiet, coastal town of Conwy tired, with Charlotte full of cold. Their journey had been pleasant enough and uneventful but, by the time they got to their destination, the weather had turned 'wet and wild'.[52] Their lodgings, which overlooked the thirteenth-century ruins of Conwy Castle, were very comfortable – the accommodation 'very good'.[53]

In all likelihood, it was here at the Castle Hotel that Charlotte first donned the voluminous pink-and-white wrapping gown that she had ordered as part of her wedding trousseau just a few weeks before.[54] The long, capacious Pepto-Bismol pink gown with matching frilled cape was a relaxed, intimate garment, designed to be worn in the presence of her new husband. Much like our modern-day dressing gown or house coat, front closing wrappers were typically worn in the morning at breakfast, or when the wearer was carrying out light, domestic tasks. Fewer, less constrictive undergarments were worn beneath these loose-fitting wrappers, allowing women to move more freely. But, in consequence, they were only deemed appropriate in private, familial settings.[55] Therefore, though it is hard for a modern onlooker to locate sensuality in Charlotte's rose-hued, high-necked, floor-length ensemble, it must nonetheless be viewed as an item of allure – something bought specifically for life as a married woman.

Charlotte's choice of pink for this intimate raiment is significant.[56] Though pink is, to us, a highly gendered colour, with strong connotations of femininity, sweetness, even love, these meanings were not nearly so fixed in the 1850s. Less than fifty years before, men had habitually worn suits of pink silk or velvet as part of their Court dress.[57] And, though by the middle decades of the nineteenth century male clothing was much more sombre in tone, pink waistcoats, banyans and smoking caps were not uncommon.[58] Pink cannot, therefore, be viewed as an inevitable choice for this intimate item of clothing. Indeed, despite a scouring of all the major archives of nineteenth-century fashion in Europe and America, few examples of pink wrappers have

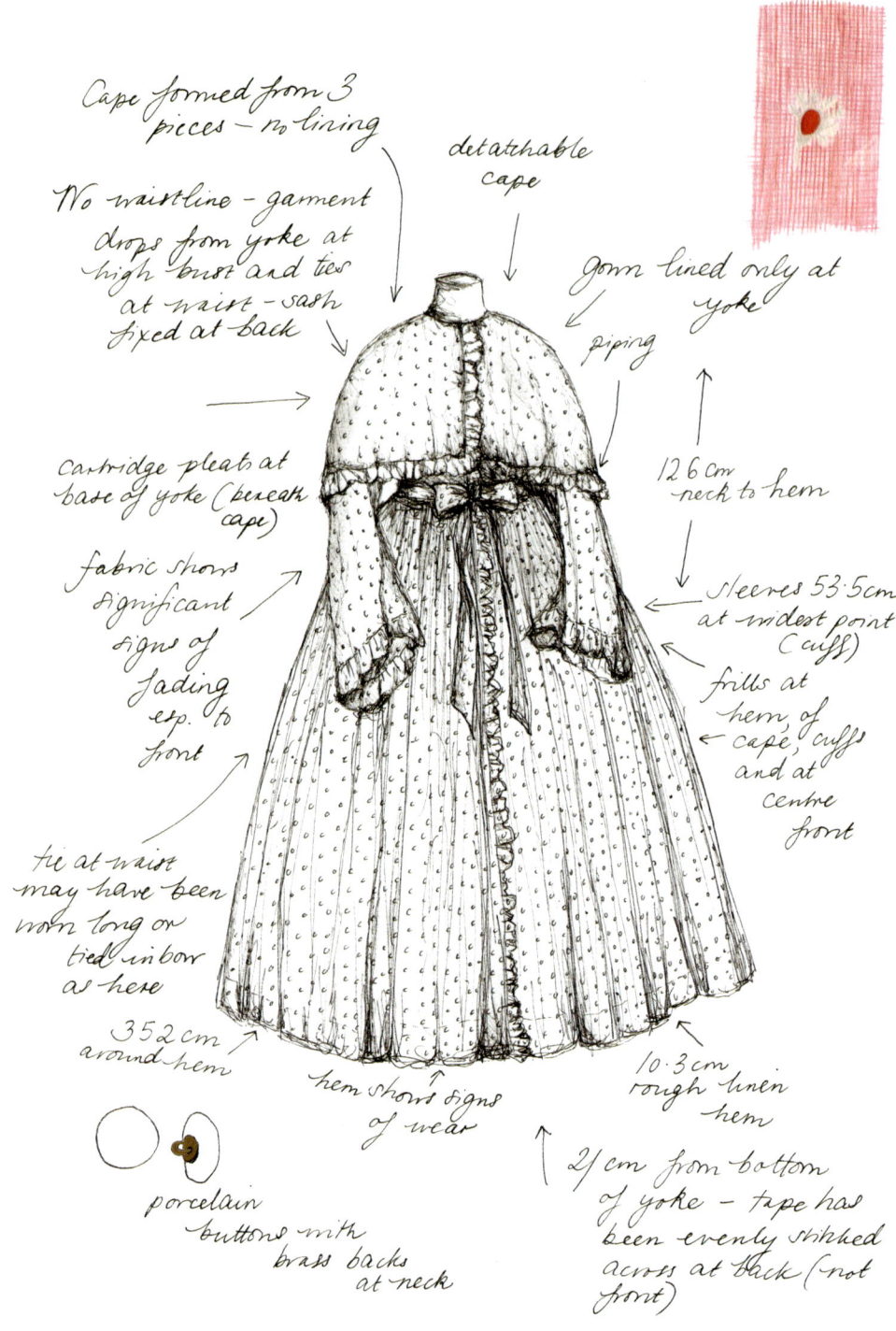

10.4 Charlotte Brontë's pink cotton wrapping gown or 'wrapper', D51

been found.[59] The majority from this period are far more solemn, favouring autumnal tones and paisley patterns or stripes.[60]

In her choice of fabric, Charlotte was not, then, following the fashions. Neither did she have a particular predilection for bright pink, there are no other such fiercely pink garments in her surviving wardrobe.[61] Rather, it seems likely that there were other motivations at play, motivations that are better understood through the eyes of her protagonist, Lucy Snowe. In *Villette*, Lucy dons a pink gown to a concert – 'a grand affair held in the large salle'.[62] It is not a gown of her choosing. Mrs Bretton, her godmother, was responsible for the alien 'pink dress'.[63] Her aim is to call Lucy out from the shadows. She literally prises her from her usual dark clothes in an attempt to secure her goddaughter's future. And, as Lucy's eventual union proves, she is right to do it. It is because of the pink dress that Paul Emmanuel first recognizes Lucy not simply as a female colleague, but as a sexual being. The colour arouses Monsieur Paul's volcanic jealousy. In his desirous mind, the gown transitions from pink to red – the colour of passion, even female 'degeneracy'.[64] Yet, though he claims to disapprove of Lucy's changed appearance, he cannot help but later admit that the pink dress 'had the merit of looking rather well'.[65]

Obviously there is no way of knowing whether Charlotte's pink wrapping gown triggered a similarly aphrodisiacal reaction in Mr Nicholls. It is hard to believe that after waiting so long for Charlotte, he needed much in the way of encouragement. As for his new wife, we can only imagine what she made of her first real sexual experience. The passionate declarations of love in her books imply that she was neither prudish nor unfeeling, and, as Juliet Barker writes, 'though she did not love Mr Nicholls when she married him, she had never found him physically repugnant'.[66] So, though her heavy cold might, as some have suggested, have delayed the consummation of their marriage, her letters, written from North Wales and then from Ireland, suggest that she did not find intimate relations with Arthur offensive.[67] In fact, all subsequent letters are brimming with tender references to 'my dear husband', suggesting new intimacies had strengthened their bond.[68]

But it was not only oxytocin that would deepen Charlotte's feelings for her new husband. After travelling around North Wales and then catching the packet steamer from Anglesey to Dublin, they remained in the city seeing

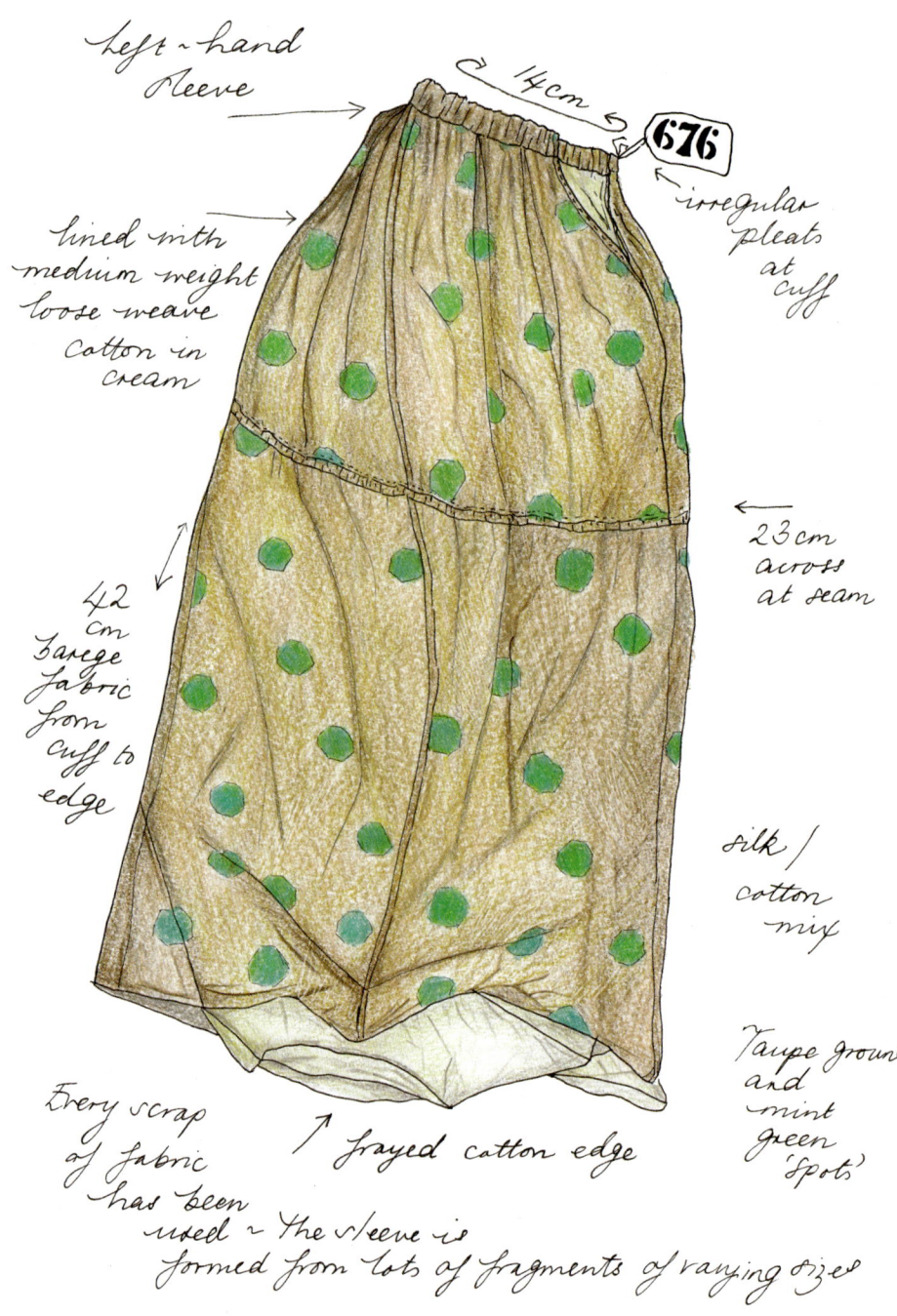

10.5 Surviving sleeve of Charlotte Brontë's green spot barège gown, D119.2

the sights. It was whilst here that Charlotte was first introduced to Arthur's brother and cousins and their 'gentle English manners' and high education.[69] The strength of her enthusiasm suggests that she had begun marriage with extremely low expectations of Arthur and particularly of his Irish heritage – ironic given that she herself was of Irish descent on her father's side, and from a financially constrained family too.

Nicholls's childhood home in Banagher proved even more surprising. She found his uncle's house, where Arthur had lived from the age of six, 'very large', 'lofty and spacious' and looking 'externally like a gentleman's country seat'.[70] On seeing this grand house, Charlotte, who had firmly believed herself superior to her husband in almost every way, began to perceive him quite differently. As she wrote to Miss Wooler: 'My dear husband appears in a new light here in his own country. More than once I have had deep pleasure in hearing his praise on all sides'. Nicholls had, by this point, exceeded all her expectations. In the last lines of the letter to her old headmistress, Charlotte's transformed perspective of 'Mr. N.' is revealed: 'I feel thankful to God for having enabled me to make what seems a right choice – and I pray to be enabled to repay as I ought the affectionate devotion of a truthful, honourable, unboastful man.'[71]

Nicholls's standing in his local community might have taken Charlotte unawares, but it seems that, sartorially at least, she was well-prepared for her trip. Though she found herself in rather more salubrious surroundings than she had expected, her barège gown, ordered in Halifax before her wedding, would have served her well. She had purchased the material that she described in the letter to Gaskell as 'drab barège with a green spot in it' at the same time as she had bought the silk for her 'Going Away Dress'. Only fragments of this dress now remain, but the pieces now held at the Parsonage suggest that the gown had large, voluminous sleeves that were closed at the wrist with a narrow, gathered cuff. The shape of the surviving skirt panels indicate that the skirt of the gown was long and full. A cream calico lining remains visible on both the existing sleeves and on the back bodice, and, though the skirt has now been dismantled, it is likely that, in keeping with other barège dresses of the period, this was also lined.[72] As the fabric is so sheer, the lining and, worse still, the body itself, could be seen through the barège – a fact that caused some consternation in the contemporary press. Indeed, in 1850, the satirical

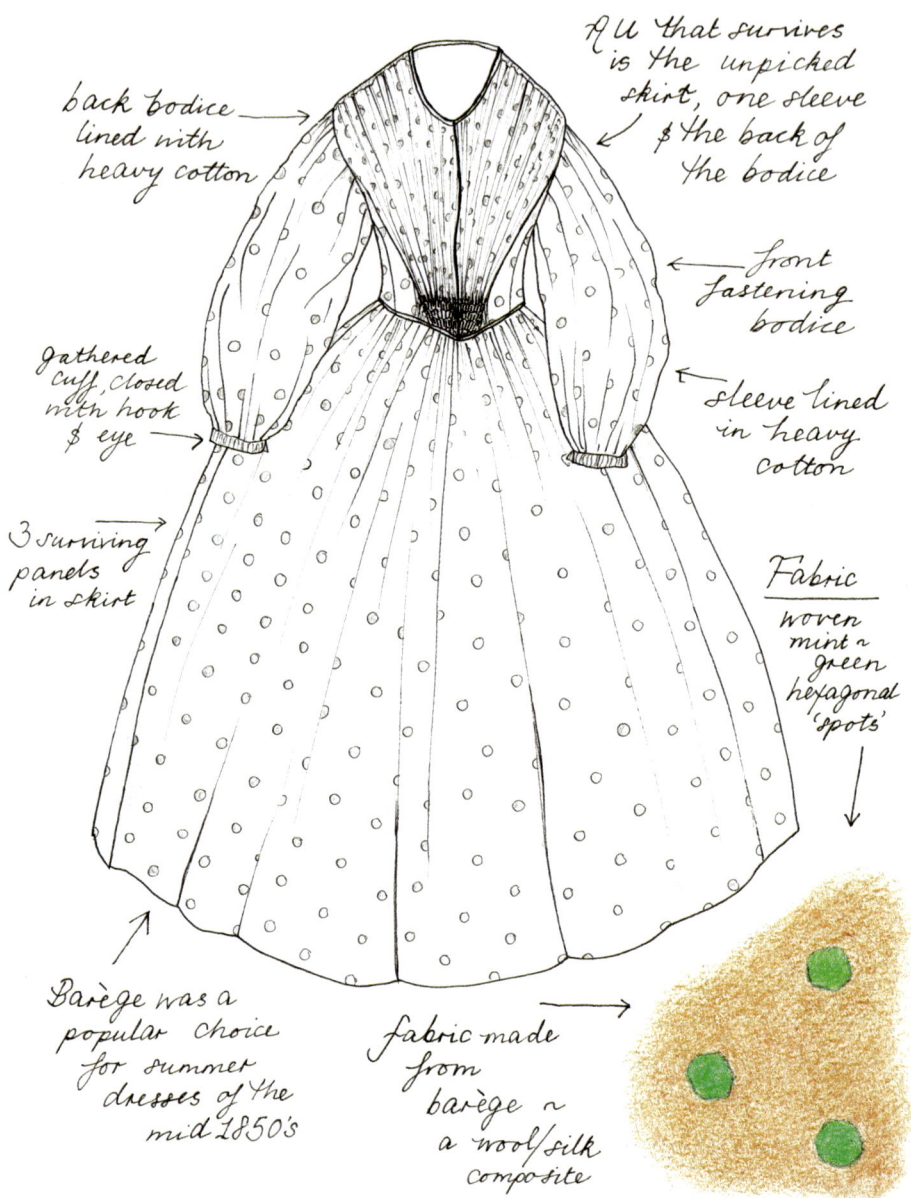

10.6 Front view of feasible reconstruction of Charlotte Brontë's 1850 barège spot dress

magazine *Punch* printed a cartoon in which a lady in a gossamer, barège dress was depicted with her ankles showing through the fabric of her gown. Beneath the cartoon was printed the warning, 'A friendly hint to young ladies who wear those delightful barège dresses. Always let the slip (or whatever that mysterious garment is called) be as long as the outer dress!'[73] As the daughter and now wife of a clergyman, Charlotte almost certainly heeded this advice.

In order to artistically recreate the gown as it might have been in 1854, numerous other surviving dresses were considered. The fine woollen warp and silk weft fabric was very popular in the 1850s and some examples remain.[74] The majority feature a softly pleated bodice, capacious pagoda sleeves and a flounced skirt. There are no stitch marks on the surviving fragments to suggest that the skirt on Charlotte's gown was ever flounced and it is therefore likely that, in common with earlier choices, it was much simpler in its silhouette. As with all gowns of the period, numerous petticoats would have been worn as undergarments, to give the skirt a rounded, sweeping shape.

In the 1850s, some lightweight gowns were made with two bodices – one for evening and one for day.[75] As Charlotte makes no mention of this in her letter, it is likely that the gown was either made in one piece or, like the 'Going Away Dress', was formed of a skirt and bodice. The surviving part of the bodice is relatively short in length, and as there is no visible waistband, it is probable that it was joined to the skirt at the waist – certainly there are pin marks at the top of the skirt. In any case, the fabric, which originated in Barèges in south-western France, is likely to have been made in a mill in or around Bradford, Huddersfield or Leeds and thus close to the Brontës' home.[76] Barège was most often used in spring and summer gowns, as its sheer, lightweight qualities complemented a warmer climate. Therefore, though the weather in Ireland was characteristically wild that June, once made up, Charlotte's optimistic purchase would have been considered wholly appropriate and, given the lively green spot and the popularity of the fabric amongst the upper- and middle-classes, even quite fashionable.

The honeymoon took the Nicholls' all around Ireland. After leaving Banagher, they had travelled along the banks of the River Shannon, past Lough Derg and then on to Limerick. From here, they journeyed across country to

Kilkee on the west coast. They stayed in a small inn that they had booked in advance. The West End Hotel did not quite live up to their expectations, but the sandy bay and majestic cliffs of Kilkee did not disappoint. Arthur wrote to his friend George Sowden, 'It was most refreshing to sit on a rock and look out at the broad Atlantic foaming at our feet.'[77]

From Kilkee they travelled south to Tralee and Killarney, then further south to Glengarriff, Cork and finally back to Dublin. They saw lakes and mountain passes, streams and moorland. The trip was near perfect, but for the accident that Charlotte had when riding a horse at the Gap of Dunloe. However, even the day of this incident had proved happy. The pair had enjoyed the resplendent scenery of the narrow mountain pass that separates the MacGillycuddy's Reeks mountain range in the west from the Purple Mountain Group in the east on horseback. But, as they traversed the tricky mountain trail, the horse reared up and Charlotte was thrown from a height and down to the stones below. Miraculously, she was 'neither bruised by the fall or touched by the horse's hoofs' but that did not stop her feeling for '[her] husband – [her] father'.[78] That her very first thoughts were for the wellbeing of her husband and not her father shows how things had changed since her wedding in June.[79] In the weeks that had passed, Charlotte's feelings had certainly been transformed – the honeymoon had achieved all that the tenacious Arthur had hoped.

The new Mr and Mrs Nicholls were on excellent form when they finally arrived back in Haworth. Charlotte was well rested, and Arthur, who had previously been ravaged by lovesickness, had gained more than twelve pounds in weight.[80] This was just as well. In their absence, Patrick's health had deteriorated, and it was immediately evident that Nicholls would need to carry out much of his father-in-law's work as well as his own. Arthur soon found himself rushed off his feet and Charlotte was required to help pick up the slack. If she had expected to return to her former quiet, focused existence in Haworth – one in which she had time to write – this was not to be the case. From the outset, Arthur presumed that Charlotte would now always subjugate her own interests to his own; that she would see it as her duty not only to care for him and meet his needs, but also those of her father and the wider parish community.[81]

Her wifely and daughterly duties, coupled with her work in the community soon proved all-encompassing. She had, of course, been involved in the life of the parish before she married and had therefore run Sunday School classes and entertained parishioners and local dignitaries on her father's behalf. But, in charting her post-marital activities through her letters, a marked spike in parochial activities is evident.[82] When she did finally get round to writing to her friends, she spoke of her increased community interaction. Remarkably though, especially given Charlotte's previous sense of isolation when in Haworth, her letters demonstrate that she began to throw herself into this new life with some considerable enthusiasm. For what appears to be the first time, she took pleasure in the 'happiness' of her parishioners.[83] She wrote of the gratitude that she felt for the 'hearty welcome' that was extended to the couple on their return from honeymoon and described how, by way of thanks, she arranged 'a supper and tea-drinking' for the 'Singers, Ringers, Sunday-School Teachers and all the scholars of the Sunday and National Schools – amounting to some 500 Souls'.[84] This generous act was an indicator of change – of Charlotte's desire to throw herself into the role of Mrs Arthur Nicholls and cement herself as matriarch in the community.

Charlotte's new occupations did not entirely eclipse her previous life as famed author, though it was notably diminished. After her engagement to Nicholls, the number of letters written to Smith and Elder lessened dramatically, but she continued to write and receive correspondence from Gaskell and from other 'literary coteries'.[85] Invitations to formal events were also received, though these were often declined.[86] Her smart 'Going Away Dress', which, beyond its symbolic role, had been designed with her writerly life very much in mind, would have been pulled out her wardrobe again. This time, it would have been worn at her meeting in Haworth with Sir James Kay-Shuttleworth and his friend on 11 November 1854. It might also have travelled with her to her more extended visit to Gawthorpe Hall in January 1855.[87] So too might her green spotted barège, for the Kay-Shuttleworths were known for their grand dinners and it seems likely that Charlotte would seek to make use of her modish new gowns, in spite of the chillier weather.

These meetings and visits suggest that, though Charlotte's life had altered dramatically, she had entered marriage with no desire to turn her back entirely upon the side of fame that she had enjoyed, or on those real friends that she made as a result of her celebrity. But, on returning to Haworth post-honeymoon, she would find that, even if she had wished to, she simply had less opportunity to write.

Nicholls has long been heralded the man who 'had murdered a great literary talent'.[88] Certainly, he saw his wife as his natural helpmate and companion and, being a man of exacting standards, Charlotte quickly found that only a 'small portion of each day' could be called her 'own'.[89] Eight weeks after her wedding, she wrote to Margaret Wooler, 'my own life is more occupied than it used to be; I have not so much time for thinking; I am obliged to be more practical, for my dear Arthur is a very practical as well as a very punctual, methodical man'.[90]

It is worth noting that if Nicholls appears dictatorial, saturnine, demanding in this description, he was only cut from the same cloth as those male protagonists who had appeared in her fantasies and dominated her experience.[91] In a letter to John Foster, written just prior to Brontë's marriage, Gaskell outlined what she saw as the reason behind her friend's attraction to Nicholls: 'I am sure that Miss Brontë could never have borne not to be well ruled and ordered ... She would never have been happy but with an exacting, rigid, law-giving, passionate man.'[92] Whether this observation was based on Gaskell's friendship with Brontë, upon familiarity with her novels or from a mixture of the two, it cannot be disputed that there was a passive/assertive duality present in Charlotte and, consequently, in her work. Indeed, as Nicholls's biographer, Alan Adamson writes:

> Part of the power of Charlotte Brontë's fiction derives from the collision of two opposing images of women: Shirley Keeldar, strong, independent, her mind filled with visions of titanic females bestriding the earth, and Helen Burns, passive and submissive, ever obedient to some superior will. In her fiction, Charlotte separated and dramatized the collision, but in her own life these two aspects of her remained inseparable.[93]

The more submissive side of Charlotte, that one who had allowed herself to be clothed in alien garments by Mrs Smith, might well have caused her to acquiesce in her husband's domination of her time. Significantly, the change of focus apparent in Brontë's life was neither unforeseen nor unwelcome. Soon after her engagement she had written to George Smith, 'In the course of the year that is gone – Cornhill and London have receded a long way from me – the links of communication have waxed very frail and few. It must be so in this world. All things considered – I don't wish it otherwise.'[94]

Leaving behind the stresses and strains of a public life had been a key deciding factor in her acceptance of Nicholls's proposal. And, despite her altered existence and chosen inconspicuousness, little regret can be perceived in her letter to Margaret Wooler written in September 1854:

> Haworth is – as you say – a very quiet place ... few take courage to penetrate so remote a nook. Besides, now that I am married I do not expect to be an object of much general interest. Ladies who have won some prominence (call it either <u>notoriety</u> or celebrity) in their single life – often fall quite into the background when they change their names; but if true domestic happiness replace Fame—the exchange <is>'will' indeed be for the better.'[95]

The uneasy relationship between her female gender and fame is once again made apparent – marriage would arguably make no discernible difference to a newly married male celebrity. Yet, though clearly aware of inequality, Charlotte does not rail against it. Instead, she directs her focus forward and onto 'true domestic happiness' – a state that, speaking as she was just three months into marriage, had not yet been fully realized but that experience had already taught her was within her grasp.

Her hopeful assertion that 'the exchange would be for the better' was soon proved right. Brontë found unexpected delight in her new duties.[96] And, despite having lived there all her life, she found she could make friends in Haworth after all, for where she had previously struggled to integrate, her status as married woman allowed her to enter society with a new, unprecedented confidence. Thus, to Ellen she wrote, 'my life is changed indeed – to be wanted continually – to be constantly called for and occupied seems so strange: yet it is marvellously good ... as far as my experience of matrimony goes, I think it tends to draw you out of and away from yourself.'[97]

Charlotte's use of alliteration accentuates her incredulity. Her language is emphatic – she seems almost unwilling to believe that she is 'wanted continually', that she is 'constantly called for'. She is clearly as surprised as anyone at the strength of her enjoyment in the midst of her domestic and parochial chores. The feelings engendered are 'marvellously good'. Most revealing of all, however, is Brontë's perception of 'matrimony'. Her physical state is recalled, and doubtless, therefore, her lifelong battle with plainness. But, with her life now joined to that of another, her thoughts have been drawn beyond her own physicality. Marriage has directed her attention 'out of and away' from 'herself' and from those things that previously dominated her existence and occupied her mind. The combination of Nicholls's adoration, his constant need of her and her continual occupation had done for Brontë what fame could not. It had offered a measure of freedom from her persistent inner scrutiny. And, ironically, though she was busier than she had ever been, she had found rest.

The consequences of Charlotte's newfound contentment were far-reaching. Married life had proved invigorating, even health-giving. The long, increasingly cold Yorkshire autumn and winter that had habitually ravaged her body had little impact. In November 1854 she wrote to Margaret Wooler,

> For my own part – it is long since I have known such comparative immunity from headaches, sickness and indigestion as during the last three months ... My life is different from what it used to be ... may God make me thankful for it! I have a good, kind attached husband and every day makes my own attachment to him stronger.[98]

It was as if, as Nussey noted to Smith some years later, 'a halo of happiness seemed to surround her – a holy calm [that] pervaded her even in moments of excitement.'[99]

Charlotte's transformation was remarkable, but it would be wrong to claim that her complicated relationship with her own appearance had no bearing on her life post-marriage. Though generally surrounded by familiar faces and strengthened by her position as both clergyman's wife and famed author, she continued to struggle with the scrutiny (real or imagined) of others. Tension can once again be traced in those circumstances where she felt inferior or was forced to confront strangers alone. In a letter to Ellen she wrote, 'Arthur will go to the Consecration of Heptonstall Church – D.V. but I don't mean to accompany him – I hardly like coming in contact with all the Mrs. Parsons.'[100] The 'Mrs. Parsons' are presented as an existential threat. They are grouped together, the word 'all' implying that they assemble in large numbers. In this setting, her husband's position offered no protection against the dissecting eyes of the other clergy wives. Her celebrity status no doubt proved an even greater hindrance, increasing interest in her person and consequently deepening her social anxiety.

Despite these setbacks, overall, Charlotte remained happier and healthier than she had perhaps ever been and, though writing had been temporarily supplanted by domestic life, at the close of 1854 her thoughts returned to those stories that she had begun in the late spring of 1853. She revisited *Willie Ellin*, a tale that would eventually become *Emma*, the first twenty pages of Brontë's final novel. Though destined to remain ever unfinished by her own hand, her recommencement of it can be viewed as a sign of her renewed mind and more rested body.[101]

Her writing proved neither all-consuming nor rapid, but the resurrection of Charlotte Brontë the novelist underscores the centrality of literary production to her life. The headstrong Charlotte, who had tenaciously sent off manuscript after manuscript to every major publisher in London had re-emerged, revitalized by love and by happiness. In a letter to Smith, written after Charlotte's death, Nicholls evoked his wife's enthusiasm for the creative process and for the sharing of her work. After all, these were pursuits that both she and her sisters had always found stimulating:

> as we sat by the fire listening to the howling of the wind around the house my poor wife suddenly said, 'If you had not been with me I must have been writing now' – She then ran upstairs, brought down and read aloud the beginning of her New Tale – When she had finished, I remarked, 'The Critics will accuse you of repetition as you have again introduced a school' – She replied, 'O, I shall alter that – I always begin two or three times before I can please myself'. But it was not to be …[102]

Nicholls later vehemently denied accusations that he had discouraged his wife from further publication and from her writing.[103] His early pride in her works supports his defence, but he clearly understood the negative impact that 'the Critics' to whom he referred had had upon his wife.[104] No doubt he had witnessed the seismic bearing that censure, whether directed toward her work or to her appearance, had had upon her in the past and was keen to protect her from it in the future.

Whether Charlotte would ever have returned to any form of public life is not known. She was not given the opportunity to develop her story, to decide whether to publish her work once again or to consciously shape her future relationship with celebrity. It is possible that the inner Shirley Keeldar might have triumphed – that Charlotte, emboldened by her husband's love and her elevated position in her local community, would have summoned the courage to return to the fray. It is conceivable that she would have drawn from her real experience of love to produce works of great merit. It is equally possible that the seemingly passive Helen Burns would instead have prevailed and that the once famous author would have disappeared into deliberate, relative obscurity – choosing instead a life of stability and parochial duty. Had this been the case, her wardrobe would have come to reflect this change. Undoubtedly, the conspicuous nature of her 'Going Away Dress' suggests that, at the time of its manufacture, the author did not envisage a life devoid of all prominence. However, it is important to remember that its acquisition occurred before she had experienced marriage and domestic happiness and therefore before she was in full possession of the facts.

At the time that Charlotte chose her 'Going Away Dress', she probably did not anticipate that within little more than six months of its manufacture she would be pregnant – effectively relegating the dress to the side-lines. Her marriage settlement, drawn up in May 1854, had made provision for the possibility of children, though, given Charlotte's age and state of health, there was no certainty. She tentatively announced the pregnancy to Ellen in mid-January 1855, 'don't conjecture – dear Nell – for it is too soon yet – though I have certainly never before felt as I have done lately'.[105] Even at this early point, she was suffering from 'continual faint sickness' but much worse was to come. Within just a few days, Charlotte was confined to bed, too unwell even to respond to letters of concern from Ellen. By this time, Arthur and Patrick were so anxious for her health that they sent to Bradford for the doctor. Dr

MacTurk pronounced that though her sickness 'would be of some duration', he was of the belief that 'after a few weeks' 'her health [would] again return'.[106]

But Charlotte's health did not return. In fact, she continued to deteriorate. On 17 February she made her will. Overturning the arrangements of her marriage settlement in which she had made provision for Patrick, she now left everything to Arthur. Any reservations that she had had about Nicholls had long since passed. She wrote to Ellen, 'I find in my husband the tenderest nurse, the kindest support – the best earthly comfort that ever woman had. His patience never fails, and it is tried by sad days and Broken nights.'[107]

As was to be expected, friends rallied round, offering help and advice, love and comfort. Ellen kept in close touch with Arthur and Patrick by letter, sent medicines, and Martha, beside herself with anguish, busied herself with practical tasks and nursing care. Margaret Wooler, in an attempt to focus

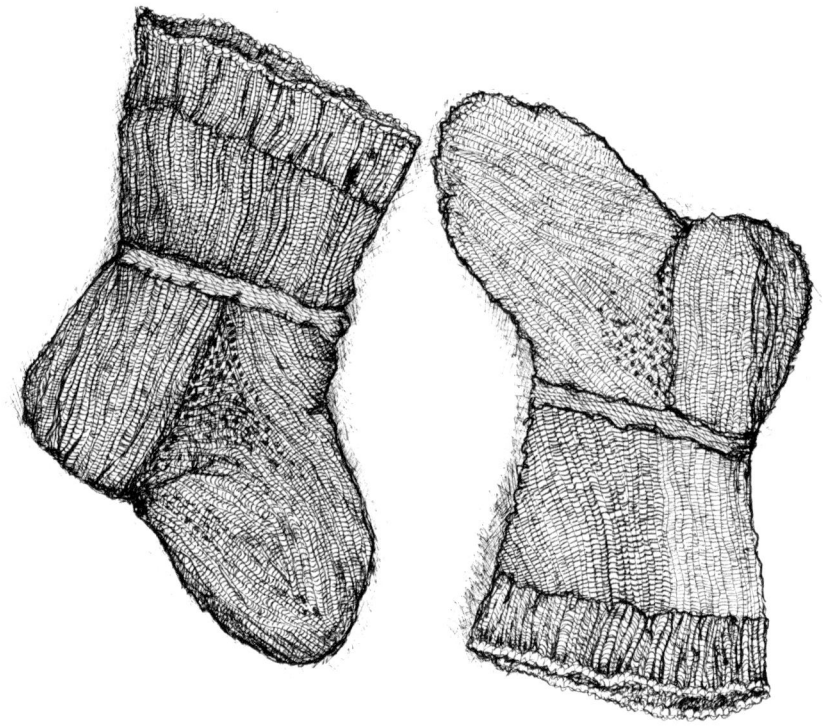

10.7 *Knitted baby socks sent by Elizabeth Smith for Charlotte Brontë's unborn baby, SG35/6B*

Charlotte's attentions on the future, sent a cotton lawn baby's bonnet featuring drawn thread work, self-coloured embroidery and a lace insert.[108] A pair of knitted baby socks, made by Charlotte whilst staying with the Smiths in London, are thought to have been returned to her by Elizabeth Smith for the child that was to come.[109]

These little gifts and messages of reassurance hint at Charlotte's low emotional state. Her friends, many of whom had known her for many years, knew just how connected Charlotte's physical health was to her state of mind. Martha tried desperately to encourage her to look forward to the new baby, but Charlotte could only reply 'I dare say I shall be glad sometime, but I am so ill – so weary.'[110]

Even despite the devoted care of all those around her, Charlotte faded away. It seemed as though Patrick's worst fears had been realized. Going into the parsonage kitchen he said, 'I told you, Martha, that there was no sense in Charlotte's marrying at all, for she was not strong enough for marriage.'[111] Clearly, it was not marriage itself to which Patrick referred, rather it was to its then inevitable consequences. He had buried far too many young women in his time as parish priest to underestimate the dangers of pregnancy and childbirth – especially to someone as delicate and small-framed as Charlotte.

In the weeks before she died, Charlotte wrote to Amelia Taylor, 'my sufferings are very great – my nights are indescribable – sickness with scarce a reprieve – I strain until what I vomit is mixed with blood'.[112] She soon became so thin that, according to Tabitha Brown, 'light showed through her hand when it was held up and her face was so drawn that she looked like a little old woman'.[113] In her final surviving letter Charlotte wrote to Ellen of her now 'skeleton emaciation'.[114] Though her words were chosen to convey the severity of her current illness, through them she reveals an implicit but characteristic hypersensitivity to her physicality and to the reactions of others, which had dogged her since her youth. Indeed, it seems as though Brontë's profound awareness of her appearance continued to the grave. It had only been the love of her 'dear patient constant Arthur' that had proved an unexpected distraction from persistent self-scrutiny.[115] That this reprieve from her lifelong battle had been so short only makes her untimely death all the more poignant.

By the third week of March, Charlotte had slipped into what Elizabeth Gaskell described as a 'low wandering delirium'. According to the biographer, she woke only intermittently. In her last days she stirred into consciousness, woken by her husband's desperate prayers. On seeing him she whispered, 'Oh, I am not going to die am I? He will not separate us; we have been so happy.'[116]

Charlotte took her last breath in the early hours of 31 March 1855. She was thirty-eight years old. Her unborn child died with her. Her distraught husband immediately threw himself on the bed with loud and violent sobs but Patrick, in contrast, walked silently away, leaving Martha and Tabitha to close Charlotte's eyes and prepare her body for burial.

In the hours that followed, her oldest friend and confidante, Ellen Nussey, arrived in Haworth to be met with the news that Charlotte had died. With the help of Martha and Tabitha, Ellen set about arranging the evergreens and blooms that would decorate her friend's 'lifeless form'. As she did so, she could not help but recall 'the flowers [she had] spread in her honour at her wedding breakfast' only nine months before.[117]

We do not know which garments the women chose for Charlotte as they readied her body for her coffin, but just like the receiver into which she had first been placed as a crying, writhing baby, they would mark, indeed they would witness, a crucial moment of her time on earth. In keeping with contemporary customs, she would have been dressed in a smart outfit that had particular significance for family or friends. Though her 'Going Away Dress' and her wedding dress might have been obvious choices, their survival excludes them. But whatever she wore, whatever she was lain in, it is poignant to think that the chosen ensemble, just like Charlotte's own body, has long since turned to dust in the vault of St Michael and All Angels' crypt where she was laid to rest on Wednesday 3 April 1855. It has gone silent to the grave, taking its last secrets with it.

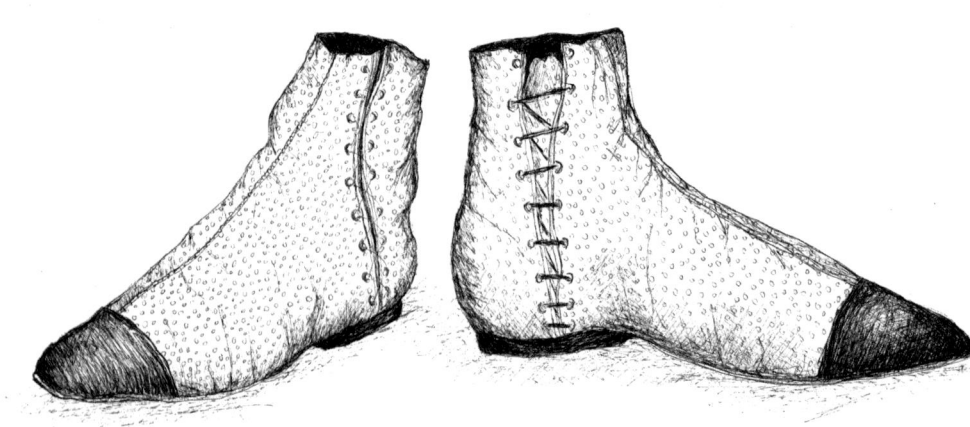

11.1 *Charlotte Brontë's spotted canvas and leather boots, D96*

11

Afterlives

Despite what one might be tempted to think, Charlotte's death did not mark the end for the clothes she had owned and worn. Certainly it was a kind of ending, but, for the most part, it was not *the* end. Indeed, with the exception of those that ventured with her into the darkness and dankness of the vault, each of Charlotte's garments and accessories began a new phase of life that spring. Their subsequent stories are as varied and distinct as the items themselves, for this great mass of things, this family of bonnets and gloves and gowns and stockings would not stay together for long.

As is so often the case with the clothes left behind, grief played a big part in their fate – or in their initial fate at very least. Nicholls was deeply affected by the loss of his wife but did not view them as vestiges of death or solemn reminders of sickness and sadness. He was not repelled by the lostness of them. Rather, he saw them as potent, material connectors to the woman he had loved; as living things in which something of Charlotte, something of the intimacy that they had shared and the life they had led, still resided. He was, in consequence, fiercely protective of the things his wife had worn and was only made more so by the fans and souvenir hunters, scandal mongers and gossip merchants who bombarded Charlotte's remaining family and friends with requests for objects and information – a phenomenon greatly inflamed by the publication of Elizabeth Gaskell's sensational biography in 1857, which saw floods of visitors pour into Haworth and endless letters arrive at the parsonage.

Arthur had been strongly against Gaskell's book from the start. Mindful of some of the more sensitive aspects of Charlotte's life that could, and indeed did, become public knowledge, he had grave concerns about its potential consequences. But the prospect of a complimentary memoir, written by an author of renown, had wakened Patrick's deep, paternal pride and there appeared to be no stopping him. It was a decision that both men would come to bitterly regret.

Though he viewed everything Charlotte had worn as sacrosanct, Nicholls did not keep it all for himself. Perhaps at his dying wife's instigation, some garments were passed on to Martha – the woman who had so faithfully served and watched over her mistress down through the years. These were valued both for their usefulness as garments to be worn and enjoyed, for Martha had not money enough for such things herself, but also as mementoes of love, long friendship and fidelity. He bequeathed numerous other items too to those who had known Charlotte, including a hand-stitched, whitework collar given to Martha Carr née Hodgkinson, a favourite student who had attended the Haworth National School where Arthur had taught, and Charlotte had sometimes assisted.[1]

There were, though, many things that Arthur did retain, not least Charlotte's wedding gown, some flowers from her wedding bonnet and her black satin slippers. These he would not be parted from – even when faced with the unexpected prospect of leaving Haworth for good.

Death had been creeping up on the eighty-four-year-old Patrick Brontë for some time and yet when, after a series of violent convulsions, it did finally come, it was still a surprise to all. He had defied the odds so many times. He had outlived his wife, and then, one after another, his six children. It seemed as if he might live out the years of which his loved ones had together been robbed. But, when Nicholls found him unconscious, early on the morning of 7 June 1861, it was apparent that he was fading fast. His death later that evening wrought real and genuine grief of the like Arthur could not have imagined in the months before his engagement to Charlotte. Their differences had long since been put to bed, and an honest closeness had developed between them – one confirmed by Patrick's decision to leave the vast majority of his estate to his 'beloved and esteemed Son-in Law … for his own absolute benefit'.[2]

By the time Patrick died, Arthur had been living and working in the parish of Haworth for sixteen years. Ever since Patrick's second stroke in 1853, he had calmly and capably carried out an increasing portion of Patrick's clerical duties alongside his own. It was not surprising, therefore, that Nicholls's formal instatement as officiating minister at Haworth was considered by all to be a certainty. But, in spite of his many years of good service, the trustees made quite a different decision. Whether they wished to dissociate the parish from the Brontës and their increasing fame or merely to assert their ultimate authority, it was the Reverend John Wade who secured the post, meaning Arthur was soon forced to face a triple bereavement – the loss of the closest thing he had to a father, his home and his employment.

After the ignominy of Haworth, Arthur could not be persuaded to apply for a new clerical post. Rather, he made the decision to return to Ireland, the land of his birth. The clothes that he had saved accompanied him – safely cradled in the wooden Rowntree's box as they were tossed and turned by the Irish Sea. Other possessions went too, as many as he could carry with him. There was Charlotte's jewellery, her paintbox, the Reverend Brontë's gun, the imposing grandfather clock that had faithfully kept them all to time. There was George Richmond's 1850 chalk portrait, Branwell's oil paintings of his sisters and a huge quantity of the Brontë siblings' early work. These were the things that summed up life for him in Haworth. These were the things that he could not bear to be parted from.[3]

Martha went with him to Banagher to help him settle in, but perhaps also to see what life in another place was like. But though she was warmly welcomed by Nicholls's family and friends, and even gained a reputation for her immaculate English sponge cakes and gingerbread biscuits, by late 1862 Martha and all the things that she had been gifted were back in Haworth. Though she returned to Ireland to visit Arthur on at least six more occasions over the coming years, it was here that she resided with her mother until 1868 when she moved to nearby Saltaire to live with her sister and brother-in-law, Ann and Benjamin Binns.[4] Martha moved back to Haworth in 1877 where, ever reluctant to sell any more of the precious clothes and objects than poverty absolutely dictated, she spent the remainder of her life alone, in a small, rather damp house just a ten-minute walk away from the Haworth Parsonage, surrounded by all the remaining things that she treasured. Martha Brown died on 19 January 1880 aged just fifty-one. All her worldly goods, including those bequeathed to her by Arthur and by Charlotte, were split between her five, large-familied, financially constrained sisters.

Arthur Bell Nicholls's life in Ireland was very different to the one that he had left behind in Yorkshire. He was a farmer now and spent his days working the land and tending the twenty acres that surrounded Hill House on the outskirts of Banagher.[5] His recently widowed aunt, Harriette Lucinda Bell, and cousin, Mary Anna Bell, who owned the house, were in much need of help and Arthur, keen to honour the woman who had sacrificially brought him up, set about gaining the new skills that he would need to make the farm a success.

Arthur's life was much changed, but he did not forget Charlotte or the love that they had shared. The things that he had brought with him continued to bring solace and to connect him with those that he had loved and lost, and particularly with the wife that he had for so long adored. In honour of Charlotte and her achievements, he displayed many of the objects that he had saved about Hill House, ensuring that those that came to visit were immediately confronted with a 'multitude of Brontë relics'.[6] And even when, in the late summer of 1864, Arthur made the surprising decision to marry his cousin Mary, a woman twelve years his junior, the material reminders of his first wife were not swept from view. Rather, as he gained a greater foothold at the farmhouse, the quantity of Brontë memorabilia placed on show multiplied. For from the very outset Nicholls had made it clear that he had 'buried his heart' with Charlotte and that if he and Mary were to marry, his second wife would have no choice but to live beneath the shadowy presence of his first.[7] To her great credit, this she duly did – even going so far as to accompany visitors to the drawing room to view George Richmond's chalk portrait of Charlotte and quietly utter, 'She was a very clever woman'.[8]

It would be easy to assume that Arthur's move to the relative isolation of Banagher would deter the many souvenir hunters and biographers who still voraciously sought to obtain a little piece of the famed author, Charlotte Brontë. This was not the case. Arthur and Mary's quiet life was all too often punctuated by the uninvited arrival of persistent individuals, keen to arrange a meeting with Charlotte's former husband or to purchase a piece of Brontë memorabilia. A few, most notably the cogent biographer Clement Shorter, were successful in wearing Nicholls down, and left clutching handfuls of manuscripts and letters.[9] Most were turned away empty handed. But when Arthur died of bronchitis on 2 December 1906, aged eighty-seven, Charlotte's possessions could no longer be kept together in the way that they had since their arrival in Ireland more than forty years before. Over the coming years, Mary arranged several sales of Brontëana via Sotheby's, to raise much-needed money upon which to live.[10] Some things, like Charlotte's wedding dress and some other, more personal items, such as the author's amethyst engagement ring or gold, garnet brooch, were shared amongst close relatives, but the vast majority of the long-treasured things were sold. By December 1916, the year after Mary's own death, nothing was left.[11]

Arthur and Martha's deaths had marked a juncture in the lives of Charlotte's surviving garments – or of those that had remained with them at least. For once those who had lived and loved and walked with the author were dead, their futures had suddenly become far more precarious. Of those many garments that Martha had bequeathed to her family, some were worn, cut up, or refashioned, made to fit new owners and to witness *their* daily lives. Others were inevitably sold, for though Martha's numerous relatives had felt some emotional attachment, indeed some items have continued to be proudly kept and cherished by subsequent generations, as demand for Brontë memorabilia grew and their financial needs became more urgent, so too did the family's interest in selling. After all, it was the natural order of things. And now, the garments that the author had worn on her back, that had borne close witness to the minutiae and the magnificence of her life, had been pushed out into the world to fend for themselves.

Of course, it would be wrong to assume that Charlotte's clothes faced exactly the same fates as do our own after death. Her fame did, to a large extent, offer them considerable protection. Though no longer witnesses to her *life*, those garments and accessories now owned by museums, collectors and enthusiasts had transitioned into witnesses of, and indeed active participants in, her *legacy*. They had not, unlike the things we tend now to consign to the charity shops, become entirely disconnected from their original owner. Rather, they had morphed into ennobled curios whose value now lay, not in their practicality or in the sentiment that they engendered, but in their close association with one of the greatest writers of the nineteenth century.

11.2 *Feasible reconstruction of muslin dress*

The formation of the Brontë Society in December 1893 and the subsequent opening of the Brontë Museum in the upper floor of the Yorkshire Penny Bank in 1895, only cemented their worth. As the Society's reputation and buying power grew, the Brontës' things began to migrate back to Haworth with surprising rapidity. Some had remained close, some were donated by members of Martha's extended family, some were returned by proud and dedicated locals, whilst others travelled many miles, sometimes even traversing vast oceans. When, in 1928, the contents of the museum were finally moved back to their rightful place inside the Haworth Parsonage, many of Charlotte's clothes were displayed in the very rooms in which they had been cut out and meticulously stitched together. When viewed within the context of the house, surrounded by some of the many other things that the Brontës' had owned and used, it was often said that the clothes were imbued with a sort of haunting presence, not based in reality of course, but wholly moving and evocative, nonetheless. Yet, even despite their redolence and their potent ability to affect and to connect, the garments and accessories were still widely viewed as curiosities of 'deep interest' rather than valid sources of biography or of culture, as artefacts that define a point on the map of human existence or consciously and unconsciously express the absolute individuality of the person who had owned and worn them.[12] As such, though enjoyed by countless visitors, they were not yet freed to fully communicate.

A great number of years would pass before Charlotte's ever-growing, surviving wardrobe would at last be given the chance to speak. A revolutionary transformation of attitudes towards material things, particularly within academic circles, would have to take place before historic clothing, and indeed any artefacts, would begin to be regarded as deserving of serious study and consideration. What has come to be known as the 'Material Turn', which began with a revival of interest in the fields of archaeology and anthropology and, spurred on by the teachings of Karl Marx, was combined with a rediscovery of the importance of objects in the formation of a society, sought to write nature, bodies and things into history, into the humanities.[13] But this new emphasis on matter did not begin in earnest until the last decades of the twentieth century – some fifty years after the return of Charlotte's clothes to the parsonage.[14]

As the years passed, forward-thinking scholars began to be inspired to cross disciplinary boundaries and look more closely at the many other types of objects or physical places and spaces connected with the Brontës, including the very bricks and mortar of the parsonage itself. These many studies have helped to join the large and small dots of history and deepen our understanding of the Brontë family's life and works and the world in which they all lived.[15] But, though great strides had been made in many new and previously overlooked areas, though much new knowledge had been unearthed, a further forty years would pass before the garments themselves, the things that Arthur and Martha had so treasured, would be visited in any depth – before dress, that great scholarly unmentionable, could, at last, be mentioned.[16]

When, nine years ago, my research into Charlotte's surviving wardrobe first began, there was no way of knowing where it would all lead. The vast collection was, after all, made up of close to 150 items, each representing a different period or facet of the author's life, and each with its own unique story to tell. It was a constantly moveable feast, with new pieces arriving just as others were being discounted, and new information challenging earlier hypotheses.[17] The work was not fast. It could not be, for every testimony had to be taken, recorded and authenticated – a slow and methodical process that sometimes took many months and many forms. There were stumbling blocks, dead ends and myth, that great confuser, proved itself a persistent and ever-present adversary; one only confounded through the quiet, yet meticulous building of evidence wrought from places far and wide.

It was not until the last years that any kind of picture began to emerge and even then it could not ever be said to be whole. It was a puzzle with missing pieces; a glass obscured darkly. For too many garments have never made it back to the Brontë Parsonage Museum and, for endless reasons, many witnesses' stories are far from complete. Some still hold secrets within, that only new additions to the collection or new technology can help reveal to the generations of scholars yet to come. But even with these challenges, by the end, if such a finite word should or could ever be uttered, something could be said for certain. These gowns and bonnets and bags and boots have presented to us a very different Charlotte Brontë. Their testimonies have revealed a woman who is at once more rounded, more three-dimensional than any yet met before. She is braver, bolder and yet more vulnerable. She is less isolated, less parochial, more Victorian and more globalized. She is more fashion conscious, more rigid, more open to change. She defies long-held preconceptions and conforms where conformity was least expected. She shows herself to be uncertain, self-hating, but also provocative, strong, unerring and tenacious. As such, this body of evidence – this ordinary, extraordinary, varied, tangible body of evidence has more than proved its worth.

Glossary of Terms

A la paresseuse A form of corset lacing that allows the wearer to tighten their own corset.

Alpaca A supple textile of the wool of the alpaca, a species of the South American camelid.

Alpaca Orleans A lightweight, plain-weave fabric made with a cotton warp and an alpaca weft.

Alum A chemical compound typically formed from hydrated double sulphate salt of aluminium and potassium.

Angria A kingdom invented by Charlotte and Branwell Brontë between 1834–9. It is situated on the eastern borders of the Glass Town Federation (or Verdopolis).

Ankle-cuffs The decorated cuff of a moccasin that is traditionally joined to the neck of the shoe.

Baleen A filter-feeder system inside the mouths of baleen whales. This supple, pliable keratinous material is used to add strength and structure to corsets or garments.

Barège A light, loose-weave wool and silk dress fabric resembling gauze.

Baste To tack through layers of fabric before they are sewn in place.

Beaver bonnet Heavy, waterproof bonnet formed from the fur of a beaver.

Bertha A deep collar of lace or muslin that falls in a continuous band and covers a low neckline.

Bias In which a fabric is cut or pulled diagonally across the weave.

Biot The front row of feathers on the wing of a bird – specifically goose, duck, turkey or chicken – and widely used in millinery.

Bishop sleeve A long, voluminous sleeve that is gathered at the wrist.

Block print A print in which a pattern is transferred onto the surface of a fabric using a wooden block that has been cut to form a relief shape.

Blonde Fine, continuous bobbin lace originally made from undyed silk.

Bobbin lace An openwork mesh made by braiding, twisting and knotting fine threads that have been wound on bobbins.

Body dysmorphia A mental health condition in which an individual is preoccupied by flaws in their appearance and how they are perceived by others. Their views are often far removed from reality.

Bombazine A twilled dress fabric of worsted and silk or cotton often used to make mourning clothes.

Book muslin A fine, diaphanous material, which was folded in a book-like manner when sold by the piece.

Brontëana i) Relics that once belonged to the Brontës.
ii) Name given to Brontë-related items that can be purchased in a giftshop.

Busk A flat, ruler-like object that is inserted into a channel in the front of a corset. Typically made from wood, whalebone or metal and frequently embellished.

Busk point A lace used to tie the busk in position in the corset. Two holes are often present at the base through which this is threaded.

Bust enhancers Pads that are sewn inside a corset to give the impression of a larger bust.

Calash A folding head-covering made to protect women's hair in the late eighteenth century.

Cambric A lightweight, closely woven cotton.

Cape A short cloak worn as outerwear.

Changeant silk Also known as shot silk, an iridescent silk formed from two different coloured warp and weft threads.

Chemise A female undergarment worn to separate the dress from the body. Low-necked, short-sleeved and composed of either linen or cotton.

Chemisette A sleeveless, muslin or light cotton half-shirt that was worn to fill in a low-necked dress.

Childbed linen Infant garments and bedding.

Chip bonnet A bonnet formed from pulped or shaved wood.

Clout A piece of cloth used to form a nappy.

Coburg A wool and cotton twilled stuff often used in mourning wear.

Cochineal A red colourant made from the Dactylopius coccus beetle.

Daguerreotype The first widely available form of photograph.

Demi-full dress Smart evening wear.

Demi-full sleeves Sleeves that finish at mid-forearm.

Ditsy print A fine, floral, printed, often cotton fabric.

Dye An organic molecule with absorption bands in the visible spectrum region that is used to change the colour of cloth, or another material. Dyes can be 'natural' or synthetic.

Early life adversity Adversity that takes place in infancy or youth.

En tablier Trimmings placed on the front skirt of a gown, and which form a triangular shape.

Eyelets Holes made either side of a corset or bodice through which a lace or ribbon is then laced. Originally, these were hand-stitched, but, later, made from bone, wood or metal.

Figured fabric A fabric that has been deliberately woven with a pattern that shows on the upper surface. This is achieved by changes made to the warp and weft.

Flax Blue-flowered plant from which linen is made. This term is sometimes applied to the fabric itself.

Flounce A strip of gathered material or lace that has been sewn at its upper edge to the main body of a skirt or sleeve.

Fluorescence The emission or luminescence of light by a substance that has absorbed light or another form of electromagnetic radiation. Typically, this excitation is caused by the absorption of energy from incident radiation or particles, such as X-rays or electrons.

Full dress The very smartest, most formal of evening attire.

Furbelow An alternative term used to describe a flounce or decorative frill.

Gall A gallnut is often produced by oak trees as a defence against parasitic wasps. It can be used to produce a lasting rich brown or yellow dyestuff.

Glacé silk A glossy, taffeta silk fabric with a high sheen.

Glass Town The earliest created kingdom of the Brontë siblings.

Glazed cotton A strong cotton fabric that has a shiny surface as a result of chemical or physical finishing processes that cause a sheen to appear on the upper surface of the fabric.

Goffering iron A long, thin, barrel-shaped iron used to press ruffles.

Gusset A triangular piece of material that is inserted into a garment or pattern to add extra width to the piece.

Haematein An oxidized form of haematoxylin, used in dyeing and printing.

Haematoxylin A black, dark blue or violet dye extracted from the heart of a logwood tree.

Half-long sleeves Sleeves that are cut to finish at the elbow.

Heliotrope A vivid purple.

Indigo A natural blue-green dye extracted from the leaves of plants from the *Indigofera* genus.

Infrared The region of the electromagnetic spectrum that includes wavelengths from 0.78 to about 300 μm. Infrared rays are longer than visible rays from the red spectrum that are felt as heat.

Jacquard weaving A complex system of weaving first invented by Joseph-Marie Jacquard in 1804. The process uses a series of perforated cards that regulate the lifting and lowering of warp threads to create an often elaborate and complicated design.

Kid leather A soft, pliable leather made from the hide of young goats.

Knife pleats A specific type of pleating that is sharply pressed and where each pleat is three layers of fabric thick and yet all folded in one direction.

Lawn Fine plain-weave linen or cotton that has a silky finish. This fabric was historically made in France, but, later, also in Britain.

Lining A layer of fabric used to add warmth to a garment or to smooth/cover unsightly or rough inside seams. Typically made from cotton or linen.

Leg of mutton Sleeves composed of voluminous puffed shoulders and upper arms that then taper to a narrowed lower arm and wrist.

Leghorn straw Italian straw or straw bonnets associated with Livorno (Legorno) in Italy.

Lorgnettes Spectacles on a handle.

Lunar caustic Another name for silver nitrate, an inorganic compound used to produce indelible ink.

Mercerization The process of refining and strengthening cellulosic fibres by dipping the thread or fabric in caustic soda or sulphuric acid. This process allows the fabric or threads to absorb considerably more dye.

Mixed stuffs A general term used to describe mixed-fibre fabrics often with a woollen warp and a silk or cotton weft.

Mordant A substance, typically an inorganic oxide, that is added to a dye vat to help the dye fix to the fabric.

Morning dress Dress worn in the day and never past six pm. Note difference to mourning dress, which was worn during periods of mourning.

Muslin A very lightweight cotton with a loose weave.

Nankeen A durable, cotton cloth with a yellow tinge.

Napkins Nineteenth-century word for nappies.

Orchil/Orcein A lichen-based dye that produces a red or purple tint.

Oxytocin A peptide hormone released by the posterior pituitary gland during periods of social bonding, childbirth and reproduction.

Pagoda sleeves Term used to describe the wide, bell-shaped sleeve of the 1860s that flared from the elbow.

Pantalettes White drawers with legs that poked out beneath the skirt.

Paramatta A high-quality tweed associated with mourning dress.

Passementerie Ornamental braids or trimmings, which include cords, froggings, buttons or tassels.

Pattens An outer, protective shoe worn to elevate the feet from mud or rough terrain.

Pelisse A ladies' coat or jacket.

Pilche An outer nappy designed to protect the clothes from leaks.

Pinking A raw edge of fabric cut in zig-zags or scallops using a sculpted metal implement.

Piping The insertion of a fabric-covered cord that stiffens and adds decoration to seams or to the edges of garments.

Placket A deliberate opening in a piece of clothing and/or the piece of fabric sewn beneath it.

Plaid A chequered or tartan twill cloth.

Prussian blue A dark blue pigment produced through the oxidation of ferrous ferrocyanide salts.

Raman spectroscopy A spectroscopic technique used to establish the vibrational modes of molecules.

Resilience factors Those patterns of positive adaptation that are drawn upon in the face of significant risk or adversity – these factors are learned and not innate.

Sartorial Of or connected to clothing, to tailoring or to the style of dress.

Sateen i) A (typically) cotton fabric with a shiny, satin upper surface.
ii) A fabric made using the satin weave structure but made with spun (mercerized, carded or combed) yarns instead of filament (loose yarns).

Satin i) A close warp-faced weave that is deliberately formed to give a lustrous, smooth surface to the upper side of the fabric. The weave is so close that the warp threads largely cover the weft threads.
ii) A lustrous silk fabric made using the satin weave.

Self-concept clarity The extent to which beliefs about the self are clearly and confidently delineated, defined and become consistent and stable over time.

Self-efficacy The extent to which one considers oneself to have the ability to exert control over one's own motivation, behaviour and social environment.

SEM EDX (Scanning Electron Microscopes) employ electron beams to obtain key information from the nanoscale. They rely on interaction with some form/excitation of X-rays (EDX).

Shift A women's undergarment worn next to the skin to absorb dirt and oils from the body.

Spectra (Specifically Electromagnetic) Spectra refers to all frequencies of electromagnetic radiation and to the particular distribution of electromagnetic radiation released or absorbed by that specific object.

Spencer Short jacket with long sleeves and a high neckline, popular during the Regency period.

Starch A stiffening substance that is applied to fabric to make it more rigid and crease resistant.

Staylace A lace used to close a corset or pair of stays.

Stays A pair of boned, laced, bodices worn under clothes from the late sixteenth century until the end of the nineteenth century.

Straight pins Common, straight pins used in sewing or in the closure of clothing.

Strait-laced i) Wearing a corset or stays tightly laced.
ii) Having unwaveringly strong morality.

Stuff A thickly woven cloth, often formed from wool.

Sumptuary laws Laws designed to limit what could be worn based on social rank and wealth. They controlled which fabrics, colours, buttons, embroideries and furs could be worn and by whom.

Tamboured Embroidery technique that involves stretching fabric and embroidering a chain-like stitch to embroider or attach beads, sequins or feathers using a tambour hook.

Tight-lacing The practice of lacing a corset extremely tight in order to lessen the size and girth of the natural waist.

Tippet A long scarf or shawl of fur or lace.

Tucker A piece of lace, linen or lawn worn beneath a bodice or as an insert worn to cover a low-fronted dress.

Tulle A very fine net fabric made from silk threads.

Twill A fabric (often wool based) formed from a weave that is characterized by diagonal lines produced by a series of floats that have been staggered in the warp direction.

Ugly bonnet Brim and bonnet protector made from silk or cotton and reed. Descendant of the calash.

Ultramarine blue A natural mineral dye that comes from lapis lazuli. It can be simulated by heating sulphur, clay, soda ash and some form of reducing agent.

Vamp The part of a shoe upper, covering the top of the foot. In Iroquois moccasins, these are typically formed from velvet or leather.

Vandyke points Large zigzags that imitate the notable, pointed collars and cuffs so apparent in the work of Van Dyck.

Velvet A clothing or upholstery fabric made from silk, cotton or wool and characterized by a short, dense but extremely soft warp pile.

Warp Yarns that run the entire length of the cloth (vertically). They are stronger than the weft yarns.

Weft Yarns that weave in and out horizontally and at right angles with the warp threads of the cloth.

Worsted A wool-based yarn, which is carded and combed to produce a smooth, even surface. It was a speciality of the West Riding of Yorkshire.

Wrapper or wrapping gown A printed cotton or wool dressing-gown-like garment worn by women in the mornings when at home.

Tables

Table 1: Clothing Requirements in Accordance with Events Detailed in Charlotte Brontë's Extant Letters

Criteria Set for the Classification and Organization of Data

- The information on which this table has been based, has been taken directly from Charlotte Brontë's extant letters, which have been included in the comprehensive collection, *The Letters of Charlotte Brontë*, ed. by Margaret Smith, 3 vols. (Oxford: Oxford University Press, 1995, 2000, 2004).
- Not all the letters written by Charlotte have survived. Equally, not all events that occurred in her life will have been referred to within these letters. The data must therefore be viewed as indicative rather than comprehensive.
- When an 'event' constitutes a visit or a prolonged period of time in one place or situation, it has been counted as one unless other 'events' that took place within that period were noted by Brontë within a letter. For example, her arrival in Brussels in 1842 is counted as one event, but her visits to Mary and Martha Taylor, whilst there, have been individually counted.
- The numbers of 'events' cannot be viewed as indicative of the numbers of garments owned by Brontë in any given year. In the first instance, Brontë clearly wore clothes on days when events did not occur or were not documented, and also, the same clothes would have been worn on numerous occasions.

- Though the chart documents changing sartorial requirements, each 'event' should not be viewed as suggestive of ownership of a necessary garment. For example, Charlotte Brontë *required* clothing for the opera when she first visited George Smith in 1848 but did not have the appropriate 'conspicuous' garments 'either with her or in the world'. Therefore, the event has been included within the category 'Distant Event Requiring Conspicuous Clothing' even though this clothing did not, at that time, exist.

- For the purposes of this chart, the term 'Local Events' includes all events that took place within a twenty-five-mile radius of Haworth and can be considered part of Brontë's typical, daily activities. Included within this are places of education and of work – Roe Head School, Dewsbury (25 miles away), Stonegappe (9 miles) and Rawdon (13.5 miles). Also included are the homes of friends – Ellen Nussey (Birstall, 15.6 miles), Mary and Martha Taylor (Hunsden, 14.8 miles).

- For the purposes of this chart, the term 'Distant Events' refers to all events that took place outside of a twenty-five-mile radius of Haworth.

- The term 'Events Requiring Everyday Clothing' refers here to garments that would typically make up a lower-middle-class woman's wardrobe and that, pre-fame, were worn by Brontë on a day-to-day basis. For example, this would include day-dresses in cotton, wool or muslin, silk gowns for evening, special occasions or for work (as governess), mourning wear, acceptable outerwear, headwear and accompanying accessories, as well as night and underwear. As specified by Charlotte Brontë herself, all of these would have been 'high-made country garments' and were limited in number.

- The term 'Events Requiring Conspicuous Clothing' refers here to garments that fall outside the expected perimeters of 'Everyday Clothing' for a lower-middle-class woman. It can be presumed that these garments would have been costlier, more fashionable or more ostentatious than those typically worn either by Brontë or by women of Brontë's socio-economic group at that time.

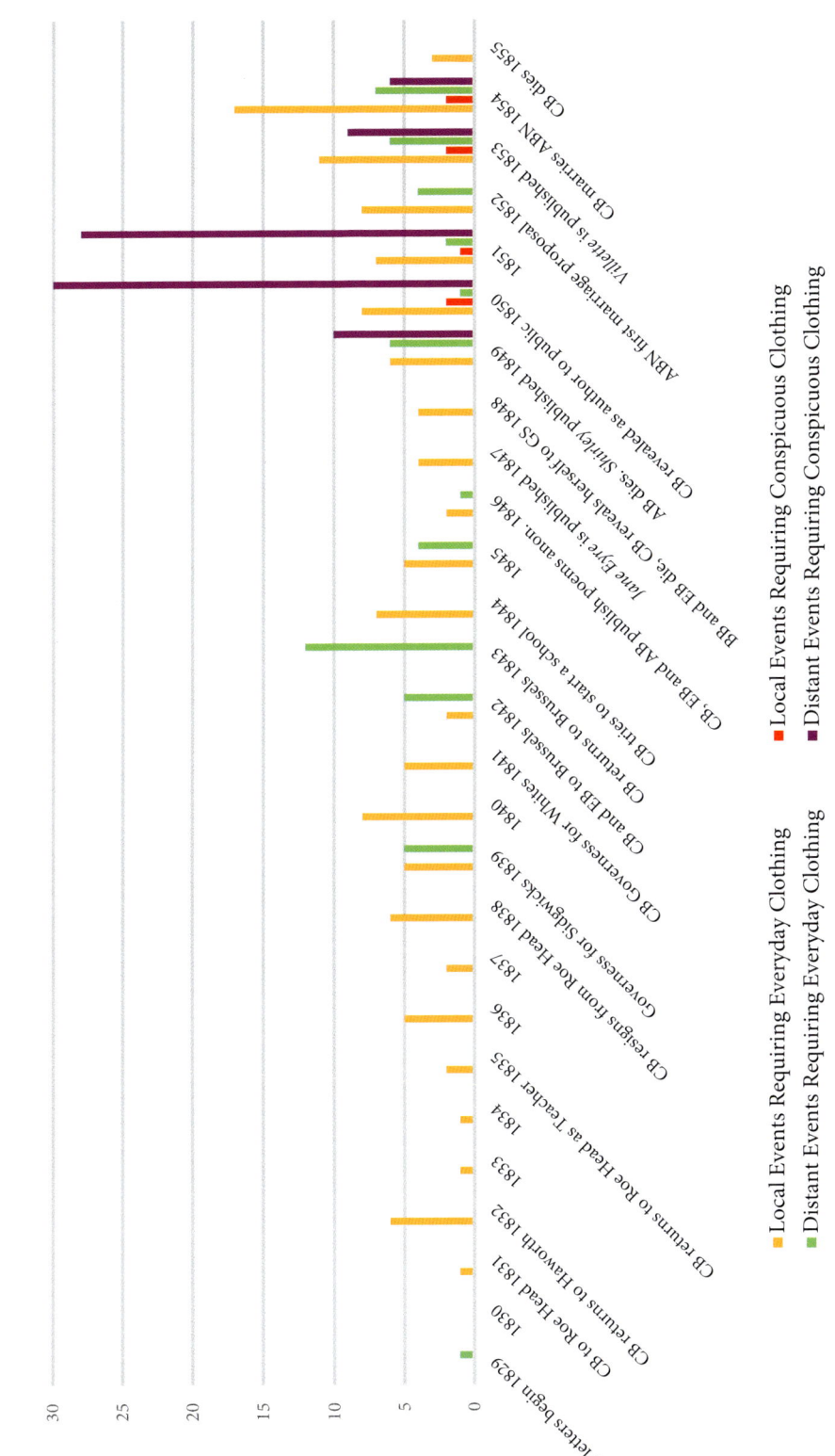

Table 1 Clothing requirements in accordance with events detailed in *Charlotte Brontë's* extant letters

Table 2: References to the Making, Receiving and Buying of Charlotte Brontë's Clothing in her Surviving Letters

Criteria Set for the Classification and Organization of Data

- The information on which this table has been based, has been taken directly from Charlotte Brontë's extant letters as included in the comprehensive collection, *The Letters of Charlotte Brontë*, ed. by Margaret Smith. 3 vols. (Oxford: Oxford University Press, 1995, 2000, 2004). Inevitably, these volumes do not include all letters ever written by Charlotte Brontë. Equally not all letters written by Charlotte are likely to have survived. The first surviving letter was written in 1829 and the last in March 1855. All references fall between these two dates.

- The term 'Clothing' here encompasses all types of garments and accessories including umbrellas and parasols, shoes and bonnets, but excludes jewellery, though much remains.

- Only those references which have clear connection to Charlotte Brontë's *own* wardrobe have been considered.

- The numbers of 'references' cannot be viewed as indicative of the total number of garments made, received or bought by Charlotte Brontë in any given year. Rather, this table only documents those referred to within her surviving letters.

- For the purposes of this table, the phrase 'Clothing Gifts Received by CB' signifies all references to the receiving of gifts by Charlotte Brontë. It should be noted that in almost every case, these 'gifts' were handmade by the giver. Often, though not exclusively, this giver was Ellen Nussey. Yet, as the majority of letters that have survived are to Ellen Nussey, this is not surprising.

- The phrase 'Clothing Purchases Made' refers here to all items of clothing purchased by or on behalf of Charlotte Brontë and documented within the surviving letters.
- For the purposes of this table, the phrase, 'References to the Sewing of Garments' signifies all references found within the surviving letters, to the making of Charlotte Brontë's clothing and of sewing. This 'making' could refer to both Charlotte Brontë herself as manufacturer, but also, to others who made clothing on her behalf.

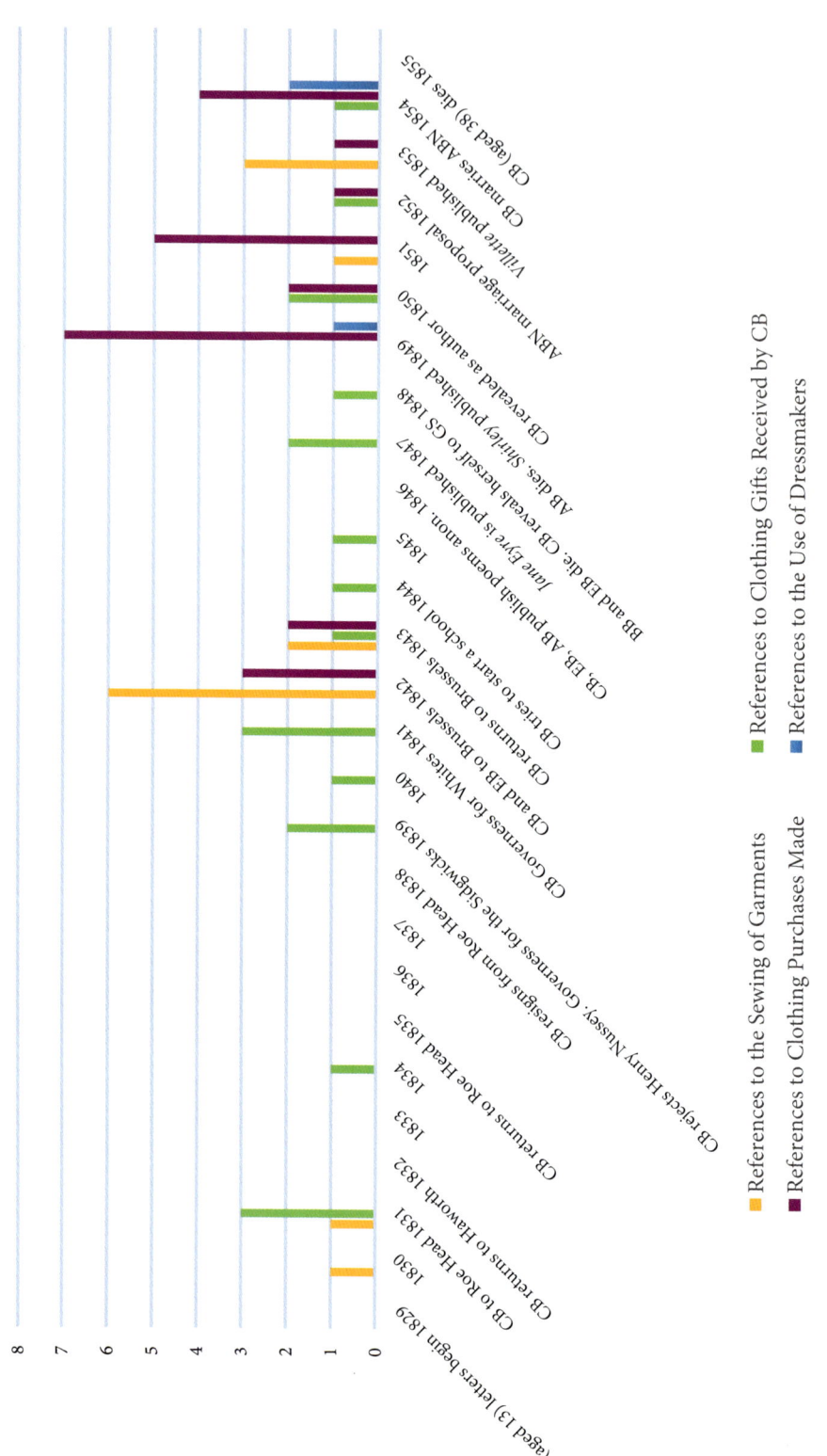

Table 2 References to the making, receiving and buying of Charlotte Brontë's clothing in her surviving letters

Notes

Chapter One

1 Anne Thackeray Ritchie, *Chapters from Some Memoirs* (London: Macmillan and Co., 1894), 60.

2 Elizabeth Wilson, *Adorned in Dreams* (London: Virago Press, 1987), 3.

3 This number does not include Charlotte Brontë's jewellery and is approximate because a small quantity of garments cannot be attributed categorically.

Chapter Two

1 Luke Howard, *The Climate of London Deduced from Meteorological Observations Made in the Metropolis and at Various Places Around it*, Vol. 1 (London: J. and A. Arch Cornhill, Longman, 1833).

2 Ibid., 42.

3 Elizabeth Cleghorn Gaskell, *The Life of Charlotte Brontë*, Vol. 1 (London: Smith, Elder and Company, 1857), 44.

4 William Moss, *An Essay on the Management, Nursing and Diseases of Children, From Birth and on the Treatment and Diseases of Pregnant and Lying-In Women with Remarks on the Domestic Practice of Medicine*, 2nd ed. (Egham: C. Boult and F.N. Longman, 1794), 34.

5 See Patrizia Calefato, 'Fashion and Worldliness: Language and Imagery of the Clothed Body', *Fashion Theory*, 1:1 (1997), 72. doi: 10.2752/136270497779754534; and Igor Kopytoff, 'The Cultural Biography of Things', in *The Social Life of Things: Commodities in Cultural Perspective*, ed., Arjan Appadurai (Cambridge: Cambridge University Press, 1986), 67.

6 Throughout infancy and early childhood, the signals of gender were subtle, and, at first glance, many garments appeared unisex, meaning even Branwell is likely to have worn some of Charlotte's cast-offs.

7 C. Willett and Phillis Cunnington, *The History of Underclothes* (New York: Dover Publications, 1992), 98.

8 Free, unfettered play, much of it outdoors, was advocated by the time of Charlotte's birth. The eighteenth-century philosopher, Jean-Jacques Rousseau's influence had ensured that children were now encouraged to be bold, adventurous and inquisitive – to run, jump, shout and laugh as they learned through their play. For more see Virginia Smith, *Clean: A History of Personal Hygiene and Purity* (Oxford: Oxford University Press, 2008), 250 and Jean-Jacques Rousseau, *Émile, ou De l'éducation* (Republique de Genève et France: A La Haye, 1762).

9 Beverley Lemire, *Dress, Culture and Commerce: The English Clothing Trade Before the Factory* (Basingstoke: Macmillan, 1997), 127.

10 A china doll with a full-skirted long dress made from material once worn by Charlotte Brontë remains at the parsonage, proving fabric was repurposed in this way. 'China Doll', Date unknown, Earthenware, cotton, braid (H153), BPM, Haworth. Two patchwork quilts also remain and, though thought to have been made later, demonstrate the remodelling of old clothes in this way. 'Patchwork Quilt', Date unknown, Cotton (D144), BPM, Haworth and 'Patchwork Quilt', Date unknown, Cotton, Velvet, Silk (D145), BPM, Haworth.

11 George Graham, William Farr, Horace Mann, *Census of Great Britain, 1851. Population Tables*, Vol. 2 (London: George Edward Eyre, 1854), 714.

12 Deborah Wynne, 'Reading Victorian Rags: Recycling, Redemption, and Dickens's Ragged Children', *Journal of Victorian Culture*, 20:1 (2015), 34–49 and William White, *History, Gazetteer and Directory of the West-Riding of Yorkshire, with the City of York and Port of Hull, Etc.*, Vol. 2 (Leeds: Baines and Newson, 1838), 50.

13 For many Christian families, the christening was an important occasion and one that often marked the first time a woman and her newborn ventured out into public. A corkscrew, used to open the bottles of Holy Water from Jordan, that was used at the Brontë children's christenings, has also survived. See: 'Corkscrew', D/U, Iron, (1814-04-23 – 1820-01-17), BPM, Haworth.

14 The cap is in private ownership but has excellent provenance.

15 Elizabeth Firth, 'Diary – 1815', *Elizabeth Firth Manuscripts* (MS 58), University of Sheffield Library.

16 Ibid.

17 Patterns were routinely passed from friend to friend or amidst family. See Tambour embroidery and bonnet patterns, Mary Mansen, *Design Book, 1827* (T. 213-1968), V&A Museum, London.

18 See: Joanne Bailey, *Parenting in England 1760-1830: Emotion, Identity, and Generation* (Oxford: Oxford University Press, 2012) and Anthony Fletcher, *Growing Up in England: The Experience of Childhood, 1600–1914* (Oxford: Oxford University Press, 2010).

19 Sophia Frances Anne Caulfield and Blanche C. Saward, *The Dictionary of Needlework* (London: A.C. Bradley, 1882), 252.

20 For example, Unwin's Ready-made Linen Warehouse, 57 Lombard Street, London, sold 'Childbed Linen and Baby clothes' in 1817 and S. Turner and M. Broadbent's of Leeds sold 'Childbed Linen and Baby clothes' in 1819. See also Margaret Spufford, *The Great Reclothing of Rural England: Petty Chapmen and their Wares in the Seventeenth Century* (London: Hambledon Press, 1984); Beverley Lemire, 'Peddling Fashion: Salesmen, Pawnbrokers, Tailors, Thieves and the Second-hand Clothes Trade *c.* 1700–1800', *Textile History*, 22:1 (1991), 67–82.

21 Advertisement for 'Jane Booth of Mill-Hill Leeds' and the sale of 'Child-bed Linen of different Qualities, Children's stays and caps', in *Leeds Intelligencer* (Leeds, England), 15 May 1813, 3.

22 Alice Dolan, 'The Fabric of Life: Linen and Life Cycle in England, 1678–1810', PhD thesis, University of Hertfordshire, 2015, 30 and R. Whittock, *The Complete Book of Trades or the Parents' Guide and Youths' Instructor* (London: John Bennett, 1837), 131.

23 See: 'Baby's Long Gown', 1810–1820, Cotton, Cotton Ties (B.174-1993), V&A, London; John Constable, 'A baby, perhaps Maria Louisa Constable', 1819, Pencil drawing on paper, 555 mm × 434 mm (D.235-1888), V&A, London.

24 Linda Baumgarten, *What Clothes Reveal: The Language of Clothing in Colonial and Federal America* (New Haven and London: The Colonial Williamsburg Foundation in association with Yale University Press, 2011), 158.

25 Morwenna and John Rendle-Short, *The Father of Childcare, William Cadogan (1711–1797)* (Bristol: John Wright and Sons, 1966), 20. Also quoted in William Buchan, *Domestic Medicine; or the Family physician* ... (Edinburgh: Balfour, Auld and Smellie, 1769), 16.

26 Twelve-year-old Nancy Garr arrived from Bradford in 1816 and was joined by her sister Sarah in 1818. They remained with the Brontës until 1825.

27 John Locke, *Some Thoughts Concerning Education* (London: A. & J. Churchill, 1693) and Jean-Jacques Rousseau, *Émile, ou De l'éducation* (Republique de Genève et France: A La Haye, 1762) and William Buchan, *Domestic Medicine; or, A treatise on the prevention and cure of diseases by regimen and simple medicines; With an appendix containing a dispensatory. For the use of private practitioners* (London: W. Strahan, 1774).

28 Iris Brooke, *English Children's Costume, 1775–1920* (London: Dover Publications, 2003), 32.

29 For examples see: 'Combinations', Cambric, early 1800s (T.211-1934), V&A Museum, London; 'Pantalets', Cotton with broderie anglaise, 1802–1820 (C.I.46.77.2) The Metropolitan Museum of Art, New York; 'Three ladies and a child', 1825, Engraving, paper, ink (2002.139/2990), Museum of London, London.

30 Phebe Lucas Glaisyer (1816–1904), 'Recollections of my Childhood' in John Lucas, *Phebe's Hitchin Book* (Hitchin: Hitchin Historical Society Publication), 40.

31 See: J.D. Ingres, 'Harriet Montagu and her sister', 1818, Pencil on paper, Private Collection.

32 Lucas Glaisyer, 'Recollections', 40.

33 The shift from silks to cottons can be seen clearly in the clothing diaries of Barbara Johnson. In 1779 Johnson had thirty-one silk dresses, but only six more were acquired between the years 1780 and 1800. However, in this later period, she obtained seventeen cotton gowns, highlighting this fashionable trend towards cotton over silk. See: Barbara Johnson, *A Lady of Fashion: Barbara Johnson's Album of Style and Fabrics,* ed., Nathalie Rothstein (London: Thames and Hudson, 1987).

   For an early example see 'Cotton day dress', *c.* 1810, White cotton with coffee and red print (CIRC.307-1922), V&A, London.

34 Phebe Lucas wore white muslin for Sunday best and was given a 'new white muslin frock and silk spencer' to attend her brother's wedding in 1827. Lucas Glaisyer, 'Recollections', 63.

35 Patrick Brontë, 'Letter to the Editor', *Leeds Mercury* (Leeds Yorkshire), 16 March 1843, 6.

36 In 1819, Phebe Lucas Glaisyer got into trouble with her uncle for 'clattering along the brick passage in my pattens'. Lucas Glaisyer, 'Recollections of my Childhood', 51. 'Pattens belonging to Elizabeth Branwell (Aunt Branwell)', are also held at the BPM. See: 'Pattens', Wood, metal, *c.* 1820s, (D25.1/2), BPM, Haworth.

37 'The Home of the Brontës', *People's Friend* (Dundee D.C. Thompson and Company), Monday 02 September 1895, 3.

38 'Leather mules', Leather, 1830s, (2004/331), owned by the Hutton family, but currently held at the BPM, Haworth.

39 'Letter from Patrick Brontë to Richard Burn, 27 January 1820' (MS ADM 1820), Borthwick Institute of Historical Research, University of York.

   Though the living at Thornton was said to be £140 per annum, Patrick received only £127 as he was expected to pay dues (£5) and contributions (£6–£8) out of his salary.

40 Patrick's salary amounted to approximately £170 per annum, compared to the £140 he received in Thornton.

41 Ann Dinsdale, *At Home with the Brontës: The History of Haworth Parsonage and its Occupants* (Stroud: Amberley Publishing, 2013), 25.

42 'Letter from Elizabeth Gaskell to John Forster, September 1853', in *The Letters of Mrs Gaskell,* eds, J.A.V. Chapple and Arthur Pollard (Manchester: Manchester University Press, 1966), 244.

43 Phyllis Bentley, *The Brontës and their World* (London: Thames and Hudson, 1972), 19.

44 Juliet Barker, *The Brontës*, 2nd ed. (London: Abacus Books), 106–7. [Reproduced with kind permission of the Licensor (Little Brown) through PLSclear and also Andrew Lownie Literary Agency.] The three mills were Bridge House, Ebor Mill and Mytholmes, with the rest between Oxenhope and Stanbury.

45 Ibid., 106–7.

46 Philip Rhodes, 'A Medical Appraisal of the Brontës', *Brontë Society Transactions*, 16:2 (1972), 102–9.

47 Ann Dinsdale, 'Mrs Brontë's Nurse', *Brontë Studies*, 30:3 (November 2005), 258–9.

48 A. Swedlund and A. Donta, 'Scarlet Fever Epidemics of the Nineteenth Century: A Case of Evolved Pathogenic Virulence?' in *Human Biologists in the Archives: Demography, Health, Nutrition and Genetics in Historical Populations*, eds, D. Herring and A. Swedlund (Cambridge: Cambridge University Press, 2002), 159–77.

49 'Letter from Patrick Brontë to John Buckworth, 27 November 1821' in John Buckworth, *The Cottage Magazine*, 11 (1822), 245–6.

50 Before the invention of antibiotics, 15–20 per cent of all children who contracted scarlet fever died.

51 Dinsdale, 'Mrs Brontë's Nurse', 258–9.

52 Anne Buck, *Clothes and the Child: A Handbook of Children's Dress in England 1500–1800* (Carlton, Bedford: Ruth Bean, 1996), 143–4.

53 William Dearden, 'The Rev. P. Brontë', *Bradford Observer* (Bradford, England), 20 August 1861, 7.

54 Ibid., 8.

55 'Letter from Patrick Brontë to John Buckworth, 27 November 1821', 245–6.

56 'Sampler finished by Charlotte Brontë on 22 July 1822, aged six', Cotton, 1822 (S7), BPM, Haworth.

57 Dearden, 'The Rev. P. Brontë', 8.

58 Ibid., 8.

59 R.A.H., 'School for Clergymen's Daughters', in *The Christian Guardian, Church of England Magazine* (London: Seeley and Sons), January 1828, 278.

60 Kate Stephenson, *The Cultural History of School Uniform* (Exeter: Exeter University Press, 2022), 1.

61 William Shakespeare, *Macbeth* (London: Macmillan Collector's Library, 2016), 1.3.95–104, 11.

62 The school prospectus reprinted in part in *The Christian Guardian* stipulated that the 'girls will all appear in the same dress'. 'The School for Clergymen's Daughters', *The Christian Guardian (and Church of England) Magazine*, January 1828, 320.

63 Ibid., 320.

64 Barker, *The Brontës*, 141.

65 Kelley Swain, 'Purple', *The Lancet Psychiatry*, 4:12 (2017), 908. https://doi.org/10.1016/S2215-0366(17)30450-9.

66 Maria Hayward, *Rich Apparel: Clothing and the Law in Henry VIII's England* (London: Routledge, 2009), 28. And Swain, 'Purple', 908.

67 Simon Frith, 'Socialization and Rational Schooling: Elementary Education in Leeds before 1870', in *Popular Education and Socialization in the Nineteenth Century*, ed., Phillip McCann (London: Methuen, 1977), 69.

68 See 43, Hatton Garden, London, the site of St Andrew Parochial School or Blewcoat School, Caxton Street, London.

69 Jayne Shrimpton, 'Uniform Appearance: What Did Our Ancestors Wear in Institutions?', *Family Tree*, 4 (1 March 2021), 11–14.

70 Ami Kobayashi, 'Book Review: A Cultural History of School Uniform', *Paedagogica Historica*, 57:6 (February 2021), 755.

71 Stephenson, *Cultural History of School Uniform*, 14.

72 Currer Bell (Charlotte Brontë), *Jane Eyre: An Autobiography* (New York: Harper and Brothers, 1848), 19.

73 Charlotte Brontë, *Jane Eyre,* 18.

74 Charlotte Brontë, *Jane Eyre,* 18.

75 Charlotte Brontë, *Jane Eyre,* 25.

76 Charlotte Brontë, *Jane Eyre,* 25.

77 Charlotte Brontë, *Jane Eyre,* 25.

78 See Elizabeth Cleghorn Gaskell, *The Life of Charlotte Brontë*, Vol. 11 (Leipzig: Bernhard Tauchnitz, 1859), 62 and 'Letter from "Clericus" to Arthur Bell Nicholls', CMR, MS, Private Collection.

79 'Letter from "Clericus" (CMR) to Arthur Bell Nicholls', 26 May 1857, MS, Private Collection.

80 Ellen Nussey, 'Reminiscences of Charlotte Brontë (1831–1855)', *Scribner's Monthly*, 2:1 (May 1871), 19.

81 All Charlotte's surviving clothes support this notion, for example, her corset is markedly small in size and bust pads have been inserted to augment her slight figure. Also, on 12 April 1851, Charlotte asked her friend, Ellen Nussey, to purchase on her behalf 'chemisettes of small size' as 'the full woman's size don't fit'. See 'Letter from Charlotte Brontë to Ellen Nussey, 12 April 1851', MS (Bonnell 235), BPM, Haworth.

82 'Letter from Charlotte Brontë to Mary Taylor, 4 September 1848', MS (MMS ID: 992984659423601631), John Rylands University Library, University of Manchester, Manchester.

83 'Letter from Charlotte Brontë to Ellen Nussey, 9 October 1848', MS (Ashley MS 2452), The British Library, London.

84 'Charlotte Brontë to Mary Taylor, 4 September 1848'.

85 Anna Krugovoy Silver, *Victorian Literature and the Anorexic Body* (Cambridge: Cambridge University Press, 2002), 82.

86 Silver writes extensively on the issue of hunger and repression as shown in Brontë's novels. She makes a strong connection between actual hunger and sexual repression, suggesting that the rejection of food correlates to a lack of romantic love. Silver also raises the issue of Emily Brontë's potential anorexia but does not go so far as to state Charlotte suffered from the same disease.

87 'Letter from Charlotte Brontë to Miss Margaret Wooler, 28 August 1848', MS (Brontë(C)/5: 110009974), Fitzwilliam Library, Cambridge.

88 Gaskell, *The Life of Charlotte Brontë*, Vol. 1, Chapters IV and V.

89 Following the publication of Gaskell's biography, which made bold claims about the school, a debate ensued. Witnesses argued that the Clergy Daughters' School could not be held responsible for the deaths of Maria and Elizabeth, and that Charlotte's description of Lowood bore little resemblance to the establishment. Brontë maintained that her description was truthful, but that she regretted that the characters had proved recognisable.

90 Christine Alexander and Margaret Smith, *The Oxford Companion to the Brontës* (Oxford: Oxford University Press, 2006), 131.

91 See Charlotte Brontë, *Jane Eyre*, 28–9.

Chapter Three

1 'Brown Umbrella', Cotton, wood, leather, metal, 1830s (D128), BPM, Haworth.

2 Helene Moglen, *Charlotte Brontë: The Self Conceived* (Wisconsin: University of Wisconsin Press, 1984), 26.

3 Christine Alexander, *The Early Writings of Charlotte Brontë* (Oxford: Basil Blackwell, 1983), 12.

4 Bob Duckett, 'Where Did the Brontës Get Their Books?', *Brontë Studies*, 32:333 (2007), 203.

5 Jennie Batchelor, *The Lady's Magazine (1770–1832) and the Making of Literary History* (Edinburgh: Edinburgh University Press, 2022), 13–14.

6 'Letter from Charlotte Brontë to Hartley Coleridge, 10 December 1840', MS (MS-0859, Container 13.5), Harry Ransom Center, The University of Texas, Austin.

7 Batchelor, *The Lady's Magazine,* 24.

8 'Letter from Charlotte Brontë to Hartley Coleridge, 10 December 1840'.

9   Susie L. Steinbach, *Understanding the Victorians: Politics, Culture and Society in Nineteenth Century Britain* (London: Taylor & Francis, 2012), 74.

10 Nick Holland, *Aunt Branwell and the Brontë Legacy* (Barnsley: Pen and Sword, 2018), 35.

11 Moglen, *The Self Conceived*, 25.

12 For more, see Juliet Barker, 2010. *The Brontës*, 2nd ed. (London: Abacus Books, 2010), 179–97; Alexander, *Early Writings of Charlotte Brontë*, 1–61; and Charlotte Brontë, *Juvenilia 1829–1835*, ed., Juliet Barker (London: Penguin Classics, 1996), vii–109.

13 Juvenilia can be accessed at the BPM; The Morgan Library; New York Public Library; The Huntington Library; The Harry Ransom Humanities Research Center, Texas; The Houghton Library, Harvard University and The British Library.

14 Barker, *The Brontës*, 195.

15 'Plummer, Thomas' in Christine Alexander and Margaret Smith, *The Oxford Companion to the Brontës* (Oxford: Oxford University Press, 2006), 370.

16 Barker, *The Brontës*, 202.

17 There is considerable disparity between Brontë's pre- and post-fame portraits. George Richmond's portrait (George Richmond, *Charlotte Brontë*, Chalk, 1850, 23⅝ in. × 18¾ in. (NPG1452), National Portrait Gallery, London) commissioned by Charlotte's editor, George Smith, and later used as the basis for a frontispiece to Gaskell's biography, is, in effect, an 'airbrushed' image. Though Patrick Brontë was pleased with the portrait, Charlotte's friend Mary Taylor considered it a 'flattered likeness'. She argued that she 'had rather the mouth and eyes had been nearer together and shown the veritable square face and large disproportionate nose.' (Letter from Mary Taylor to Elizabeth Gaskell, 30 July 1857, included in *The Brontës: Interviews and Recollections*, ed., H. Orel (Iowa: Iowa University Press, 1997), 114. The famous Thompson portrait (John Hunter Thompson, *Charlotte Brontë*, 1855, Oil on canvas, 348 mm × 413 mm (P25), BPM, Haworth), which now hangs in the parsonage, and depicts a pretty, fresh-faced woman, was not drawn from life and yet continues to be the image most often associated with post-fame Charlotte. Created by a friend of Branwell Brontë for the delectation of the newly flourishing and lucrative Brontë tourist industry, it highlights a persistent desire, and one continued to this day, to beautify those whose abilities we most admire. For more, see Eleanor Houghton, 'Decoding Clothing: Charlotte Brontë, Plainness and the Language of Dress', PhD thesis, University of Southampton, 2020, Chapter 1.

18 For detailed information see ibid. See also, 'Mary Taylor on Charlotte Brontë' quoted in David Harrison, *The Brontës of Haworth: Yorkshire's Literary Giants* (Victoria: Trafford Press, 2002), 233; George Smith, 'Charlotte Brontë' in *Cornhill Magazine*, 9 (December 1900), 782; Dr T.P. Browne, 'A Phrenological Estimate of the Talents and Dispositions of a Lady', 29 June 1851, included in *The Brontës: Interviews and Recollections*, ed., Harold Orel (Iowa: University of Iowa Press, 1997), 93.

19 See Elizabeth Gaskell, *Life of Charlotte Brontë,* Vol. 2, 155; Frances Grundy, 'The Decline and Fall of Branwell Brontë 1741–1848', in *Pictures of the Past: Memories of Men I Have Met and Places I Have Seen* (London: Griffith and Farran, 1879), 73–4; see also Charlotte Brontë, 'Self Portrait, 1843', drawing included in 'Letter from Charlotte Brontë to Ellen Nussey, 6 March 1843', Paper, 90 × 136 mm (BS50.4), BPM, Haworth.

20 George Smith, 'Charlotte Brontë', 778–95; Ellen Nussey, 'Reminiscences of Charlotte Brontë', *Scribner's Monthly*, 2:1 (1871), 18–31; Gaskell, 'Letter from Elizabeth Gaskell to Catherine Winkworth, 25 August 1850' (BC MS 19c Gaskell/04/24), Brotherton Collection, University of Leeds, Leeds.

21 Charlotte was extremely short-sighted and, as her surviving glasses prove, required -10 dioptres lenses. Gaskell, 'Letter from Elizabeth Gaskell to Catherine Winkworth, 25 August 1850'; Nussey, 'Reminiscences of Charlotte Brontë', 18–31; T. Wemyss Reid, *Charlotte Brontë: A Monograph* (London: Macmillan and Co., 1877), 39–43; Gaskell, *Life of Charlotte Brontë*, Vol. 1, 99; Harriet Martineau, 'Charlotte Brontë's Reaction to Criticism (1849)' in Harriet Martineau, *Autobiography*, ed., Maria Weston Chapman (Boston: James R. Osgood, 1877), 23.

22 Gaskell, *Life of Charlotte Brontë*, Vol. 1, 99, 126, 127 and Vol. 2, 155; Matthew Arnold, quoted in Ellis H. Chadwick, *In the Footsteps of the Brontës*, 2nd ed. (Cambridge: Cambridge University Press, 2011), 420; G.H. Lewes, reported in 'Letter from George Eliot to Charles and Cara Bray, 5 and 12 March 1853' in *The George Eliot Letters*, Vol. 2, ed., Gordon Haight (New Haven: Yale University Press, 1954), 92; George Smith, 'Charlotte Brontë', 778–95; 'Letter from William Makepeace Thackeray to Miss Lucy Baxter, 11 March 1853', in *The Letters and Private Papers of William Makepeace Thackeray*, Vol. 3, ed., Gordon Norton Ray (Harvard: Harvard University Press), 232–3.

23 Gaskell, *Life of Charlotte Brontë*, Vol. 1, 101.

24 Mary Taylor quoted in Gaskell, *Life of Charlotte Brontë*, Vol. I, 106.

25 Nussey, 'Reminiscences', 60.

26 Mary Taylor quoted in Gaskell, *Life of Charlotte Brontë*, Vol. I, 106.

27 Lena Goodman, 'Marriage Calculations in the Eighteenth Century: Deconstructing the Love vs. Duty Binary', *Proceedings of The Western Society of French History*, 33 (2005), 143–62.

28 Lawrence Stone, *Family, Sex and Marriage 1500–1800* (New York: Harper Perennial, 1979).

29 Florence Nightingale, *Cassandra*, ed., Myra Stark (New York: Feminist Press, City University of New York, 1979), 44.

30 *The Science of Dress for Ladies and Gentlemen* (London: Groombridge and Sons, 1856), 16.

31 Sara Stickney Ellis, *The Women of England: Their Social Duties and Domestic Habits* (London: Fisher, 1839), 72–3.

32 Jane Megan Northrup, *Reflecting on Cosmetic Surgery: Body Image, Shame and Narcissism* (London and New York: Routledge, 2012), 34.

33 Steve Gores, *Psychosocial Spaces: Verbal and Visual Readings of British Culture, 1750–1820* (Detroit: Wayne State University Press, 2000), 36.

34 Naomi Wolf, *The Beauty Myth* (London: Vintage Classics, 2015), 8.

35 The phrase 'true womanhood' was used by mid-nineteenth-century authors who wrote about the subject of women. For more see Barbara Welter, 'The Cult of True Womanhood: 1820–1860' (PDF), *American Quarterly*, 18:2 (1966), 151–74.

36 Sharon Marcus, *Between Women: Friendship, Desire, and Marriage in Victorian England* (Princeton: Princeton University Press, 2007), 107.

37 See Laura Mulvey, 'Visual Pleasure and Narrative Cinema', *Screen*, 16 (Autumn 1975), 6–18. Also, Andy Symonds, 'Explainer: What Does the "Male Gaze" Mean, and What About a Female Gaze?', *The Conversation*, 5 January 2016 [Accessed 26 June 2019]. http://theconversation.com/explainer-what-does-the-male-gaze-mean-and-what-about-a-female-gaze-52486.

38 Mary Taylor quoted in Gaskell, *Life of Charlotte Brontë*, Vol. I, 107.

39 Ibid., 106–7.

40 Ibid., 106.

41 'Letter from Charlotte Brontë to Ellen Nussey, 7 July 1836', HM 24412, Huntingdon Library, San Marino, California.

42 See Fraser, *Charlotte Brontë*, 68 and 'Letter from Charlotte Brontë to Mrs Franks, May 1831' (Bonnell Stores 38), BPM, Haworth.

43 Barker, *The Brontës*, 207.

44 Mary Taylor quoted in Gaskell, *Life of Charlotte Brontë*, Vol. I, 106.

45 Nussey, 'Reminiscences', 58–83.

46 Charlotte Brontë, *Jane Eyre*, 6.

47 Lenny R. Vartanian and Lydia Hayward, 'Self-Concept Clarity and Body Dissatisfaction', in *Self-Concept Clarity: Perspectives on Assessment, Research and Applications*, eds, Kenneth G. DeMarree and Jennifer Lodi-Smith (New York: Springer, 2018), 195–218; L.R. Vartanian, K. Nicholls and J. Fardouly, 'Testing the Identity Disruption Model among Adolescents: Pathways Connecting Adverse Childhood Experiences to Body Dissatisfaction', *Journal of Youth and Adolescence*, 52 (2023), 134–48.

Self-concept clarity is defined by J.D. Campbell, P.D. Trapnell, S.J. Heine, I.M. Katz, L.F. Lavallee and D.R. Lehman in 'Self-Concept Clarity: Measurement, Personality Correlates, and Cultural Boundaries', *Journal of Personality and Social Psychology*, 70 (1996), 141–56.

48 See: Mental Health Foundation, *Body Image Report – Executive Summary*, 2022 [Accessed 2 December 2022]. https://www.mentalhealth.org.uk/explore-mental-health/articles/body-image-report-executive-summary and Vartanian and Hayward, 'Self-Concept Clarity and Body Dissatisfaction', 195.

49 Catherine Sebastian, Stephanie Burnett and Sarah-Jayne Blakemore, 'Development of the Self-Concept During Adolescence', *Trends in Cognitive Sciences*, 12:11 (2008), 141–6; M.B. Spencer, D.P. Swanson and V. Harpalani, 'Development of the Self', in *Handbook of Child Psychology and Developmental Science: Socioemotional Processes*, ed., Michael Lamb and R.M. Lerner (Hoboken: Wiley, 2015), 753.

50 C.K. Higa-McMillan, J.Y. Takishima-Lacasa and K. Ramsey, 'Self-Consciousness' in *Encyclopaedia of Adolescence*, ed., R.J.R. Levesque (Springer: Cham, 2018), 3347–55.

51 Susan Harter, 'Emerging Self-Processes during Childhood and Adolescence', *The Handbook of Self and Identity*, eds, June Price Tangney and Mark R. Leary (New York: Guilford Press, 2012), 696.

52 Gaskell, *Life of Charlotte Brontë*, Vol. 1, 109.

53 See Barker, *The Brontës*, 205.

54 Nussey, 'Reminiscences', 24.

55 Ibid., 58–83.

56 Barker, *The Brontës*, 213.

57 'Letter from Charlotte Brontë to Ellen Nussey, 21 July 1832', HM 24403, Huntington Library, San Marino, California.

58 Margaret Beetham, *A Magazine of Her Own: Domesticity and Desire in the Woman's Magazine 1800–1914* (London and New York: Routledge, 1996), 30.

59 Compare Charlotte Brontë, 'Lady Jephia Bud', 6 December 1829, Wash over pencil on paper, 97 × 64 mm (Bonnell Collection: 2696), The Morgan Library, New York; with Charlotte Brontë, 'Portrait of a lady with wreath, 24 July 1832', Pencil on paper, 146 × 103 mm (C7), BPM, Haworth.

60 Collars of this sort were popular in the 1830s. They were not commonly worn in portraits unless the subjects were married and/or of middle age or older.

61 Sleeve puffs, down-filled armbands that were worn on the arm, were habitually worn by the upper- and middle-classes. They were not practical and encumbered movement, but ensured sleeves always remained voluminous. 'Sleeve puff', Cotton and down, 1830s (T.212-1917), V&A Museum, London.

62 See: Patrick Branwell Brontë, 'John Brown', c. 1835–9, Oil on canvas, 770 × 620 mm (B20) BPM, Haworth; Patrick Branwell Brontë, 'Henry Foster of Denholme', c. 1838–9, Oil on canvas, 380 × 295 mm (B44), BPM, Haworth.

63 Patrick Branwell Brontë, 'Miss Margaret Hartley', c. 1838–9, Oil on canvas, 330 × 273 mm (B2), BPM, Haworth; Patrick Branwell Brontë, 'Mrs Isaac Kirby', c. 1838–9, Oil on canvas, 350 × 300 mm (B24), BPM, Haworth.

64 Jane Sellars, 'Portraits of the Brontës' in *The Brontës in Context*, ed., Marianne Thormählen (Cambridge: Cambridge University Press, 2012), 126. See also Lucasta Miller, *The Brontë Myth* (London: Jonathan Cape, 2001).

65 Brontë, *Juvenilia 1829–1835*, 115.

66 'Letter from Charlotte Brontë to Ellen Nussey, 4 July 1834', HM 24408, Huntington Library, San Marino, California.
    For evidence of her reading see also Charlotte Brontë, 'High Life in Verdopolis', 20 February–20 March 1834, MS (MS 34255) owned by BPM, Haworth but held by The British Museum, London.

67 Charlotte Brontë, 'The Green Dwarf: A Tale of the Perfect Tense, by Lord Charles Albert Florian Wellesley', 1833, MS (MS-0526) Harry Ransom Center, University of Texas at Austin.

68 Charlotte Brontë, *The Green Dwarf with a Foreword by Libby Purves* (London: Hesperus Classics, 2003), viii.

69 Ibid., 23.

70 Quote by Lady Caroline Lamb née Ponsonby, included in Morgan Sydney, *Lady Morgan's Memoirs: Autobiography, Diaries and Correspondence*, Vol. 2, 3 Vols. (Leipzig: Bernhard Tauchnitz, 1863), 322.
    For examples of Byronic heroes see: Charlotte Brontë, 'Arthur Adrian Marquis of Douro (1)', c. 1833, Pencil on paper, 195 × 112 mm (C28), BPM, Haworth; Charlotte Brontë, 'Arthur Adrian Marquis of Douro (2)', c. 15 October 1833, Pencil on paper, 99 × 80 mm, Private owner; Charlotte Brontë, 'Alexander Soult', c. 15 October 1833, Pencil on card, 100 × 85 mm, Private owner; Charlotte Brontë, 'Young Military Man', c. 1833–4, Pencil on card, 102 × 66 mm (B15), BPM, Haworth. For more on these images see Christine Alexander and Jane Sellars, *The Art of the Brontës* (Cambridge: Cambridge University Press, 2005).

71 Charlotte Brontë, 'Zenobia Marchioness of Ellrington (Countess of Blessington)', 15 October 1833, Pencil on paper, 90 × 79 mm, Private owner.

72 Charlotte Brontë, 'Young Woman with "Fairy Legend"', c. 1833–4, Pencil on paper, 113 × 84 mm (C94), BPM, Haworth.

73 Charlotte Brontë, 'English Lady (Lady Jersey)', 15 October 1834, Pencil on card, 227 × 169 mm (Bonnell 2), BPM, Haworth; Charlotte Brontë, 'Sketch of a "'beautiful lady'"', c. January 1834, Pencil on paper, 135 × 122 mm (Bonnell 89), BPM, Haworth.

74 'Letter from Charlotte Brontë to Ellen Nussey, 2 July 1835', HM 24410, Huntington Library, San Marino, California.

75 Barker, *The Brontës*, 272 and 'Letter from Patrick Brontë to Mrs Elizabeth Firth Franks, 6 July 1835' (Bonnell Stores: BS 184), BPM, Haworth.

76 'Draft Letter from Charlotte Brontë to Hartley Coleridge, December 1840', MS (Bonnell Collection, 2696), The Morgan Library, New York.

77 Ellis Bell, 'Prefatory Note' to Charlotte Brontë, *Wuthering Heights, a New Edition Revised, with a Biographical Notice of the Authors, a Selection of Their Literary Remains, and a Preface by Currer Bell* (London: Smith, Elder and Company, 1850), 370.

78 See: Charlotte Brontë, 'Roe Head Journal, 11 August 1836' (Bonnell 98(1)), BPM, Haworth.

79 M.W. Stevens, D. Dorstyn, P.H. Delfabbro and D.L. King, 'Global Prevalence of Gaming Disorder: A Systematic Review and Meta-Analysis', *Australia and New Zealand Journal of Psychiatry*, 55:6 (June 2021), 553–68.

80 See: Monica Kim, 'The Good and Bad of Escaping to Virtual Reality', *The Atlantic*, 18 February 2015 [Accessed 16 January 2023], https://www.theatlantic.com/health/archive/2015/02/the-good-and-the-bad-of-escaping-to-virtual-reality/385134/ and Peter Vorderer and Bernhd Henning, 'Psychological Escapism: Predicting the Amount of Television Viewing by Need for Cognition', *Journal of Communication*, 51:1 (2001), 100–20, http://berndhenning.de/joc-nfc.pdf.

81 Charlotte Brontë, 'Roe Head Journal', 4 February 1836 [Autograph manuscript of a diary entry and two prose fragments], The Morgan Library & Museum, MA 2696.18, The Henry Houston Bonnell Brontë Collection, Bequest of Helen Safford Bonnell, 1969.

82 Ibid. and Charlotte Brontë, *Villette by Currer Bell, Author of 'Jane Eyre' and 'Shirley'* (New York: Harper and Brothers, 1853), 211.

83 Charlotte Brontë, 'The Adventures of Captain Hastings, Otherwise known as Henry Hastings by Charles Townshend', 24 February–26 March 1839 (HEW 1.4.14), Houghton Library, Harvard University.

84 'Letter from Charlotte Brontë to Ellen Nussey, 5 May 1838', MS (Bonnell Stores, 164), BPM, Haworth.

85 Charlotte Brontë, 'Roe Head Journal, 11 August 1836' (Bonnell 98(1)), BPM, Haworth.

86 Charlotte Brontë, 'The Adventures of Captain Hastings', pt. 2, 28, Seq. 68.

87 'Letter from Charlotte Brontë to Ellen Nussey, 12 March 1839', MS (Gr E2), BPM, Haworth.

88 Ibid.

89 'Letter to Charlotte Brontë to Henry Nussey, 5 March 1839', MS, Private collection.

90 See Barker, *The Brontës*, 366–7.

91 'Letter from Charlotte Brontë to Henry Nussey, 5 March 1839'; Hall and Davidoff specifically explore middle-class marital expectations, practices and gender roles. They include detailed case studies of provincial middle-class marriages of the period and explore the diminished role of the spinster. Spinster's precarious existence and limited work options are accentuated, as is the 'pejorative label given to [them] throughout [their] lives'. In the light of these clearly defined, aesthetically orientated marital and non-marital roles, it is clear that Brontë would have understood that to be a spinster, and moreover a plain spinster, was to operate in the hinterlands of polite society. Catherine Hall and Leonore Davidoff, *Family Fortunes: Men and Women of the English Middle Class 1780–1850* (London and New York: Routledge, 1987), 273.

92 'Letter from Charlotte Brontë to Ellen Nussey, 26 May 1840', MS (BS 44.5), BPM, Haworth.

93 Charlotte Brontë, *Jane Eyre*, 155.

Chapter Four

1 'Letter from Charlotte Brontë to Ellen Nussey, 2 October 1838', MS (Bonnell Stores, 40:3), BPM, Haworth.

2 'Letter from Charlotte Brontë to Ellen Nussey, 2 July 1835', HM 24410, Huntington Library, San Marino, California.

3 'Letter from Charlotte Brontë to Emily Brontë, 8 June 1839', MS, Untraced, included in Margaret Smith (ed.), *The Letters of Charlotte Brontë, Volume One, 1829–1847* (Oxford: Oxford University Press). Reproduced with permission of the Licensor through PLSclear, 191.

4 'Letter from Charlotte Brontë to Ellen Nussey, 30 June 1839', The Morgan Library & Museum, MA 2696.24, The Henry Houston Bonnell Brontë Collection, Bequest of Helen Safford Bonnell, 1969; and 'Letter from Charlotte Brontë to Emily Brontë, 8 June 1839', 191.

5 'Letter from Charlotte Brontë to Emily Brontë, 8 June 1839', 191.

6 Ibid., 191.

7 Arthur Christopher Benson, *The Life of Edward White Benson*, Vol. 1 (New York: Macmillan, 1899), 12.

8 'Letter from Charlotte Brontë to Emily Brontë, 8 June 1839', 191.

9 From July 1839 until March 1841.

10 'Letter from Charlotte Brontë to Ellen Nussey, 24 October 1839', HM 24419, Huntington Library, San Marino, California.

11 Patrick Brontë, *A Funeral Service for the Late Rev. William Weightman* (Halifax: J.U. Walker, 2 October 1842), 10.

12 'Letter from Charlotte Brontë to Ellen Nussey, ?3 March 1841', MS, Untraced included in Smith, *Letters, Volume One*, 246 and Barker, *The Brontës*, 411.

13 'Letter from Charlotte Brontë to Ellen Nussey, ?3 March 1841' and 'Letter from Charlotte Brontë to Ellen Nussey, ?21 March 1841', MS (Bonnell Stores, 47.5), BPM, Haworth.

14 'Letter from Charlotte Brontë to Ellen Nussey, ?3 March 1841', 246.

15 'Charlotte Brontë's Governess Dress', c. 1839–43, Silk (D11), BPM, Haworth.

16 Stock books were meticulously searched by the author and later by Sarah Laycock, curator. During the November 2018 and February 2019 trips, over 180 dossier files and all 184 issues of the Brontë Society journal *Brontë Transactions* were studied.

17 Due to the data protection guidelines of the BPM, the exact date and name of donor, though known, has been withheld.

18 Thomas Carlyle, *Thomas Carlyle's Collected Works*, Vol. 2 (London: Chapman and Hall, 1837), 319.

19 With grateful thanks to Linda Pierson and Ann Dinsdale of the BPM for their help in locating this text and their generous sharing of knowledge.

20 Jocelyn Kellett, *Haworth Parsonage: The Home of the Brontës* (Haworth: The Brontë Society, 1977), 54.

21 J.A. Erskine Stuart, *The Brontë Country: Its Typography Antiquities and History* (London: Longman, 1888), 82.

22 Michael Baumber, 'That "Vandal" Wade the Reverend John Wade and the Demolition of the Brontë Church', *Brontë Society Transactions*, 22:1 (1997), 96–112.

23 See Kellett, *Haworth Parsonage*, 54 and Ann Dinsdale, *At Home with the Brontës: The History of Haworth Parsonage and its Occupants* (Stroud: Amberley Publishing, 2013).

24 There is some precedent for placing shoes within the walls of buildings to bring luck, but garments are not often found in this way. See Kayt Hawkins, *50 Finds from Childhood: Objects from the Portable Antiquities Scheme* (Stroud: Amberley Publishing, 2024), 30–1.

25 Kellett, *Haworth Parsonage*, 54.

26 Harriet Martineau, 'Charlotte Brontë's Reaction to *Criticism* (1849)' in *Autobiography*, Vol. 2, ed. Maria Weston Chapman (Boston: James R. Osgood, 1877), 21–5.

27 For example, the skirt of the brown silk dress is 98 cm, the 'Thackeray Dress' skirt is 98 cm at the back of the skirt and 85.5 cm at the front. The 'Paisley Dress' is 98 cm long from waist to hem.

28 The gown has not undergone stylistic changes or been altered in size or shape. There are, however, two lines of machine stitching barely visible on the front panel of the skirt. As this is a drop-down panel, it would have been subject to considerable wear. It is therefore likely that this change took the form of a repair, probably prior to its display and before more modern conservation practices were employed.

29 For more on leg o'mutton or gigot sleeves, see: François Boucher, *20,000 Years of Fashion: The History of Costume and Personal Adornment* (New York: H.N. Abrams, 1987), 351.

30 See University of Rhode Island 'Fashion Plate – Une Conversation La Mode, 1832,' Historic Textile and Costume Collection [Accessed 4 September 2024], https://uritextilecollection.omeka.net/items/show/148 and 'Fashion Plate – Evening Dress and Costume Antique, 1833,' Historic Textile and Costume Collection [Accessed 4 September 2024], https://uritextilecollection.omeka.net/items/show/149 for outlandishly large sleeves. For early 'deflated' sleeves see 'Morning Visiting Dress, 1835,' Fashion plate, Scripps College, Ella Strong Denison Library, Macpherson Collection, Costume Plates of Myrtle Tyrrell Kirby, box 5.

31 To see 1842/3 change in sleeves see 'Promenade Dresses, May 1842,' *The Court Magazine and Monthly Critic and Lady's Magazine and Museum*, May 1842.

32 Bessie Rayner Parkes, 'The Profession of the Teacher', in *Essays on Women's Work* (London: Alexander Strahan Publisher, 1866), 88.

33 Lady Lucile Duff Gordon, *Discretions and Indiscretions* (Jarrold: London, 1932), 60.

34 Sarah Stickney Ellis, *The Women of England: Their Social Duties and Domestic Habits* (London: Fisher, 1839), 463.

35 Prof. Kathryn Hughes writes about the loss of caste in her book, *The Victorian Governess* (London and Rio Grande: The Hambledon Press, 1993), 13, 177, 28, 33.

36 The Countess of Blessington, *The Governess* (London: Longman, 1839), 136.

37 Ibid., 12.

38 Rayner Parkes, *Essays on Women's Work*, 88.

39 Millicent Bell, 'Class, Sex and the Victorian Governess: James' Turn of the Screw' in *New Essays on Daisy Miller and the Turn of the Screw*, ed., Vivian Pollak (Cambridge: Cambridge University Press, 1993), 91.

40 George Stephen, *The Guide to Service: For the Governess* (London: Charles Knight and Co., 1844), 304.

41 Charlotte Brontë, *Jane Eyre*, 46.

42 Charlotte Brontë, *Jane Eyre*, 65.

43 'According to one estimate for the 1850s, "the highest wage was £30 per year."' See: Bridget Hill, *Women Alone: Spinsters in England, 1660–1850*, Yale University Press, 2001, 64. Quoted with permission of the Licensor through PLSclear.

44 For an early example, see '1822–1830 White muslin gown with woven chequered pattern' in Nancy Bradfield, *Costume in Detail 1730–1930* (London: Eric Dobby Publishing Ltd, 1995), 117–18. For more on maternity wear see, Lydia Semler, Jana Hill and Ilea Magdelina Bonner, *A History of Maternity Wear Design, Patterns, and Construction* (New York and Abingdon: Routledge, 2024).

45 Aprons were commonly worn over morning dress or day dress. (See: Louis-Marie Lanté, 'Fashion Plate, 10 September 1834', Hand coloured engraving (E.22396:209-1957), V&A, London.) These could be made from a hard-wearing fabric such as cotton or linen, or from less practical but more decorative lawn, silk or even velvet. See: 'Cotton apron with whitework', 1830–1869, Cotton, whitework, insets of broderie anglaise (T.952-1913), V&A, London. Or, for more decorative aprons see: 'Plaid Silk Apron', 1840, Silk (MA. 1979.7.45), Historic Clothing Collection, Smith College, Northampton and 'Striped silk apron decorated with green and white trim', 1837–50, Silk (T.747-1913), V&A, London and 'Black velvet apron with embroidery', 1830–40, Velvet, silk, cotton (T.131-1963) V&A, London.

46 Sarah Josepha Buell Hale, 'A Lady', *The Workwoman's Guide: Containing Instructions to the Inexperienced in Cutting out and Completing Those Articles of Wearing Apparel …* (London: Simpkin, Marshall and Company, 1838), 74.

47 See, 'Women's tie-on pockets', V&A, London [Accessed 18 September 2024], https://www.vam.ac.uk/articles/womens-tie-pockets.

48 Charlotte Brontë, *Villette*, 66.

49 Not even Lucy Snowe's dress pocket was safe from the surveillance of Madame Beck.

50 Charlotte Brontë, *Jane Eyre*, 123.

51 Burman and Fennetaux include another such anecdote in their book. They explain how Elizabeth Woodcock survived 'eight days buried in a snow-drift' in 1799 by tying a coloured handkerchief extracted from her pocket to a stick and thrusting it out where it was spotted by a passing local farmer. See Barbara Burman and Arianne Fennetaux, *The Pocket: A Hidden History* (New Haven: Yale University Press, 2020), Reproduced with permission of the Licensor through PLSclear, 172–3.

52 William Makepeace Thackeray, *Vanity Fair: A Novel Without a Hero* (New York: Harper and Brothers, 1848).

53 Charles Dickens, 'David Copperfield' in *The Works of Charles Dickens* (New York: Hurd and Houghton, 1867), 19.

54 Dinah Craik, *John Halifax, Gentleman* (Leipzig: Berhard Taschnitz, 1857), 176.

55 Hughes, *The Victorian Governess*, 126.

56 Thackeray, *Vanity Fair*, 51.

57 Nelly Weeton, *Journal of a Governess 1811–25*, Vol. 2, ed., Edward Hall (Oxford: Oxford University Press, 1936–9), 379.

58 Charlotte Brontë, *Jane Eyre*, 95.

59 Ibid., 79.

60 Mary Anne Caton, 'The Aesthetics of Absence: Quaker Women's Plain Dress in the Delaware Valley, 1790–1900' in *Quaker Aesthetics: Reflections on a Quaker Ethic in American Design and Consumption*, eds, Emma Jones Lapsansky and Anne Verplanck (Philadelphia: University of Pennsylvania, 2003), 251.

61 For examples, see: 'Black Silk Quaker Dress', c. 1840, American (1976.1223.3), The Metropolitan Museum of Art, New York (Black silk dress with centre front opening and drawstring, fall-front skirt); 'Quaker, Light Brown Silk Dress', 1840–55, American (00.221.8), New Bedford Whaling Museum, Massachusetts (Silk dress with front fastening and drawstring, fall-front dress); 'Brown Silk Quaker Dress with Open Bodice', American, 1820–30 (20.4.1), Newport Historical Society, Rhode Island (Silk dress with front fastening and drawstring, fall-front dress). Anne Sanders Wilson, 'Paper Doll- Quaker Dress', Watercolour on paper, 1832 (T.361:15-1998), V&A Museum, London.

62 Fox asserted that as qualification for ministry was given by the Holy Spirit and not earned through learning, all had equal right to minister, including women and children. See H. Larry Ingle, *First Among Friends, George Fox and the Creation of Quakerism* (Oxford: Oxford University Press, 1994).

63 William Howitt, 'The Quakeress', *Sheffield Iris*, 48 (17 February 1835), 4.

64 Carol Mattingly, 'Appropriate[ing] Dress: Women's Rhetorical Style in Nineteenth Century America', in *Studies in Rhetorics and Feminisms* (Carbondale and Edwardsville: Illinois University Press, 2002), 17.

65 'The Revival of Quakerism' in *Edinburgh Review or Critical Journal* CLXXIV (Edinburgh: Longman Greens and Co., London 1891), 203.

66 Howitt, 'The Quakeress', 4.

67 Charles Lamb, 'A Quakers' Meeting –1823', in *The Works of Charles Lamb*, ed., Thomas Noon Talfourd (New York: Harper and Brothers 1838).

68 Suzanne Keen, 'Quaker Dress, Sexuality, and the Domestication of Reform in the Victorian Novel', *Victorian Literature and Culture*, 30 (2002), 217.

69 Ibid., 212.

70 See W. Pearson Thistlethwaite, *Yorkshire Quarterly Meeting of the Society of Friends 1665–1966* (published by author, 1979) and H.R. Hodgson in '[Brighouse] Monthly Meeting Properties', in *The Society of Friends in Bradford: A Record of 270 Years* (Bradford: Percy Lund, Humphries & Co., 1926), 65–86.

71 There are four references to Quakers in *Jane Eyre*: Jane describes her own black dress, 'Quaker-like as it was' (Chapter X); Jane depicts herself as being 'in my usual Quaker trim, where there was nothing to retouch – all being too close and plain,

braided locks included, to admit of disarrangement' (Chapter XIV); Jane describes Grace Poole's warning to her to lock her door as being delivered 'with the demureness of a Quakeress' (Chapter XVI); Jane's description of herself as a 'plain Quakerish governess' who does not need or want Rochester's jewels (Chapter XXIV). There are seven references in *Shirley* and one in *Villette*.

72 Charlotte Brontë, *Jane Eyre*, 97.

Chapter Five

1   'Letter from Charlotte Brontë to Ellen Nussey, 19 July 1841', MS (Bonnell Stores, 104/0.5), BPM, Haworth.
2   'Letter from Charlotte Brontë to Ellen Nussey, 17 October 1841' (Harry Elkins Widener Collection 1.5.4), Houghton Library, Harvard University.
3   'Letter from Charlotte Brontë to Ellen Nussey, 7 August 1841', HM 24428, Huntington Library, San Marino, California.
4   Ibid.
5   Ibid.
6   'Letter from Charlotte Brontë to Elizabeth Branwell, 29 September 1841', MS, Untraced, included in Margaret Smith (ed.), *The Letters of Charlotte Brontë, Volume One, 1829–1847*, Vol. 1, 3 vols (Oxford: Oxford University Press, 1995), 268–9.
7   Ibid., 268–9.
8   Anthony Trollope, *The Warden* (London: Longmans, Green, Reader and Dyer, 1866), 165.
9   A map of Brussels as it was in 1842/3 can be seen at (P76), BPM, Haworth.
10 Juliet Barker, *The Brontës*, 2nd ed., London: Abacus Books, 2010), 445.
11 Charlotte Brontë, *Villette* (New York: Harper and Brothers, 1853), 105. Eyewitnesses said Brontë's description in *Villette* exactly matches the Pensionnat garden.
12 These sums are based on the figures included in 'Prospectus for "Maison d'Èducation Pour Les Jeunes Demoiselles Sous la Direction, de Madame Heger – Parent", Rue d'Isabelle 32, á Bruxelles', 1842: MS (SB:2065.103), BPM, Haworth; and research carried out by Juliet Barker and included in *The Brontës*, 1062, n. 114.
13 'Letter from Charlotte Brontë to Ellen Nussey, May 1842', MS (BS50.2) BPM, Haworth.

14 See 'A Funeral sermon for the late Rev. William Weightman, M A. preached in the Church of Haworth, on Sunday the 2nd of October 1842 by the Rev. Patrick Bronte,' 1842 (SB:2281.29), BPM, Haworth.

15 'Letter from Branwell Brontë to Francis Grundy, 29 October 1842', MS, Untraced, included in Barker, *The Brontës*, 474.

16 It has been purported that Ellen Nussey insisted that Charlotte's corset should never been placed on show and that as a result, though it has long been held at the parsonage, it has never been displayed.

17 For examples, see 'Stays. Pale blue glazed woollen damask over stiff, whalebone foundation, lined with white linen', United Kingdom, 1740–60 (1947.1622), Manchester City Galleries, and 'Stays and Busk', Watered silk, whalebone, linen, Dutch, 1660–80 (T.14&A-1951), V&A, London.

18 Norah Waugh, *Corsets and Crinolines* (London and New York: Routledge, 1954), 75. Also, 'Cotton Corset', 1825–35, Cotton, cord, cotton thread, British (T.57-1948), V&A, London.

19 'Cotton corset', 1840, Cotton, bone, cotton thread, European (C.1. 42.74.12), The Metropolitan Museum of Art, New York; 'Cotton corset', 1840, Cotton, bone, cotton thread, European (C.1. 37.45.93), The Metropolitan Museum of Art, New York.

20 Valerie Steele, *The Corset: A Cultural History* (New Haven: Yale University Press, 2003), 29. Reproduced with permission of the Licensor through PLSclear.

21 Linda Sparks, *The Basics of Corset Building: A Handbook for Beginners* (New York: St Martin's Press, 2005), 37.

22 Eleri Lynn, *Underwear Fashion in Detail* (London: V&A Publishing, 2014), 128.

23 Lynn, *Underwear*, 119.

24 For strapless corset see: 'Cotton corset', 1839–41, Silk metal lace, American or European (38.23.10b-d), The Metropolitan Museum of Art, New York.

25 For more on the processes in involved in closely studying dress see Ingrid Mida and Alexandra Kim, *The Dress Detective* (London: Bloomsbury Visual Arts, 2019).

26 Mercerization is a refining and strengthening process applied to cellulosic fibres. It involves dipping the thread or fabric in caustic soda or sulphuric acid. This enables the fibres to absorb more water and more dye, making the dye cloth brighter and deeper in hue. This process was not common until 1880.
   This research has centred mainly in Europe. Advice has been sought from many experts in the field, including weaving and jacquard loom specialist, James Laycock of Ashleigh Textiles, Haworth; Historical Corset Collector, Melanie Talkington of Lace Embrace Atelier, Toronto; Frieda Sorber, Historical Collection Curator, MoMu, Antwerp; Adrian Dickinson of Paragon Textiles, Huddersfield (the only remaining commission pattern weavers in the world) and Leen Heyvaert at the Stadsmuseum, Lokeren.

27 'Woven Riding Corset by Charles Bayer', 1878–85, Linen, silk and whalebone (T.114&A-1938), V&A, London and 'Rare example of a Woven Cotton Corset', c. 1860, [Accessed 7 January 2017], www.antiquecorsetgallery.com.

28 Michel Chevalier, *Exposition Universelle de 1867: Rapports du Jury International, Bruxelles*, Vol. 4 (Paris: Paul Dupont, 1868), 310–13.

29 By 1846, Werly was selling modified 'medicinal corsets' in Britain, and by the early 1850s J. Tinsley of Leeds, T. Gallaway, also of Leeds and J. M'Clintock and Co. of Barnsley were all making seamless woven corsets. See: Henry Schroder, *The Annals of Yorkshire from the Earliest Period to the Present Time*, Vol. 2 (Leeds: George Crosby, 1852), 292.

30 Thanks to Leen Van de Wiele for her help in locating this information.

31 Michel Perrot, *Revue de l'Exposition des Produits de l'Industrie Nationale en 1841* (Bruxelles: Chez L'Ateur, 1841), 332.

32 The Royal Commission for the Exhibition of 1851. *Exhibitions of the Works of the Industry of All Nations – Reports by the Juries: On the Subjects in the Thirty Classes into Which the Exhibition Was Divided*, Vol. 1 (London: William Clowes and Sons, 1852), 483.

33 See 'Honorable Mention – Mathieu Van Beneden and J.B. Van Beneden-Bruers' in Michel Perrot, *Revue de l'Exposition des Produits de l'Industrie Nationale en 1841* (Bruxelles: Chez L'Ateur, 1841); 'Porcelain Card for J.B. Van Beneden-Bruers, Bruxelles, c. 1830–1840', 'Inventaris van de collective porseleinkaarten' (4419) Liberaal Archif Iconographie, Ghent, Belgium. The corsets were also made available to buy at Vve. Verberckmoes, Rue Court de Marais, Ghent for Virginie Van Caneghem.

34 Saint-Josse-ten-Noode is one of nineteen municipalities located in the Brussels-Capital Region of Belgium. It covered much of the centre of Brussels.

35 *Almanach Royal et du Commerce de Belgique, pour l'An 1838* (Bruxelles: Impremerie Balleroy, 1838), 487.

36 For more on the prevalence of industrial espionage in the Industrial Revolution, see John R. Harris, *Industrial Espionage and Technology Transfer: Britain and France in the 18th Century* (London and New York: Routledge, 2017).

37 In 1841, J.B. Van Beneden's premises were in Marche au Bois, but by 1851, at 26, Rue de l'Ecuyer. It is known that his premises were located in the centre of Brussels from the 1830s onwards. It is not known when Madame Van Beneden's shop moved from Rue de Paroissien to the Galerie de la Reine, but this move had taken place by 1851. The Galerie de la Reine was not fully built until 1846, so this cannot be where Brontë purchased her corset.

38 The busk has not been tested, so it is possible it is made from either steel or iron. Yet, though steel was used to make busks by the 1840s, it typically flakes as it corrodes and as there is no such evidence of flaking despite deterioration, iron is more likely.

39 For attractive examples see: 'American Scrimshaw Corset Busks', *c.* 1845, Ivory, baleen, ink (1956.103), American Heritage Collection, Colby Museum of Art, Waterville, Maine.

40 To understand the size, construction and weight of the busk (because it cannot be removed from the woven casing), the author commissioned a copy to be made.

41 Lynn, *Underwear*, 73 and 'Practical Instructions for Stay Making', in *Godey's Lady's Book*, eds, Sarah J. Hale and Louis Godey (Philadelphia: Louis Godey, July–December 1857), 165.

42 Brontë's cotton corset cover, *c.* 1840 (D130), BPM, Haworth, measures 21.02 inches at the waist. This would have been worn over the corset and up to five petticoats, so is still remarkably small. Her *c.* 1838 muslin, 'Paisley Dress' (D8), BPM, Haworth, measures 22.5 inches at the waist when closed. *Godey's Lady's Book* of 1857 (Sarah Hale, Josepha Buell and Louis Antoine Godey (eds), *Godey's Lady's Book*, Vol. 54–5 (Philadelphia: Louis Godey, 1857) suggests that 4 inches should be allowed for clothes when measuring a corset. Though the arrival of the crinoline in 1856 may have altered this measurement slightly, a large increase would still be expected. See 'Practical Guide for Stay-Making' in Sarah Josepha Buell Hale and Louis Antoine Godey, *Godey's Lady's Book*, 165.

43 George Smith, 'Chapter VII. Charlotte Brontë' in *Recollections of a Long and Busy Life*, MS, National Library of Scotland, MSS.23191-23192, 11.

44 'Letter from George Gissing to his sister Ellen Gissing, 3 July 1888', *Letters of George Gissing to Members of His Family, Collected and Arranged by Algernon and Ellen Gissing* (London: Constable and Company, 1926), 218.

45 See Virginia Smith, *Clean: A History of Personal Hygiene and Purity* (Oxford: Oxford University Press, 2008).

46 Lynn, *Underwear*, 73. Lynn's statement has been confirmed by extensive study of corsets dated to between 1820 and 1840 held at Bath Museum of Fashion, Hampshire Cultural Trust, Berrington Hall and York Castle Museum. No such obvious evidence of tight lacing was found.

47 Steele, *The Corset*, 2.

48 See: Alison Gernsheim, *Victorian and Edwardian Fashion: A Photographic Survey* (New York: Dover Publications, 1981); Vanda Foster, *A Visual History of the Nineteenth Century* (London: Batsford Ltd, 1984); J. Anderson Black, Madge Garland and Frances Kennett, *A History of Fashion* (London: Orbis Publishing, 1983); Aileen Ribeiro and Cally Blackman, *A Portrait of Fashion* (London: National Portrait Gallery, 2015); Richard Ormond, *Early Victorian Portraits*, Vols 1 and 2 (London: HMSO, 1973).

49 Catharine Esther Beecher, *A Treatise on Domestic Economy: For the Use of Young Ladies at Home, and at School* (Boston: Thomas Webb, 1843), 116.

50 Beecher, *A Treatise on Domestic Economy*, 116–17.

51 For examples see The Royal College of Surgeons of England, 'On the Ill Effects of Insufficient Exercise, Constrained Positions, and Tight Stays on the Health of Young Women', *The Penny Magazine* (28 February 1833), 77–81. And Dr Warren, 'Dangers of Tight-lacing', in *The Fireside Friend, or Female Student: Being Advice to Young Ladies on the Important Subject of Education* (Boston: Marsh, Capen, Lyon and Webb, 1840), 70.

52 Steele in her work, *The Corset*, outlines these strong views, and most particularly those of Helene E. Roberts, 'The Exquisite Slave: The Role of Clothes in the Making of the Victorian Woman', *Signs: Journal of Women in Culture and Society*, 2 (Spring 1977), 554–69; Lois Banner, *American Beauty* (New York: Knopf, 1983); Leigh Summers, *The Sexual Politics of Corsetry: 1850–1900* (Parkville: University of Melbourne, 1999).

53 Steele, *The Corset*, 1.

54 Steele, *The Corset*, 35.

55 Anna Krugovoy Silver, *Victorian Literature, and the Anorexic Body* (Cambridge: Cambridge University Press, 2002), 30. As Steele points out in *The Corset*, 48, however, working-class women were, conversely, envisioned as being large and strong like men.

56 Valerie Steele, *Fashion and Eroticism* (Oxford: Oxford University Press, 1985), 108.

57 Madame Roxey Caplin, *Health and Beauty, or Corsets Constructed in Accordance with the Physiological Laws of the Human Body* (London: Darton and Company, 1854), 42.

58 Quoted in Fernand Libron and Henry Clouzot, *Le Corset Dans l'Art et les Mouers du XIIIe au XXe Siècles* (Paris: Self-Published 1933), 50.

59 Daniel Roche, *The Culture of Clothing and Fashion in the Ancien Régime* (Cambridge: Cambridge University Press, 2014), 123.

60 According to Simon Place, 'by 1824, even the poorest streetwalker in London wore a corset', included in Michael Mason, *The Making of Victorian Sexuality* (Oxford: Oxford University Press, 1994), 29.

61 First used in the sixteenth century – 'strait' meaning 'narrow', 'close-fitting', 'binding' and 'laced' meaning 'to fasten with laces or ties', later combined to 'strict in manners, prudish' [Accessed 27 February 2023], https://www.etymonline.com/word/strait-laced, and Bryan A. Garner, *Garner's Modern Usage* (Oxford, Oxford University Press 2022), 1041 and 603.

62 Steele, *The Corset*, 35.

63 Linda Nochlin quoted in Marcia Pointon, *Naked Authority: The Body in Western Painting 1830–1908* (Cambridge: Cambridge University Press, 1990), 119.

64 David Kunzle, *Fashion and Fetishism: Social History of the Corset, Tight-lacing and Other Forms of Body Sculpture* (Maryland: Rowmand and Littlefield, 1982), 152.

65 'Letter from Charlotte Brontë to Ellen Nussey, 6 March 1843'.

66 Amelia Faye Rauser, *Caricature Unmasked: Irony, Authenticity, and Individualism in Eighteenth Century Prints* (Newark: University of Delaware Press, 2008), 15.

67 Wemyss Reid (1842–1905) wrote, 'there is a little caricature sketched by herself lying before me as I write. In it all the more awkward of her physical points are ingeniously exaggerated.' Wemyss Reid did not know Brontë, but he did know Ellen, thus the 'more awkward physical points' are clearly based in truth, despite having been exaggerated – and consequently fit with the expectations of caricature. See T. Wemyss Reid, *Charlotte Brontë: A Monograph* (London: Macmillan and Co., 1877), 28.

68 'Letter from George Gissing to Ellen Gissing, 3 July 1888', in *Papers of George Gissing and his Family, 1870–1937* (The George Gissing Collection: GB 133 GRG/1), University of Manchester Library, Manchester.

69 'Letter from Mary Taylor to Ellen Nussey c. 24 September 1842', MS (Brontë Family Works and Letters, Box 1), The Harry Ransom Humanities Research Center, University of Texas, Austin.

70 'Letter from Constantin Heger to Zöe Heger', quoted in Gaskell, *Life of Charlotte Brontë*, Vol. 1, 245.

71 Murnen and Byrne have defined hyperfemininity as an exaggerated adherence to a feminine gender role as it relates to heterosexual relationships. See Sarah Murnen and Donn Byrne, 'Hyper-femininity: Measurement and Initial Validation of the Construct', *The Journal of Sex Research*, 28 (1991), 479–89.

72 Roche, *The Culture of Clothing*, 123.

73 Marianne Thormählen, *The Brontës and Religion* (Cambridge: Cambridge University Press, 2004), 30.

74 'Letter from Charlotte Brontë to Ellen Nussey, May 1842', MS (BS50.2), BPM, Haworth.

75 Charlotte Brontë, *Villette*, 109.

76 Ibid., 78. Translates to: 'Because when you're dead – you'll burn in Hell right away!'/'Do you really believe that?'
  'Certainly I believe it: everyone knows it: and besides, the priest told me so.'

77 Charlotte Brontë, *Jane Eyre*, 156.

78 'Letter from Charlotte Brontë to Ellen Nussey, 2 April 1845', HM 24437, Huntington Library, San Marino, California.

79 Ibid.

80 See Barker, *The Brontës*, 484–504; Claire Harman, *Charlotte Brontë A Life* (London: Penguin, 2016), 170–81.

81 'Letter from Mr Westwood (a friend of the Hegers) to unknown recipient, 21 February 1870', MS (52298), John Hay Library, Brown University, New York.

82 'Letter from Constantin Heger to unidentified former pupil, not dated,' MS, Untraced, but included in Edith Weir, 'New Brontë Material Come to Light', *Brontë Society Transactions*, 11:59 (1946), 256–7.

83 Moglen, *The Self Conceived*, 63.

84 Barker, *The Brontës*, 493.

85 'Letter from Charlotte Brontë to Ellen Nussey, May 1842'.

86 'Letter from Charlotte Brontë to Branwell Brontë, 1 May 1843', MS (Ashley 161), The British Library, London.

87 Ibid.

88 Letter from Charlotte Brontë to Emily Brontë, 29 May 1843, MS, Untraced, included in Smith, *Letters,* Vol. 1, 320.

89 'Letter from Charlotte Brontë to Ellen Nussey ?Late June 1843', The Morgan Library & Museum. MA 2696.26. The Henry Houston Bonnell Brontë Collection. Bequest of Helen Safford Bonnell, 1969.

90 'Letter from Charlotte Brontë to Ellen Nussey 13 October 1843', HM 24433, Huntington Library, San Marino, California.

91 She would later write to Ellen, 'I returned to Brussels after Aunt's death against my conscience – prompted by what then seemed an irresistible impulse – I was punished by my selfish folly by a total withdrawal for more than two years of happiness and peace of mind. I could hardly accept success if I were to err again in the same way.' 'Letter from Charlotte Brontë to Ellen Nussey, 14 October 1846', HM 24449, Huntington Library, San Marino, California.

92 Charlotte Brontë, *Villette*, 154.

93 See J.C. Russell, *Russell's General Atlas of Modern Geography,* 1836, unnumbered page, sketch of an unnamed girl, The Morgan Library & Museum, PML 129886, Bequest of Helen Safford Bonnell,1969.

94 For more on the significance and standing of this self-portrait see, Eleanor Houghton, 'Decoding Clothing: Charlotte Brontë, Plainness and the Language of Dress', PhD thesis, University of Southampton, 2020, 51–5 and Harman, *Charlotte Brontë A Life*, 179.

95 Harman, *Charlotte Brontë A Life,* 179.

96 Charlotte Brontë, *Jane Eyre*, 62.

97 Charlotte Brontë, *Jane Eyre*, 62.

98 Shahidha Bari, *Dressed: The Secret Life of Clothes* (London: Jonathan Cape, 2019), 33.

99 Kunzle, *Fashion and Fetishism*, 17.

100 'Letter from Charlotte Brontë to Emily Brontë, 1 October 1843', MS, Untraced, included in Smith, *Letters of Charlotte Brontë*, Vol. 1, 331.

101 'Letter from Charlotte Brontë to Emily Brontë, 19 December 1843', MS, Untraced, included in Smith, *Letters of Charlotte Brontë*, Vol. 1, 339.

Chapter Six

1 'Letter from Charlotte Brontë to Ellen Nussey, 13 December 1846', HM 24450, Huntington Library, San Marino, California.

2 For more see: Juliet Barker, *The Brontës*, 2nd ed. (London: Abacus Books, 2010), 552 and 1078, n. 86.

3 It is not known whether Anne left Thorp Green as a direct consequence of Branwell's relationship with Mrs Robinson. It is likely that she knew of the longstanding affair but is thought to have handed in her notice some weeks before Branwell was finally found out.

4 'Letter from Charlotte Brontë to Ellen Nussey? December 1845', MS, Untraced, included in Smith, *Letters*, Vol. 1, 441–2. 'Letter from Charlotte Brontë to Constantin Heger, 24 October 1844', MS (Add. 38723B), The British Library, London.

5 Charlotte Brontë, 'Biographical Notice of Ellis and Acton Bell', in Ellis and Acton Bell, *Wuthering Heights and Agnes Grey* (London: Smith, Elder and Company, 1850), vii.

6 Ibid., vii.

7 'Letter from Charlotte Brontë to Aylott & Jones, 31 January 1846', MS (Bonnell Stores 169), BPM, Haworth.

8 Barker, *The Brontës*, 573 and 'Letter from Charlotte Brontë to Aylott and Jones, 3 March 1846', MS (Bonnell 174) BPM, Haworth.

9 Charlotte Brontë, 'Biographical Notice', x.

10 'Letter from Charlotte Brontë to Aylott and Jones, 6 April 1846' (Bonnell 179), BPM, Haworth.

11 Jane Tozer and Sarah Levitt, *Fabric of Society: A Century of People and Their Clothes 1770–1870* (Carno: Laura Ashley Ltd, 1983), 71.

12 *The Mirror of Literature, Amusement and Instruction Containing Original Essays*, Vol. VIII (London: J. Limbird, 1826), 158.

13 For examples, see (D22.1/2; D38; D52 1/2), BPM, Haworth.

14 Tozer and Levitt, *Fabric of Society*, 71.

15 For more on Haworth's sanitation see: Benjamin Herschel Babbage, 'Report … on a Preliminary Inquiry into the Sewerage, Drainage, and Supply of Water, and the Sanitary Condition of the Inhabitants of the Hamlet of Haworth', *Public Health Act* (London: W. Clowes and Sons, 1850).

16 'Lady's Washing Book' in *The Workwoman's Guide: Containing Instructions to the Inexperienced in Cutting out and Completing Those Articles of Wearing Apparel & Which Are Usually Made at Home: Also Explanations on Upholstery, Bonnet-Making, Straw Plaiting, Knitting Etc.* (London: Simpkin, Marshall and Company, 1838), 234.

17 Ibid., 235.

18 'Letter from Charlotte Brontë to Ellen Nussey, 21 December 1839', HM 24420, Huntington Library, San Marino, California. See also: Anne Brontë, 'Diary Paper, 31 July 1845', William Self, Private Collection. A toy iron, presumably used to teach children how to iron, has also survived. See: 'Replica Iron', D/U, Brass and wood (H165), BPM, Haworth.

19 'Letter from Charlotte Brontë to Ellen Nussey, ?28 December 1839', MS, Beinecke Collection, Yale. For more on Charlotte's references to the making of clothing in her letters see Table 1.

20 Tozer and Levitt, *Fabric of Society*, 74.

21 *The Workwoman's Guide*, 1838, v.

22 For more on the place of centrality of sewing to women's lives see Serena Dyer, *Material Lives: Women Makers and Consumer Culture in the Eighteenth Century* (London: Bloomsbury Visual Arts, 2021) and Barbara Burman (ed.), *The Culture of Sewing: Gender, Consumption and Home Dressmaking* (Oxford: Berg, 1999).

23 Mary Wollstonecraft, *A Vindication of the Rights of Women, with Strictures on Political and Moral Subjects* (London: T. Fisher Unwin, 1891), 126.

24 'Letter from Jane Austen to Cassandra Austen, Saturday 5 to Tuesday 8 March 1814' (CHWJA:JAHLTR.9), Jane Austen's House Museum, Chawton, Hampshire; and 'Letter from Charlotte Brontë to Emily Brontë 8 June 1839', MS, Untraced, included in Smith, *Letters*, Vol. 1, 192.

25 'Corset Cover', Cotton and lace (D168), BPM, Haworth; and 'Cotton Chemise', Cotton with broderie anglaise (D130), BPM, Haworth.

26 Charlotte Brontë made Ellen Nussey a small, beaded purse (see. Fig. 0.1). Fascinatingly, it bears uncanny similarity to one made and owned by Jane Austen (Crochet Beaded Purse, Hampshire Cultural Trust, WINCH:LH 868.4.).

27 'Berlin wool tapestry bag', Wool, cotton, cord (D31), BPM, Haworth.

28 See: 'Embroidery Styles: An Illustrated Guide', V&A Museum [Accessed 17 August 2023], https://www.vam.ac.uk/articles/embroidery-styles-an-illustrated-guide.

29 All references to the production of clothing were traced and documented by the author. See: Eleanor Houghton, 'Decoding Clothing: Charlotte Brontë, Plainness and the Language of Dress', PhD thesis, University of Southampton, 2020.

30 'Letter from Charlotte Brontë to Ellen Nussey, 10 May 1851', HM 24479, Huntington Library, San Marino, California.

31 'Paisley Dress', Muslin, linen, metal, 1840–5 (D8), BPM, Haworth.

32 For similar examples see: 'White muslin, broad stripes roller printed in mauve, yellow, red and green, with designs inspired by hieroglyphics and ancient Roman decoration', 1836–9, Muslin, cotton (1947.2057), Manchester Art Gallery, Manchester; 'White striped muslin gown, printed with stem and leaf design in green, mauve, brown and red', 1847–9, Muslin, cotton (1947.2297), Manchester Art Gallery, Manchester; 'White striped muslin gown printed with grass design in green, purple and rose-pink', 1837–9, Muslin, cotton (1947.2064), Manchester Art Gallery, Manchester.

33 Sonia Ashmore, *Muslin* (London: V&A Publishing, 2012).

34 'Fragment of muslin dress worn by Charlotte Brontë', 1840s (D148), BPM, Haworth.

35 'Patchwork quilt', Silk, velvet, cotton with wadding, unfinished (D145), BPM, Haworth.

36 C. Holmes Cautley, 'Old Haworth Folk Who Knew the Brontës', *Cornhill Magazine*, July 1910, 81–2.

37 'Fawn Tartan Cloak', Wool, cotton (D16), BPM, Haworth and 'Purple, Blue, Sand and Green Cloak', Wool, cotton (D17), BPM, Haworth.

38 For examples see: C. Willett Cunnington and Phyllis Cunnington, *Handbook of English Costume in the Nineteenth Century* (London: Faber and Faber, 1973), 434.

39 Samford Bamford, *Dialect of South Lancashire or Tim Bobbin's Tummus and Meary …* (Manchester, 1850), 5. See also: 'Red Cloak', British, Broadcloth, 1770–80 (2018-4), Colonial Williamsburg Museum, Virginia; 'Scarlet Woollen, Hooded Cloak', Wool, 1800–20 (1951.114), Manchester Galleries, Manchester.

40 See: John C. Russell, 'The Blind Beggar and his Granddaughter', Oil on canvas, 90.6 × 70.03 cm, date unknown (B.M.1029), The Bowes Museum, Barnard Castle; 'Cloak', Red wool broadcloth, mohair shag, 1775–1810 (1989-402), Colonial Williamsburg Museum, Virginia.

41 Sue Felshin, 'Making a Short Cloak' [Accessed 18 April 2023], https://people.csail.mit.edu/sfelshin/revwar/short-cloaks/.

42 With tremendous thanks to James Laycock for his expertise and for the time spent looking at the Brontë cloaks.

43 Michael Baumber, 'Haworth in the Time of the Brontës' in *The Brontës in Context (Literature in Context)*, ed., Marianne Thormälen (Cambridge: Cambridge University Press, 2002), 11.

44 See: 'Double cape, tartan cloak', worsted, *c.* 1800–10 (M.1930.272), National Museums Scotland, Scotland; 'Royal Stewart tartan cloak', worsted, *c.* 1830 (A.1993.209), National Museums Scotland, Scotland; 'Tartan Cloak', worsted, 1815 (1956–4), Colonial Williamsburg Museum, Virginia; 'Lady's Travelling Cloak', worsted, 1820–30 (NT 1360836), National Trust, Killerton, Devon.

45 For more on the popularity of tartan during the Georgian period, see: 'Royal Stuart Tartan Cloak c. 1830', National Museums Scotland [Accessed 18 April 2023], https://www.nms.ac.uk/explore-our-collections/stories/scottish-history-and-archaeology/highland-style/highland-style-sub-pages/royal-stewart-tartan-cloak-c1830/.

46 Charlotte Brontë, *Jane Eyre*, 23.

47 Joe Wheat, *Blanket Weaving in the Southwest*, ed., Anne Lane Hedlund (Tucson: University of Arizona Press, 2003).

48 Frederick J. Glover, 'Philadelphia Merchants and the Blanket Trade 1820–1860', *Pennsylvania History*, 28:2 (April 1961), 121–41.

49 'Letter from Thomas Cook to Mr Abbott, 26 September 1826', in *The Documents of Wormalds and Walker Ltd* (BUS/Wormwalds), Brotherton Library, University of Leeds, Leeds.

50 For more on the impact of globalization on fabrics and fashion see *Disseminating Dress: Britain's Fashion Networks 1600–1970*, eds, Serena Dyer, Jade Halbert and Sophie Littlewood (London: Bloomsbury, 2022).

51 1840s Brontë bonnet, fawn silk with chestnut and sand ombré ribbons, (D104) BPM, Haworth.

52 See: Linda Welters, 'The Fashion of Sustainability,' in *Sustainable Fashion: Why Now? A Conversation Exploring Issues, Practices, and Possibilities*, eds, Janet Hethorn and Connie Ulasewicz (New York: Fairchild Books, 2008), 8.

53 It has long been purported that D102, colloquially known as the 'shared dress' was worn by all the sisters. Beyond that found within the dress itself, no evidence has been found to support this claim, but the gown has clearly been drastically reworked, and it is certainly possible that it was a originally owned by one of her taller sisters. (Emily's coffin suggests that she was 5ft 6 or 7 in. Anne's height is unknown, but she was taller than Charlotte.) The current measurements are not drastically different from other surviving dresses known to have belonged to Charlotte, but there are anomalies – most notably, the waist and bust are slightly larger, and the skirt slightly longer.

54 Karen Tranberg Hansen, 'The Anthropology of Secondhand Clothes,' in *Encyclopedia of Clothing and Fashion*, ed., Valerie Steele (Detroit: Charles Scribner's Sons, 2005), 151.

55 Elizabeth Sanderson, 'Nearly New: The Second-Hand Clothing Trade in Eighteenth-Century Edinburgh,' *Costume*, 31 (1997), 38.

56 Anne Brontë, 'Diary Paper, 31 July 1845', MS, William Self, Private Collection included in Smith, *Letters,* Vol. 1, 410; 'Letter from Charlotte Brontë to Ellen Nussey, 8 December 1851', MS (B.S. 84.5), BPM, Haworth.

57 Gaskell, Elizabeth Cleghorn Gaskell. 1857. *The Life of Charlotte Brontë*, Vol. 1 (London, Smith Elder and Company), 11.

58 Ibid., 11.

59 William Makepeace Thackeray, 'Letter to Lucy Baxter, 11 March 1853', included in *The Brontës: Interviews and Recollection*, ed., Harold Orel (Iowa: University of Iowa Press), 106.

60 In *Agnes Grey*, Anne Brontë had already created a plain heroine. Though this fact was not central to the book, she had set an all-important precedent.

61 For more on Charlotte's attitudes to beauty and plainness as revealed in *Jane Eyre*, see chapter entitled 'The Plainness Manifesto' in Eleanor Houghton, 'Decoding Clothing: Plainness and the Language of Dress', Vol. 1.

62 See J.E.C. Welldone, 'The Brontë Family at Manchester', in *Cornhill Magazine*, Volume XXVIII, June 1910 (London: Smith, Elder and Company), 494.

63 'Letter from Charlotte Brontë to Smith, Elder and Company, 7 August 1847', MS (SG 3), BPM, Haworth. Charlotte Brontë, 'Biographical Notice', 361.

64 'Letter from Charlotte Brontë to Smith, Elder and Company, 12 September 1847', MS (SG 1B), BPM, Haworth.

65 'Letter from Charlotte Brontë to Smith, Elder and Company, 19 October 1847', MS (M.L. Parrish Collection, Miscellaneous Correspondence, 9ALsS, Box 14, Folder 1), Princeton University Library, Princeton, New Jersey.

66 Elizabeth Rigby, 'Vanity Fair and Jane Eyre', *Quarterly Review* (December 1848), 153–85.

67 Anne Isabella Thackeray Ritchie, *Chapters from Some Memoirs* (London: Macmillan and Co., 1894), 60.

68 George Henry Lewes quoted in *Cornhill Magazine* (December 1900), 171–2; Unsigned Review, *Critic* (30 October 1847) in *The Critical Heritage: The Brontës*, ed., Miriam Allott (London: Routledge 2001), 78; George Henry Lewes, 'Jane Eyre – An Autobiography, edited by Currer Bell', *Westminster Review* (January 1848), 581-4; Unsigned Review, '*Critic,* October 1847', in *The Critical Heritage: The Brontës*, ed., Miriam Allott (Oxford: Routledge 2001), 73–4; Albany William Fonblanque, '"Review" 27 November 1847, *The Examiner*', in *The Critical Heritage: The Brontës*, ed., Miriam Allott (Oxford: Routledge, 2001), 76–8.

69 'Letter from Charlotte Brontë to William Smith Williams, 28 October 1847', The Morgan Library & Museum, MA 2696.34, The Henry Houston Bonnell Brontë Collection. Bequest of Helen Safford Bonnell, 1969.

70 Elizabeth Rigby, 'Vanity Fair and Jane Eyre', *Quarterly Review*, 84:127 (December 1848), 153–85.

71 'Letter from Charlotte Brontë to William Smith Williams, 21 December 1847', MS (Pforzheimer Papers: MISC 0191), Carl H. Pforzheimer Collection of Shelley and His Circle, New York Public Library, Astor, Lenox, and Tilden Foundations.

72 'Letter from Charlotte Brontë to William Smith Williams, 21 December 1847'.

73 *Agnes Grey* was published by Newby under the pseudonym of Acton Bell; Emily's (Ellis Bell's) *Wuthering Heights* made up the first two volumes of the publication, and *Agnes Grey* the third. The original edition of the novel, published in 1847, had numerous orthographic and punctuation errors. These were rectified by Charlotte in the second edition, published in 1850 by Smith, Elder and Company.

74 'Letter from Sampson Low to George Smith, June 1848', quoted by Charlotte Brontë in 'Letter to Mary Taylor, 4 September 1848', MS (University MSS EL B91 F/1), John Rylands Library, University of Manchester.

75 'Letter from Charlotte Brontë to Mary Taylor, 4 September 1848'.

76 Letter from George Smith described in 'Letter from Charlotte Brontë to Mary Taylor, 4 September 1848'.

77 'Letter from Charlotte Brontë to Mary Taylor, 4 September 1848'.

78 George Smith, 'Charlotte Brontë', 91.

79 'Letter from Charlotte Brontë to Mary Taylor, 4 September 1848'.

80 Ibid.

81 Lucasta Miller, *The Brontë Myth* (London: Jonathan Cape, 2001), 16.

82 Maura C. Ives, 'Introduction', in *Women Writers and the Artifacts of Celebrity in the Long Nineteenth Century*, eds, Maura C. Ives, Ann R. Hawkins (Farnham: Ashgate, 2012), 4.

83 'Letter from Charlotte Brontë to Mary Taylor, 4 September 1848'.

84 Ibid., Smith Williams was also in the carriage, in 'full dress'.

85 For more see, Jennifer Hall-Witt, *Fashionable Acts: Opera and Elite Culture in London, 1780–1880* (Durham: University of New Hampshire Press, 2007), 40 and Penelope Byrde, *Nineteenth Century Fashion* (London: Batsford, 1992), 128.

86 'Letter from Charlotte Brontë to Mary Taylor, 4 September 1848'.

87 Ibid.

88 Ibid.

89 Charlotte Brontë, 'Cash Book 1848–1849' (BS 22, 10), BPM, Haworth.

90 'Paisley Parasol', Wool, wood, metal, fringing, *c.* 1840s/50s (D133), BPM, Haworth.

91 'Black and White Silk Parasol', Silk, wood, fringing, *c.* 1840s/50s (D106), BPM, Haworth.

92 'Letter from Charlotte Brontë to Mary Taylor, 4 September 1848.'

93 Ibid.

94 George Smith, Sidney Lee and Leslie Smith (eds), *A Memoir* (London: Private Circulation, 1902), 88 and 91.

Chapter Seven

1 Robert Keefe, *Charlotte Brontë's World of Death* (Austin and London: University of Texas Press, 1979), 130.

2 See: Emma I. Langan, 'The Brontës and Tuberculosis Immunity', *Brontë Studies*, 46:2 (2021), 210–22.

3 'Letter from Charlotte Brontë to Ellen Nussey, 9 October 1848', MS (2452 Ashley), The British Library, London.

4 'Letter from Charlotte Brontë to William Smith Williams, 2 October 1848', MS (2696), The Morgan Library, New York.

5 'Letter from Charlotte Brontë to Ellen Nussey, 9 October 1848', MS (Ashley 2452), The British Library, London.

6 Pat Jalland, *Death in the Victorian Family* (Oxford University Press: Oxford, 1996), 212.

7 'Memorial Card for Patrick Branwell Brontë', Embossed white card with black edging and bold print (SB:910), BPM, Haworth.

8 See: 'Bradford and Leeds Fashion Combined with Economy in Silks, Shawls, Delaines, Muslins, Mantles and Bonnets', in *The Bradford Observer*, Bradford (Thursday 19 April 1849), 8.

   Mourning Warehouses in Hull and London offered mourning garments for loan, suggesting this was a common practice. See: 'General Mourning Warehouse, 54 Market Place, Hull' advertisement in *The Hull Advertiser*, Hull (29 September 1848), 1.

9 Lou Taylor, *Mourning Dress* (Abingdon: Routledge, 2009), 35.

10 Anne Buck, *Dress in Eighteenth Century England* (London: Batsford, 1979), 60. Leigh Weatherall Dickson, '"Only Four Months a Widow": The Storytelling Wardrobe of Lady Susan in Whit Stillman's Love and Friendship' (2016), in *After Austen Reinventions, Rewritings, Revisitings*, ed., Lisa Hopkins (London: Springer International Publishing, 2018), 177–96.

11 Jalland, *Death in the Victorian Family*, 300 and Lou Taylor, *Mourning Dress*, 252.

12 Branwell was buried on 28 September 1848.

13 For example, The Leeds Mourning Warehouse in Briggate and The London General Mourning Warehouse in Regent Street promised to compose well-fitting mourning wardrobes at 'the shortest notice'. See: 'Advertisement for 'Frederic Forster Family Mourning' in *Yorkshire Post and Leeds Intelligencer*, Leeds (15 February 1876), 1; and 'Advertisement for 'The London General Mourning Warehouse', *The Illustrated Weekly Times*, London (25 March 1843), 48.

14 Thackeray, *Vanity Fair*, 366.

15 Elizabeth Gaskell, *Mary Barton*, Vol. 1 (London: Chapman and Hall, 1848), 66–7.

16 Charlotte Brontë, *Jane Eyre*, 127.

17 'Essay on Mourning' in *Walker's Hibernian Magazine*, Dublin (November 1786), 561–3 and Arnold van Geneep, 'The Rites of Passage', in *Death Mourning and Burial: A Cross Cultural Reader*, ed., Antonius C.G.M. Robben (Oxford: Blackwell Publishing: 2004), 213–22.

18 Throughout the eighteenth century, tuberculosis had come to be known as the 'White Plague' due to the paleness of its patients. See: 'History of World TB Day', Centers for Disease, Control and Prevention [Accessed 4 May 2023], https://www.google.com/url?sa=t&source=web&rct=j&opi=89978449&url=https://stacks.cdc.gov/view/cdc/52419/cdc_52419_DS1.pdf&ved=2ahUKEwjNvZTcwJONAxVwWUEAHdiFB8YQFnoECBYQAQ&usg=AOvVaw1PlEBsSnxlLiznYp_urYH1.

19 Gaskell, *Life of Charlotte Brontë*, Vol. 2, 84.

20 Ibid., 84.

21 'Letter from Charlotte Brontë to William Smith Williams, 20 December 1848', MS (PAL01846), Ella Strong Dennison Library, Claremont Colleges, California.

22 'Emily Jane Brontë Funeral Card', Printed white card with black border (SB:1956), BPM, Haworth.

23 'Funeral Garlands' in *The Book of Days: A Miscellany of Popular Antiquities*, ed., R. Chambers (London: W. and R. Chambers, 1863), 274.

24 'Charlotte Brontë's Cashbook 1848/9', MS (B.22.9), BPM, Haworth. Miss Young's shop did not open until late in November 1848 and Charlotte did not visit Leeds until after Emily's death but might have been there before she went to Scarborough with Anne in May, though no mention is made in her correspondence.

25 A black, silk parasol remains at the parsonage, see: 'Black, silk parasol, silk, metal wood, exact date unknown' (D77), BPM, Haworth. For similar example see 'Mourning bonnet', *c.* 1845, Black ciré, muslin form with stiffening to the brim, wire, silk (NT 1349748), Snowshill Wade Costume Collection, Gloucestershire, National Trust; 'Mourning Poke Bonnet,' *c.* 1845, Black dyed straw, silk (2009.300.5622a–c), Brooklyn Museum Costume Collection at The Metropolitan Museum of Art, New York.

26 Several pieces of jewellery formed from Brontë hair have survived. Though some have been made from hair taken from Emily and Anne (J12), BPM Haworth, others are thought to have been made entirely from Emily's hair (J51), BPM, Haworth. For more see: Deborah Lutz, *The Brontë Cabinet* (London and New York: W.W. Norton and Company, 2015), Chapter 7. Advertisement for 'Naismith's Hair-Cutting and Perfumery' who fashioned 'ornamental hair of every description' in J. Ibbetson, *Ibbetson's Directory of the Borough of Bradford* (Bradford: J. Ibbetson, Bridge Street, 1845), 18; Advertisement for 'Winspear's Fancy Hair Work', in *The Yorkshire Gazette* (18 July 1840), 4.

27 One of Charlotte's surviving bracelets, the main body of which has been formed from Emily and Anne's hair, also features large cut and set amethysts. See: 'Hair Bracelet set with amethysts' (J14), BPM, Haworth.

28 Emily Brontë, [Long Neglect Has Worn Away], MS (Bonnell 127(11) h.), BPM, Haworth.

29 Lou Taylor, *Mourning Dress*, 240.

30 Helen Sheumaker, *Love Entwined: The Curious History of Hairwork in America* (Philadelphia: University of Pennsylvania State, 2007), 66.

31 'Jet Brooch', Black carved jet (J69), BPM, Haworth; 'Jet Bracelet', Black carved jet (J75.1), BPM, Haworth; 'Jet Bracelet', Black carved jet (J75.2), BPM, Haworth.

32 Helen Muller, *Jet Jewellery and Ornaments* (Haverfordwest: Shire Publications, 1980), 3.

33 Muller, *Jet Jewellery*, 5 and 13; Grahame Clark, *Symbols of Excellence: Precious Metals of Expressions of Status* (Cambridge: Cambridge University Press, 1986), 30 and Lou Taylor, *Mourning Dress*, 237.

34 'Jet Necklace', Polished, black carved jet beads and metal clasp (J69), BPM, Haworth; 'Jet Bracelet', Black carved jet (J78), BPM, Haworth.

35 'Letter from Charlotte Brontë to William Smith Williams, ?13 January 1849', MS (Bon 205, 1-2), BPM, Haworth.

36 Ibid., 1–2.

37 'Letter from Charlotte Brontë to William Smith Williams, 1 February 1849', MS (Gr. F7, p. 4), BPM, Haworth.

38 'Letter from Charlotte Brontë to Ellen Nussey, 16 May 1849', HM 24465, Huntington Library, San Marino, California.

39 'Letter from Charlotte Brontë to William Smith Williams, 27 May 1849', MS, Untraced, included in Smith, *Letters*, Vol. 2 (Oxford: Oxford University Press), Reproduced with permission of the Licensor through PLSclear, 213.

40 'Charlotte Brontë's Cashbook 1848/9', (MS B.22.9), BPM, Haworth; and Ellen Nussey, 'An Account of Anne Brontë's Death' in T. Wemyss Reid (ed.), *Charlotte Brontë: A Monograph* (London: Macmillan and Co., 1877), 95–6.

41 Nussey, 'An Account' in Wemyss Reid, *Charlotte Brontë*, 95.

42 Large numbers of ugly bonnets remain. Most are formed from blue silk or cotton. Five such examples, all composed of silk, whalebone/reed (HMCMS:AOC1002.2, HMCMS:BWM1964.654, HMCMS:C2009.79, HMCMS:C2009.80 and HMCMS:AOC1002.1) can be found at the Hampshire Cultural Trust, Winchester, Hampshire.

43 For more on the calash bonnet, see Serena Dyer, *Bergère, Poke and Cottage: Understanding Early Nineteenth Century Headwear* (Derby: Codnor Books, 2011), 10. For example see 'Calash', 1700/1790, Silk, ribbon, cotton (HMCMS:C1976.31.31), Hampshire Cultural Trust, Winchester, Hampshire.

44 William Powell Frith, *Ramsgate Sands*, Oil on canvas, 77 cm × 155.1 cm, 1851–4, (RCIN 405068), Royal Collections Trust, London, © His Majesty, King Charles III 2023.

45 'Letter from Charlotte Brontë to William Smith Williams, 30 May 1849', MS (Berg Coll MSS 186119: b.2.f.14–15), Henry W. and Albert A. Berg Collection of English and American Literature, New York Public Library, Astor, Lenox and Tilden Foundations.

46 Nussey, 'An Account' in Wemyss Reid, *Charlotte Brontë*, 96.

47 'Letter from Charlotte Brontë to Patrick Brontë, 29 May 1849', MS, Untraced, but described in Gaskell's *Life of Charlotte Brontë,* Vol. 2, 110–11.

48 'Letter from Charlotte Brontë to William Smith Williams, 4 June 1849', MS (Ashley 2452), The British Library, London.

49 See Julia Samuel, *Grief Works: Stories of Life, Death and Surviving* (London: Penguin Books, 2017).

50 'Pair of Beaded Moccasins with Ankle Cuffs', Deerskin, velvet, glass, late 1840s (D124.1/2), BPM, Haworth. For more on the story of Charlotte's beaded Iroquois moccasins see Eleanor Houghton, 'Charlotte Brontë's Moccasins: The Wild West Brought Home' in *Charlotte Brontë, Embodiment and the Material World*, eds, Justine Pizzo and Eleanor Houghton (Cham: Palgrave Macmillan, 2020), 171–204.

51 For list of items see 'Object Dossier for D124', BPM.

52 For more on the evocation of the moccasins in *Shirley*, see Houghton, 'Charlotte Brontë's Moccasins', 189–90.

53 It is the policy of the BPM to preserve the anonymity of donors, so all names, where available, have been omitted. see: Houghton, 'Charlotte Brontë's Moccasins', 191.

54 'Letter from Charlotte Brontë to Patrick Brontë, 9 June 1849', MS, Fragments in six different locations, compiled in Smith, *Letters*, Vol. 2, 218.

55 Charlotte and Ellen had visited the Hudsons of Easton Farm, Bridlington in 1839. See: 'Letter from Charlotte Brontë to Ellen Nussey, 24 October 1839', HM 24419, Huntington Library, San Marino, California.

56 'Letter from Charlotte Brontë to Ellen Nussey, 4 July 1849', MS (B.S. 62), BPM, Haworth

57 'Letter from Charlotte Brontë to William Smith Williams, 25 June 1849', MS (B.S. 70), BPM, Haworth and 'Letter from Charlotte Brontë to William Smith Williams, 13 June 1849', MS (Ashley 172), The British Library, London.

58 'Letter from Charlotte Brontë to Ellen Nussey, 14 July 1849', MS (BS71.24), BPM, Haworth.

59 'Letter from Charlotte Brontë to William Smith Williams, 26 July 1849', MS (Bon 210), BPM, Haworth and 'Letter from Charlotte Brontë to William Smith Williams, 25 June 1849', MS (BS70), BPM, Haworth; 'Letter from Charlotte Brontë to William Smith Williams, 29 August 1849', MS, formerly in the collection of Sir Alfred Law and now secured for public ownership.

60 'Letter from Charlotte Brontë to William Smith Williams, *c*. 15 September 1849', MS (Bon 212), BPM, Haworth.

61 Elizabeth Rigby (unsigned), 'Vanity Fair and Jane Eyre' in *Quarterly Review*, 84:167 (December 1848), 153–85.

62 'Literature: Reviews of New Books – *Shirley: A Tale* by the Author of *Jane Eyre*', *Bell's New Weekly Messenger* (Sunday 18 November 1849).

63 The Literary Examiner, '*Shirley*: A Tale by Currer Bell', *The Examiner*, London (Saturday, 3 November 1849), 6.

64 'Letter from Charlotte Brontë to William Smith Williams, 1 November 1849', The Morgan Library & Museum, MA 2696.38, The Henry Houston Bonnell Brontë Collection, Bequest of Helen Safford Bonnell, 1969.

65 'Letter from Charlotte Brontë to Elizabeth Cleghorn Gaskell, 17 November 1849', MS (B.S.71.7 (a)), BPM, Haworth.

66 'Letter from Charlotte Brontë to Elizabeth Cleghorn Gaskell, 17 November 1849'.

67 'Letter from Charlotte Brontë to William Smith Williams, 15 November 1849', HM 24392, Huntington Library, San Marino, California.

68 Advertisement for 'Dr Winns "True Anticardium Paris Black Reviver"' in *The Morning Herald* (Wednesday 28 April 1841), 8.

69 'Letter from Charlotte Brontë to Ellen Nussey, 26 November 1849,' MS (Bon 217), BPM, Haworth; and 'Letter from Charlotte Brontë to Ellen Nussey, 16 November 1849', MS (B.S. 104/35) BPM, Haworth.

70 'Letter from Charlotte Brontë to Ellen Nussey, 26 November 1849.'

71 James M. Volo and Dorothy Denneen Volo, *The Antebellum Period* (Westport: Goodwood Press, 2004), 150.

72 'Velvet beaded mittens', Velvet, cotton, glass (D50.1/2), BPM, Haworth; 'Lace fingerless mittens', Cotton, (D79.1/2), BPM, Haworth. 'Letter from Charlotte Brontë to Rev Patrick Brontë, 5 December 1849', MS (Berg Coll MSS 186119: b.1.f.1), Henry W. and Albert A. Berg Collection of English and American Literature, New York Public Library, Astor, Lenox and Tilden Foundations and 'Last Three Nights of Macready's First Series of Farewell Performances', in *Bell's Weekly Messenger* (Sunday 2 December 1849), 8.

73 'Semi-circular, black lace veil', (D169), BPM, Haworth; 'Spanish lace veil', Silk, (D88), BPM, Haworth; 'Black Lace Bonnet Veil', Silk (D98), BPM, Haworth.

The author was commissioned to study George Eliot's clothing for the Exploring Eliot Foundation and Nuneaton/Herbert Museums in 2021. For George Eliot's Lace Mantilla see 'Black veil,' Silk, (X/EN155), Nuneaton Museum, Nuneaton.

74 Charlotte Brontë, *Villette*, 198.

75 Eneas Sweetland Dallas, 'Dyes and Dyeing' in *Once a Week*, Fourth Series, Vol. V (London: Sweeting and Co., 1877), 68.

76 'Black sateen, rabbit fur lined pumps with ribbon ties and rosette flourish' (D93), BPM, Haworth.

77 'Black Silk Stockings', Silk (D23.1/2), BPM, Haworth.

78 Elizabeth Semmelhack, *Heights of Fashion: A History of the Elevated Shoe* (Pittsburgh: Periscope Press, 2008); Alison Matthews David, *Fashion Victims*, Kindle Edition (London: Bloomsbury Publishing, 2017), 44.

79 'Black canvas, low heeled boots with shiny black leather toes, laced' (D3.1/2), BPM, Haworth; 'Dark brown spotted canvas, low heeled boots with soft leather toe, laced' (D96.1/2), BPM, Haworth.

80 Charlotte asked Ellen to buy cork insoles to help warm Anne's and her shoes, as the cold was so biting. See: 'Letter from Charlotte Brontë to Ellen Nussey, ?22 January 1849', HM 24464, Huntington Library, San Marino, California.

81 'Letter from Charlotte Brontë to Mrs Smith, 17 December 1849', MS (SG 29), BPM, Haworth.

82 'Letter from Charlotte Brontë to Ellen Nussey, ?5 December 1849', The Morgan Library & Museum. MA 2696.27, The Henry Houston Bonnell Brontë Collection, Bequest of Helen Safford Bonnell, 1969.

83 'Letter from Charlotte Brontë to Revd. Patrick Brontë, 5 December 1849', MS (Berg Coll MSS 186119: b.1.f.1), Henry W. and Albert A. Berg Collection of English and American Literature, New York Public Library, Astor, Lenox and Tilden Foundations; 'Letter from Lucy Martineau to Jack Martineau, 10 December 1849', Private Collection; Harriet Martineau, *Memorials of Harriet Martineau,* ed., Maria Weston Chapman (Boston: James R. Osgood, 1877), 24.

84 'Letter from Charlotte Brontë to Ellen Nussey, 19 December 1849', MS (Berg Coll MSS 186119: b.1.f.17), Henry W. and Albert A. Berg Collection of English and American Literature, New York Public Library, Astor, Lenox and Tilden Foundations.

85 'Letter from Charlotte Brontë to Rev Patrick Brontë, 5 December 1849.'

86 'Broderie anglaise blouse', Cotton with black trim (D171), BPM, Haworth.

87 For examples see: 'Plate II – Fashions for July 1848', *The London and Paris Ladies' Magazine,* ed., The Honourable Mrs Ford (Simpkin, Marshall and Co., 1848).

88 For Charlotte's 'Lace chemisettes', Lawn, lace (D90, D109), BPM, Haworth; 'Black and white chequered handkerchief', Silk (D113), BPM, Haworth.

89 'Lavender, grey, white and black barége shawl' (D188), BPM, Haworth.

90 For examples see: 'Purple, black silk and velvet half mourning gown', *c.* 1855–65, Silk, velvet, cotton (1974-14-6), Litchfield Historical Society, Litchfield, Connecticut; 'Purple and black calico printed by Thomas Hoyle and Sons', *Journal of Design and Manufactures, September 1849 – February 1850* (Chapman and Hall, London, 1850), 108.

91 'Two round buttons and a spool of purple thread' (H176.5), BPM, Haworth.

92 W. and G. Audsley, *Color in Dress: A Manual for Ladies* (Philadelphia: George MacLean, 1870), 47.

93 Peter Stallybrass, 'Worn Worlds: Clothes Mourning, And the Life of Things' in *Cultural Memory and the Construction of Identity,* eds, Dan Ben-Amos and Liliane Weissberg (Wayne State University Press, 1999), 28.

94 Elizabeth Wilson, *Adorned in Dreams: Fashion and Modernity* (London: Virago Press, 1987), 1.

95 Ann Rosalind Jones and Peter Stallybrass, *Renaissance Clothing and the Materials of Memory* (Cambridge: Cambridge University Press, 2000), 3. Charlotte Brontë, *Villette,* 34.

96 Karl Marx, 'Wage Labour and Capital' in *Neue Rheinische Zeitung,* 5 April, 8 and 11, 1849.

97 'Letter from Charlotte Brontë to William Smith Williams, 13 June 1849', MS (Ashley 172), The British Library, London.

98 'White cotton stockings marked E2' and 'White cotton stockings marked AB5' (D39, D33), BPM, Haworth; 'AB Handkerchief', White cotton with cotton trim (D189), BPM, Haworth.

99 'Child's silk bodice', Silk, brass (2000/2.2), BPM, Haworth.

100 'Tortoiseshell comb', Spanish style, tortoiseshell (J73), BPM, Haworth; and A.F. Mary Robinson, *Emily Brontë* (Boston: Roberts Brothers, 1883), 286.

101 'Anne Brontë's Blood-stained handkerchief', Cotton (D19), BPM, Haworth.

102 See particularly, 'Shawls' (D99, D121, D26), BPM, Haworth.

103 Stallybrass, 'Worn Worlds: Clothes and Mourning'.

Chapter Eight

1 'Letter from Charlotte Brontë to Ellen Nussey, ?11 March 1850', MS, Untraced, included in Margaret Smith (ed.), *The Letters of Charlotte Brontë, Volume Two, 1848–1851*, Vol. 2 (Oxford: Oxford University Press, 2000). Reproduced with permission of the Licensor through PLSclear.

2 'Letter from Charlotte Brontë to William Smith Williams, 16 March 1850', MS (BS75.51), BPM, Haworth.

3 'Letter from Charlotte Brontë to Ellen Nussey, 19 March 1850', MS (BS75.52), BPM Haworth.

4 'Letter from Charlotte Brontë to Laetitia Wheelwright, 25 March 1850', MS (Berg Coll MSS 186119: b.2. f. 3-4), Henry W. and Albert A. Berg Collection of English and American Literature, New York Public Library, Astor, Lenox and Tilden Foundations.

5 'Letter from Charlotte Brontë to William Smith Williams, 16 March 1850'.

6 'Letter from Charlotte Brontë to George Smith, 19 November 1849', MS (Berg Coll MSS 186119: b.2.f.1), Henry W. and Albert A. Berg Collection of English and American Literature, New York Public Library, Astor, Lenox and Tilden Foundations.

7 Sidney Lee, 'Charlotte Brontë in London', *Brontë Transactions,* 4:19 (based on an address given Spring 1909), 116.

8 'Thackeray Dress', *Alpaca Orleans*, velvet, cotton, brass (D129.1/2), BPM, Haworth.

9 Sotheby, Wilkinson and Hodge, *Catalogue of Valuable Illuminated and Other Manuscripts, Autograph Letters, Oriental Drawings and Printed Books ... Held on 13, 14 and 15 December 1916 at No. 3 Wellington Street, The Strand, Soho* (London: Dryden Press, 1916), 93.

10 For more see: Eleanor Houghton, 'Unravelling the Mystery: Charlotte Brontë's 1850 "Thackeray Dress"', *Costume,* 50:2 (2016), 194–219.

11 The fragments, together with a shoe purported to have been Charlotte's, were found in the New York Public Library.

12 Martha is known to have had a hand in making this gown, see Sotheby, Wilkinson and Hodge, *Catalogue of Valuable Illuminated and Other Manuscripts*, 93.

13 'Fashions for April 1850', *La Belle Assemblée*, January to June 1850, Vol. 32 (London: Joseph Rogerson, 1850).

14 The meeting was between Eleanor Houghton and renowned electrochemists Prof. Philip Bartlett and Prof. Andrea Russell of the University of Southampton. Prof. Russell subsequently pulled together a team consisting of her PhD students Danai Panagoulia and Alex Keeler and the author, to carry out the experiments and analyze the results. Later, help was also kindly given by Tim Smith and Dr Hazel Garvie-Smith of Renishaw plc, Wotton-under-Edge.

15 K. Kavkler and A. Demšar, 'Examination of Cellulose Textile Fibres in Historical Objects by Micro-Raman Spectroscopy', *Spectrochimica Acta Part A: Molecular and Biomolecular Spectroscopy*, 78:2 (2011), 740–6; Bronwyn Cosgrove, Andrea L. Woodhead and Jeffrey Church, 'The Purple Coloration of Four Late 19th Century Silk Dresses: A Spectroscopic Investigation', *Spectrochimica Acta Part A: Molecular and Biomolecular Spectroscopy*, 154 (2016), 185–92.

16 In 1830, Outram of Greetland, Halifax had produced a cloth from alpaca fleece, but this was sold as a curiosity at a high price and was not mass produced.

17 See: *Catalogue of Animal Products Belonging to her Majesty's Catalogue of the Collection of Animal Products … Exhibition of 1851, Exhibited in the South Kensington Museum* (London: William Clowes and Sons, 1858), 24.

18 Robert Balgarnie, *Sir Titus Salt Baronet: His Life and Its Lessons* (London: Hodder and Stoughton, 1878), 62 and Charles Dickens, 'The Great Yorkshire Llama Drama', in *Household Words* (Leipzig: Bernhard Tauchnitz, 1853), 8–14.

19 According to John James in his book *The History of Bradford and Its Parish*, 'In 1849 there set in a demand for fancy alpaca goods consisting of mottled and mixed wefts'. See John James, *The History of Bradford and Its Parish* (Bradford: Longmans, Green, Reader and Dyer, 1866), 235.

20 Rosemary Rees, Nigel Kelly and Jane Shuter, *Living through History: Britain 1750–1900* (Oxford: Heinemann, 1998).

21 Broad Oak Works at Accrington are known to have printed some of Salt's alpaca cloth. See: Benjamin Hargreaves, *Messrs. Hargreaves' Calico Print Works at Accrington, and Recollections of Broad Oak* (Accrington: E. Bowker, 1884), 68; Frederick A. Gatty of Accrington (who had formed a partnership with Frederick Steiner) and Professor Emile Kopp, also of Accrington, both worked on chemical innovations specifically aimed at fixing dyes to mixed fibres. See: *Practical Mechanics Journal*, Vol. VI (London: George Herbert, 1854), 271.

22 See: Henry Cole and Richard Redgrave, *The Journal of Design and Manufacture*, Vol. 2 (London: Chapman and Hall, 1850), 22; Linda Parry, *British Textiles: 1700 to the Present* (London: V&A, 2010), 10; *Exhibition of the Works of All Industry of All*

Nations 1851: Reports by the Juries, ed., Charles Wentworth Dilke (London: William Clowes and Sons, 1852), 742–3.

23 See Houghton, 'Unravelling the Mystery', 206.

24 Vittoria Guglielmi, Silvia Bruni and Federica Pozzi, 'The Identification of Ancient Textile Dyes by Surface-Enhanced Raman Spectroscopy (SERS) on Silver and Gold Colloids', in *5th International Congress on the Application of Raman Spectroscopy in Art and Archaeology*, ed., RAA (Bilbao: Researchgate, 2009); Stephen Batchelor, Laurence Abbott, Lindsay Smith and John Moore, 'Resonance Raman and UV-Visible Spectroscopy of Black Dyes on Textiles', *Forensic Science International*, 202 (2010), 54–63; Jolanta Was-Gubala and Waldemar Machnowski, 'Application of Raman Spectroscopy for Differentiation among Cotton and Viscose Fibers Dyed with Several Dye Classes', *Spectroscopy Letters*, 47 (2014), 527–35.

25 Alex J. Keeler, Danai Panagoulia, Hazel Garvie-Cook, Eleanor Houghton and Andrea Russell, 'Following the Threads: A Raman Spectroscopic Investigation of Charlotte Brontë's Thackeray Dress', University of Southampton in Collaboration with Renishaw plc (2017), 2.

26 The following sources were consulted as efforts were made to establish how the dyes might have been chosen and applied: Edward Parnell, *Dyeing and Calico Printing* (London: Taylor, Walton and Maberly, 1849); Charles O'Neill and A.A. Fesquet, *A Dictionary of Dyeing and Calico Printing* (Philadelphia: Henry Carey Baird, 1869); Charles O'Neill, *Chemistry of Calico Printing, Dyeing, and Bleaching: Including Silken, Woollen, and Mixed Goods Practical and Theoretical … These Subjects for the Years 1868 and 1859* (Manchester: Dunhill, Palmer and Company, 1860); Philip Sykas, 'Identifying Printed Textiles in Dress 1740-1890', ed., DATS (Manchester & London: DATS in partnership with the V&A, 2007); Mary Schoeser and Celia Rufey, *English and American Textiles: From 1790 to the Present* (London: Thames & Hudson, 1989); David Jenkins (ed.), *The Cambridge History of Western Textiles*, Vol. 2 (New York: Cambridge University Press, 2003).

27 The fabric was tested for zinc, aluminium, iron, copper and chrome, but though it is very likely that a mordant or combination of mordants was used, none was detected.

28 R.J. Clark, I.M. Bell and P.J. Gibbs, 'Raman Spectroscopic Library of Natural and Synthetic Pigments (Pre-Approximately 1850)', Christopher Ingold Laboratories, University College London, 2007 [Accessed 18 February 2019], http://www.ucl.ac.uk/chem/resources/raman/speclib.html.

29 Parnell, *Dyeing and Calico Printing*, 222.

30 See: 'Letter from William Makepeace Thackeray to Mrs Elizabeth Smith, 6 June 1850' (Rare Books 3200006), Huntington Library, San Marino, California.

31 Professor Archer, 'Wool and its Applications' in *British Manufacturing Industries* (London: Edward Stanford, 1877), 51.

32 Charlotte Brontë, *Shirley: A Tale* (New York: Harper and Brothers, 1850), 289.

33 Daniel Miller, *Stuff* (Cambridge: Polity Press, 2010), 40.

34 James Burnley, *West Riding Sketches* (London: Hodder and Stoughton, 1875), 12.

35 William Makepeace Thackeray, '"The Last Sketch" (1847–1855) [Introduction to Emma, an Unfinished Novel by Charlotte Brontë]', *Cornhill Magazine*, London (April 1860), 488.

36 'Letter from Charlotte Brontë to Ellen Nussey [12 June 1850]', HM 24471, Huntington Library, San Marino, California.

37 Thackeray, 'The Last Sketch', 488.

38 Ibid., 488.

39 According to Anne Isabella Thackeray, present at the dinner were Mrs Crowe, Mrs Brookfield, Mr and Mrs Thomas Carlyle, Mrs Elliot and Miss Perry, Mrs and Miss Proctor and most of her father's habitual friends. See Anne Isabella Thackeray Ritchie, *Chapters from Some Memoirs* (London: Macmillan and Co., 1894), 62–3.

40 Thackeray Ritchie, *Chapters from Some Memoirs*, 60–5; and Charles and Frances Brookfield, 'A Party for Charlotte Brontë (1850–1851)', in Charles Hallam Brookfield, *Mrs Brookfield and Her Circle* (London: Sir Isaac Pitman and Sons, 1906), 354–5.

41 Thackeray Ritchie, *Chapters from Some Memoirs*, 60–5.

42 Lewis Melville, *The Life of William Makepeace Thackeray*, Vol. 1 (London: Hutchinson and Company, 1899), 261.

43 See: Lee, Smith and Stephen, *George Smith*, 96.

44 See: Thackeray Ritchie, *Chapters from Some Memoirs*, 65; and Houghton, 'Unravelling the Mystery', 196; and Lee, Smith and Stephen, *George Smith*, 98.

45 George Smith, *A Memoir*, eds, Sidney Lee and Leslie Smith (London: Private Circulation, 1902), 97. See also quote by an acquaintance of Charlotte's who claimed 'I've known that lady sit silent throughout a whole evening! Fancy that! Never opened her lips; but her eyes were busy all the time!' in 'Charlotte Brontë' in *Hebden Bridge Times* (Hebden Bridge, Yorkshire), 13 August 1897, 7.

46 Ibid., 98.

47 'Letter from Charlotte Brontë to Ellen Nussey, 29 April 1850' (Bon B.S. 104/40.5), MS, BPM, Haworth.

48 'Letter from Charlotte Brontë to Mary Taylor, 4 September 1848', Untraced, in Smith, *Letters*, Vol. 2, 113.

49 For more, see Houghton, 'Unravelling the Mystery'.

50 Thackeray Ritchie, *Chapters from Some Memoirs*, 60; and 'Mittens', Cream crochet, cotton (D118), BPM, Haworth.

51 'Charlotte Brontë's Appearance, 1850' in Hester Ritchie, *Letters of Anne Thackeray Ritchie, with Forty-Five Additional Letters from her Father, William Makepeace*

Thackeray (London: John Murray, 1924), 269–70. Anne is probably referring to the curled and looped hairstyles popular in the 1850s. See: 'Le Bon Ton, Fashion Plate *c.* 1850' (E.1995-1888), V&A, London.

52 Brookfield, 'A Party for Charlotte Brontë (1850–1851)', 304. For examples of hair pieces see: 'Sample of plaited hair', 1830–50, Hair, silk (T.259I-1916), V&A, London; 'Sample of plaited hair', 1820–1850, Hair, silk (T.259A-1916), V&A, London.

Aware of her mistake, Charlotte later had the headdress 'rearranged as I wished- it is now a very different matter to the bushy, tasteless thing it was before'. See: 'Letter from Charlotte Brontë to Ellen Nussey 9? December 1852', MS, Untraced, included in Smith, *Letters,* Vol. 3, 91.

53 'Letter from Charlotte Brontë to Laetitia Wheelwright, 17 December 1849', MS (B.S. 72), BPM, Haworth and 'Letter from Charlotte Brontë to Ellen Nussey, 19 December 1849' in MS (Berg Coll MSS 186119: b.1.f.17), Henry W. and Albert A. Berg, *Collection of English and American Literature*, New York Public Library, Astor, Lenox and Tilden Foundations.

54 'Letter to ?Mrs. Gaskell from Unknown Author, September 1853', included in Elizabeth Cleghorn Gaskell, *The Life of Charlotte Brontë*, Vol. 2, 297.

55 'Letter from Charlotte Brontë to Ellen Nussey, ?5 December 1849', MS (MA 2696), The Morgan Library, New York.

56 Birgitta Nedalmann, 'Georg Simmel as an Analyst of Antonymous Dynamics: The Merry Go Round of Fashion', in *Georg Simmel and Contemporary Sociology*, ed., B.S. Phillips, M. Kaern and Robert S. Cohen (Boston: Kluwer Academic Publishers, 1990), 251.

57 Phillippe Perrot, *Fashioning the Bourgeoisie: A History of Clothing in the Nineteenth Century* (Princeton: Princeton University Press, 1994), 82. Though he places focus on post-Revolution France, Perrot argues that bourgeois dress had replaced the multiplicity of aristocratic costumes, but that beneath its superficial uniformity, subtle levels of meaning had been carefully cultivated.

58 Georg Simmel, *On Individuality and Social Forms: Selected Writings*, ed. Donald N. Levine (Chicago: Chicago University Press, 1971), 311.

59 Perrot, *Fashioning the Bourgeoisie*, 85.

60 A nobiliary particle is used in a surname in many cultures to signal the nobility of a family. In England and Wales this was originally the Latin word 'de' (Elizabeth de Hoton), but later came to be replaced by 'of' (John of Gaunt).

61 Roche, *The Culture of Clothing*, 6–7.

62 See Table 1 for a chart detailing the changing type and quantity of clothing required by Charlotte between the years 1829 and 1855, and specifically, how her need for conspicuous clothing grew in the years of fame (1849–53). See also Table 2 for references to Charlotte's purchasing of clothing, which again increased exponentially between 1849 and 1851.

63 Perrot, *Fashioning the Bourgeoisie*, 6.

64 Lawrence and E.M. Hanson, *Four Brontës: The Lives and Works of Charlotte, Branwell, Emily and Anne Brontë* (London: Oxford University Press, 1949), 294–8.

65 Brookfield, 'A Party for Charlotte Brontë (1850–1851)', 355.

66 'Letter from Charlotte Brontë to Ellen Nussey, 26 November 1849', MS (Bon 217), BPM, Haworth.

67 'Letter from Charlotte Brontë to Ellen Nussey, ?27 July 1849', MS (MS 24466), Huntington Library, San Marino; 'Letter from Charlotte Brontë to Ellen Nussey, 10 May 1851', HM 24479, Huntington Library, San Marino, California; 'Letter from Charlotte Brontë to Ellen Nussey, 29 April 1849', MS (Bon 219), BPM, Haworth.

68 For example, see 'Letter from Charlotte Brontë to Mrs. Gaskell? Early June 1854', MS (BS.9.7), BPM, Haworth.

69 See Ellis H. Chadwick, *In the Footsteps of the Brontës*, 2nd ed. (Cambridge: Cambridge University Press, 2011), 461.

70 'Letter from Charlotte Brontë to Ellen Nussey, 10 May 1851.'

71 Despite the efforts to boost British industry, bonnets formed from leghorn straw (from Legorno, now Livorno, Italy) were the most sought after. The straw of Charlotte's bonnet remains in almost perfect condition and, with the exception of some small pieces that have been added to the brim, has been woven in one piece from the centre of the crown outward. Though the silk lining has now faded, the jacquard ribbons are also of high quality. 'Straw bonnet with pink ribbons', Straw, silk, cotton (D140), BPM, Haworth.

   For examples of fashionable bonnets, see: 'London and Paris Fashions for July 1851', Hand-coloured lithograph (E.1166-1959), V&A, London and 'Fashion Plate', 1851, Hand-coloured lithograph (E.1250-1959), V&A, London.

72 Attribution was established by the author after close examination of the garment and all key documents within the collection. 'Blue-and-cream striped silk gown with floral embellishments and bows', Silk, calico, bone, metal, 1850s (D10), BPM, Haworth.

73 'Paisley Dress', Muslin, linen, metal, 1840–5 (D3), BPM, Haworth.

74 See Barbara Burman and Ariane Fennetaux, *The Pocket: A Hidden History 1640–1900* (New Haven: Yale University Press, 2020), 42.

75 For an example of a gown featuring a small, similarly sized pocket made for holding a watch see '1849–1850 Deep Violet, Printed, Fine Wool Dress' in Nancy Bradfield, *Costume in Detail 1730–1930* (London: Eric Dobby Publishing Ltd, 1995), 187.

76 For example of gowns featuring skirts 'en tablier' see: Hippolyte Damours, 'Modes de Paris', *Petit Courrier des Dames, Journal des Modes*, 15 January 1839 (NPG D47776), National Portrait Gallery, London and 'Walking Dresses', *Les Modes Parisiennes* (Paris: Moine Impr. Des Noyes, 1848), 47.

77 Penelope Byrde, *Nineteenth Century Fashion* (London: Batsford 1992), 128. Brontë's extant wardrobe contains more examples of such embellishments.

78 For examples, see 'Front Fastening Silk Day Dress with Tiered Bell Sleeves and Passementerie', 1850s (38), John Bright Collection, London; 'Fashions for September 1850', included in La Belle Assemblée (London, 1850); 'Silk Day Dress with Ruched Silk Trim, 1850–1855' (CE0004114A), Museo del Traje, Madrid).

79 For examples see: Collars, lawn/cotton (D66.2, D110. D122, D146, D63, D103.1), BPM, Haworth.

80 'Lady's Dinner Dress, The Paris and London Fashions', *The Lady's Newspaper*, London (20 May 1848) included in *The Lady's Newspaper from January to June 1848*, Vol. III, 410–11.

81 'Letter from Charlotte Brontë to Ellen Nussey, 26 August 1850', HM 24473, Huntington Library, San Marino, California.

82 'Letter from G.H. Lewes to George Smith' included Thomas James Wise and John Alexander Symington, *Shakespeare Head Brontë*, Vol. 3 (Oxford: Oxford University Press, 1932), 171–2.

83 'Royal Italian Opera', *The Illustrated London News*, London (8 June 1850), 10.

84 James Laver, *Costume and Fashion: A Concise History*, 5th edn (London: Thames and Hudson, 2014), 174.

85 'Dress for the Elderly Lady, 25 October 1850', in *The Lady's Newspaper*, July to December 1851, Vol. X (Robert Palmer: London), 225.

86 G.H. Lewes, reported in 'Letter from George Eliot to Charles and Cara Bray, 5 and 12 March 1853' in *The George Eliot Letters*, Vol. 2, ed., Gordon Haight (New Haven: Yale University Press, 1954), 92.

87 'Letter from Mary Taylor to Ellen Nussey, 15 August 1850', Untraced, included in Smith, *Letters*, Vol. 2, 443.

88 Gaskell, *The Life of Charlotte Brontë*, Vol. 1, 100.

89 William Dearden, 'Nancy Garr', *Bradford Observer* (20 August 1857), 8; 'Nancy Wainwright: Charlotte Brontë's Nurse', *Illustrated Weekly Telegraph*, London (10 January 1885), 1.

90 William Dearden, 'Nancy Garr', *Bradford Observer*, Bradford (20 August 1857), 8; and also 'Letter from Patrick Brontë to Elizabeth Cleghorn Gaskell, 30 July 1857', MS (EL B121, 3), John Rylands Library, University of Manchester, Manchester.

91 For definition of 'conspicuous consumption' see Thorstein Veblen, *Conspicuous Consumption* (London: Penguin, 2005).

92 For examples of ribbons and bows see: (D182, D183, D184, D66.1, D95, D138, D54, D61.2), BPM, Haworth.

93 Whilst Brontë did make some money from her books, according to her marriage settlement, this was estimated at *c*. £1,678. On her father's death, she was set to inherit just £300. See Barker, *The Brontës*, 887.

94 For example, Brontë drew on real-life experience in her description of the actress Vashti who is based on Rachel, whom she saw with Smith 'more than once' and also the scene of the fire is based on an incident at Devonshire House when Dickens gave a performance. See George Smith, *A Memoir*, eds, Sidney Lee and Leslie Smith (London: Private Circulation 1902), 103.

95 Sidney Lee was George Smith's business partner. In Sir Sidney Lee and Leslie Stephen, *The Dictionary of National Biography: Founded in 1882 by George Smith* (London: Oxford University Press, 1925) and Sir Sidney Lee, 'Charlotte Brontë in London', in *Brontë Transactions*, 4:19, 95–120.

96 Smith, *A Memoir*, 103

97 Charlotte Brontë, *Villette*, 198.

98 Charlotte Brontë, *Villette*, 198.

99 Charlotte Brontë, *Villette*, 209.

100 Charlotte Brontë, *Villette*, 209.

101 Gaskell, *Life of Charlotte Brontë*, Vol. 2, 208.

102 James Pope-Hennessey, *Monckton Milnes: The Flight of Youth 1851–1885* (London: Constable and Company, 1951), 65.

103 Gaskell, *Life Charlotte Brontë*, Vol. 2, 290. It should be noted that Brontë did not meet Gaskell until 1849, and thus post fame.

104 Gaskell, *Life Charlotte Brontë*, Vol. 2, 290.

105 George Smith, 'Charlotte Brontë', 92.

106 Gaskell, *The Life of Charlotte Brontë*, Vol. 1, 348.

107 Emily Dickinson, '"Hope" is the thing with feathers,' 1891 (Packet X, Mixed Fascicles, (46b), J254, Fr314), Houghton Library, Harvard University.

108 John Stores Smith, 'Personal Reminiscences: A Day with Charlotte Brontë (1850)', *The Free Lance: A Journal of Humour and Criticism (Manchester)*, 3 (14 March 1868), 86.

109 Stores Smith, 'Personal Reminiscences', 87.

110 'Letter from Charlotte Brontë to Sydney Dobell, 28 June 1851', MS, Untraced in Smith, *Letters*, Vol. 2, 651–2.

111 'Letter from Charlotte Brontë to Amelia Taylor, 7 June 1851', MS (BC MS 19c Brontë/03/02/14), Brotherton Library, University of Leeds, Leeds.

112 Gaskell, *The Life of Charlotte Brontë*, Vol. 1, 348.

113 Brontë spoke these words to a writer who visited her in Haworth in 1850. Stores Smith, 'Personal Reminiscences', 87.

114 Alison Chapman, 'Achieving Fame and Canonicity', in *Cambridge Companion to Victorian Women's Literature, 1830–1890*, ed., Linda Peterson (Cambridge: Cambridge University Press, 2015), 76.

115 For information on Brontë's visits to the Great Exhibition see Barker, *The Brontës*, 794–5, 798–9. For details of her visit to Pentonville, Newgate, Foundling Hospital and Bethlehem Hospital see 'Letter from Charlotte Brontë to Ellen Nussey, 19 January 1853', HM 26002, Huntington Library, San Marino, California.

116 Pope-Hennessey, *Monckton Milnes*, 66.

Chapter Nine

1 'Letter from Richard Monckton Milnes to Mrs Gaskell, 30 January 1854', MS (FMS Am 1943.1), Houghton Library, Harvard University.

2 'Letter from Charlotte Brontë to Mrs Rand, 26 May 1845', The Morgan Library & Museum, MA 2696.33, The Henry Houston Bonnell Brontë Collection, Bequest of Helen Safford Bonnell, 1969.

3 'Letter from Charlotte Brontë to Ellen Nussey, 10 July 1846', MS (Gr. E. 10.), BPM, Haworth.

4 'Letter from Charlotte Brontë to Patrick Brontë, 2 June 1852', The Morgan Library & Museum, MA 2696.44, The Henry Houston Bonnell Brontë Collection, Bequest of Helen Safford Bonnell, 1969.

5 'Letter from Charlotte Brontë to Ellen Nussey, 28 January 1850', MS (N/A), Houghton Library, Harvard University.

6 'Letter from Charlotte Brontë to Ellen Nussey, 2 January 1853', MS (BS86.1), BPM, Haworth.

7 'Letter from Charlotte Brontë to Ellen Nussey, [?28 July 1851]', MS (Add. MS c/80/7) Trinity College, University of Cambridge.

8 'Letter from Charlotte Brontë to Ellen Nussey, 15 December 1852', MS (Berg Coll MSS 186119: b.1.f.24-25), Henry W. and Albert A. Berg Collection of English and American Literature, New York Public Library, Astor, Lenox and Tilden Foundations.

9 Ibid.

10 Ibid.

11 Christine Alexander and Margaret Smith, *The Oxford Companion to the Brontës* (Oxford: Oxford University Press, 2006), 342.

12 'Letter from Charlotte Brontë to Margaret Wooler, 12 April 1854', MS (Brontë(C)/26), Fitzwilliam Library, Cambridge.

13 'Letter from Charlotte Brontë to Ellen Nussey, 6 April 1853', MS (Grolier E24), BPM, Haworth.

14 Elizabeth Gaskell, *Life of Charlotte Brontë*, Vol. 2, 289.

15 Ibid., Vol. 1, p. 292.

16 Alan Adamson, *Mr Charlotte Brontë* (London: McGill-Queen's University Press, 2008), 44; and 'Letter from Charlotte Brontë to Ellen Nussey, 16 May 1853'.

17 'Letter from Charlotte Brontë to Ellen Nussey, 6 April 1853', MS (Grolier E24), BPM, Haworth.

18 'Letter from Charlotte Brontë to Ellen Nussey, 27 May 1853', MS (Grolier E25), BPM, Haworth; 'Letter from Charlotte Brontë to Ellen Nussey, 16 May 1853', in Charlotte Brontë, MS (Correspondence II; Robert H. Taylor Collection of English and American Literature, RTC01), Manuscripts Division, Department of Special Collections, Princeton University Library.

19 'Letter from Charlotte Brontë to Mrs Gaskell, 18 June 1853', MS, Untraced, included in Margaret Smith (ed.), *The Letters of Charlotte Brontë, Volume Three, 1852–1855*, Vol. 3 (Oxford: Oxford University Press, 2004), Reproduced with permission of the Licensor through PLSclear, 177.

20 'Letter from Mary Taylor to Ellen Nussey, 24 February 1854', MS (Ashley 5768), The British Library, London.

21 'Letter from Charlotte Brontë to Elizabeth Gaskell, 15 November 1853', MS (BS, 91.5), BPM, Haworth.

22 'Draft Letter by ?Mrs Smith to Charlotte Brontë, 22 November 1853', MS (SG 87), BPM, Haworth.

23 'Letter from Charlotte Brontë to George Smith, December 1853', MS (SG 88), BPM, Haworth.

24 'Letter from Charlotte Brontë to Ellen Nussey, 11 April 1854', MS (Pforzheimer Collection: MISC 0060), New York Public Library.

25 Quoted in 'Letter from Mrs Gaskell to John Forster, 17 May 1854', MS (MS.2262), National Library of Scotland, Scotland. This was untrue. In her marriage settlement, the money stipulated was £1,678 9s. 9d. See Juliet Barker, *The Brontës*, 2nd ed. (London: Abacus Books, 2010), 891.

26 Charlotte is recalling the book of Gen. 29 (NIV), in which Jacob must work for Laban for seven years to earn the hand of his beautiful and shapely daughter, Rachel.

27 'Letter from Charlotte Brontë to Ellen Nussey, 20 April 1840', HM 24426, Huntington Library, San Marino, California.

28 Currer Bell, *Jane Eyre: An Autobiography* (New York: Harper and Brothers, 1848), 171.

29 Kristin Harris Walsh, '"You Just Nod and Pin and Sew and Let Them Do Their Thing": An Analysis of the Wedding Dress as Artifact and Signifier', *Ethnologies*, 7:2 (2005), 239.

30 Nicholls's curate salary was £100 a year in May 1845. This was a real wage price of £9,404.00 as of summer 2023. www.measuringworth.com.

31 Letter from Charlotte Brontë to ?Mrs Gaskell Early June 1854', MS (BS.9.7), BPM, Haworth.

32 'Conscience', OED Online [Accessed March 2023], https://oed.com/view/Entry/39460; Defined as: 'senses involving consciousness of morality or what is considered right'; or the modifying adjective that denotes 'a generally or legally agreed sense of what is right or just'; or 'a consciousness of acting or having acted rightly, or of being virtuous'.

33 'Letter from Charlotte Brontë to Ellen Nussey [15 April 1854]', MS (BS. 95.2), BPM, Haworth.

34 Zoe Burke, 'National Wedding Survey: The Average UK Wedding 2025; Brides Editors, 'This Is What American Weddings Look Like Today', *Brides*, 15 August 2021 [Accessed 27 June 2023], https://www.brides.com/gallery/american-wedding-study.

35 N.F.R. Crafts, Average age at first marriage for women in mid-nineteenth century England and Wales: a cross section study, Warwick Economic Research Papers, University of Warwick, No. 92: 1976, 4.

36 Edwina Ehrman, *The Wedding Dress: 300 Years of Bridal Fashions* (London: V&A Publishing, 2014), 56–9. Queen Frederika of Baden also wore white at her marriage to King Gustav IV of Sweden in 1797.

37 Clara de Chatelain, *Bridal Etiquette* (London: Ward and Lock, 1856), 12.

38 See item 93 in Her Majesty's Stationery Office, *A Catalogue of Pictures, Drawings and Sketches of the Late William Mulready: Part One – the Oil Paintings* (London: George Eyre and William Spottiswoode, 1864), 20.

39 Alison Toplis, *The Clothing Trade in Provincial England 1800–1850* (Abingdon: Routledge, 2016), 140.

40 'Letter from Charlotte Brontë to Ellen Nussey, 27 July 1849', HM 24466, Huntington Library, San Marino, California.

41 According to Margaret Ross, Nicholls's great-niece. See 'Descriptive Notes by Jean Agnew', *Wedding Replica File* (undated, 4), BPM, Haworth.

42 H.K. Bell, 'Charlotte Brontë's Husband. His Later Life and Surroundings (1855–1906)' in *Cornhill Magazine*, Vol. LXII (January 1927), 42–6.

43 Frances Bell, Nicholls's second wife's niece, later wrote: 'Well there was a press? [][] in the lobby, which was never opened for many, many years. But the second wife one day said that she might as well look what was in it and if I do not mistake the wedding things were there.' See, 'Letter from Frances Bell', Date unknown, in *Wedding Dress Replica File*, BPM, Haworth.

44 A note included in the *Wedding Replica File* recounts Donald Hopewell, President of the Brontë Society from 1974–82. Drawing on unknown 'Belfast' sources, he states 'Mr. Nicholls took [the wedding dress] to Ireland with him and it was kept in the bottom drawer of a tallboy which had originally stood in Charlotte Brontë's bedroom in Haworth. With the wedding dress were shoes, gloves, a kind of stole, and a few little flowers which apparently came from the lining of the bonnet. These were kept in a box that had Rowntrees of Scarborough on it.' That these items were kept together is also confirmed by Margaret Ross. See: 'Descriptive Notes by Jean Agnew', *Wedding Replica File*, BPM, Haworth.

45 According to Ross, a silk sash, lengths of coloured ribbon, a silk bookmark, some visiting cards and a pair of black satin shoes were also included. See: 'Descriptive Notes by Jean Agnew', *Wedding Replica File*, BPM, Haworth.

46 See: Elizabeth McCrum, 'Destruction of Ulster Museum's Textile and Costume Collection', *Costume*, 12 (April 1978), 105–9.

47 'Letter from Frances Bell', included in *Wedding Replica File*, BPM, Haworth.

48 Agnew states that Ross had 'had the excitement of trying on the dress on a visit to Banagher and realized how tiny it was'.

49 The drawings have not been located since.

50 Gaskell was in close contact with Brontë prior to her wedding. She wrote, 'At the beginning of May, Miss Brontë left home to pay three visits before her marriage. The first was to us. She remained only three days, as she had to go to the neighbourhood of Leeds, there to make such purchases as were required for her marriage. Her preparations, as she said, could neither be extensive nor expensive.' Elizabeth Cleghorn Gaskell, *Mary Barton*, Vol. 1 (London: Chapman and Hall, 1880), 420.

51 Gaskell, *Life of Charlotte Brontë*, Vol. 2, 16.

52 'Going Away Dress', Silk, cotton, 1854 (D741/2), BPM, Haworth; and 'Barège Dress', barège, cotton, 1854 (D119.1/2, D28.1/2), BPM, Haworth.

53 Ellis H. Chadwick, *In the Footsteps of the Brontës*, 2nd ed. (Cambridge: Cambridge University Press, 2011), 458. See also: Diary of Yorkshireman, 'Charlotte Brontë's Bonnet', *The Yorkshire Evening Post*, Yorkshire (10 February 1943), 4. Two Americans who had to change trains at Leeds were quoted by Henrietta, Janet and Beatrice Mary Walker as saying 'Leeds! Leeds! What is it noted for?' 'Oh!' was the reply, 'it is the place where Charlotte Brontë bought her trousseau.'

54 'Advertisement for Beech and Barrell's of London', *The Indian News and Chronicle of Eastern Affairs* (London: January 1850).

55 See 'Muslin Wedding Dress', c, 1855, European (M.2007.211.755), LACMA, Los Angeles; 'Wedding Dress', Muslin, 1851 (T.367&A-1988), V&A, London; 'Wedding Dress worn by Scea Beata Myhrman', Muslin, silk, cotton, 1854 (192688), Nordic Museum/Nordiska Museet, Stockholm; 'Wedding Dress', Muslin 1855–61 (N/A), Palais Galliera, Musée de la Mode de la Ville de Paris, Paris.

56 'Wedding Dress', Muslin, 1851 (T.367&A-1988), V&A, London. The dress and petticoat are associated with a horsehair lace bonnet.

57 See: 'Illustration of the Empress of the French [Empress Eugenie], in her Bridal Costume', *The Illustrated London News*, 5 March 1853, 188.

58 Chadwick, *In the Footsteps of the Brontës*, 460.

59 Gaskell, *Life of Charlotte Brontë*, Vol. 2, 316 and quote from Sexton's relative in Chadwick, *In the Footsteps of the Brontës*, 460.

60 Gaskell, *Life of Charlotte Brontë*, Vol. 2, 316.

61 A biot is a stiff feather from the front edge of a wing.

62 The earliest known usage of the poem 'Something Old, Something New, Something Borrowed Something Blue' was in May 1876; see G.F., 'Weddings', *Notes and Queries*, Oxford University Press, Volume s5-V (20 May 1876), 408. This suggests that the practice was adopted well before the inclusion of this in the volume. Brontë's blue feather could be attributed to this tradition.

63 See: Diary of Yorkshireman, 'Charlotte Brontë's Bonnet', 4.

64 'Straw Bonnet with Pink Silk Ribbon' (D140), BPM, Haworth, is a leghorn bonnet trimmed with pink ribbons and lined with silk that has now faded to very pale pink/white.

65 'Advertisement – Hunt and Hall, Millinery', *Leeds Intelligencer*, Leeds (22 April 1854), 1.

66 The bonnet did not go to Ireland with the rest of the wedding garments, though some stems of the orange blossom adornments were taken.

67 'Letter from Charlotte Brontë to? Mrs Gaskell, early June 1854 – Fragment'; see also 'Wedding Dress Fashion Plate', *Le Conseiller Des Dames & Desmoiselles*, Paris, March 1853.

68 *The Etiquette of Courtship and Matrimony: With a Complete Guide to the Forms of a Wedding* (London: David Bogue, 1852), 69.

69 Orange blossom was worn by Hera for her marriage to Zeus and was also by Juno, the goddess of marriage. It is a symbol of fertility and purity because the plant blooms and bears fruit simultaneously.

70 *The Times* newspaper wrote that 'Her Majesty wore no diamonds on her head, nothing but a simple wreath of orange blossom', *The Times* (11 February 1840), 4. Between 1839 and 1846, Albert subsequently presented Victoria with a beautiful orange blossom parure to mark the significant moments in their lives. See, Royal

Collection Trust's Press Office, 'How Queen Victoria and Prince Albert Expressed Their Love through Flowers Is Explored in a New Exhibition, Royal Collection Trust, London, Tuesday, 12 July 2016' [20 August 2018], https://www.royalcollection.org.uk/about/press-office/press-releases/how-queen-victoria-and-prince-albert-expressed-their-love-through.

71 See: 'Wedding wreath, orange blossom made from green and white feathers on silk thread wrapped wire with silk ribbons, worn by Elizabeth Wroughton Richards, Hampshire', 1854 (T.6-2008), V&A, London.

72 Erving Goffman, *Gender Advertisements* (New York: Harper and Row, 1987), 20–1.

73 Fred Davis, *Fashion, Culture, and Identity* (Chicago: Chicago University Press, 1992), 82.

74 Davis, *Fashion, Culture, and Identity*, 82.

75 See Note to 'Letter from Charlotte Brontë to Harriet Martineau, 9 December 1849', MS, Untraced, in Smith, *Letters*, Vol. 2, 304. Anne Isabella Ritchie née Thackeray quoted in Chadwick, *In the Footsteps of the Brontës*, 399; John Stores Smith, 'Personal Reminiscences A Day with Charlotte Brontë (1850)', *The Free Lance: A Journal of Humour and Criticism*, 3 (14 March), 86.

76 H.L.J., 'Aesthetics of Dress: Art of a Bonnet', *Blackwood's Magazine,* Edinburgh (February 1845), 247.

77 *Charlotte Brontë 'Wedding Veil'*, Lace, wire, satin, silk, ribbon, 1854 (D97), BPM, Haworth; 'Letter from Charlotte Brontë to? Mrs Gaskell, early June 1854 – Fragment'.

78 Rachel Terry, 'Additions to the Brontë Society Collections: Further Details and New Items', *Brontë Society Transactions*, 27 (November 2002), 251.

79 Charlotte Brontë, *Jane Eyre*, 108.

80 Ibid., 112.

81 Gaskell, *Life of Charlotte Brontë*, Vol. 2, 316.

82 A bertha is a large collar made from lace or another fine fabric. 'Letter from Frances Bell', included in *Wedding Replica File*, BPM, Haworth. Princess Eugenie wore a lace bertha at her wedding ceremony in 1853.

83 Margaret Ross. See 'Descriptive Notes by Jean Agnew', *Wedding Replica File*, BPM, Haworth, undated. and repeated in another note included in the *Wedding Replica File*, that recounts the reminiscences of Donald Hopewell, President of the Brontë Society from 1974–82.

84 Chadwick, *The Footsteps of the Brontës*, 460. Charlotte Brontë, Wedding Shawl, silk and wool, *c.* 1854 (D78), BPM, Haworth. This shawl is on long-term loan from Bradford Museums and Galleries, who acquired it from the buyer at the sale in 1886.

85 An advertisement from 1855 stated that shawls sold at The Great Shawl and Cloak Emporium, Regent Street, London, ranged in price from a 'woollen wrap of ten shillings to the elaborately worked India of One Hundred and Fifty Guineas', included in Edmund Lodge Esq, *The Peerage of the British Empire*, Vol. 24 (London Saunders and Otley, 1855), 30. In the Binns Sale of 1886, another shawl sold for 25 shillings, while the so-called 'wedding shawl', sold for '£4 15s'.

86 'Sandalled shoes' are frequently referred to in contemporary literature. *Englishwomen's Domestic Magazine* (Vol. 2, 228) of 1866, uses the phrase, as does Marie-Pauléne Rose Blaze de Bury, *Germania in 1850; Its Courts, Camps, and People*, Vol. 2 (London: Henry Colburn, 1851), 61. They feature 'thin soles', but no firm descriptions remain and no examples of obviously sandalled shoes, of the type that could be worn over 'white stockings' have been found. H.K. Bell, 'Charlotte Brontë's Husband. His Later Life and Surroundings (1855–1906)' in *Cornhill Magazine*, London, Vol. LXII (January 1927), 42–6.

87 Margaret Ross. See 'Descriptive Notes by Jean Agnew', *Wedding Replica File*, BPM, Haworth.

88 'Letter from Frances Bell', in *Wedding Replica File*, BPM, Haworth.

89 'Black Satin Slippers', Leather, silk (D93), BPM, Haworth.

90 For example see: 'Satin Wedding Shoes,' 1854, Silk, satin, leather, lined with cotton and kidskin, imported from Paris (T.4:1,2-2008), V&A, London.

91 Lucy Johnston, *Nineteenth Fashion in Detail* (London: V&A Publishing, 2010), 78.

92 'Letter from Frances Bell', included in *Wedding Replica File*, BPM, Haworth.

93 (D36, D92, LI.2005.10), BPM, Haworth, are all pairs of kid leather gloves with single fastenings at the wrist that remain at the parsonage.

94 'Letter from Charlotte Brontë to Ellen Nussey, 11 April 1854', MS (Pforzheimer Collection: MISC 0060), The Carl H. Pforzheimer Collection of Shelley and His Circle, New York Public Library, Astor, Lenox and Tilden Foundations.

95 Charlotte Brontë, *Villette*, 300, 363 and 364.

96 Ibid., 184.

97 Brontë describes Ginevra as being, 'obliged to be well dressed, and she had not money to buy variety of dresses. All her thoughts turned on this difficulty; her whole soul was occupied with expedients for effecting its solution. It was wonderful to witness the activity of her otherwise indolent mind on this point, and to see the much-daring intrepidity to which she was spurred by a sense of necessity, and the wish to shine.' Charlotte Brontë, *Villette*, 80.

98 Charlotte Brontë, *The Professor*, Fair Copy, 1850, The Morgan Library & Museum. MA 31. Purchased by J. Pierpont Morgan before 1908.

99 Charlotte Brontë, *Jane Eyre*, 105 and 110.

100 Ibid., 105.

101 'Charlotte Brontë's Wedding', *Yorkshire Post and Leeds Intelligencer,* Leeds (Thursday 14 August 1913), 6.

102 'Brown striped gown worn by Ellen Nussey for Charlotte Brontë's Wedding', 1854, Striped silk (2003/16), BPM, Haworth and 'Straw and silk Pork Pie Hat', 1854 (D1), BPM, Haworth.

103 'Charlotte Brontë's Wedding: An Excerpt from the *Keighley News* for 27 October 1923' included in Margaret Smith, *The Letters of Charlotte Brontë, Vol. Three, 1852–1855* (Oxford: Oxford University Press, 2004), 359.

104 Barker, *The Brontës,* 894.

Chapter Ten

1 Going Away Dress, Silk, cotton, brass (D74.1/2), BPM, Haworth.

2 'Letter from Charlotte Brontë to Ellen Nussey [15 April 1854]', MS (B.S.95.2), BPM, Haworth.

3 Ellen Binns received a real price value of £150.80 for the dress. (Amount calculated using www.measuringworth.com as of summer 2023)

4 'Fragment of Going Away Dress,' Silk (D134), BPM, Haworth was sold by Ellen Binns at the Saltaire Sale in 1887 and was placed in an envelope labelled 'piece of dress worn by CB'; 'Fragment of Going Away Dress,' Silk, cardboard (D135) was given to the Brontë Society in 1950; (D136) is an annotated card that contains scraps of four different fabrics – all worn towards the end of Brontë's life. (D107.2) is another annotated card, but this has only a small piece of the striped silk. It was given to the museum in 1921.

5 On (D107.2), BPM Haworth, is also written, 'Those who saw the wedding said she tripped along like a fairy.'

6 'Letter from Charlotte Brontë to Elizabeth Gaskell,? early June 1854'.

7 Chadwick, *In the Footsteps of the Brontës,* 459.

8 Clement Shorter, *Charlotte Brontë and Her Circle,* 2nd ed. (London: Hodder and Stoughton, 1896), 332, n. 3.

9 It is possible that the garment was loaned to the Brontë Society for safe-keeping and was therefore mentioned in the catalogue of 1896 but not sold to the Brontë Society until 1907. Lewis Hainsworth, *A Descriptive Catalogue of Objects in the Museum of the Brontë Society at Haworth* (Haworth: Brontë Society Museum and Library, 1896), 23.

10 Juliet Barker, *Sixty Treasures of the Brontë Parsonage Museum* (Haworth: Brontë Society, 1988), Item 51.

11 Jane Sellars, *Charlotte Brontë (British Library Writers' Lives)* (London: British Library Publishing, 1997), 109.

12 Rachel Terry, 'Additions to the Brontë Society Collections: Further Details and New Items', *Brontë Society Transactions*, 27 (November 2002), 252, 251.

13 See: Brontë Catalogue Object Display Card for (D74.1), BPM, Haworth [Accessed 12 August 2024], http://Brontë.adlibsoft.com/detail.aspx?parentpriref.

14 Anita Quye, Julie H. Wertz and David France, 'Turkey Red Prints: Identification of Lead Chromate, Prussian Blue and Logwood on Turkey Red Calico', *Studies in Historical Textiles*, Conservar Património: 31 (April): 31–9.

15 In 1856, William Perkin discovered mauveine dye. More synthetic dyes were then produced, and these were often more resistant to environmental changes.

16 It was not until the 1980s that the Bonnell Store was made environmentally stable.

17 Renishaw plc invited us to their headquarters at Wotton-under-Edge where we were given access to a Renishaw inVia Qontor Raman microscope, StreamLine Technology and WiRE 4 software. Hazel Garvie-Cook and Tim Smith guided the experiments.

18 Scanning Electron Microscopy or SEMs utilize electron beams to retrieve information from a sample at the nanoscale. The main type of signals that are detected are the backscattered electrons (BSEs) and secondary electrons (SEs), which generate a greyscale image of the sample at very high magnifications. SEM is often used in conjunction with Energy Dispersive X-ray detection (EDX) as in this case. This allows different information about the elements within the sample to be identified. See Antonis Nanakoudis, 'EDX Analysis with a Scanning Electron Microscope (SEM): How Does It Work?', in *Desktop Electron Microscopy Solutions*, Thermo Fisher Scientific, 21 June 2018 [Accessed 12 August 2024], https://blog.phenom-world.com/edx-analysis-scanning-electron-microscope-sem.

19 Hazel Garvie-Cook, 'Raman Analysis of Charlotte Brontë's Dresses', ed., Renishaw plc. (Unpublished document: Renishaw plc, 2016), 15.

20 Garvie-Cook, 'Raman Analysis of Charlotte Brontë's Dresses', 15.

21 Valentine Walsh, Nicholas Eastaugh, Tracey Chaplin and Ruth Siddall, *Pigment Compendium: A Dictionary and Optical Microscopy of Historical Pigments*, Arts, Museum and Heritage Studies (London: Routledge, 2008), 224.

22 Parnell, *Dyeing and Calico Printing*, 684.

23 Nick Umney and Shayne Rivers, *Conservation of Furniture* (Oxford: Butterworth/Heinemann 2003), 325. Ultramarine blue is lightfast but is extremely susceptible to mineral oils or acid vapours. These rapidly destroy the blue colour.

24 For example, note the practice of mixing indigo with cochineal to produce 'beautiful violets on silk'. William Nicholson, *A Dictionary of Practical and Theoretical Chemistry* ... (London: Richard Phillips 1808), 203.

25 After much research, the author identified these particular dyestuffs as those most likely to have been used to produce red or purple shades in the 1850s.

26 The Renishaw inVia Raman microscope, equipped with 785 nm laser excitation, that was used to carry out these experiments at the University of Southampton, has a red laser, as the dyes we were identifying are also red, this can be the cause of difficulties. A green laser might have produced better results, but access to such a laser was not then available. The problem is not uncommon – see: Karen A. Trentelman and Catherine M. Schmidt, '1064 Nm Dispersive Raman Micro-Spectroscopy for the in-Situ Identification of Organic Red Colourants', *e-Preservation Science*, 6 (2009), 10–21.

27 Isabella Whitworth and Zvi C. Koren, 'Orchil and Tyrian Purple: Two Centuries of Bedfords from Leeds', *Ambix*, 63 (2016), 244–67, © 2016 Society for the History of Alchemy and Chemistry, reprinted by permission of Informa UK Limited, trading as Taylor & Francis Group, www.tandfonline.com on behalf of 2016 Society for the History of Alchemy and Chemistry. Reproduced with permission of the Licensor through PLSclear.

28 Ibid., 246.

29 American Silk Society and Gideon B. Smith, *Journal of the American Silk Society, and Rural Economist*, Vols 1–2 (Baltimore: American Silk Society, 1839), 50.

30 M. Clark, *Handbook of Textile and Industrial Dyeing – Principles, Processes and Types of Dye*, Vol. 1 (Oxford: Woodhead Publishing, 2011), 536.

31 Erin Hammeke, 'Logwood Dye on Paper', 6 April 2019 [Accessed 27 June 2023], https://www.ischool.utexas.edu/~cochinea/pdfs/e-hammeke-04-logwood.pdf.

32 D. Cardon and P.C.M. Janson, *Dyes and Tannins, Plant Resources of Tropical Africa* 3 (Nederland: PROTA Foundation, 2005), 83–4 and Bart Kahr, Scott Lovell and J. Anand Subramony, 'The Progress of Logwood Extract', *Chirality*, 10 (1998), 66–77.

33 See: Nicholson, *A Dictionary of Practical and Theoretical Chemistry*; See under LOG; 'Dyeing: Of Dyeing Silk Violet or Purple', in *The Encyclopaedia Britannica, Or Dictionary of Arts, Sciences, and of General Literature* (Edinburgh: Adam and Charles Black, 1855), 312; Edward Roberts, *A Manual Containing Directions for Sowing, Transplanting and Raising of the Mulberry Tree* (Baltimore: Samuel Sands, 1839), 90; Peter Barlow, *The Encyclopaedia of Arts, Manufactures, and Machinery* (London: John Joseph Griffin and Company, 1851), 539; William Crookes, *A Practical Handbook of Dyeing and Calico Printing* (London: Longmans, Green and Co., 1874), 342, 346, 347, 348; Edward Parnell, *Dyeing and Calico Printing* (London: Taylor, Walton and Maberly, 1849), 581.

34 A.J. Valente, *Rag Paper Manufacture in the United States, 1801–1900: A History, with Directories of Mills and Owners* (Jefferson: McFarland and Company, 2010), 174.

35 Parnell, *Dyeing and Calico Printing*, 266. Here, brazilwood and logwood are used concurrently to produce 'marone' or 'crimson'. The cuffs, collar and hem of the dress and the fringing on the bodice have not yet been analysed.

36 Walsh et al., *Pigment Compendium*, 60.

37 Brazilwood on wool with alum as a mordant gives a greyscale contrast of 3.0 after exposure to 7.8 million lux hours. See Tim Padfield and Sheila Landi, 'The Light Fastness of the Natural Dyes', *Studies in Conservation*, 11 (1966), 181–96.

38 Judith H. Hofenk de Graff, *The Colourful Past: Origins, Chemistry and Identification of Natural Dyestuffs* (Switzerland: Abegg-Stiftung and Archetype Publications, 2004), 147.

39 Other experiments could be carried out in the future. For more information on the microchemical experiments that could definitively confirm the presence of logwood or brazilwood see Hofenk de Graff, *The Colourful Past*, 237–8 and 147–8.

40 As a result of this research, efforts have now been made to ensure the garments are housed in more environmentally controlled surroundings. Coverings have been made from conservation calico. The presence of Prussian blue has also meant that attention will now be paid to the use of insecticides, which can cause severe colour reaction in textiles. See: Sophie Rowe, 'The Effect of Insect Fumigation by Anoxia on Textiles Dyed with Prussian Blue', *Studies in Conservation*, 49 (2004), 259–70.

41 Linda Pierson, researcher at the Brontë Parsonage Museum, has carried out important work on the 1851 census records. This proved very helpful in my research.

42 'Letter from Charlotte Brontë to Ellen Nussey, 11 June 1854', MS (Grolier E. 28), BPM, Haworth.

43 See: Anthony van Dyck (1599–1641), Charles I, 1635–before June 1636, Oil on canvas, 84.4 × 99.4 cm (RCIN 404420), © Royal Collection Trust/© His Majesty King Charles III, 2024.

44 'Fashions for November', *Yorkshire Gazette* (4 November 1854), 7.

45 See 'Travelling Dress', 1855–6, *Le Moniteur des Dames et Demoiselles* (b17509853), The Metropolitan Museum of Art, New York; Moritz Von Schwind, *The Visit (In the Artist's House)*, 1855, Oil on canvas, 72 × 51 cm (AKG43625), Neue Pinakothek, Munich.

46 'Fringed Silk Day Dress', 1854/6, Silk, fringing, cotton (YORCM:BA3602), York Castle Museum, York.

47 It is possible, though unlikely, that this dress may instead have been worn by Hannah Walker of Rawdon, who married Charles Thompson Grimshaw in 1855.

48 'Letter from Charlotte Brontë to? Mrs Gaskell, early June 1854 Fragment.'

49 Brontë visited Leeds, Keighley or Halifax with relative frequency in the years 1848 onwards.

50 See Table 1 for references to Charlotte's increased purchasing of clothing in the year 1854 as she accumulated clothes for her wedding trousseau.

51 Susan and Robert Cochrane, *Mr Dear Boy, The Life of Arthur Bell Nicholls B.A., Husband of Charlotte Brontë* (London: Highgate Publications, 1999), 55.

52 'Letter from Charlotte Brontë to Ellen Nussey, 29 June 1854', MS (Berg Coll MSS 186119: b.1.f.29-30), Henry W. and Albert A. Berg Collection of English and American Literature, New York Public Library, Astor, Lenox and Tilden Foundations.

53 'Letter to Dear Sir from Mr Nicholls, 10 August 1903', MS (B.S. 285.75), BPM, Haworth.

54 Pink wrapping gown and cape, Cotton, 1854 (D51.1/2), BPM, Haworth.

55 Patricia Cunningham, *Reforming Women's Fashion, 1850–1920* (Kent: Kent State University Press, 2003), 7.

56 The heavy cotton fabric is composed of Z-spun yarns woven at 18 × 18 threads per centimetre. The pattern has been surface-printed onto the cotton and therefore the reverse remains undyed. A single pink/red colour has been used, in different densities. The pattern consists of a very fine vertical pin-stripe, punctuated with stylized leaf shapes that have been left in relief. At the centre of each of these white leaves has been placed a bright red dot. These have been placed in a diapered design, and positioned a considerable distance apart, making the repeat relatively large.

The vivid crimson print is likely to have been achieved through the use of cochineal, a popular dyestuff used throughout the nineteenth century. This supposition is supported by the extensive fading. Cochineal carmine absorbs luminous energy easily, resulting in oxidation, which in turn causes decomposition and discolouration. See: L.M.R. Bowers and S.J.S. Sobeck, 'Impact of Medium and Ambient Environment on the Photo-Degradation of Carmine in Solution and Paints', *Journal of Dyes and Pigments*, Vol. 127 (2015), No. 18–24 and Yan Luo, Mengya Li and Juan Du, 'Esterification of Cochineal Carmine Used For Dyeing Cationic Modified Cotton with High Color Fastness', *Journal of Engineered Fibers and Fabrics*, 12:2 (2017), 61.

57 Court suit, 1780–1800, British, Wool, cotton, silk (2013.516a–c), The Metropolitan Museum of Art, New York.

58 'Man's Waistcoat', 1845–50, Pink silk satin, silk, glazed cotton (T.1-1954), V&A, London.

59 'Pink wrapper', Cotton, 1850s (2004.013.002), Goldstein Museum of Design, University of Minnesota.

60 'Dressing Gown', 1850s, Silk, American or European (C.I.69.32.4a, b), The Metropolitan Museum of Art, New York; 'Wrapping Gown', 1855, Silk, British

(1972.184.5), The Metropolitan Museum of Art, New York; 'Wrapping Gown', 1840s, Cotton, American (C.I.44.35), The Metropolitan Museum of Art, New York.

61 Charlotte's leghorn straw bonnet (D140) does have a pale pink/now whitened lining and pink ribbons, but the pink cannot be viewed as dominant. There is a also a very pale pink bonnet (D141), but this also dates to this later period.

62 Brontë, *Villette*, 198.

63 Ibid., 198.

64 Ibid., 320.

65 Ibid., 320.

66 Juliet Barker, *The Brontës*, 2nd ed. (London: Abacus Books, 2010), 894.

67 Rebecca Fraser, *Charlotte Brontë: A Writer's Life* (New York: Pegasus Books, 2008), 468.

68 'Letter from Charlotte Brontë to Catherine Wooler, 18 July 1854', MS (Brontë(C)/33: 110010002), Fitzwilliam Museum, Cambridge; Barker, *The Brontës*, 894.

69 'Letter from Charlotte Brontë to Catherine Wooler, 10 July 1854', MS (Brontë(C)/28: 110009997), Fitzwilliam Museum, Cambridge.

70 'Letter from Charlotte Brontë to Margaret Wooler, 10 July 1854'.

71 Ibid.

72 Numerous fragments of the original barège dress remain at the parsonage. These are numbered D119.1, D119.2, D28.1, D28.2. Other pieces also exist in different collections.

73 'Barège Dresses', *Punch*, London, Vol. 19 (1850), 18.

74 For examples, see 'Dress with fan-front bodice and tiered skirt, wool barège, 1850s' (682), The Irma G. Bowen Historic Clothing Collection, University of New Hampshire; 'Woman's Dress, 1855–65, Silk Gauze' (CD:053830), National Museum of American History, The Smithsonian Museum, New York.

75 See 'Silk Gauze' ensemble with two interchangeable bodices, 1855 (1992.31.2a–c), Metropolitan Museum of Art, New York.

76 *Guidebook to the Industrial Revolution with Facts, Figures and Observations on the Manufactures and Produce Exhibited* (London: Partridge and Oakey, 1851), 105.

77 'Letter from Arthur Bell Nicholls to George Sowden, 10 August 1854', MS (BS 247), BPM, Haworth.

78 See 'Letter from Charlotte Brontë to Catherine Winkworth, 27 July 1854', Special Collections, Leeds University Library. Brotherton Collection (MS 19c Brontë/C8).

79 Barker, *The Brontës*, 897.

80 Cochrane, *Mr Dear Boy*, 63.

81 Alan Adamson, *Mr Charlotte Brontë* (London: McGill-Queen's University, 2008), 67.

82 See Table 1, *Clothing Requirements in Accordance with Events Detailed in Charlotte Brontë's Letters*. For more detailed charts, see also Eleanor Houghton, 'Decoding Clothing: Charlotte Brontë, Plainness and the Language of Dress', PhD thesis, University of Southampton, 2020.

83 See 'Letter from Charlotte Brontë to Margaret Wooler, 22 August 1854', MS (Brontë(C)/29: 110009998), Fitzwilliam Museum, Cambridge; and 'Letter from Charlotte Brontë to Ellen Nussey, 31 October 1854', MS (B.S. 96.5), BPM, Haworth.

84 'Letter from Charlotte Brontë to Ellen Nussey, 29 August 1854', MS (Bon 251), BPM, Haworth.

85 For detailed information on Charlotte's letters, see Houghton, 'Charlotte Brontë: Decoding Clothing, Plainness and the Language of Dress', Vol. 3. Monckton Milnes continued to correspond with Charlotte and later with Patrick Brontë.

86 Two weeks before her marriage, Brontë received an invitation from the Mayor of Oxford for an 'Evening Reception in the Town Hall'. See: 'The Mayor and Mayoress of Oxford to C. Brontë, 15 June 1854', MS (HAOBP), BPM, Haworth. Brontë also invited Gaskell and her husband to come and stay in the autumn of 1854, but they were unable to come. See Barker, *The Brontës*, 900.

87 'Letter from Charlotte Brontë to Ellen Nussey, 14 November 1854, MS (Ashley 168), The British Library, London; and 'Letter from Charlotte Brontë to Sir J. Kay-Shuttleworth, 5 January 1855', MS, Cely-Trevilian Collection, Royal Society of Antiquaries.

88 Adamson, *Mr Charlotte Brontë*, 72.

89 'Letter from Charlotte Brontë to Ellen Nussey, 7 September 1854.'

90 'Letter from Charlotte Brontë to Margaret Wooler, 16 September 1854', MS (Brontë(C)/30: 110009999), Fitzwilliam Library, Cambridge.

91 Barker, *The Brontës*, 740.

92 Moglen, *The Self Conceived*, 232–3 and 'Letter from Elizabeth Gaskell to John Foster, 23 April 1854', MS (Add. 38794), The British Library, London.

93 Adamson, *Mr Charlotte Brontë*, 72.

94 'Letter from Charlotte Brontë to George Smith, 25 April 1854', MS (SG 90), BPM, Haworth.

95 'Letter from Charlotte Brontë to Margaret Wooler, 19 September 1854', MS (Brontë(C)/30: 110009999), Fitzwilliam Library, Cambridge.

96 Barker, *The Brontës*, 899.

97 'Letter from Charlotte Brontë to Ellen Nussey, 9 August 1854', MS (BS96.1), BPM, Haworth.

98 'Letter from Charlotte Brontë to Margaret Wooler, 15 November 1854', MS (Brontë(C)/31: 110010000), Fitzwilliam Library, Cambridge.

99 'Letter from Mrs Gaskell to John Forster, 17 May 1854', MS (MS.2262), National Library of Scotland, Scotland.

100 In using the term, the 'Mrs. Parsons' Brontë was referring to the wives of the local clergymen. 'Letter from Charlotte Brontë to Ellen Nussey to ?20 October 1854', The Morgan Library & Museum, MA 2696.29, The Henry Houston Bonnell Brontë Collection, Bequest of Helen Safford Bonnell, 1969.

101 Charlotte Brontë, *Emma*, 27 November 1853, MS, Taylor Collection, Princeton University Library, Princeton and printed in *The Cornhill Magazine*, April 1860, 485–98 with Introduction by Thackeray entitled 'The Last Sketch'.

102 'Letter from Arthur Bell Nicholls to George Smith, 11 October 1859', MS, MS.43112, Smith, Elder and Company Archives, National Library of Scotland, Edinburgh.

103 Nicholls strenuously denied that he stopped Brontë from writing and wrote to Clement Shorter and later to Mrs Ward strongly underscoring this. See Shorter, *The Brontës Life and Letters*, Vol. 2, 366; 'Letter from Arthur Bell Nicholls to Mrs Humphry Ward, 28 November 1899', MS (H.Mss.0927), Mrs Humphry Ward Papers Special Collections, The Claremont Colleges Library, Claremont, California.

104 Barker describes Nicholls's pride and enjoyment of Brontë's work. See: Barker, *The Brontës*, 740.

105 'Letter from Charlotte Brontë to Ellen Nussey, 19 January 1855', MS (B.S. 99), BPM, Haworth.

106 'Letter from A.B. Nicholls to Ellen Nussey, 1 February 1855', Leeds University Library, Brotherton Collection (MS 19c Brontë/C11); and 'Letter from Patrick Brontë to James Kay-Shuttleworth, 3 February 1855', Leeds University Library, Brotherton Collection (MS 19c Brontë/F2).

107 'Letter from Charlotte Brontë to Ellen Nussey on or after 21 February 1855' (B.S. 101), BPM, Haworth.

108 'Baby bonnet', Cotton, 1850s (D111), BPM, Haworth.

109 'Knitted baby socks', 1850s (SG35/6B), BPM, Haworth. Charlotte was knitting the baby socks, presumably for a friend, in January 1850. See 'Letter from Charlotte Brontë to Mrs Elizabeth Smith, 9 January 1850', MS (S.G.31/4B), BPM, Haworth.

110 'Letter from Charlotte Brontë to Amelia Taylor, early March 1855', MS (B.S. 102), BPM, Haworth; and Gaskell, *Life of Charlotte Brontë*, Vol. 2, 322.

111 John Lock and W.T. Dixon, *A Man of Sorrow: The Life, Letters and Times of the Rev Patrick Brontë* (London: Praeger Publishers, 1965), 452.

112 'Letter from Charlotte Brontë to Amelia Taylor, Late February 1855', MS (B.S. 103), BPM, Haworth.

113 Lock and Dixon, *Man of Sorrow*, 475.

114 'Letter from Charlotte Brontë to Ellen Nussey, early March 1855', MS (B.S. 100), BPM, Haworth.

115 Ibid.

116 Gaskell, *Life of Charlotte Brontë*, Vol. 2, 324.

117 'Letter from Ellen Nussey to George Smith, 1 June 1860', MS, MS.43113, Smith, Elder and Company Archives, National Library, Edinburgh, Scotland.

Chapter Eleven

1 See: 'Collar, said to have belonged to Charlotte Brontë, with two letters by Arthur Bell Nicholl's' Sotheby's Sale, 10 December 2019, Lot 92 [Accessed 13 July 2023], https://www.sothebys.com/en/buy/auction/2019/english-literature-history-childrens-books-and-illustrations-2/Brontë-family-collar-said-to-have-belonged-to. The collar is now part of the Brontë Collection (D180), BPM, Haworth.

2 Patrick Brontë, 'Last Will and Testament', 20 June 1855, MS (Bon 75), BPM, Haworth.

3 Christine Alexander, 'Arthur Bell Nicholls and the Adamson Saga: New Discoveries of Brontë Memorabilia', *Brontë Studies*, 31:3 (2006), 202.

4 Frances E. Bell, *A Hundred Years of Life* (Bath: Privately Printed, n.d.). See also: Alan Adamson, *Mr Charlotte Brontë* (London: McGill-Queen's University, 2008), 129.

5 'Letter from Arthur Bell Nicholls to Mr. Sutcliffe, 5 November 1861' (BS249.5), BPM, Haworth and Adamson, *Mr Charlotte Brontë*, 174.

6 Clement K. Shorter, *Charlotte Brontë and Her Circle* (London: Hodder & Stoughton, 1896), 501 and Clement K. Shorter, *Charlotte Brontë* (London: Hodder and Stoughton, 1905), 231.

7 Bell, *A Hundred Years of Life*.

8 Bell, *A Hundred Years of Life* and Adamson, *Mr Charlotte Brontë*, 134

9 See Alexander and Smith, *The Oxford Companion to the Brontës*, 344 and 544–5 and Alexander, 'Arthur Bell Nicholls and the Adamson Saga', 202.

10 Sotheby's Sales took place on the 26 July 1907, 19 July 1914 and one after Mary's death on 15 December 1916.

11 For more on the items left to Mary's relatives, see Alexander, 'Arthur Bell Nicholls and the Adamson Saga', 194–209.

12 Virginia Woolf, 'Haworth, 1904,' in *The Guardian*, London (21 December 1904) and reprinted in Virginia Woolf, *Books and Portraits of Virginia Woolf*, ed., Mary Lyon (London: The Hogarth Press, 1979), 194–7 and Peter Miller, 'Introduction' in *Cultural Histories of the Material World*, ed., Peter Miller (Ann Arbor Ann: University of Michigan Press, 2013), 20.

13 Frank Trentmann, 'Materiality in the Future of History: Things, Practices, and Politics' in *Special Issue, Journal of British Studies*, 48:2 (April 2009), 283–307.

14 I. van der Tuin, 'The Material Turn in the Humanities' for NWO, Dutch Research Council, 1 February 2011 to 28 August 2014, File Number: 275-20-029 [Accessed 31 July 2023], https://www.nwo.nl/en/projects/275-20-029; Giorgio Reillo, 'The "Material Turn" in World and Global History', *Journal of World History*, 33:2 (2022); Anne Gerritsen and Giorgio Riello (eds), *The Global Lives of Things: The Material Culture of Connections in the Early Modern World* (London: Routledge, 2015).

15 Ivan Gaskell and Sarah Ann Carter (eds), 'Introduction' in *The Oxford Handbook of History and Material Culture* (Oxford: Oxford University Press, 2020), 1.

16 Anne Brydon and Sandra Niessen (eds), 'Introduction' in *Consuming Fashion: Adorning the Transnational Body – Dress, Body, Culture* (London: Bloomsbury, 1998), ix–x.

17 For example, it was not until after writing my journal article, Houghton, 'Unravelling the Mystery', that I discovered (via a series of scientific experiments) that the fabric of Charlotte's 'Thackeray Dress' was composed, not of cotton and wool, but of cotton and alpaca and that it was, therefore, an innovative fabric.

Select Bibliography

NOTE: Many of the letters cited throughout the book are included in: Charlotte Brontë, *The Letters of Charlotte Brontë*, Vol. 1 18–1847, ed., Margaret Smith (Oxford: Oxford University Press).

A Lady. 1808. *The Lady's Economical Assistant, or The Art of Cutting out, and Making the Most Useful Articles of Wearing Apparel, without Waste: Explained by the Clearest Directions, and Numerous Engravings, of Appropriate and Tasteful Patterns: Designed for Domestic Use by a Lady; Designed for Domestic Use*. London: John Murray.

Abbott, Mr. 1826. 'Letter to Mr Abbott.' The Documents of Wormalds and Walker BUS/Wormwalds, Brotherton Library, University of Leeds.

Adamson, Alan. 2008. *Mr Charlotte Brontë*. London: McGill-Queen's University.

'Advertisement for Beech and Barrell's of London.' *The Indian News and Chronicle of Eastern Affairs*. January 1850.

'Advertisement for Dr Winns "True Anticardium Paris Black Reviver".' *The Morning Herald*. 28 April 1841.

'Advertisement for "Frederic Forster Family Mourning".' *Yorkshire Post and Leeds Intelligencer*. 15 February 1876.

'Advertisement for "The London General Mourning Warehouse".' *The Illustrated Weekly Times*. 25 March 1843, 48.

Agnew, Jean. n.d. 'Descriptive Notes by Jean Agnew.' Wedding Replica File, BPM.

Alexander, Christine. 1983. *The Early Writings of Charlotte Brontë*. Oxford: Basil Blackwell.

Alexander, Christine. 2006. 'Arthur Bell Nicholls and the Adamson Saga: New Discoveries of Brontë Memorabilia.' *Brontë Studies*, 31 (3): 194–209. https://doi.org/10.1179/147489306X132246.

Alexander, Christine, and Jane Sellars. 2005. *The Art of the Brontës*. Cambridge: Cambridge University Press.

Alexander, Christine, and Margaret Smith. 2006. *The Oxford Companion to the Brontës*. Oxford: Oxford University Press.

Alexander, Christine, with Mandy Swann. 2020. *The Diary Papers of Emily and Anne Brontë*. Sydney: Juvenilia Press.

Almanach Royal et du Commerce de Belgique, pour l'An 1838. 1838. Bruxelles: Impremerie Balleroy.

American Silk Society and Gideon B. Smith. 1839. *Journal of the American Silk Society, and Rural Economist*. Vols. 1–2. Baltimore: American Silk Society.

Anderson Black, J., Madge Garland and Frances Kennett. 1983. *A History of Fashion*. London: Orbis Publishing.

Archer, Professor. 1877. 'Wool and Its Applications.' In *British Manufacturing Industries*. London: Edward Stanford, 1–56.
Ashmore, Sonia. 2012. *Muslin*. London: V&A Publishing.
Audsley, W., and G. Audsley. 1870. *Color in Dress: A Manual for Ladies*. Philadelphia: George MacLean.
Austen, Jane. 1814. 'Letter to Cassandra Austen.' (CHWJA: JAHLTR.9). Jane Austen's House Museum, Chawton, England.
Bailey, Joanne. 2012. *Parenting in England 1760–1830: Emotion, Identity, and Generation*. Oxford: Oxford University Press.
Balgarnie, Robert. 1878. *Sir Titus Salt Baronet: His Life and Its Lessons*. London: Hodder and Stoughton.
Bamford, Samford. 1850. *Dialect of South Lancashire or Tim Bobbin's Tummus and Meary*. Manchester.
Banner, Lois. 1983. *American Beauty*. New York: Knopf.
'Barège Dresses.' *Punch*. Vol. 19. July–December 1850: 18.
Bari, Shahidha. 2019. *Dressed: The Secret Life of Clothes*. London: Jonathan Cape.
Barker, Juliet. 1988. *Sixty Treasures of the Brontë Parsonage Museum*. Haworth: Brontë Society.
Barker, Juliet. 1996. 'Introduction.' In *Charlotte Brontë: Juvenilia: 1829–1835*. London: Penguin Classics, vii–xxi.
Barker, Juliet. 2010. *The Brontës*. 2nd ed. London: Abacus Books.
Barlow, Peter. 1851. *The Encyclopaedia of Arts, Manufactures, and Machinery*. London: John Joseph Griffin and Company.
Bassett, Lynne Z. 2001. *Textiles for Regency Clothing 1800–1850: A Workbook of Swatches and Information*. Arlington: Q Graphics Production Co.
Batchelor, Jennie. 2022. *The Lady's Magazine (1770–1832) and the Making of Literary History*. Edinburgh: Edinburgh University Press.
Batchelor, Stephen, Laurence Abbott, Lindsay Smith and John Moore. 2010. 'Resonance Raman and UV-Visible Spectroscopy of Black Dyes on Textiles.' *Forensic Science International*, 202: 54–63.
Baumber, Michael. 1997. 'That "Vandal" Wade the Reverend John Wade and the Demolition of the Brontë Church.' *Brontë Society Transactions*, 22 (1): 96–112.
Baumber, Michael. 2002. 'Haworth in the Time of the Brontës.' In *The Brontës in Context (Literature in Context)*, ed. Marianne Thormälen. Cambridge: Cambridge University Press, 9–17.
Baumgarten, Linda. 2011. *What Clothes Reveal: The Language of Clothing in Colonial and Federal America*. New Haven and London: The Colonial Williamsburg Foundation in Association with Yale University Press.
Beecher, Catharine Esther. 1843. *A Treatise on Domestic Economy: For the Use of Young Ladies at Home, and at School*. Boston: Thomas Webb.
Beetham, Margaret. 1996. *A Magazine of Her Own: Domesticity and Desire in the Woman's Magazine, 1800–1914*. London and New York: Routledge.
Bell, Currer. 1848. *Jane Eyre: An Autobiography*. New York: Harper and Brothers.
Bell, Currer. 1850. 'Prefatory Note.' In *Ellis Bell, Wuthering Heights, a New Edition Revised, with a Biographical Notice of the Authors, a Selection of Their Literary Remains, and a Preface by Currer Bell*. London: Smith, Elder and Company, xix–xxiv.

Bell, Frances E. n.d. *A Hundred Years of Life*. Bath: Privately Printed.
Bell, H.K. 1927. 'Charlotte Brontë's Husband. His Later Life and Surroundings (1855–1906).' *Cornhill Magazine*, XII (January): 42–6.
Bell Nicholls, Arthur. 1854. 'Letter to George Sowden.' (MS. B.S. 247). BPM.
Bell Nicholls, Arthur. 1855. 'Letter to Ellen Nussey.' (MS. MS 19c Brontë/C11). Brotherton Collection, University of Leeds.
Bell Nicholls, Arthur. 1859. 'Letter to George Smith.' (MS. MS File 8, no. 3). Smith, Elder and Company Archives, National Library of Scotland.
Bell Nicholls, Arthur. 1899. 'Letter to Mrs Humphry Ward.' (MS. H.Mss.0927). Mrs Humphry Ward Papers, The Claremont Colleges Library, Claremont, California.
Bell Nicholls, Arthur. 1903. 'Letter to Dear Sir.' (MS. B.S.285.75). BPM, Haworth.
Bell, Millicent. 1993. 'Class, Sex and the Victorian Governess: James' Turn of the Screw', in *New Essays on Daisy Miller and the Turn of the Screw*, ed. Vivian Pollak. Cambridge: Cambridge University Press, 91–120.
Benson, Arthur Christopher. 1899. *The Life of Edward White Benson*. Vol. 1. New York: Macmillan.
Bentley, Phyllis. 1972. *The Brontës and their World*. London: Thames and Hudson.
Blaze de Bury, Marie-Pauléne Rose. 1851. *Germania in 1850: Its Courts, Camps, and People*. Vol. 2. 2 vols. London: Henry Colburn.
Blessington, The Countess of (ed.). 1834–47. *Heath's Book of Beauty*. London: Longman, Rees, Orme, Brown, Green, and Longmans.
Blessington, The Countess of. 1839. *The Governess*. London: Longman.
Bogle, M. 1978. 'Artificial Weighting and the Deterioration of Silk.' *AIC Preprints, Sixth Annual Meeting of the American Institute for Conservation of Historic and Artistic Works*. Fort Worth, Texas, 31–40.
Boucher, François. 1987. *20,000 Years of Fashion: The History of Costume and Personal Adornment*. New York: H.N. Abrams.
Bowers, L.M.R., and S.J.S. Sobeck. 2015. 'Impact of Medium and Ambient Environment on the Photo-Degradation of Carmine in Solution and Paints.' *Journal of Dyes and Pigments*, 127: 18–24.
Bradfield, Nancy. 1995. *Costume in Detail, 1730–1930*. London: Eric Dobby Publishing Ltd.
'Bradford and Leeds Fashion Combined with Economy in Silks, Shawls, Delaines, Muslins, Mantles and Bonnets.' *The Bradford Observer*, 19 April 1849, 8.
Brides Editors. 15 August 2021. 'This Is What American Weddings Look Like Today.' https://www.brides.com/gallery/american-wedding-study.
Briggs, Asa. 1988. *Victorian Things*. London: Batsford Ltd.
Brontë Catalogue Object Display Card for (D74.1), BPM, Haworth, http://Brontë.adlibsoft.com/detail.aspx?parentpriref.
Brontë, Anne. 31 July 1845. 'Diary Paper', William Self, Private Collection.
Brontë, Charlotte. 1829. 'The History of the Year.' (MS. B80 (11)). BPM, Haworth.
Brontë, Charlotte. 1830. 'Albion and Marina: A Tale by Lord Charles Wellesley.' (WCSC_MS_EPC_10). Wellesley College Special Collections. https://libcat.wellesley.edu/Record/in00000641718.
Brontë, Charlotte. 1832. 'The Bridal: Autograph Manuscript Signed: [Haworth], 1832 July 14 and Aug. 20.' (MA 2614). The Henry Houston Bonnell Brontë Collection, The Morgan Library, New York.

Brontë, Charlotte. 1833. 'The Green Dwarf: A Tale of the Perfect Tense, by Lord Charles Albert Florian Wellesley.' Brontë Family Collection. Harry Ransom Center, University of Texas at Austin. https://hrc.contentdm.oclc.org/digital/collection/p15878coll3/id/477/rec/1.
Brontë, Charlotte. 1834. 'High Life in Verdopolis.' MS. Haworth. 34255. BPM held by British Library.
Brontë, Charlotte. 1836. 'Autograph Manuscript of a Diary Entry and Two Prose Fragments.' [Roe Head School, Mirfield]. The Henry Houston Bonnell Brontë Collection, Bequest of Helen Safford Bonnell, 1969, Morgan Library, New York.
Brontë, Charlotte. 1836. 'Passing Events.' MS. (MA 30.1). The Morgan Library, New York.
Brontë, Charlotte. 1836. 'Roe Head Journal.' MS. (Bonnell 98(7)). BPM, Haworth.
Brontë, Charlotte. 1839. 'The Adventures of Captain Hastings, Otherwise known as Henry Hastings by Charles Townshend.' (HEW 1.4.14). Widener Collection, Houghton Library, Harvard University.
Brontë, Charlotte. 1848. 'Cash Book.' Haworth. BS 22, 10. BPM.
Brontë, Charlotte. 1850. *Shirley: A Tale*. New York: Harper and Brothers.
Brontë, Charlotte. 1850. 'Biographical Notice of Ellis and Acton Bell', in Ellis and Acton Bell, *Wuthering Heights and Agnes Grey*. London: Smith, Elder and Company, xix–xxiv.
Brontë, Charlotte. 1853. 'Emma.' MS. Taylor Collection. Princeton University Library.
Brontë, Charlotte. 1853. *Villette by Currer Bell, Author of 'Jane Eyre' and 'Shirley'*. New York: Harper and Brothers.
Brontë, Charlotte. (Currer Bell). 1857. *The Professor*. 2 vols. London: Smith, Elder and Company.
Brontë, Charlotte. 1874. *Shirley: A Tale*. London: Smith, Elder and Company.
Brontë, Charlotte. 1996. *Juvenilia 1829–1835*, ed. Juliet Barker. London: Penguin Classics.
Brontë, Charlotte. 2003. *The Green Dwarf with a Foreword by Libby Purves*. London: Hesperus Classics.
Brontë, Charlotte, Ellis Bell and Acton Bell. 1850. 'Biographical Notice of Ellis and Acton Bell.' In *Wuthering Heights and Agnes Grey*. London: Smith, Elder and Company, v–xiv.
Brontë, Charlotte, and Emily Brontë. 1997. *The Belgian Essays: A Critical Edition*, ed. Sue Lonoff. New Haven: Yale University Press.
Brontë, Charlotte, Emily Brontë and Anne Brontë. 2010. *Tales of Glass Town, Angria, and Gondal: Selected Early Writings*, ed. Christine Alexander. Oxford: Oxford University Press.
Brontë, Emily. Unknown. '[Long Neglect Has Worn Away].' MS. Bonnell 127 (11). BPM.
Brontë, Patrick. 1842. *A Funeral Service for the Late Rev. William Weightman*. Halifax: J.U. Walker.
Brontë, Patrick. 1843. 'Letter to the Editor.' *Leeds Mercury*, 16 March, 6.
Brontë, Patrick. 1855. 'Last Will and Testament.' Bon 75. BPM.
Brontë, Patrick. 1857. 'Letter to Elizabeth Cleghorn Gaskell.' MS. EL B121. University of Manchester, John Rylands Library.
Brooke, Iris. 2003. *English Children's Costume, 1775–1920*. London: Dover Publications.
Brookfield, Charles and Frances. 1906. 'A Party for Charlotte Brontë (1850–1851).' In Charles Hallam Brookfield, *Mrs Brookfield and Her Circle*. London: Sir Isaac Pitman and Sons, 354–5.

Browne, Dr. T.P. 1997. 'A Phrenological Estimate of the Talents and Dispositions of a Lady', 29 June 1851. In *The Brontës: Interviews and Recollections*, ed. Harold Orel. Iowa: University of Iowa Press, 93–5.

Brownmiller, Susan. 1984. *Femininity*. New York: Simon and Schuster.

Brydon, Anne, and Sandra Niessen, eds. 1998. 'Introduction *Consuming Fashion: Adorning the Transnational Body – Dress, Body, Culture*. London: Bloomsbury, ix–x.

Buchan, William. 1769. *Domestic Medicine; or the Family Physician …* Edinburgh: Balfour, Auld and Smellie.

Buchan, William. 1774. *Domestic Medicine; or, A Treatise on the Prevention and Cure of Diseases by Regimen and Simple Medicines; With an Appendix Containing a Dispensatory. For the Use of Private Practitioners*. London: W. Strahan.

Buck, Anne. 1979. *Dress in Eighteenth Century England*. London: Batsford.

Buck, Anne. 1996. *Clothes and the Child: A Handbook of Children's Dress in England 1500–1900*. Bedford: Ruth Bean.

Buckworth, John. 1822. 'Letter from Patrick Brontë to John Buckworth, 17 November 1821', *The Cottage Magazine*, 11: 245–6.

Burke, Zoe. 2025. 'National Wedding Survey: The Average UK Wedding'. https://www.hitched.co.uk/wedding-planning/organising-and-planning/the-average-wedding-cost-in-the-uk-revealed/.

Burman, Barbara (ed.). 1999. *The Culture of Sewing: Gender, Consumption and Home Dressmaking*. Oxford: Berg.

Burman, Barbara, and Ariane Fennetaux. 2020. *The Pocket: A Hidden History 1640–1900*. New Haven: Yale University Press.

Burman, Hannah. 2018. 'British Quaker Women's Fashionable Adaptation of Their Plain Dress, 1860–1914', *Costume*, 52 (2): 240–60.

Burnley, James. 1875. *West Riding Sketches*. London: Hodder and Stoughton.

Byrde, Penelope. 1992. *Nineteenth Century Fashion*. London: Batsford.

Byrde, Penelope. 1999. *Jane Austen Fashion: Fashion and Needlework in the Works of Jane Austen*. Ludlow: Excellent Press.

Cacioli, Jon-Paul, and Alexander J. Mussap. 2014. 'Avatar Body Dimensions and Men's Body Image.' *Body Image*, 11 (2): 146–55. https://doi.org/10.1016/j.bodyim.2013.11.005.

Calefato, Patrizia. 1997. 'Fashion and Worldliness: Language and Imagery of the Clothed Body.' *Fashion Theory*, 1 (1): 69–90. doi:10.2752/136270497779754534.

Campbell, J.D., P.D. Trapnell, S.J. Heine, I.M. Katz, L.F. Lavallee and D.R. Lehman. 1966. 'Self-Concept Clarity: Measurement, Personality Correlates, and Cultural Boundaries.' *Journal of Personality and Social Psychology*, 70 (1996): 141–56.

Caplin, Madame Roxey. 1854. *Health and Beauty, or Corsets Constructed in Accordance with the Physiological Laws of the Human Body*. London: Darton and Company.

Cardon, D., and P.C.M. Janson. 2005. *Dyes and Tannins, Plant Resources of Tropical Africa 3*. Nederland: PROTA Foundation.

Carlyle, Thomas. 1837. *Thomas Carlyle's Collected Works*. Vol. 2. 34 vols. London: Chapman and Hall.

Catalogue of Animal Products Belonging to Her Majesty's Catalogue of the Collection of Animal Products Belonging to Her Majesty's Commissioners for the Exhibition of 1851, Exhibited in the South Kensington Museum. 1858. London: William Clowes and Sons.

Caton, Mary Anne. 2003. 'The Aesthetics of Absence: Quaker Women's Plain Dress in the Delaware Valley, 1790–1900.' In *Quaker Aesthetics: Reflections on a Quaker Ethic in American Design and Consumption*, eds Emma Jones Lapsansky and Anne Verplanck. Philadelphia: University of Pennsylvania, 246–71.

Caulfield, Sophia Frances Anne, and Blanche C. Saward. 1882. *The Dictionary of Needlework*. London: A.C. Bradley.

Centers for Disease, Control and Prevention. 2023. 'History of World TB Day.' 15 February. https://www.cdc.gov/tb/worldtbday/history.htm#:~:text=In%20the%20 1700s%2C%20TB%20was,all%20these%20men%20of%20death.

Chadwick, Ellis H. 2011. *In the Footsteps of the Brontës*. 2nd ed. Cambridge: Cambridge University Press.

Chambers, R. (ed.). 1863. 'Funeral Garlands'. In *The Book of Days: A Miscellany of Popular Antiquities*. London: W. and R. Chambers, 246–71.

Chapman, Alison. 2015. 'Achieving Fame and Canonicity.' In *The Cambridge Companion to Victorian Women's Writing*, ed. Linda Peterson. Cambridge: Cambridge University Press, 73–86.

Chapple, J.A.V., and Pollard, Arthur. 1966. *The Letters of Mrs Gaskell*. Manchester: Manchester University Press.

'Charlotte Brontë.' 1987. *Hebden Bridge Times*. 13 August, 7.

'Charlotte Brontë's Wedding.' 1913. *Yorkshire Post and Leeds Intelligencer*. Thursday 14 August, 6.

Chatelain, Clara de. 1856. *Bridal Etiquette*. London: Ward and Lock.

Chevalier, Michel. 1868. *Exposition Universelle de 1867: Rapports du Jury International, Bruxelles*. Vol. 4. 13 vols. Paris: Paul Dupont.

Clark, Grahame. 1986. *Symbols of Excellence: Precious Metals of Expressions of Status*. Cambridge: Cambridge University Press.

Clark, M. 2011. *Volume 1: Handbook of Textile and Industrial Dyeing – Principles, Processes and Types of Dyes*. Vol. 1. Oxford: Woodhead Publishing.

Clark, R.J., I.M. Bell and P.J. Gibbs. 2007. 'Raman Spectroscopic Library of Natural and Synthetic Pigments (Pre-Approximately 1850).' Christopher Ingold Laboratories, University College London. 2007. http://www.ucl.ac.uk/chem/resources/raman/speclib.html.

'Clericus.' 1857. 'Letter from "Clericus" to Arthur Bell Nicholls July 1857.' Private Collection.

C.M.R. 1857. 'Letter from CMR to Arthur Bell Nicholls, July 1857'. MS. Private Collection.

Cobbett, William. 1837. *Advice to Young Men and (Incidentally) to Young Women in the Middle and Higher Ranks of Life*. London: Anne Cobbett.

Cochran, Matthew D., and Mary Beaudry. 2006. 'Material Culture Studies and Historical Archaeology.' In *The Cambridge Companion to Historical Archaeology*, eds Dan Hicks and Mary Beaudry. Cambridge: Cambridge University Press, 191–204.

Cochrane, Susan and Robert. 1999. *Mr Dear Boy: The Life of Arthur Bell Nicholls B.A., Husband of Charlotte Brontë*. London: Highgate Publications.

Cole, Henry, and Richard Redgrave. 1850. *The Journal of Design and Manufacture*. Vol. 2. London: Chapman and Hall.

The Complete Book of Trades or the Parents' Guide and Youths' Instructor. 1837. London: John Bennett.

Cook, Daniel Thomas. 2004. *The Commodification of Childhood: The Children's Clothing Industry and the Rise of the Child Consumer*. Durham and London: Duke University Press.

Cosgrove, Bronwyn, Andrea L. Woodhead and Jeffrey Church. 2016. 'The Purple Coloration of Four Late 19th Century Silk Dresses: A Spectroscopic Investigation.' *Spectrochimica Acta Part A: Molecular and Biomolecular Spectroscopy*, 154: 185–92.

Crafts, Nicholas F. 1976. *Average Age at First Marriage for Women in Mid-Nineteenth Century England and Wales: A Cross Section Study*. A Warwick Economic Research Paper, No. 92, 4.

Craik, Dinah. 1857. *John Halifax, Gentleman*. Leipzig: Bernhard Tauchnitz.

Crookes, William. 1874. *A Practical Handbook of Dyeing and Calico Printing*. London: Longmans, Green and Co.

Cunningham, Patricia. 2003. *Reforming Women's Fashion, 1850–1920*. Kent: Kent State University Press.

Cunnington, C. Willett, and Phyllis Cunnington. 1973. *Handbook of English Costume in the Nineteenth Century*. London: Faber and Faber.

Cunnington, C. Willett, and Phyllis Cunnington. 1992. *The History of Underclothes*. New York: Dover Publications.

Davis, Fred. 1992. *Fashion, Culture, and Identity*. Chicago: Chicago University Press.

Dearden, William. 1857. 'Nancy Garr.' *Bradford Observer*. 20 August 1857.

Dearden, William. 1861. 'The Rev. P. Brontë.' *Bradford Observer*. 27 June, 1861, 7.

Diary of a Yorkshireman. 1943. 'Charlotte Brontë's Bonnet.' *The Yorkshire Evening Post*. 10 February 1943, 4.

Dickens, Charles. 1853. 'The Great Yorkshire Llama Drama.' In *Household Words*, 8–14. Leipzig: Bernhard Tauchnitz.

Dickens, Charles. 1867. 'David Copperfield.' In *The Works of Charles Dickens*. Vol. 1. 35 vols. New York: Hurd and Houghton.

Dickinson, Emily. 1891. '"Hope" Is the Thing with Feathers.' (Packet X, Mixed Fascicles, (46b), J254, Fr314). Houghton Library, Harvard University.

Dickson, Leigh Weatherall. 2018. '"Only Four Months a Widow": The Storytelling Wardrobe of Lady Susan in Whit Stillman's Love and Friendship' (2016). In *After Austen Reinventions, Rewritings, Revisitings*, ed. Lisa Hopkins. London: Springer International Publishing, 177–96.

Dilke, Charles Wentworth (ed.). 1852. *Exhibition of the Works of All Industry of All Nations 1851: Reports by the Juries …* London: William Clowes and Sons.

Dinsdale, Ann. 2005. 'Mrs Brontë's Nurse.' *Brontë Studies*, 30 (3): 258–9.

Dinsdale, Ann. 2013. *At Home with the Brontës: The History of Haworth Parsonage and its Occupants*. Stroud: Amberley Publishing.

Dolan, Alice. 2015. 'The Fabric of Life: Linen and Life Cycle in England, 1678–1810.' PhD thesis, University of Hertfordshire.

Downing, Sarah Jane. 2012. *Fashion in the Time of Jane Austen*. Oxford: Shire Publications.

'Dress for the Elderly Lady', 25 October 1850.' 1851. In *The Lady's Newspaper, July to December 1851, Volume the Tenth*. London: Robert Palmer.

Ducheneaut, Nicolas, Don Ming-Hui Wen, Nicholas Yee and Greg Wadley. 2009. *Body and Mind: A Study of Avatar Personalization in Three Virtual Worlds*. Proceedings of CHI 2009. https://doi.org/10.1145/1518701.1518877.

Duckett, Bob. 2007. 'Where Did the Brontës Get Their Books?' *Brontë Studies*, 32 (3): 193–206.

Duff Gordon, Lady Lucile. 1932. *Discretions and Indiscretions*. London: Jarrold.

Dyer, Serena. 2011. *Bergère, Poke and Cottage: Understanding Early Nineteenth Century Headwear*. Derby: Codnor Books.

Dyer, Serena. 2021. *Material Lives: Women Makers and Consumer Culture in the Eighteenth Century*. London: Bloomsbury Visual Arts.

Dyer, Serena, Jade Halbert and Sophie Littlewood (eds). 2022. *Disseminating Dress: Britain's Fashion Networks 1600–1970*. London: Bloomsbury.

Eastop, Dinah and Agnes Timar-Balazsy. 2008. *Chemical Principles of Textile Conservation*. London: Routledge.

The Edinburgh Review or Critical Journal. 1891. 'The Revival of Quakerism.' July, CLXXIV edition.

Ehrman, Edwina. 2014. *The Wedding Dress: 300 Years of Bridal Fashions*. London: V&A Publishing.

Ellis, Samantha. 2017. 'The Brontës Very Real and Raw Irish Roots.' *The Irish Times*, 11 January. https://www.irishtimes.com/culture/books/the-brontës-very-real-and-raw-irish-roots-1.2932856.

Erskine Stuart, J.A. 1888. *The Brontë Country: Its Typography Antiquities and History*. London: Longman.

'Essay on Mourning.' *Walker's Hibernian Magazine*. November 1786, 561–3.

The Etiquette of Courtship and Matrimony: With a Complete Guide to the Forms of a Wedding. 1852. London: David Bogue.

'Fashions for April 1850.' In *La Belle Assemblée*. January to June 1850, Vol. 32. London: Joseph Rogerson, 252–6.

'Fashions for November.' *Yorkshire Gazette*. 4 November 1854, 3.

'Fashions for September 1850.' In *La Belle Assemblée*. September 1850, 188–93.

'Fashion Plate – Une Conversation La Mode, 1832,' Historic Textile and Costume Collection. https://uritextilecollection.omeka.net/items/show/148.

'Fashion Plate – Evening Dress and Costume Antique, 1833', Historic Textile and Costume Collection. https://uritextilecollection.omeka.net/items/show/149.

Felshin, Sue. n.d. 'Making a Short Cloak.' https://people.csail.mit.edu/sfelshin/revwar/short-cloaks/.

Finden, Edward Francis, William Brockedon and William Finden. 1833. *Finden's Illustrations of the Life and Works of Lord Byron*. 3 vols. London: John Murray.

Firth, Elizabeth. 1815. 'Diary Entry for 1815, Elizabeth Firth Manuscripts.' MS (MS 58). University of Sheffield Library. https://www.sheffield.ac.uk/library/special/efirth.

Fletcher, Anthony. 2010. *Growing Up in England: The Experience of Childhood, 1600–1914*. Oxford: Oxford University Press.

Fonblanque, Albany William. 2001. '"Review" 27 November 1847, *The Examiner*.' In *The Critical Heritage: The Brontës*, ed. Miriam Allott. Oxford: Routledge, 76–8.

Ford, The Honourable Mrs. 1848. 'Plate II – Fashions for July 1848.' *The London and Paris Ladies' Magazine*. London: Simpkin, Marshall and Co.

Foster, Vanda. 1984. *A Visual History of the Nineteenth Century*. London: Batsford Ltd.

Fraser, Rebecca. 2008. *Charlotte Brontë: A Writer's Life*. New York: Pegasus Books.

Frith, Simon. 1977. 'Socialization and Rational Schooling: Elementary Education in Leeds before 1870.' In *Popular Education and Socialization in the Nineteenth Century*, ed. Phillip McCann. London: Meuthen and Co., 67–92.

Garner, Bryan A. 2022. *Garner's Modern Usage*. Oxford: Oxford University Press.

Garvie-Cook, Hazel. 2016. 'Raman Analysis of Charlotte Brontë's Dresses.' Unpublished document, Renishaw plc.

Gaskell, Elizabeth Cleghorn. 1850. 'Letter from Elizabeth Gaskell to Catherine Winkworth, 25 August 1850.' Brotherton Collection, University of Leeds (BC MS 19c Gaskell/04/24).

Gaskell, Elizabeth Cleghorn. 1854. 'Letter to John Foster.' MS (Add. 38794). British Library, London.

Gaskell, Elizabeth Cleghorn. 1857. *The Life of Charlotte Brontë*, Vol. 1. London: Smith, Elder and Company.

Gaskell, Elizabeth Cleghorn. 1859. *The Life of Charlotte Brontë*. Vol. 1. 2 vols. Leipzig: Bernhard Tauchnitz.

Gaskell, Elizabeth Cleghorn. 1880. *Mary Barton*. Vol. 1. 2 vols. London: Chapman and Hall.

Gaskell, Ivan, and Sarah Anne Carter. (2020). 'Introduction.' In *The Oxford Handbook of History and Material Culture*. Oxford: Oxford University Press.

Geneep, Arnold van. 2004. 'The Rites of Passage.' In *Death Mourning and Burial: A Cross Cultural Reader*, ed. Antonius C.G.M. Robben. Oxford: Blackwell Publishing, 213–22.

'General Mourning Warehouse, 54 Market Place, Hull.' *The Hull Advertiser*, 29 September 1848.

Gerin, Winifred. 1967. *Charlotte Brontë: The Evolution of Genius*. Oxford: Oxford University Press.

Gernsheim, Alison. 1981. *Victorian and Edwardian Fashion: A Photographic Survey*. New York: Dover Publications.

Gerritsen, Anne, and Giorgio Riello (eds). 2015. *The Global Lives of Things: The Material Culture of Connections in the Early Modern World*. London: Routledge.

G.F. 1876. 'Weddings: Something Old, Something New, Something Borrowed Something Blue.' *Notes and Queries*. Oxford: Oxford University Press. S5-V (20 May 1876): 408.

Gissing, George. 1926. 'Letter from George Gissing to his Sister Ellen Gissing, 3 July 1888.' In *Letters of George Gissing to Members of His Family, Collected and Arranged by Algernon and Ellen Gissing*. London: Constable and Company.

Glover, Frederick J. 1961. 'Philadelphia Merchants and the Blanket Trade 1820–1860.' *Pennsylvania History*, 28 (2): 121–41.

Goffman, Erving. 1987. *Gender Advertisements*. New York: Harper and Row.

Goodman, Lena. 2005. 'Marriage Calculations in the Eighteenth Century: Deconstructing the Love vs. Duty Binary.' *Proceedings of The Western Society of French History*, 33: 143–62.

Gores, Steve. 2000. *Psychosocial Spaces: Verbal and Visual Readings of British Culture, 1750–1820*. Detroit: Wayne State University Press.
Graham, George, William Farr and Horace Mann. 1854. *Census of Great Britain, 1851. Population Tables*. Vol. 2. London: George Edward Eyre.
Grundy, Frances. 1897. 'The Decline and Fall of Branwell Brontë 1741–1848.' In *Pictures of the Past: Memories of Men I Have Met and Places I Have Seen*. London: Griffith and Farran, 73–4.
Guglielmi, Vittoria, Silvia Bruni and Federica Pozzi. 2009. 'The Identification of Ancient Textile Dyes by Surface-Enhanced Raman Spectroscopy (SERS) on Silver and Gold Colloids.' *5th International Congress on the Application of Raman Spectroscopy in Art and Archaeology*, ed. RAA. Bilbao: Researchgate.
Guidebook to the Industrial Revolution with Facts, Figures and Observations on the Manufactures and Produce Exhibited. 1851. London: Partridge and Oakey.
Hacke, Marei. 2008. 'Weighted Silk, History, Analysis and Conservation.' *IIC Reviews in Conservation*, 9, 3–15. http://dx.doi.org/10.1179/sic.2009.54.Supplement-1.3.
Haight, Gordon, ed. 1954. *The George Eliot Letters*. Vol. 2. New Haven: Yale University Press.
Hainsworth, Lewis. 1896. *A Descriptive Catalogue of Objects in the Museum of the Brontë Society at Haworth*. Brontë Society Museum and Library.
Hale, Sarah Josepha. 1868. *Manners: Or, Happy Homes and Good Society All Year Round*. Boston: J.E. Tilton and Co.
Hale, Sarah Josepha, and Louis Antoine Godey (eds). 1857. *Godey's Lady's Book*. Vol. 54–5. Philadelphia: Louis Godey.
Hale, Sarah Josepha, and Louis Godey (eds). 1857. 'Practical Guide for Stay Making'. *Godey's Lady's Book*, Vol. 54–5. Philadelphia: Louis Godey, 165.
Hall, Catherine, and Leonore Davidoff. 1987. *Family Fortunes: Men and Women of the English Middle Class 1780–1850*. London and New York: Routledge.
Hall-Witt, Jennifer. 2007. *Fashionable Acts: Opera and Elite Culture in London, 1780–1880*. Durham: University of New Hampshire Press.
Hammeke, Erin. 2004. 'Logwood Dye on Paper (PDF).' Austin: University of Texas.
Hanson, Lawrence, and E.M. Hanson. 1949. *Four Brontës: The Lives and Works of Charlotte, Branwell, Emily and Anne Brontë*. London: Oxford University Press.
Hargreaves, Benjamin. 1884. *Messrs. Hargreaves' Calico Print Works at Accrington, and Recollections of Broad Oak*. Accrington: E. Bowker.
Harman, Claire. 2016. *Charlotte Brontë A Life*. London: Penguin.
Harper, Douglas. n.d. 'Etymology of Strait-Laced.' In *Online Etymology Dictionary*. https://www.etymonline.com/word/strait-laced.
Harris, John R. 2017. *Industrial Espionage and Technology Transfer: Britain and France in the 18th Century*. London and New York: Routledge.
Harris Walsh, Kristin. 2005. '"You Just Nod and Pin and Sew and Let Them Do Their Thing": An Analysis of the Wedding Dress as an Artifact and Signifier.' *Ethnologies*, 27 (2): 239–59.
Harrison, David. 2002. *The Brontës of Haworth: Yorkshire's Literary Giants*. Victoria: Trafford Press.

Harter, Susan. 2012. 'Emerging Self-Processes during Childhood and Adolescence.' In *The Handbook of Self and Identity*, eds June Price Tagney and Mark R. Leary. New York: Guilford Press, 680–715.

Harvey, Karen. 2009. 'Introduction.' In *History and Material Culture: A Student's Guide to Approaching Alternative Sources*. London and New York: Routledge, 1–23.

Hawkins, Kayt. 2024. *50 Finds from Childhood: Objects from the Portable Antiquities Scheme*. Stroud: Amberley Publishing.

Heger, Madame. 1842. 'Prospectus for "Maison d'Èducation Pour Les Jeunes Demoiselles Sous la Direction, de Madame Heger – Parent". Rue d'Isabelle 32, á Bruxelles.' (SB:2065.103). BPM, Haworth.

Her Majesty's Stationery Office. 1864. *A Catalogue of Pictures, Drawings and Sketches of the Late William Mulready: Part One – the Oil Paintings*. London: George Eyre and William Spottiswoode.

Herman, Bernard L. 1992. *The Stolen House*. Charlottesville and London: University Press of Virginia.

Herschel Babbage, Benjamin. 1850. 'Report ... on a Preliminary Inquiry into the Sewerage, Drainage, and Supply of Water, and the Sanitary Condition of the Inhabitants of the Hamlet of Haworth.' *Public Health Act* (11 & 12 Vict., cap. 63) (London: W. Clowes and Sons).

Hill, Bridget. 2001. *Women Alone. Spinsters in England 1660–1850*. New Haven, CT: Yale University Press.

H.L.J. 1845. 'Aesthetics of Dress: Art of a Bonnet.' *Blackwood's Magazine*, February, 247.

Hodgson, H.R. 1926. '[Brighouse] Monthly Meeting Properties.' In *The Society of Friends in Bradford: A Record of 270 Years*. Bradford: Percy Lund, Humphries and Co.

Hofenk de Graff, Judith H. 2004. *The Colourful Past: Origins, Chemistry and Identification of Natural Dyestuffs*. Switzerland: Abegg-Stiftung and Archetype Publications.

Holland, Nick. 2018. *Aunt Branwell and the Brontë Legacy*. Barnsley: Pen and Sword.

Hollander, Anne. 1993. *Seeing Through Clothes*. Oakland: University of California Press.

Hollander, Anne. 2016. *Fabric of Vision Dress and Drapery in Painting*. London: Bloomsbury Academic.

Hollander, Anne. 2016. *Sex and Suits: The Evolution of Modern Dress*. London, Oxford and New York: Bloomsbury.

Holmes Cautley, C. 1910. 'Old Haworth Folk Who Knew the Brontës.' *Cornhill Magazine*. July: 76–84.

Houghton, Eleanor. 2016. 'Unravelling the Mystery: Charlotte Brontë's 1850 "Thackeray Dress."' *Costume*, 50 (2): 194–219.

Houghton, Eleanor. 2020. 'Charlotte Brontë's Moccasins: The Wild West Brought Home.' In *Charlotte Brontë, Embodiment and the Material World*, eds Justine Pizzo and Eleanor Houghton. Cham: Palgrave Macmillan, 171–204.

Houghton, Eleanor. 2020. 'Decoding Clothing: Charlotte Brontë, Plainness and the Language of Dress.' PhD thesis, University of Southampton.

Howard, Luke. 1833. *The Climate of London Deduced from Meteorological Observations Made in the Metropolis and at Various Places Around It*. Vol. 1. 2 vols. London: J. and A. Arch Cornhill, Longman.

Howitt, William. 1835. 'The Quakeress.' *Sheffield Iris*. 17 February, 4.

Hughes, Kathryn. 1993. *The Victorian Governess*. London and Rio Grande: The Hambledon Press.
Hughes, Kathryn. 2016. *The Governess-Video and Transcript*. Discovering Literature: Romantics and Victorians. London: The British Library. https://www.bl.uk/romantics-and-victorians.
Ibbetson, J. 1845. 'Advertisement for "Naismith's Hair-Cutting and Perfumery".' In *Ibbetson's Directory of the Borough of Bradford*. Bradford: J. Ibbetson, 18, 57, 58.
'Illustration of the Empress of the French [Empress Eugenie], in her Bridal Costume.' 1853. *The Illustrated London News*. 5 March, 188.
Ingelow, Jean. 1864. *Studies for Stories*. London: Alexander Strahan.
Ingle, H. Larry. 1994. *First Among Friends, George Fox and the Creation of Quakerism*. Oxford: Oxford University Press.
Ives, Maura C. 2012. 'Introduction.' In *Women Writers and the Artifacts of Celebrity in the Long Nineteenth Century*, eds Maura C. Ives and Ann R. Hawkins. Farnham: Ashgate, 4.
Jalland, Pat. 1996. *Death in the Victorian Family*. Oxford: Oxford University Press.
James, John. 1866. *The History of Bradford and Its Parish*. Bradford: Longmans, Green, Reader and Dyer.
Jameson, Anna. 1846. *On the Relative Social Position of Mothers and Governesses*. London: Spottiswoode and Shaw.
Jenkins, David. 2003. *The Cambridge History of Western Textiles*. Vol. 2. Cambridge: Cambridge University Press.
Johnson, Barbara. 1987. *A Lady of Fashion: Barbara Johnson's Album of Style and Fabrics*, ed. Nathalie Rothstein. London: Thames and Hudson.
Johnston, Lucy. 2010. *Nineteenth Fashion in Detail*. London: V&A Publishing.
Jones, Ann Rosalind, and Peter Stallybrass. 2000. *Renaissance Clothing and the Materials of Memory*. Cambridge: Cambridge University Press.
Kafai, Yasmin B., Deborah A. Fields and Melissa S. Cook. 2010. 'Your Second Selves: Player-Designed Avatars.' *Games and Culture*, 5 (1): 23–42.
Kahr, Bart, Scott Lovell and J. Ananad Subramony. 1998. 'The Progress of Logwood Extract.' *Chirality*, 10: 66–77.
Kavkler, K. and A. Demšar. 2011. 'Examination of Cellulose Textile Fibres in Historical Objects by Micro-Raman Spectroscopy.' *Spectrochimica Acta Part A: Molecular and Biomolecular Spectroscopy*, 78 (1): 740–6.
Kawamura, Yuniya. 2004. *Fashion-Ology: An Introduction to Fashion Studies*. Oxford and New York: Berg.
Keefe, Robert. 1979. *Charlotte Brontë's World of Death*. Austin: University of Texas Press.
Keeler, Alex J., Danai Panagoulia, Hazel Garvie-Cook, Eleanor Houghton and Andrea Russell. 2017. 'Following the Threads: A Raman Spectroscopic Investigation of Charlotte Brontë's Thackeray Dress.' Southampton: University of Southampton and Renishaw plc.
Keen, Suzanne. 2002. 'Quaker Dress, Sexuality, and the Domestication of Reform in the Victorian Novel.' *Victorian Literature and Culture*, 30: 211–36.
Kellett, Jocelyn. 1977. *Haworth Parsonage: The Home of the Brontës*. Haworth: The Brontë Society.

Kennedy, Thomas C. 2017. 'Quakers: Gender and Equality.' In *The Oxford History of Protestant Dissenting Traditions: The Nineteenth Century*, eds Thomas Larsen and Micheal Ledger-Thomas. Oxford: Oxford University Press, 79–98.

Kim, Monica. 2015. 'The Good and the Bad of Escaping to Virtual Reality.' *The Atlantic*, 18 February. https://www.theatlantic.com/health/archive/2015/02/the-good-and-the-bad-of-escaping-to-virtual-reality/385134/.

Kobayashi, Ami. 2021. 'Book Review: A Cultural History of School Uniform.' *Paedagogica Historica*, 57 (6): 755–7.

Kopytoff, Igor. (1986). 'The Cultural Biography of Things.' In *The Social Life of Things: Commodities in Cultural Perspective*, ed. Arjan Appadurai. Cambridge: Cambridge University Press, 64–91.

Krugovoy Silver, Anna. 2002. *Victorian Literature and the Anorexic Body*. Cambridge: Cambridge University Press.

Kunzle, David. 1982. *Fashion and Fetishism: Social History of the Corset, Tight-lacing and Other Forms of Body Sculpture in the West*. Maryland: Rowman & Littlefield.

'Lady's Dinner Dress, Paris and London Fashions.' 1848. *The Lady's Newspaper*, 20 May, 29.

'Lady's Washing Book.' 1838. In *The Workwoman's Guide: Containing Instructions to the Inexperienced in Cutting out and Completing Those Articles of Wearing Apparel & Which Are Usually Made at Home: Also Explanations on Upholstry, Bonnet-Making, Straw Plaiting, Knitting Etc*. London: Simpkin, Marshall and Company, 234.

Lamb, Charles, and Thomas Noon Talfourd. 1838. 'A Quakers' Meeting – 1823.' In *The Works of Charles Lamb*. New York: Harper and Brothers, 56–63.

Langan, Emma I. 2021. 'The Brontës and Tuberculosis Immunity.' *Brontë Studies*, 46 (2): 210–22.

Lanté, Louis-Marie. 'Fashion Plate, 10 September 1834,' Hand coloured engraving, (E.22396:209-1957), V&A, London.

'Last Three Nights of Macready's First Series of Farewell Performances.' 1849. *Bell's Weekly Messenger*. 2 December.

Laver, James. 2014. *Costume and Fashion: A Concise History*. 5th ed. London: Thames and Hudson.

Lee, Sir Sidney, and Leslie Stephen. 1925. *The Dictionary of National Biography: Founded in 1882 by George Smith*. London: Oxford University Press.

Lee, Sir Sidney. 1909. 'Charlotte Brontë in London.' *Brontë Transactions*, 4 (19): 95–120.

Lemire, Beverley. 1991. 'Peddling Fashion: Salesmen, Pawnbrokers, Tailors, Thieves and the Second-Hand Clothes Trade c.1700–1800.' *Textile History*, 22 (1): 67–82.

Lemire, Beverley. 1997. *Dress, Culture and Commerce: The English Clothing Trade Before the Factory*. Basingstoke: Macmillan.

Lévi-Strauss, Monique. 2013. *Cashmere: A French Passion 1800–1880*. London: Thames and Hudson.

Lewes, George Henry. 1848. 'Jane Eyre – An Autobiography, Edited by Currer Bell.' *Westminster Review*, January, 581–4.

Leyland, Francis A. 1886. 'Letter from Branwell Brontë to Francis Grundy, October 1845.' In *The Brontë Family, With Special Reference to Branwell Brontë*, 2: 92. London: Hurst and Blackett Publishers, 46–7.

Li, Yuhang, and Sally Promey. 2014. 'Sensory Devotions: Hair Embroidery and Gendered Corporeal Practice in Chinese Buddhism.' In *Sensational Religion: Sensory Cultures in Material Practice*. New Haven and London: Yale University Press, 355–74.

Libron, Fernand, and Henry Clouzot. 1933. *Le Corset Dans l'Art et les Mouers du X111e au XXe Siècles*. Paris: Self-Published.

Lipovetsky, Gilles. 2004. *The Empire of Fashion: Dressing Modern Democracy*. Princeton and Oxford: Princeton University Press.

The Literary Examiner. 1849. 'Shirley: A Tale by Currer Bell', *The Examiner*, Saturday 3 November, 6.

'Literature: Reviews of New Books – Shirley: A Tale by the Author of Jane Eyre.' 1849. *Bell's New Weekly Messenger*. 18 November, 5, 6.

Lock, John, and W.T. Dixon. 1965. *A Man of Sorrow: The Life, Letters and Times of the Rev. Patrick Brontë*. London: Praeger Publishers.

Locke, John. 1693. *Some Thoughts Concerning Education*. London: A. & J. Churchill.

Lodge Esq., Edmund. 1855. *The Peerage of the British Empire*. Vol. 24. London: Saunders and Otley.

'LOG.; Dyeing: Of Dyeing Silk Violet or Purple.' 1855. In *The Encyclopaedia Britannica, Or Dictionary of Arts, Sciences, and of General Literature*. Edinburgh: Adam and Charles Black, 312–13.

'The London General Mourning Warehouse.' 1843. *The Illustrated Weekly Times*, 25 March, 48.

Lucas Glaisyer, Phebe. 2009. 'Recollections of my Childhood.' In *Phebe's Hitchin Book*, ed. John Lucas. Hitchin: Hitchin Historical Society, 3–107.

Luo, Yan, Mengya Li, and Juan Du. 2017. 'Esterification of Cochineal Carmine Used For Dyeing Cationic Modified Cotton with High Color Fastness.' *Journal of Engineered Fibers and Fabrics*, 12 (2): 60–6.

Lutz, Deborah. 2015. *The Brontë Cabinet*. London and New York: W.W. Norton and Company.

Lynn, Eleri. 2014. *Underwear Fashion in Detail*. London: V&A Publishing.

Malhoney, Francis. 1833. 'Gallery of Literary Characters: Miss Landon No. XII.' *Fraser's Magazine*.

Mansen, Mary. 1827. *Design Book, 1827*. T. 213-1968. V&A Museum, London.

Marcus, Sharon. 2007. *Between Women: Friendship, Desire, and Marriage in Victorian England*. Princeton: Princeton University Press.

Martineau, Harriet. 1877. 'Charlotte Brontë's Reaction to *Criticism* (1849).' In *Autobiography*, ed. Maria Weston Chapman. Vol. 2. Boston: James R. Osgood.

Martineau, Harriet, and Maria Weston Chapman. 1877. *Memorials of Harriet Martineau*, ed. Maria Weston Chapman. Boston: James R. Osgood.

Marx, Karl. 1849. 'Wage Labour and Capital.' *Neue Rheinische Zeitung*. 5 April.

Mason, Michael. 1994. *The Making of Victorian Sexuality*. Oxford: Oxford University Press.

Matthews David, Alison. 2017. *Fashion Victims*. Kindle Edition. London: Bloomsbury.

Mattingly, Carol. 2002. *Appropriating Dress: Women's Rhetorical Style in Nineteenth Century America*. Carbondale and Edwardsville: Illinois University Press.

'The Mayor and Mayoress of Oxford to C. Brontë'. 1854. MS (HAOBP). BPM, Haworth.

McCrum, Elizabeth. 1978. 'Destruction of Ulster Museum's Textile and Costume Collection.' *Costume*, 12 (April): 105–9.

Melville, Lewis. 1899. *The Life of William Makepeace Thackeray*. Vol. 1. 2 vols. London: Hutchinson and Company.

Mental Health Foundation. 2022. 'Body Image Report – Executive Summary.' https://www.mentalhealth.org.uk/explore-mental-health/articles/body-image-report-executive-summary.

Messinger, Paul. 2007. 'On the Relationship between My Avatar and Myself.' *Journal of Virtual Worlds Research*, 1 (November): 1.

Mida, Ingrid, and Alexandra Kim. 2019. *The Dress Detective*. London: Bloomsbury Visual Arts.

Miller, Daniel. 2010. *Stuff*. Cambridge: Polity Press.

Miller, Janet, and Barbara Reagan. 1989. 'Degradation in Weighted and Unweighted Historic Silks.' *JAIC Online*, 28 (2:4): 97–115.

Miller, Lucasta. 2001. *The Brontë Myth*. London: Jonathan Cape.

Miller, Peter. 2013. 'Introduction.' In *Cultural Histories of the Material World*, ed. Peter Miller. Ann Arbor: University of Michigan Press, 1–32.

The Mirror of Literature, Amusement and Instruction Containing Original Essays. 1826. Vol. VIII. London: J. Limbird.

Moglen, Helene. 1984. *Charlotte Brontë: The Self Conceived*. Wisconsin: University of Wisconsin Press.

Monckton Milnes, Richard. 1854. 'Letter to Mrs Gaskell, 30 January 1854.' (MS. fMS Am 1943.1). Houghton Library, Harvard University.

Monckton Milnes, Richard. 1857. 'Commonplace Book'. MS. Papers of Richard Monckton Milnes, Lord Houghton. Trinity College Cambridge. https://archives.trin.cam.ac.uk/index.php/papers-of-richard-monckton-milnes-1st-baron-houghton.

Moore, Thomas (ed.). 1833. *The Letters and Journals of Lord Byron: With Notices of His Life*. Vol. 2. London: John Murray.

'Morning Visiting Dress, 1835', Fashion plate, Scripps College, Ella Strong Denison Library, Macpherson Collection, Costume Plates of Myrtle Tyrrell Kirby, box 5.

Moss, William. 1794. *An Essay on the Management, Nursing and Diseases of Children, From Birth and on the Treatment and Diseases of Pregnant and Lying-In Women with Remarks on the Domestic Practice of Medicine*. 2nd ed. Egham: C. Boult and F.N. Longman.

Muller, Helen. 1980. *Jet Jewellery and Ornaments*. Haverfordwest: Shire Publications.

Mulvey, Laura. 1975. 'Visual Pleasure and Narrative Cinema.' *Screen*, 16 (Autumn): 6–18.

Murnen, Sarah, and Donn Byrne. 1991. 'Hyper-femininity: Measurement and Initial Validation of the Construct.' *The Journal of Sex Research*, 28: 479–89.

Nanakoudis, Antonis. n.d. 'EDX Analysis with a Scanning Electron Microscope (SEM): How Does it Work? https://blog.phenom-world.com/edx-analysis-scanning-electron-microscope-sem. *Desktop Electron Microscopy Solutions*, Thermo Fisher Scientific (blog). https://blog.phenom-world.com/edx-analysis-scanning-electron-microscope-sem.

'Nancy Wainwright: Charlotte Brontë's Nurse.' 1885. *Illustrated Weekly Telegraph*, 10 January.

Nedalmann, Birgitta. 1990. 'Georg Simmel as an Analyst of Antonymous Dynamics: The Merry Go Round of Fashion.' In *Georg Simmel and Contemporary Sociology*, ed. B.S. Phillips, M. Kaern and Robert S. Cohen. Boston: Kluwer Academic Publishers, 243–57.

Nicholson, William. 1808. *A Dictionary of Practical and Theoretical Chemistry: With Its Application to the Arts and Manufactures and to the Explanation of the Phenomena of Nature*. London: Richard Phillips.

Nightingale, Florence. 1979. *Cassandra*, ed. Myra Stark. New York: Feminist Press, City University of New York.

Northrup, Jane Megan. 2012. *Reflecting on Cosmetic Surgery: Body Image, Shame and Narcissism*. London and New York: Routledge.

Nussey, Ellen. 1860. 'Letter to George Smith.' (File No. 2). Smith, Elder and Company Archives, John Murray Publishers.

Nussey, Ellen. 1860. 'Letter to George Smith.' (File 7. No. 5). Smith, Elder and Company Archives, National Library of Scotland.

Nussey, Ellen. 1871. 'Reminiscences of Charlotte Brontë (1831–1855).' *Scribner's Monthly*, 2: 1, 18–31.

Nussey, Ellen. Quoted in 1877. 'An Account of Anne Brontë's Death.' In *Charlotte Brontë: A Monograph*, ed. Thomas Wemyss Reid. London: Macmillan and Co., Chapter 7.

Ogarkova, Anna. 2013. 'Folk Emotion Concepts: Lexicalization of Emotional Experiences across Languages and Cultures.' In *Components of Emotional Meaning: A Sourcebook*, eds Klaus Scherer, Johnny Fontaine and Cristina Soriano. Oxford: Oxford University Press.

O'Neill, Charles. 1860. *Chemistry of Calico Printing, Dyeing, and Bleaching: Including Silken, Woollen, and Mixed Goods Practical and Theoretical*. Manchester: Dunhill, Palmer and Company.

O'Neill, Charles, and A.A. Fesquet. 1869. *A Dictionary of Dyeing and Calico Printing*. Philadelphia: Henry Carey Baird.

Oosten, T.B. van. 1994. 'Investigation into the Degradation of Weighted Silk.' In *Contributions of the Central Research Laboratory to the Field of Conservation and Restoration*, eds H. Verschoor and J. Mosk. Amsterdam: Central Research Laboratory for Objects of Art and Science, 65–76.

Orel, Harold, ed. (1997). *The Brontës: Interviews and Recollections*. Iowa: University of Iowa Press.

Ormond, Richard. 1973. *Early Victorian Portraits*. Vols 1 and 2. London: HMSO.

Padfield, Tim, and Sheila Landi. 1966. 'The Light Fastness of the Natural Dyes.' *Studies in Conservation*, 11, 181–96.

Parnell, Edward. 1849. *Dyeing and Calico Printing*. London: Taylor, Walton and Maberly.

Parry, Linda. 2010. *British Textiles: 1700 to the Present*. London: V&A Publishing.

Peacock, John. 2009. *Children's Costume: The Complete Historical Sourcebook*. London: Thames and Hudson.

Pearson Thistlethwaite, W. 1979. *Yorkshire Quarterly Meeting of the Society of Friends 1966*. Published by author.

Perrot, Michel. 1841. *Revue de l'Exposition des Produits de l'Industrie Nationale en 1841*. Bruxelles: Chez L'Ateur.

Perrot, Phillippe. 1994. *Fashioning the Bourgeoisie: A History of Clothing in the Nineteenth Century*. Princeton, NJ: Princeton University Press.

Pointon, Marcia. 1990. *Naked Authority: The Body in Western Painting 1830–1908*. Cambridge: Cambridge University Press.

Pope-Hennessey, James. 1951. *Monckton Milnes: The Flight of Youth 1851–1885*. Constable and Company.

Practical Mechanics Journal, Volume VI, April 1853–March 1854. London: George Herbert.

'Promenade Dresses, May 1842'. *The Court Magazine and Monthly Critic and Lady's Magazine and Museum*.

'Purple and Black Calico Printed by Thomas Hoyle and Sons.' 1849. *Journal of Design and Manufactures*, 2 (September).

Quaile, Sheilagh. n.d. 'Cashmere Shawls'. Smart History, The Centre for Public History. https://smarthistory.org/cashmere-shawls/.

'Queen Victoria to Prince Albert.' 1940. *The Times*. 11 February.

Quye, Anita, Julie H. Wertz and David France. 2018. 'Turkey Red Prints: Identification of Lead Chromate, Prussian Blue and Logwood on Turkey Red Calico.' *Conservar Património* (April): 31–9.

R.A.H. 1828. 'The School for Clergymen's Daughters.' *The Christian Guardian (and Church of England) Magazine*, January.

Rapports du Jury Belge de l'Exposition Universelle de Paris en 1855. 1856. Bruxelles: Imprimerie de Bols-Wittouck.

Rashaduzzamam Mithun, M.D. 2017. 'Silk and its Degumming Process.' *Textile Today*, 15 November.

Rauser, Amelia Faye. 2008. *Caricature Unmasked: Irony, Authenticity, and Individualism in Eighteenth Century Prints*. Newark: University of Delaware Press.

Rayner Parkes, Bessie. 1866. *Essays on Women's Work*. London: Alexander Strahan Publisher.

Rees, Rosemary, Nigel Kelly and Jane Shuter. 1998. *Living through History: Britain 1750–1900*. Oxford: Heinemann.

Reid, T. Wemyss. 1877. *Charlotte Brontë: A Monograph*. London: Macmillan and Co.

Reillo, Giorgio. 2022. 'The "Material Turn" in World and Global History.' *Journal of World History*, 33 (2): 193–232.

Rendle-Short, Morwenna and John. 1966. *The Father of Childcare, William Cadogan (1711–1797)*. Bristol: John Wright and Sons.

Rhodes, Philip. 1972. 'A Medical Appraisal of the Brontës.' *Brontë Society Transactions*, 16 (2): 102–9.

Ribeiro, Aileen and Cally Blackman. 2015. *A Portrait of Fashion*. London: National Portrait Gallery.

Rigby, Elizabeth. 1848. 'Vanity Fair and Jane Eyre.' *Quarterly Review*, December, 84 (127): 153–85.

Ritchie, Hester. 1924. 'Charlotte Brontë's Appearance, 1850.' In *Letters of Anne Thackeray Ritchie, with Forty-Five Additional Letters from her Father, William Makepeace Thackeray*. London: John Murray, 269–70.

Roberts, Edward. 1839. *A Manual Containing Directions for Sowing, Transplanting and Raising of the Mulberry Tree*. Baltimore: Samuel Sands.

Roberts, Helene. 1977. 'The Exquisite Slave: The Role of Clothes in the Making of the Victorian Woman.' *Signs: Journal of Women in Culture and Society*, 2: 554–69.

Robinson, A.F. Mary. 1883. *Emily Brontë*. Boston: Roberts Brothers.

Roche, Daniel. 2014. *The Culture of Clothing: Dress and Fashion in the Ancien Régime*. Cambridge: Cambridge University Press.

Rousseau, Jean Jacques. 1762. *Émile, ou De l'Éducation*. Republique de Genéve et France: A La Haye.

Rowe, Sophie. 2004. 'The Effect of Insect Fumigation by Anoxia on Textiles Dyed with Prussian Blue.' *Studies in Conservation*, 49: 259–70.

Royal Collection Trust's Press Office. 2016. 'How Queen Victoria and Prince Albert Expressed Their Love through Flowers Is Explored in a New Exhibition.' *Royal Collection Trust, London* (blog). 12 July. https://www.royalcollection.org.uk/about/press-office/press-releases/how-queen-victoria-and-prince-albert-expressed-their-love-through.

The Royal College of Surgeons of England. 1833. 'On the Ill Effects of Insufficient Exercise, Constrained Positions, and Tight Stays on the Health of Young Women.' *The Penny Magazine*, 28 February.

The Royal Commission for the Exhibition of 1851. 1852. *Exhibitions of the Works of the Industry of All Nations – Reports by the Juries: On the Subjects in the Thirty Classes into Which the Exhibition Was Divided*. Vol. 1. 2 vols. London: William Clowes and Sons.

'Royal Italian Opera.' 1850. *The Illustrated London News*. 8 June.

'Royal Stewart Tartan Cloak, c.1830.' National Museums Scotland. 18 April 2023. https://www.nms.ac.uk/explore-our-collections/stories/scottish-history-and-archaeology/highland-style/highland-style-sub-pages/royal-stewart-tartan-cloak-c1830/.

Russell, John C. 1969. *Russell's General Atlas of Modern Geography*, 1836, unnumbered page, sketch of an unnamed girl. The Morgan Library & Museum. PML 129886. Bequest of Helen Safford Bonnell.

Samuel, Julia. 2017. *Grief Works: Stories of Life, Death and Surviving*. London. Penguin Books.

Sanderson, Elizabeth. 1997. 'Nearly New: The Second-Hand Clothing Trade in Eighteenth-Century Edinburgh.' *Costume*, 31: 38–48.

Schoeser, Mary and Celia Rufey. 1989. *English and American Textiles: From 1790 to the Present*. London: Thames & Hudson.

Schroder, Henry. 1852. *The Annals of Yorkshire from the Earliest Period to the Present Time*. Vol. 2. 2 vols. Leeds: George Crosby.

The Science of Dress for Ladies and Gentlemen. 1856. London: Groombridge and Sons.

Sebastian, Catherine, Stephanie Burnett and Sarah-Jayne Blakemore. 2008. 'Development of the Self-Concept during Adolescence.' *Trends in Cognitive Sciences*, 12 (11): 441–6.

Sellars, Jane. 1997. *Charlotte Brontë (British Library Writers' Lives)*. London: British Library Publishing.

Sellars, Jane. 2012. 'Portraits of the Brontës.' In *The Brontës in Context*, ed. Marianne Thormählen. Cambridge: Cambridge University Press, 123–33.
Selwyn, David. 2010. *Jane Austen and Children*. London and New York: Continuum International Publishing.
Semler, Lydia, Jana Hill, Ilea Magdelina Bonner. 2024. *A History of Maternity Wear Design, Patterns, and Construction*. New York and Abingdon: Routledge.
Semmelhack, Elizabeth. 2008. *Heights of Fashion: A History of the Elevated Shoe*. Pittsburgh: Periscope Press.
Shakespeare, William. 2016. *Macbeth*. London: Macmillan Collector's Library.
Sheumaker, Helen. 2007. *Love Entwined: The Curious History of Hairwork in America*. Philadelphia: University of Pennsylvania State.
Shorter, Clement. 1896. *Charlotte Brontë and Her Circle*. 2nd ed. London: Hodder & Stoughton.
Shorter, Clement. 1905. *Charlotte Brontë*. London: Hodder and Stoughton.
Shrimpton, Jayne. 2021. 'Uniform Appearance: What Did Our Ancestors Wear In Institutions?' *Family Tree Magazine*. 1 March, https://www.pressreader.com/uk/family-tree/20210301/281595243273067?srsltid=AfmBOopIWsUezq7S-Rk7-dGKXDIpD8Tl5 nY9xawB2hwDxzOacdJSvXEv.
Simmel, Georg. 1971. *On Individuality and Social Forms: Selected Writings*, ed. Donald N. Levine. Chicago: Chicago University Press.
Smith, George. 1895. 'Chapter VII. Charlotte Brontë' in *Recollections of a Long and Busy Life*, MS, National Library of Scotland, MSS.23191-23192, 11.
Smith, George. 1900. 'Charlotte Brontë'. *Cornhill Magazine*, IX (December): 778–95.
Smith, George. 1902. *A Memoir*, eds Sidney Lee and Leslie Smith. London: Private Circulation.
Smith, Margaret (ed.). 1995. *The Letters of Charlotte Brontë, Volume One, 1829–1847*. Vol. 1. 3 vols. Oxford: Oxford University Press.
Smith, Margaret. (ed.). 2000. *The Letters of Charlotte Brontë, Volume Two, 1848–1851*. Vol. 2. 3 vols. Oxford: Oxford University Press.
Smith, Margaret. (ed.). 2004. *The Letters of Charlotte Brontë, Volume Three, 1852–1855*. Vol. 3. 3 vols. Oxford: Oxford University Press.
Smith, Virginia. 2008. *Clean: A History of Personal Hygiene and Purity*. Oxford: Oxford University Press.
Society for the Relief of Poor Married Women when in Childbed. 1822. *First Annual Report of the Edinburgh Society for the Relief of Poor Married Women of Respectable Character When in Child-Bed*. Edinburgh: Anderson and Bryce.
Sotheby, Wilkinson and Hodge. 1916. *Catalogue of Valuable Illuminated and Other Manuscripts, Autograph Letters, Oriental Drawings and Printed Books … Held on 13, 14 and 15 December 1916 at No. 3 Wellington Street, The Strand*. Soho, London: Dryden Press.
Sparks, Linda. 2005. *The Basics of Corset Building: A Handbook for Beginners*. New York: St Martin's Press.
Spencer, M.B., D.P. Swanson and V. Harpalani, 'Development of the Self.' In *Handbook of Child Psychology and Developmental Science: Socioemotional Processes*, eds Michael Lamb and R.M. Lerner (Hoboken: Wiley, 2015), 753.

Spufford, Margaret. 1984. *The Great Reclothing of Rural England: Petty Chapmen and their Wares in the Seventeenth Century*. London: Hambledon Press.

Stallybrass, Peter. 1999. 'Worn Worlds: Clothes Mourning And the Life of Things.' In *Cultural Memory and the Construction of Identity*, eds Dan Ben-Amos and Liliane Weissberg. Detroit: Wayne State University Press, 35–50.

Steele, Valerie. 1985. *Fashion and Eroticism*. Oxford: Oxford University Press.

Steele, Valerie. 2003. *The Corset: A Cultural History*. New Haven, CT: Yale University Press.

Steinbach, Susie L. 2012. *Understanding the Victorians: Politics, Culture and Society in Nineteenth Century Britain*. London: Taylor & Francis.

Stephen, George. 1844. *The Guide to Service: For the Governess*. London: Charles Knight and Co.

Stephenson, Kate. 2022. *The Cultural History of School Uniform*. Exeter: Exeter University Press.

Stevens, M.W., D. Dorstyn, P.H. Delfabbro and D.L. King. 2021. 'Global Prevalence of Gaming Disorder: A Systematic Review and Meta-Analysis.' *Australia and New Zealand Journal of Psychiatry*, 55 (6): 553–68.

Stickney Ellis, Sarah. 1839. *The Women of England: Their Social Duties and Domestic Habits*. London: Fisher.

Stone, Lawrence. 1979. *Family, Sex and Marriage 1500–1800*. New York: Harper Perennial.

Stores Smith, John. 1868. 'Personal Reminiscences: A Day with Charlotte Brontë (1850).' *The Free Lance: A Journal of Humour and Criticism*, 3 (14 March): 85–7.

Stripe, Nick. 2019. 'Married by 30? You're Now in the Minority'. *Office of National Statistics*, 1 April. https://blog.ons.gov.uk/2019/04/01/married-by-30-youre-now-in-the-minority/#:~:text=50%20unmarried%20women.-,The%20average%20age%20of%20marriage%2C%20for%20a%20first%2Dtime%20marriage,9%20in%2010%20in%201976.

Summers, Leigh. 1999. *The Sexual Politics of Corsetry: 1850–1900*. Parkville: University of Melbourne.

Swain, Kelley. 2017. 'Purple.' *The Lancet Psychiatry*, 4 (12): 908.

Swedlund, Alan C., and Alison K. Donta. 2002. 'Scarlet Fever Epidemics of the Nineteenth Century: A Case of Evolved Pathogenic Virulence?' In *Human Biologists in the Archives: Demography, Health, Nutrition and Genetics in Historical Populations*, eds D. Ann Herring and Alan C. Swedlund. Cambridge: Cambridge University Press, 159–77.

Sweetland Dallas, Eneas. 1877. 'Dyes and Dyeing.' In *Once a Week*. Fourth Series. Vol. V. September 1876–December 1877. London: Sweeting and Co., 68.

Sydney, Morgan. *Lady Morgan's Memoirs: Autobiography, Diaries and Correspondence*. 1863. Vol. 2. 3 vols. Leipzig: Bernhard Tauchnitz.

Sykas, Philip. 2007. *Identifying Printed Textiles in Dress 1740–1890*, ed. DATS. London: DATS in partnership with the V&A.

Symonds, Andy. 2016. 'Explainer: What Does the "Male Gaze" Mean, and What About a Female Gaze?' *The Conversation*, 5 January. http://theconversation.com/explainer-what-does-the-male-gaze-mean-and-what-about-a-female-gaze-52486.

Szolin, Kim, Daria J. Kuss, Filip M. Nuyens and Mark D. Griffiths. 2022. 'Exploring the User-Avatar Relationship in Videogames: A Systematic Review of the Proteus Effect.'

Human–Computer Interaction, August: 1–26. https://doi.org/10.1080/07370024.2022.2 103419.

Takami, Mika, and Ina Vanden Berghe. 2013. 'Caring for Queen Victoria's Privy Council Dress *c*. 1837: An Investigation of the Unique Discolouration of the Black Silk.' *E-Preservation Science*, 10: 42–9.

Taylor, G.P. 2006. 'God's Own County.' *The Guardian Newspaper*. 2 June. https://www.theguardian.com/travel/2006/jun/02/travelnews.shortbreaks.unitedkingdom.

Taylor, Lou. 2009. *Mourning Dress*. Abingdon: Routledge.

Taylor, Mary. 1842. 'Letter to Ellen Nussey c. 24 September 1842', MS (Brontë Family Works and Letters, Box 1), The Harry Ransom Humanities Research Centre, University of Texas, Austin.

Taylor, Mary. 1850. 'Letter to Ellen Nussey.' (Berg Collection 186119). The Henry W. and Albert A. Berg Collection of English and American Literature, New York Public Library, Astor, Lenox and Tilden Foundations.

Taylor, Mary. 1857. 'Letter to Elizabeth Cleghorn Gaskell, 18 Feb 1856'. Quoted in Elizabeth Cleghorn Gaskell, '*The Life of Charlotte Brontë: Volume One.*' London: Smith, Elder and Company, 125.

Terry, Rachel. 2002. 'Additions to the Brontë Society Collections: Further Details and New Items.' *Brontë Society Transactions*, 27 (November): 252.

Thackeray Ritchie, Anne Isabella. 1894. *Chapters from Some Memoirs*. London: Macmillan and Co.

Thackeray Ritchie, Anne. 1924. 'Charlotte Brontë's Appearance, 1850.' In *Letters of Anne Thackeray Ritchie, with Forty-Five Additional Letters from Her Father, William Makepeace Thackeray*. London: John Murray, 269–70.

Thackeray, William Makepeace. 1848. *Vanity Fair: A Novel Without a Hero*. New York: Harper and Brothers.

Thackeray, William Makepeace. 1853. 'Letter from William Makepeace Thackeray to Miss Lucy Baxter, 11 March 1853', in *The Letters and Private Papers of William Makepeace Thackeray*. Vol. 3, ed. Gordon Norton Ray. Harvard: Harvard University Press, 232–3.

Thackeray, William Makepeace. 1860. 'The Last Sketch' (1847–1855) [Introduction to *Emma*, an unfinished novel by Charlotte Brontë]. *Cornhill Magazine*, I (April): 487–98.

Thackeray, William Makepeace. 1997. 'Letter to Lucy Baxter, 11 March 1853.' In *The Brontës: Interviews and Recollections*, ed. Harold Orel. Iowa: University of Iowa Press, 232–3.

Thormählen, Marianne. 2004. *The Brontës and Religion*. Cambridge: Cambridge University Press.

Toplis, Alison. 2016. *The Clothing Trade in Provincial England 1800–1850*. Abingdon: Routledge.

Tozer, Jane, and Sarah Levitt. 1983. *Fabric of Society: A Century of People and Their Clothes 1770–1870*. Carno: Laura Ashley Ltd.

Tranberg Hansen, Karen. 2005. 'The Anthropology of Secondhand Clothes.' In *Encyclopedia of Clothing and Fashion*, ed. Valerie Steele. Detroit: Charles Scribner's Sons, 151.

Trapnell, P.D., J.D. Campbell, S.J. Heine, I.M. Katz, L.F. Lavallee and D.R. Lehman. 1996. 'Self-Concept Clarity: Measurement, Personality Correlates, and Cultural Boundaries.' *Journal of Personality and Social Psychology*, 70: 141–56.

Trentelman, Karen A., and Catherine M. Schmidt. n.d. '1064 nm dispersive Raman microspectroscopy for the in-situ identification of organic red colourants.' *e-Preservation Science*, 6 (2009): 10–21.

Trentmann, Frank. 2009. 'Materiality in the Future of History: Things, Practices, and Politics.' *Special Issue, Journal of British Studies*, 48 (2): 283–307.

Trollope, Anthony. 1866. *The Warden*. London: Longmans, Green, Reader and Dyer.

Tuin, I. van der 2011. 'The Material Turn in the Humanities.' *NWO, Dutch Research Council* (blog). 1 February 2011 to 28 August. File Number: 275-20-029. https://www.nwo.nl/en/projects/275-20-029.

Turner, Whiteley 1913. *A Spring-Time Saunter: Round and About Brontë Land*. Halifax: The Halifax Courier.

Umney, Nick, and Shayne Rivers. 2003. *Conservation of Furniture*. Oxford: Butterworth/Heinemann.

Underwood, Michael. 1811. *A Treatise on the Diseases of Children with the Direction of Management for Children From Birth*. 6th ed. Vol. 1. 3 vols. London: J. Callow, Medical Bookseller.

University of Rhode Island. n.d. 'Fashion Plate – Une Conversation La Mode, 1832', Historic Textile and Costume Collection, https://uritextilecollection.omeka.net/items/show/148.

University of Rhode Island. n.d. 'Fashion Plate – Evening Dress and Costume Antique, 1833', Historic Textile and Costume Collection, https://uritextilecollection.omeka.net/items/show/149

Unsigned Review. 2001. 'Critic, October 1847.' In *The Critical Heritage: The Brontës*, ed. Miriam Allott. Oxford: Routledge, 73–4.

Valente, A.J. 2010. *Rag Paper Manufacture in the United States, 1801–1900: A History, with Directories of Mills and Owners*. Jefferson: McFarland and Company.

Van Der Heide, Brandon, Erin M. Schumaker, Ashley M. Peterson and Elizabeth B. Jones. 2013. 'The Proteus Effect in Dyadic Communication: Examining the Effect of Avatar Appearance in Computer-Mediated Dyadic Interaction.' *Communication Research*, 40 (6): 838–60.

Vartanian, Lenny R. and Lydia Hayward 2018. 'Self-Concept Clarity and Body Dissatisfaction.' In *Self-Concept Clarity: Perspectives on Assessment, Research and Applications*, eds Kenneth G. DeMarree and Jennifer Lodi-Smith. New York: Springer, 195–218.

Vartanian, Lenny R., K. Nicholls and J. Fardouly. 2023. 'Testing the Identity Disruption Model among Adolescents: Pathways Connecting Adverse Childhood Experiences to Body Dissatisfaction.' *Journal of Youth and Adolescence*, 52: 134–48.

Veblen, Thorstein. 2005. *Conspicuous Consumption*. London: Penguin.

Victoria and Albert Museum. n.d. 'Embroidery Styles: An Illustrated Guide.' V&A. https://www.vam.ac.uk/articles/embroidery-styles-an-illustrated-guide.

Volo, James M., and Dorothy Denneen Volo. 2004. *The Antebellum Period*. Westport, CT: Greenwood Press.

Vorderer, Peter, and Bernhd Henning. 2001. 'Psychological Escapism: Predicting the Amount of Television Viewing by Need for Cognition.' *Journal of Communication*, 51 (1): 100–20.

'Walking Dresses.' (1848). *Les Modes Parisiennes*. Paris: Moine Impr. Des Noyes.

Walsh, Valentine, Nicholas Eastaugh, Tracey Chaplin and Ruth Siddall. 2008. *Pigment Compendium: A Dictionary and Optical Microscopy of Historical Pigments, Arts, Museum and Heritage Studies*. London: Routledge.

Ward, Mrs Humphrey, ed. 1899. 'Introduction to Charlotte Brontë's 'Villette'. London: Smith, Elder and Company.

Warren, Dr. 1840. 'Dangers of Tight-Lacing.' In *The Fireside Friend, or Female Student: Being Advice to Young Ladies on the Important Subject of Education*. Boston: Marsh, Capen, Lyon and Webb, 70.

Was-Gubala, Jolanta and Waldemar Machnowski. 2014. 'Application of Raman Spectroscopy for Differentiation among Cotton and Viscose Fibers Dyed with Several Dye Classes.' *Spectroscopy Letters*, 47: 527–35.

Watts, Alaric A., ed. 1830. *The Literary Souvenir*. London: Longman, Rees, Orme, Brown and Green.

Waugh, Norah. 1954. *Corsets and Crinolines*. London and New York: Routledge.

Weber, Jacob. 2018. 'Patterns in British Height: 1770–1845.' Oakland: Berkeley University. https://delong.typepad.com/jacob-p.-weber-heightpaperfinal-x.pdf.

Webster, Thomas. 1815. 'Health in the Nursery.' In *An Encyclopaedia of Domestic Economy Comprising Such Subjects as Are Most Immediately Connected with Housekeeping: As, The Construction of Domestic Edifices, … Preservation of Health, Domestic Medicines, & c*. Vol. 2. New York: Harper and Brothers, 11–12.

'Wedding Dress Fashion Plate.' 1853. *Le Conseiller Des Dames & Desmoiselles* (Paris). March.

Weeton, Nelly. 1936–9. *Journal of a Governess 1811–25*, ed. Edward Hall. Vol. 2. 2 vols. Oxford: Oxford University Press.

Weir, Edith. 1946. 'Review of *Letter from Constantin Heger to Unidentified Former Pupil*.' In 'New Brontë Material Come to Light.' *Brontë Society Transactions*, 11 (59): 256–7.

Welldon, J.E.C. 1910. 'The Brontë Family at Manchester.' *Cornhill Magazine*, XXVIII (June): 4–26.

Welter, Barbara (1966). 'The Cult of True Womanhood: 1820–1860' (PDF). *American Quarterly*, 18 (2): 151–74.

Welters, Linda. 2008. 'The Fashion of Sustainability.' In *Sustainable Fashion: Why Now? A Conversation Exploring Issues, Practices, and Possibilities*, eds Janet Hethorn and Connie Ulasewicz. New York: Fairchild Books, 4–26.

Wentworth Dilke, Charles. 1852. *Exhibition of the Works of All Nations 1851: Reports by the Juries*. London: William Clowes and Sons.

Westwood, Mr. (a friend of the Hégers). n.d. 'Letter to Unknown Recipient, 21 February 1870.' (MS. 52,298). John Hay Library, Brown University, Providence.

Wheat, Joe. 2003. *Blanket Weaving in the Southwest*, ed. Anne Lane Hedlund. Tuscon: University of Arizona Press.

White, William. 1838. *History, Gazetteer and Directory of the West-Riding of Yorkshire, with the City of York and Port of Hull, Etc.* Vol. 2. Leeds: Baines and Newson.

Whitworth, Isabella, and Zvi C. Koren. 2016. 'Orchil and Tyrian Purple: Two Centuries of Bedfords from Leeds.' *Ambix*, 63: 244–67.

WHO Headquarters. 2020. 'Addictive Behaviours: Gaming Disorders.' World Health Organization. 22 October. https://www.who.int/news-room/questions-and-answers/item/addictive-behaviours-gaming-disorder.

Wilson, Elizabeth. 1987. *Adorned in Dreams: Fashion and Modernity*. London: Virago Press.

Winspear, William. 1840. 'Advertisement for "Winspear's Fancy Hair Work".' *The Yorkshire Gazette*, 18 July.

Wise, Thomas James, and John Alexander Symington (eds). 1932. *The Brontës: Their Lives, Friendships and Correspondence. The Shakespeare Head Brontë*. Oxford: Basil Blackwell for the Shakespeare Head Press.

Wise, Thomas James, and John Alexander Symington (eds). n.d. 'Letter from G.H. Lewes to George Smith.' In *The Shakespeare Head Brontë*, 3: 171–2. Oxford: Oxford University Press.

Wolf, Naomi. 2015. *The Beauty Myth*. London: Vintage Classics.

Wollstonecraft, Mary. 1891. *A Vindication of the Rights of Women, with Strictures on Political and Moral Subjects*. London: T. Fisher Unwin.

Woolf, Virginia and Mary Lyon. 1979. '"Haworth 1904." *The Guardian*. 21 December 1904.' In *Books and Portraits of Virginia Woolf*. London: The Hogarth Press, 166–73.

Worth, Narnia, and Angela Book. 2014. 'Personality and Behavior in a Massively Multiplayer Online Role-Playing Game.' *Computers in Human Behavior*, 38 (September): 322–30.

Wynne, Deborah. 2015. 'Reading Victorian Rags: Recycling, Redemption, and Dickens's Ragged Children.' *Journal of Victorian Culture*, 20 (1): 34–49.

Index

Italic page numbers indicate figures. Initials are used to indicate individuals in subheadings, e.g. CB for Charlotte Brontë.

Ackroyd, Tabith 'Tabby' 55, 105, 106, 132, 135, 145, 209
Adamson, Adam 230
à la paresseuse ('lazy-lacing') system 81
alpaca mix fabrics 164–5, *see also* 'Thackeray Dress'
Angria 32
    character similar to CB, introduction of 48, 50
    inspiration for 45
    obsession with 47–8
    sharing with school friends 38–9
appearance
    anxiety about, fame and 183–5
    The Brontë Sisters (Patrick Branwell Brontë) 40, 43
    CB's awareness of her own 89–91, *90*
    continued concern with when dying 236
    in drawings, CB's 44–5
    first social experiences in London 129
    in *Jane Eyre* (CB) 119
    marriage, changing attitudes to 33–4
    during marriage, continued struggle with 232
    plain, governesses 67
    Roe Head School, CB's at 31–3, 35–8
    role in decision to marry Nicholls 193–4
    Thackeray dinner party, comments made after 170
    visit to Mrs Gaskell's 190

appetite, CB's lack of 24–5
aprons 275n45
assertive/passive duality in CB 230

baby clothes
    christening bonnet 7–8
    gowns/frocks 9
    ready-made 8–9
baby socks made by CB 235, *235*
bags, Berlin wool work *108*
baleen 84
barége evening gown *224*, 225, *226*, 227
Barker, Juliet 212, 223, 262n44, 305n115
beauty, changing trends 34–5
Beecher, Catherine Esther 87
beliefs, religious, CB's 92, 95, 117, 207
Bell, Currer
    CB revealed as 157–8
    as CB's pen name 122, 146–7
Bell, Frances 200, 206
Bell, H.K., 206
bequests of garments after death 240
Berlin wool work 107, *108*
Binns family 160, 206, 211, 212, 241, 311n85, 312n3, 312n4
birth of CB 5–6
black lace 148, *149*, 182
Blake Hall, near Mirfield, CB as governess at 54
blouse, whitework with black trim 151, *152*

blue-and-cream striped silk gown 173,
    174, 175–82, *176*
body dysmorphia 38, 183
bones, corset 84
bonnets
    blue silk ugly *141*
    childhood clothes 10–11
    christening *7*, 7–8
    fashion consciousness shown in 115
    pink lined leghorn straw *184*, 302n71
    veils 148, *149*, 205
    wedding *202*, 202–5, *205*
    wind 'ugly' 140, *141*, 142
boots and shoes 150
    childhood 11–12, *12*
    spotted canvas and leather *238*
    wedding 206–7
box of dresses concealed in a wall 57–8, 60
bracelets
    jet 137
    made from hair of EB 136
Branwell, Elizabeth 16–17, 28–9, 74, 77
Branwell, Thomas 28–9
brazilwood 216
Brontë, Anne
    clothes, use of after death 153–6
    death of Branwell 132
    illness and death 138–43
    packing of clothes after death, CB and 143
    return from Roe Head School 53
    at Roe Head School 46
    Scarborough trip 138–42
Brontë, Branwell 101, 102
    The Brontë Sisters (Patrick Branwell Brontë) 40, *42*, 43
    career as artist 45, 53
    death and funeral 131–4
Brontë, Elizabeth (sister) 18, 19
    illness and death 26
Brontë, Emily
    bracelet made from hair of 136, *136*
    clothes, use of after death 153–6, *155*
    death of Branwell 132

illness and death 134–5
poems by, CB's discovery of 102–3
return from Roe Head School 46
teaching post 53
Brontë, Maria (mother) 15, 17
    illness and death 15, 16, 17
    maternal care 8, 9
Brontë, Maria (sister) 18, 19
    illness and death 25–6
Brontë, Patrick
    after Maria's death 17
    anxiety over future for daughters 53–4
    appropriate dress, views on 178–9
    care of 105
    CB's death 236
    CB's wedding and 208
    consent for CB to marry Nicholls 193–4
    death 240
    duties at Haworth 15, 16
    education, importance of for 19–20
    European trip 75–6
    hazards of wearing cotton 11
    health on CB's return from honeymoon 228
    illness in 1830 30
    influence of on CB and sisters 27–8
    mourning clothes 132–3
    reaction to Nicholl's proposal to CB 188–9
    reliance on daughters 102
    sight, operation to restore 119
    stroke 191
The Brontë Sisters (Patrick Branwell Brontë) 40, *42*, 43
Brontë Society 245
Brookfield, Charles 172
Brookfield, Frances 169–70, 172
Brown, Martha 79, 105, 106, 132, 135, 139, 145, 158, 160, 209, 211, 235–6, 237, 240, 241–2, 243
Brownfield, Mary 198
brown silk dress 117, *116*, 117, *118*, 287n52

Brussels
    CB's return to Pensionnat Heger 78
    journey to school there 74–5
    Pensionnat Heger, CB and EB at 75–7
    return to Haworth after deaths 77–8
bullying 36, 197
Burman, Barbara 275n51
busk, corset 85, *85*, 279n38
Byron, Lord, as influence on CB 44

Chadwick, Esther 160, 172, 201, 206, 212
charity schools, colour of school uniforms 23
Charlotte Brontë (portrait by Richmond) 266n17
Charlotte Brontë (portrait by Thompson) 266n17
Chatelain, Clara de 198
childhood clothes
    bonnets 10–11
    boots and shoes 11–12, *12*
    christening bonnet *7*, 7–8
    freedom of movement, garments allowing 9–10
    gowns 10, *10*
    gowns/frocks 9
    handmade 8
    hand-me-downs 6
    laundering 6
    outdoor wear 11
    printed cotton 11
    ready-made 8–9
    unfettered play 260n8
    as unisex 259n6
christenings
    bonnet, CB's *7*, 7–8
    importance of 260n13
Clergy Daughter's School 265n89
    Brontë sisters at 20–6
cloaks
    in concealed box of dresses 58
    style 111, 113
    tartan 113
    woollen cloth *114*, 113
clogs 11

clouts 9
cochineal 316n56
collars 217, 269n60
colour
    'Going Away Dress' 212–16, *213*
    pink 221, *222*, 223
    purple, use of for school uniforms 22–3
    during second stage of mourning 151–3
    wedding dresses 198–9
    wrapping gown, pink cotton 221, 223
comb, tortoiseshell *155*
communicative witnesses, clothes as 2–4, 245–7
community interaction, CB's increase in after marriage 228–9
corset(s)
    1842 *72*
    à la paresseuse ('lazy-lacing') system 81
    bones 84
    busk 85, *85*
    cotton cover 280n42
    dating 81
    design, changes in 79
    display of 278n16
    eyelets 81
    health and 88
    impenetrable busk *85*
    inside view *80*
    morality and chastity as displayed by 93
    as object of sensuality 89
    as protective, CB's as 91, 92–3, 97–8
    reasons for wearing 88–91
    as signifier of class 89
    status of as working woman, CB's 91–2
    structure of 79–81
    tight-lacing, CB's practice of 86, 87–98, 177
    waist dimension 85–6
    woven, CB's as 81–4
cotton
    childhood clothes 11
    hazards of wearing 11

shift from silk to 262n33
wrapping gown, pink cotton 221, *222*, 223, 316n56
cupboard containing box of dresses 57–8, 60

David Copperfield (Dickens) 67
Davidoff, Leonore 272n91
Dearden, William 19
death of CB 234–7
domestic sphere 51, 68, 91
drawings, CB's, appearance and clothes in 44–5
see also portraits
dresses
  blue-and-cream striped silk 173, *174*, 175–82, *176*
  brown silk 117, *116*, 117, *118*, 287n52
  fashion consciousness shown in 115, 211, 218, 247
  fringed silk day dress *218*
  'Going Away Dress' *210*, *213*, 229
  'Governess Dress' 56–8, *59*, *61*, 274n28
  making 109–11, *110*, *112*
  'Muslin Print Dress' *100*
  'Paisley Dress' *vi*, *xiv*, *110*, 115, 173
  reconstruction of 'Muslin Print Dress' 244
  repairing/remaking 115, *116*, 117, *118*
  'Thackeray Dress' 158, *159*, 160, *161*, 162–7, *163*
  wedding dress *195*
dyes/dyeing
  black/brown, fading of 67–8
  brazilwood 216
  cochineal 316n56
  going away dress 212–16, *213*
  indigo 314n24
  lazurite 214, 215
  logwood 215, 216
  mixing of different dyes 214
  mordants 166
  orchil 214–15
  purple, use of for school uniforms 22–3

repairing/remaking of gowns and garments 117
'Thackeray Dress' 162–3, *163*, 165–6

eating, CB's relationship with 24–5
education
  appearance and 34–5
  Clergy Daughter's School 20–6
  gaps in CB's 35
  importance of for Patrick Brontë 19–20
  Roe Head School, CB at 30–3
embellishments on blue-and-cream striped gown *176*, 177–8
Emma (CB) (unfinished) 233
engagement to Nicholls 194
'en tablier', embellishments as 175

fabric
  recycling and reuse 6–7, 260n10
  see also individual types
fame
  anxiety about appearance and 183–5
  appearance, CB's continued insecurities about 168
  CB revealed as Currer Bell 157–8
  CB's relationship with 158
  dinner party at house of Thackeray 168–70
  expectation of production and 185–6
  gender and 231
  pleasurable side of 186
  Thackeray, William Makepeace, CB's meeting with 166–8
  'Thackeray Dress' 158, *159*, 160, *161*, 162–7, *163*
  vulnerability, CB's, striped silk dress and 173, *174*, 175–82, *176*
fantasy world, Brontë sisters' withdrawal to 27
fashion, CB's struggles with codes of
  blue-and-cream striped silk gown 173, *174*, 175–82, *176*
  dinner party at Thackeray's 170
  in London 170–3

fastenings
   corsets 81
   governess dress, CB's 64–5
feminine ideal, changing trends 34–5
Fennetaux, Ariane 275n51
Firth, Elizabeth 7–8, 16, 46
floral adornments on blue-and-cream striped gown *176*, 177–8
food, CB's relationship with 24–5, 264n81, 265n86
footwear
   boots 150
   childhood 11–12, *12*
   sandalled shoes 311n86
   slippers 148, 150, 206–7
   spotted canvas and leather *238*
   wedding 206–7
freedom of movement, childhood garments allowing 9–10
friendships
   growth of at Roe Head School 38–9
   see also Nussey, Ellen; Taylor, Mary
fringed silk day dress *218*
frugality, CB's concern with 179
   choice of wedding dress 197

Garr, Nancy 9, 17, 19, 179, 261n26, 303n89, 303n90
Garr, Sarah 9, 17, 19, 261n26, 303n89, 303n90
Gaskell, Elizabeth 25, 158, 172, 178–9, 183–4, 200–1, 206, 230, 236
   biography of CB 1–2, 239–40
gifts to friends, making 107, 258
Glass Town 29, 32
   character similar to CB, introduction of 48, 50
   obsession with 47–8
   sharing with school friends 38–9
gloves, wedding 207
'Going Away Dress' *210*, 213
   as back/forward-looking 211
   collar 217
   colour 212–16, *213*
   compared to Quaker wedding gown 218–19
   as fashionable 218
   provenance 211–12
   self-reliance in choice of, CB's 219–20
   sleeves 218
   style 217
   use after marriage 229
governess, CB as
   Blake Hall, near Mirfield 54
   dislike of role 70–1
   at Upper House, Rawdon 55
governess clothes
   Quaker clothes and 68–70
   salary of a governess 64
   sartorial tightrope of 66
   status and 63–4
   'temptress' governesses, stories of 66–7
   unobtrusiveness of governesses 67
'Governess Dress', CB's 53–70, *59*
   brown/black colour of 67
   dating 60–1
   fastenings 64–5
   independence and individuality shown in 70
   inside view *61*
   pockets 65–6
   unobtrusiveness of governesses 67
gowns, babies 9
The Green Dwarf: A Tale of Perfect Tense (CB) 44
green spot barége gown *224*, *225*, *226*, *227*, 229

Hainsworth, Lewis 212
hairwork *136*, 136–7, 292n26, 292n27
Hall, Catherine 272n91
hand-me-down clothes 6
Haworth
   Brontë family's move to 12–13, 15
   return from Brussels, CB's 101
   in the 1820s 13–15
   textile industry in 13–14
Haworth Parsonage *14*, 14–15
   display of CB's clothes 245

Heath's Book of Beauty 45
Heger, Constantin, CB's attachment to 76–7, 78, 93
height, CB's 60
holiday with Ellen Nussey 54–5
Hollie point 8
honeymoon 220–1, 227–8
Howitt, William 69
Hubbersty, Eleanor 198–9

identity of CB as author
    fear of revealing 125
    uncovering of 157–8
infant clothes
    christening bonnet *7*, 7–8
    gowns/frocks 9
    ready-made 8–9
influences on CB and sisters
    fantasy world, withdrawal to 27
    Patrick Brontë 27
    wooden soldiers as inspiration 29
internet gaming disorder 47
ironing of clothes 106
Iroquois moccasins *144*

Jacquard ribbon tie *180*
Jane Eyre (CB)
    anonymity of CB as author 121
    appearance as central to 119
    capsule wardrobe of a governess 64
    cloaks 113
    governesses' need to change clothes 64
    mourning clothes in 134
    personal experiences, use of in writing 11–20
    pockets 66
    publication 120–2
    'Quaker', references to clothing as 69–70, 276n71
    reception of 1, 121
    righting of wrongs 119–20
    school uniform, CB's reaction to 23–4
    unobtrusiveness of governesses 67
    wedding ensemble 208
jet jewellery 137–8

jewellery
    bracelet made from hair of EB 136, *136*
    hairwork 136, *136*, 292n26, 292n27
    jet 137–8
    wedding 207

Kellett, Jocelyn 57
knitted purse *v*, 285n26

Lady's Magazine, influence on CB 28–9, 34, 46, 74
laundering 6, 105
lazurite 214, 215
'lazy-lacing system' 81
Lee, Sidney 158, 181
leghorn straw bonnets *184*, 302n71
Leg of Mutton shaped sleeves 60–1
Lewes, George Henry 32, 122, 124, 178
logwood 214, 215, 216, 315n35
London, social experiences in
    first 126–9
    wardrobe preparation for in 1849 147–8, *149*
Lucas, Phebe 11
Lynn, Eleri 87

man's shirt, Regency *49*
marriage
    CB's changing feelings towards Nicholls 223, 225
    CB's hopes for 220
    changing attitudes to in society 33–4
    community interaction, CB's increased 228–9
    contentment, CB's in 231–2
    honeymoon 220–1, 227–8
    intimate relations 223
    literary life after 229–34
    Nicholls's family 223
    proposal, CB's refusal of 50–1
Martineau, Harriet 150, 158, 177, 186
Mary Barton (Gaskell) 133
'Material Turn' 245–6
mending of gowns and garments 115, *116*, 117, *118*

mercerization 278n26
middle classes, governesses employed by 63
Milnes, Monckton 183, 186
mittens, evening 148
moccasins, Iroquois 143–4, *144*
moors, children's play on 19, 27
mordants 166, 212, 216, 299n27
mourning clothes
    blouse, whitework with black trim 151, *152*
    Branwell Brontë's death 132–4
    dye reviver 147
    Emily Brontë's death 135
    half mourning 151–2
    London trip 1849 147–8, *149*, 150
    Maria Brontë's death 17
    meaning of for CB 134
    production of 133–4
museum cataloguing process 56–7
muslin
    fragment of floral *112*
    print dresses *100*, 109–11
    wedding dress 200–1

nappies/napkins 9
Native American weaving traditions 114
needlecase hand-sewn by CB *41*
Newby, Thomas Cautley 123, 124, 125, 289n72
Nicholls, Arthur Bell
    arrival at Brontë Parsonage 187
    CB's changing feelings towards 190–2, 223, 225, 228
    CB's fame, impact on Arthur's later life 242–3
    on CB's writing and creativity 233
    change in conduct towards CB 188
    correspondence with CB 191
    dejection after proposal rejection 189, 190
    initial interaction with CB 187–8
    Ireland, return to after CB's death 241, 242
    proposal to CB 188–9
    as protective of CB's belongings after death 239
    respect for CB's possessions, continued 242, 308n44
    sale of CB's belongings after his death 243
Nicholson, William 214
Nussey, Ellen 25, 32, 38, 39, 172, 208, 237, 278n16
Nussey, Henry 50–1

orchil 214–15

'Paisley Dress' *vi*, *xiv*, *112*, 115, 173
parasols
    black silk 292n25
    paisley *127*
    purchased after meeting publisher 128–9
    silk *128*
passive/assertive duality in CB 230
patchwork quilt 111
pattens 11–12, *12*
patterns 111, 113
Pensionnat Heger, Brussels,
    CB and EB at 75–7
    CB's return to 78
    Heger, Constantin, CB's attachment to 76–7, 78, 93
pilches/pilchers 9
pink 221, *222*, 223
pins for napkins (nappies) 9
pockets
    embroidered 65
    governess dress, CB's 65–6
    sewn-in 175
poetry, publication of volume of 103–4
political turbulence in 1848 131
portraits
    The Brontë Sisters (Patrick Branwell Brontë) 40, *42*, *43*
    Charlotte Brontë (Richmond) 266n17
    Charlotte Brontë (Thompson) 266n17
    pre-/post-fame 266n17
    self portraits by CB *90*, 95, *96*, 97

pregnancy and death of CB 234–7
printed fabric
    cotton for childhood clothes 11
    muslin dresses 109–11, *112*
    'Paisley Dress' *vi*, *xiv*, 109–11, *110*, 115
    patchwork quilt 111
The Professor (CB) 104–5
    wedding ensemble 207–8
publishers, CB's, trip to reveal identity to 123–4
pumps 148, 150
purple
    going away dress 214–15, *216*
    mourning, recovery from grief and 152–3
    use of for school uniforms 22–3
purses, knitted *v*, 285n26

Quaker clothes
    CB's governess clothes and 68–70
    Jane Eyre references 276n71
    wedding dress, going away dress comparison with 218–19

rags 7
Raman spectroscopy *163*, 163–4, 165–6, 213–14
Ratcliffe, Eleanor 160
Rauser, Amelia Faye 90–1
ready-made clothes, childhood 8–9
receiver 5–6
recycling and reuse
    fabric 6–7, 260n10
    garments 115, *116*, 117, *118*, 179
Reid, Wemyss 282n67
repairing/remaking of gowns and garments 115, *116*, 117, *118*
ribbons 17, 177, 203, 217, 302n71, 303n91
Robinson, John 208
Roe Head School
    academic studies at 39
    Anne Brontë at 46
    appearance, CB's 35–8
    CB's qualities, lesson learned about 39
    Emily Brontë at 46

friendships, growth of 38–9
offered to Brontës 73
return to Haworth from 39–40
teacher, CB as 45–6, 48
Roe Head School, CB teaching at 30–3
Ross, Margaret 200, 206, 207

salary of a governess 64
Salt, Titus 164–5
sampler, CB's 18, *18*
sarapes 114
scarlet fever at the Parsonage 16–17
school, sisters' idea of opening 73, 102
school uniform 20, *21*, 22–4
scope of CB's surviving wardrobe at the BPM 3–4
Scott, Walter, Sir, as influence on CB 43–4
Self Concept Clarity 36
'Self Portrait' (drawing by CB) *90*
self portraits by CB *90*, 95, *96*, *97*, *see also* portraits
SEM-EDX (electron microscopy-energy dispersive X-ray analysis) 212–13, *213*, 313n18
sewing clothes 106–7, *108*, 109–15, *110*, *112*, *114*, *116*, 117, *118*
Sharp, Becky, in *Vanity Fair* (Thackeray) 66–7, 133
shawls
    Emily's and Anne's 156
    paisley wool *37*
    prices 311n85
    printed wool 152, *154*
Shirley (CB) 131, 144
    CB's difficulties with 138
    knowledge and pride of Yorkshire textile trade 167
    preface 145
    work on after sisters' deaths 145
shirt, Regency man's *49*
shopping/shops
    bridal wear 198, 201, 203
    children's clothes 8–9
    corset purchase in Brussels 84
    by Ellen Nussey for CB 172

frugality, concern with 179
  as increasingly common for CB 220
  mourning clothes 133
  in York, for Scarborough trip 140
Shorter, Clement 212, 242–3
Shuttleworth, Sir James Kay and Lady Janet 157
size of CB's surviving wardrobe at the BPM 3–4
sleeve puffs 269n61
sleeves
  blue-and-cream striped gown 175
  going away dress 218
  leg of mutton shape 60–1
slippers 148, 150, 206–7
Smith, Elizabeth 147, 150, 181, 182, 192, 193, 230, 235, *235*
Smith, George 86, 87, 91, 123, 124, 125, 129–30, 147, 148, 181, 183, 184–5, 192–3, 230, 266n17
Smith Williams, William 122, 124, 126, 129, 131–2, 135, 138, 142, 148, 150, 158, 186
social experiences in London
  first 126–9
  wardrobe preparation for in 1849 147–8, *149*, 150
socks, baby, made by CB 235, *235*
stature, CB's 60
Steele, Valerie 87
Stickney Ellis, Sarah 62
striped silk gown, blue-and-cream 173, *174*, 175–82, *176*

tartan cloaks 113
Taylor, Martha 73–4, 77
Taylor, Mary 25, 32, 35, 38, 73–4, 178, 185, 266n17
teaching
  first appointment at Roe Head School, CB's 45–6
  return home from Law Hill School, AB's 53
  return home from Roe Head School, CB's 48, 50

'temptress' governesses, stories of 66–7
The Tenant of Wildfell Hall (AB) 123
Terry, Rachel 212
Thackeray, Anne 170
Thackeray, William Makepeace
  CB's meetings with 150–1, 166–8
  CB's opinion of 185
  dinner party at house of 168–70
'Thackeray Dress' 158, *159*, 160, *161*, 162–7, *163*
Thornton 5, 9, 12, 13
tie, Jacquard ribbon *180*
tight-lacing of corsets 177
  CB's practice of 86, 87–98
tortoiseshell comb 155, *155*
travel, CB's desire to 73–4
trimmings on blue-and-cream striped gown *176*, 177–8
tuberculosis 25, 26, 131, 134, 291n18

ugly bonnets 140, *141*, 142
undergarments, making 106–7
Upper House, Rawdon, CB as governess at 55

Van Beneden family 83, 84, 279n33
Vanity Fair (Thackeray) 66, 67, 133
veils
  black lace *149*
  wedding bonnet *205*, 205–6
video game addiction 47
Villette (CB) 92
  description of Ginerva 311n97
  final edits and publication 189
  gift of dress to Lucy Snowe 181–2
  pink gown worn by Lucy Snowe 221, 223
  pockets 65–6
  reception of 190
  wedding ensemble 207
virtual worlds 47, *see also* Glass Town

Wade, John 57–8
waist dimension, CB's corset and 85–6
Walker, Rachel Hannah 219

washing of clothes 6, 105
wedding
   accessories 206
   bonnet *202*, 202–5, *205*
   bonnet veil *205*, 205–6
   CB's death, storage of wedding clothes after 199–200
   choice of dress, CB's attitude towards 196–8
   comments from onlookers 201–2
   contradictions, CB's 196
   dress *195*
   footwear 206–7
   gloves 207
   jewellery 207
   muslin fabric used for dress 200–1
   paradoxical messages of ensemble 207–8
   reconstructed dress 200
   as simple and quiet 208–9
   state of mind, CB's 194, *195*
   white dress, choice of 198
Weeton, Nelly 67
Weightman, William 55, 77, 78

Werly, Jean 82, 83, 84, 279n29
Williams, William Smith 122, 124, 125, 129, 131–2, 135, 138, 142, 148, 150, 158, 186
witnesses, communicative, clothes as 2–4, 245–7
wooden soldiers as inspiration 29
Wooler, Margaret 31, 35, 39, 45, 55, 73, 142, 143, 202, 208, 225, 230, 232, 235
working women, attitudes towards 62
woven corsets, CB's as 81–4
wrapping gown, pink cotton 221, *222*, 223, 316n56
Wright, Elizabeth 199
writing
   cooperative practice 104
   decision to earn living by 102–3
   literary life after marriage 229–34
   poetry, publication of volume of 103–4
   see also individual works

Yorkshire textile trade, CB's knowledge of and pride in 167